Effective Mainstreaming

SPENCER J. SALEND

THE COLLEGE AT NEW PALTZ,
STATE UNIVERSITY OF NEW YORK

Effective Mainstreaming

MACMILLAN PUBLISHING COMPANY
NEW YORK

Editor: Robert Miller
Production Supervision: Editorial Inc./Ann Knight
Cover Design: Blake Logan
Cover illustration: Clare Wood
Photo Research: John Schultz
Illustrations: Wellington Studios, Ltd.

This book was set in Baskerville by McFarland Graphics,
printed and bound by R.R. Donnelley & Sons.
The cover was printed by Phoenix Color Corp.

Macmillan Publishing Company
866 Third Avenue, New York, New York 10022

Collier Macmillan Canada, Inc.

LIBRARY OF CONGRESS CATALOGING-IN-PUBLICATION DATA

Salend, Spencer J.
    Effective mainstreaming / Spencer J. Salend.
        p.   cm.
    Includes index.
    ISBN 0-02-405324-4
        1. Handicapped children—Education—United States.
    2. Mainstreaming in education—United States.   I. Title.
    LC4031.S25   1990   89-34041
    371.9′046′0973—dc20   CIP

Printing: 2 3 4 5 6 7   Year: 0 1 2 3 4 5 6

To Suzanne

Preface

With passage of the Education for All Handicapped Children Act of 1975 (PL94–142), the Congress challenged our nation's educational system to expand the mainstream to include students with disabilities. Although many school districts have been able to respond positively, educators are still experiencing problems meeting this challenge. This book is intended to assist you in meeting the challenge of implementing effective mainstreaming in your school.

The book has been written to be teacher-, student-, and parent-oriented. It is research-based, but it is also practical. I have tried to translate the research into practice so that it both addresses and expands the realities of the classroom setting.

The book approaches mainstreaming as an ongoing, dynamic process for all students, regardless of their disability. Thus, rather than organizing the book into chapters by disciplinary areas that focus on information about the nature and needs of students with varying disabilities, the book is organized to follow a model for effectively mainstreaming all students with special needs. Chapter titles and content relate to and address the key factors that contribute to effective mainstreaming. Within each chapter are workable guidelines and procedures for successfully mainstreaming students with a wide range of disabilities. (Chapter 1 presents an overview of the chapters.) The book is designed as a text for undergraduate, graduate, or in-service courses for teachers, ancillary support personnel, and administrators interested in teaching and providing services to mainstreamed students. Because of its focus on instructional procedures, the book also could serve as a supplementary text for a course on methods or consultation.

When writing a book, an author must develop a philosophy that becomes the framework for the text. Several philosophical assumptions concerning effective mainstreaming guided the development of this book.

As you read and think about the following assumptions, you will learn about the book and the author.

Effective mainstreaming can improve the educational system. Inherent in the concept of mainstreaming is recognition of the need to individualize the educational system for students with disabilities. The result can be an educational system that is more able to accommodate and respond to the individual needs of *all* students. Thus, changes in the educational system designed to facilitate effective mainstreaming also can benefit nonhandicapped peers, teachers, parents, ancillary support personnel, and administrators. For example, all students will benefit when a teacher modifies large group instruction to improve the performance of a mainstreamed student. Similarly, as the educational system learns to respond to the needs of parents of mainstreamed students, the system increases its ability to respond to all parents.

Effective mainstreaming involves a sensitivity to and an acceptance of cultural diversity. Society is undergoing many changes that are also changing our schools. School districts throughout the United States are serving an increasing number of students from multicultural backgrounds. Our ability to redefine the mainstream to address the unique needs of these students and their families, as well as incorporate their visions and contributions, is critical in expanding the cultural base of our educational system and promoting effective mainstreaming.

Effective mainstreaming involves collaboration among educators, parents, students, community agencies, and other available resources. When these forces are working in synergy, the likelihood for effective mainstreaming is increased. This book outlines the roles and responsibilities of educators, parents, mainstreamed students and their peers, and community agencies to promote effective mainstreaming, and offers strategies for integrating these roles so that individuals work cooperatively. All roles are important, but it is the union of these roles that leads to effective mainstreaming.

In fact, this book is a result of the collaborative efforts of my students, colleagues, friends, and relatives. The book is an outgrowth of many ideas I learned from students in Woodlawn Junior High School (Buffalo, New York) and Public School 76 (Bronx, New York) and colleagues from P.S. 76: George Bonici, Nydia Figueroa-Torres, Jean Gee, and Jean Barber. Similarly, I gained much of the information presented here through interactions with teachers, administrators, and students in the Easton (Pennsylvania) Area School District, who both welcomed me and shared their experiences.

Sections of this book are based on articles that appeared in The Pointer, Volume 27, pages 5-9, 1983, and Volume 28, pages 20-22, 50-55, 1984. Reprinted with the permission of the Helen Dwight Reid Foundation. Published by Heldref Publications, 4000 Albemarle St., N.W., Washington, D. C. 20016, Copyright 1983, 1984.

I also want to acknowledge my colleagues who provided support and guidance through all stages of the book. Sandra Fradd and Marcia Norton were instrumental in encouraging me during the initial stages. I especially want to recognize Catharine Reynolds, Meenakshi Gajria, Karen Giek, Lee Bell, and Nancy Schniedewind for supporting and inspiring me throughout the process. My deepest appreciation also goes to Lynne Crockett and Connie D'Alessandro for their invaluable assistance in preparing the accompanying graphics and coordinating the copyright permissions. I also want to thank my colleagues who compiled the appendix.

This book would not have been possible without the efforts of Robert Miller and Diane Kraut of Macmillan. I sincerely appreciate their sensitivity to me. I also am grateful to the reviewers Sandra B. Cohen, University of Virginia; Deborah Gartland, Towson State University; James A. McLoughlin, University of Louisville; Sharon F. Schoen, LaSalle University; Carol Chase Thomas, University of North Carolina, Wilmington; and Rich Wilson, Bowling Green State University. Their thoughtful and professional comments helped shape and improve the book.

I want to acknowledge my parents, Anne and Harry Salend, my son, Jack, and my mother-in-law Agnes Russ for their love and support. Finally, I dedicate this book to my collaborator in life, Suzanne Salend, in recognition of her love, intelligence, faith, and encouragement.

Contents

CHAPTER 3
Preparing Students with Disabilities   79
for Mainstreaming

CHAPTER 4

Preparing Nonhandicapped Students   135
for Mainstreaming

CHAPTER 7

Modifying Content-Area Instruction   315

CHAPTER 8

Adapting Grading and Testing for Mainstreamed Students   383

CHAPTER 9

Evaluating the Progress of Mainstreamed Students
419

CHAPTER 1

Presenting a Model for Effective Mainstreaming

(Photo: Bob Daemmrich/The Image Works)

The education and treatment of individuals with disabilities has undergone a metamorphosis. Before 1800, individuals with handicapping conditions were feared, ridiculed, abandoned, or simply ignored. As educational methods were developed in the late 1700s that showed the success of various teaching techniques, society began to adopt a more accepting and humane view of individuals with disabilities. However, the nineteenth century saw the rise of institutions for individuals with disabilities; these institutions isolated the disabled from society.

Although institutional settings played an important role in the education and treatment of individuals with disabilities until the 1970s, the early twentieth century also saw the rise of special schools and special classes within public school facilities for students with handicapping conditions. The movement toward special programs and classes was followed by a period of advocacy and acceptance, which resulted in congressional enactment of the Education for All Handicapped Children Act of 1975 (PL94-142). Although PL94-142 does not specifically mention mainstreaming, this legislation established the concept of mainstreaming as one of the prevailing philosophical goals of the education of students with handicapping conditions.

This chapter is designed to offer information concerning mainstreaming. Specifically, the chapter introduces the concepts of mainstreaming and the least restrictive environment, outlines the educational placement options available to students with disabilities, reviews the factors that contributed to the mainstreaming movement, specifies arguments for and against mainstreaming, summarizes the research on mainstreaming, and presents a model for effective mainstreaming.

The Least Restrictive Environment

Mainstreaming is rooted in the concept of the *least restrictive environment*. PL94-142 mandates the placement of students with disabilities in the least restrictive environment in which their educational needs can be met. The least restrictive environment concept requires educational agencies to educate students with disabilities with their nonhandicapped peers as much as possible. The determination of the least restrictive environment is an individual decision that is based on the student's educational needs rather than the student's disability. While the least restrictive environment concept does not mean that all students with handicapping conditions should be in regular classrooms, it does mean that students with disabilities should be removed to self-contained special education classes, specialized schools, and residential programs only when the severity of their handicapping condition is so great that the students' needs cannot be accommodated in the regular education setting.

Data collected on the least restrictive environment concept since the inception of PL94–142 indicate that similar numbers of students with disabilities are still being educated in separate facilities, and that there is great variation from state to state in the use of separate facilities for these students (Danielson & Bellamy, 1989).

Tucker (1989) suggests that the least restrictive environment provision be service-defined rather than location-bound. A service-defined approach to the least restrictive environment focuses on providing services that meet students' educational needs and help them function successfully in the regular classroom setting. Wilcox and Sailor (1982) believe that the least restrictive environment must meet six criteria. To be least restrictive, the educational placement must

- include nonhandicapped peers;
- offer opportunities for interactions between handicapped and nonhandicapped students;
- maintain a ratio of handicapped and nonhandicapped students consistent with that of the larger population;
- provide equal access to educational and nonacademic activities and facilities;
- offer all students the same schedule for and organization of activities; and
- guarantee the delivery of high-quality educational services.

A Continuum of Educational Services

A continuum of educational placements ranging from the highly integrated setting of the regular classroom to the highly segregated settings of the residential program has been established to implement the least restrictive environment (Deno, 1970; Greer, 1988). While services vary from agency to agency, the range from most to least restrictive educational placements for serving students with disabilities is outlined in the continuum of services presented in Figure 1.1. A student with a disability would be placed in one of the placement alternatives based upon that student's individual needs, skills, abilities, and motivation (Stephens, Blackhurst, & Magliocca, 1982). A student should move down the continuum to a less restrictive environment as quickly as possible, and move up the continuum to a more segregated alternative only when such a move is indicated.

FIGURE 1.1.   Continuum of Educational Services.

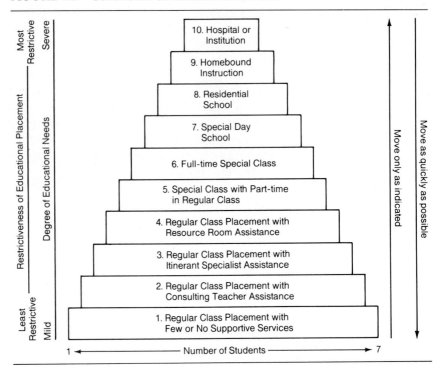

Source: Adapted from Blackhurst and Berdine (1981), Deno (1970) and Lewis & Doorlag (1987).

OPTION 1   REGULAR CLASS PLACEMENT WITH FEW OR NO SUPPORTIVE SERVICES

The least restrictive environment within the placement alternatives is the regular classroom setting with few or no supportive services. In this option, the student is educated in the regular classroom, following the same schedule as other students. The regular classroom teacher has the primary responsibility for designing and delivering the instructional program to the student. The instructional program is adapted to the needs of the mainstreamed student, and students may use adaptive devices and alternative learning strategies. While no specialized services are provided to the student, indirect services, such as in-service training to adapt the instructional program for mainstreamed students and to teach nonhandicapped students about handicapping conditions, may be offered (Lewis & Doorlag, 1987).

OPTION 2   REGULAR CLASS PLACEMENT WITH CONSULTING TEACHER ASSISTANCE

This placement option is similar to Option 1 in that the student is placed in the regular education setting for the entire day, and doesn't receive any direct special services. However, the regular classroom teacher receives consultative services from a special educator, school psychologist, guidance counselor, or other ancillary support personnel. The nature of the consultative services delivered will vary depending on the nature and severity of the handicapping condition as well as the needs of the mainstreamed student and the teacher. Typically, consultative services include obtaining specialized curricula and instructional materials, adapting instructional strategies and teacher-made tests, designing behavior management programs, and promoting social interactions between mainstreamed students and their peers. Guidelines for implementing collaborative consultation services are provided in Chapter 5.

OPTION 3   REGULAR CLASS PLACEMENT WITH ITINERANT SPECIALIST ASSISTANCE

Itinerant teachers often travel from school to school to provide direct services to students. Although the regular education program is delivered in the regular classroom setting, the student also receives weekly supportive services from itinerant teachers. Depending on the school district's arrangement, the itinerant teacher may deliver services to students within the confines of the regular classroom setting or in an area outside the classroom. For example, many speech and language therapists and migrant educators deliver services to students within the regular classroom setting. Working within the regular classroom can help promote communication between professionals and establish the link between skills taught by regular education and supportive services personnel. Occasionally, itinerant teachers working within the mainstreamed setting may provide remedial instruction to nonhandicapped students whose needs parallel those of the mainstreamed student.

OPTION 4   REGULAR CLASS PLACEMENT WITH RESOURCE ROOM ASSISTANCE

Like the itinerant teacher, the resource room teacher offers direct services to students with handicapping conditions. However, whereas the itinerant teacher often travels from school to school, the resource room teacher has a classroom within the school. Additionally, while itinerant teachers serve nonhandicapped students, mainstreamed students, and students in self-contained special education classes, the resource room teacher usually serves only students who are mainstreamed for the majority of the school day (Lewis & Doorlag, 1987). Resource room teachers provide individualized remedial instruction in specific skills (such as note taking, study skills, and so on) to small groups of students. In addition, resource teachers often provide supplemental instruction that supports and parallels the instruction the student receives in the regular classroom setting.

The resource room teacher also can help regular classroom teachers plan and implement instructional adaptations for mainstreamed students. For example, a teacher-made test adapted for mainstreamed students can be jointly constructed by the regular classroom and resource room teacher, and administered to students in the resource room.

OPTION 5   SPECIAL CLASS PLACEMENT WITH PART TIME IN THE REGULAR CLASS

In this option, the student's primary placement is in a special class setting within the same school building as their nonhandicapped peers. The student's academic program is supervised by a special educator. However, the mainstreamed student does spend some time with students from the regular classroom. While the amount of time spent in the regular classroom may vary, students in this option are placed in the regular setting only for subjects in which they can function successfully. Some students may enter the regular classroom for academic instruction, but most often the students in this option are integrated with their

Resource room teachers provide remedial instruction to small groups of students. (Photo: MacDonald Photography/Envision)

nonhandicapped peers for classes in art, music, industrial arts, and physical education.

OPTION 6   FULL-TIME SPECIAL CLASS

This placement alternative is similar to Option 5. However, contact with nonhandicapped peers takes place exclusively in a social rather than instructional setting. Students in this placement alternative share common experiences with nonhandicapped students on school buses, at lunch or recess, and during schoolwide activities (for instance, assemblies, plays, dances, and sporting events).

OPTION 7   SPECIAL DAY SCHOOLS

Students in this placement alternative attend a school different from that of their nonhandicapped peers. Placement in a special school allows for the centralization of services (Lewis & Doorlag, 1987). Thus, students' needs for services, such as physical and occupational therapy, can be delivered in a more cost-effective manner. Students attending special schools may share the common experience of riding a bus to school (often the bus students take will be different from that of their nonhandicapped peers) and returning home after school, but this option is highly restrictive and is usually used only with students with severe handicaps.

OPTION 8   RESIDENTIAL SCHOOLS

Residential programs also are designed to serve students with severe handicaps. Whereas students in a special day school return home at the end of the school day, students attending residential schools live at the school and participate in a twenty-four-hour program. Students attend the residential school during the school year or all year 'round, and see their families during holidays or family visits. In addition to delivering educational services, these programs offer the necessary comprehensive medical and psychological services that students may need.

OPTION 9   HOMEBOUND INSTRUCTION

Some students, such as those who are recovering from surgery or an illness or who have been suspended from school, may require homebound instruction. In this alternative, a teacher visits the home and delivers the instructional program in that setting. The teacher links homebound students with schools and classrooms by obtaining in-class assignments from the regular classroom teacher and delivering the student's completed assignments to the classroom teacher.

OPTION 10   HOSPITALS OR INSTITUTIONS

Placing individuals with severe handicaps into hospitals and institutions has been lessened as a result of the deinstitutionalization movement, but such placements still exist. As with all the placement options, education must be a part of any hospital or institution program. These placements should be viewed as short-term, and an emphasis should be placed on moving these individuals to a less restrictive environment.

Mainstreaming

For many students with disabilities, the least restrictive environment has been interpreted as mainstreaming into regular education classes (United States Department of Education, 1988). The United States Department of Education, in evaluating the implementation of PL94–142, found that approximately 70 percent of the students with disabilities in this country receive their instructional program in regular education settings. Data on the types of students with disabilities and the settings in which they are educated are presented in Figure 1.2. These data reveal that the extent to which students are mainstreamed varies by handicapping condition. Whereas 77 percent and 92 percent of the students with learning disabilities and speech impairments, respectively, are placed in regular classroom or resource room settings, 56 percent and 36 percent of the students with mental retardation and emotional disturbance, respectively, were educated in separate classes. Students with hearing impairments are placed in regular classrooms (19 percent), resource rooms (21 percent), separate classes (35 percent), and residential programs (11 percent). Similarly, students with visual impairments are educated in regular classrooms (32 percent), resource rooms (24 percent), separate classes (19 percent), and residential programs (10 percent). While the vast majority of students with orthopedical and other health impairments receive their instruction in settings with nonhandicapped youth, 8 percent of the students with orthopedical impairments and 18 percent of the students with health impairments also are educated in homebound or hospital environments. The most prevalent educational placement for students with multihandicaps is the separate classroom (43 percent), followed by separate day programs (19 percent) and resource room placements (15 percent).

The scope of mainstreaming varies greatly from so broad as to be defined as any interactions between students with disabilities and their nonhandicapped peers (Lewis & Doorlag, 1987) to more specific integration of students with disabilities into the social and instructional activities of the regular classroom milieu (Kaufman, Gottlieb, Agard, & Kukic, 1975;

FIGURE 1.2. Types of Disabled Students and the Settings in which They are Educated.

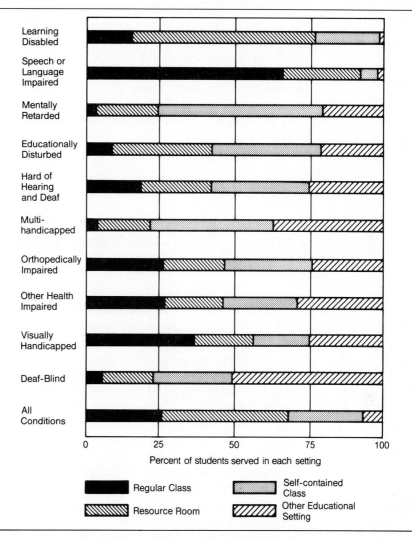

Percent of students served in each setting

Source: From data available in the *Tenth Annual Report to Congress on the Implementation of the Education of the Handicapped Act* (p. 30) by U.S. Department of Education, 1988. Washington, D.C., Author.

Turnbull & Schulz, 1979). For example, the Kaufman, et al. (1975) definition includes the component of integration, educational planning and programming, and delineation of roles and responsibilities (MacMillan & Semmel, 1977). Several definitions of mainstreaming are available in Figure 1.3.

This text defines *mainstreaming* as the carefully planned and monitored placement of handicapped students into regular education classrooms for the majority of their academic and social educational program. In this definition, the primary responsibility for the mainstreamed student's academic program lies with the regular education teacher. The academic component of the definition requires that the regular classroom environment be adapted to address the instructional needs of the mainstreamed student, while the social component requires that the mainstreamed student be assimilated into the social climate of the class and accepted by nonhandicapped peers (Kaufman, Gottlieb, Agard, & Kukic, 1975).

FIGURE 1.3. Definitions of Mainstreaming.

Each definition completes the statement, *Mainstreaming is*

- the inclusion of special students in the general educational process. Students are considered mainstreamed if they spend any part of the school day with regular class peers (Lewis & Doorlag, 1987, p. 4)

- the social and instructional integration of handicapped students in a regular education class for at least a portion of the school day (Schulz & Turnbull, 1983, p. 49)

- the education of mildly handicapped children in the least-restrictive environment. It is based on the philosophy of equal educational opportunity that is implemented through individual planning to promote appropriate learning, achievement and social normalization (Stephens, Blackhurst, & Magliocca, 1982, p. 10)

- the temporal, instructional, and social integration of eligible exceptional children with normal peers based on an ongoing, individually determined, educational planning programming process, and requires clarification of responsibility among regular and special education administrative, instructional and support personnel (Kaufman et al., 1975, p. 35)

- the carefully planned and monitored placement of students with disabilities into regular education classrooms for the majority of their academic and social educational program. The academic program within the regular education classroom should be adapted to address the instructional needs of the mainstreamed student, and the social program should be designed so that the mainstreamed student is assimilated into the social climate of the class and accepted by the nonhandicapped peers. While the primary responsibility for the mainstreamed student's academic and social program lies with the regular classroom teacher, mainstreaming is a dynamic, on-going process that requires communication and sharing information between regular and special educators, ancillary support personnel and parents (Salend, 1990)

This definition implies that mainstreaming is a dynamic, ongoing process that requires communication and sharing information between regular and special educators, ancillary support personnel, and parents. Since this definition emphasizes academic instruction and length of time spent in the regular classroom, the term *integration* will be used to refer to other planned interactions between mainstreamed and nonhandicapped students. Thus, the placement of students labelled mentally retarded into a physical education class with their regular education peers twice a week would be an example of integration, while the placement of a student with mental retardation in a regular classroom for his or her academic program with supplemental assistance from a special education teacher once a day would be considered mainstreaming.

However Reynolds and Birch (1988) delineated three aspects of mainstreaming: physical, social, and instructional. *Physical mainstreaming* requires that students with handicapping conditions are educated in the same school facilities as their nonhandicapped peers. While physical mainstreaming guarantees that all students attend and use the same facilities, it does not necessarily guarantee that there will be social and academic interactions between handicapped and nonhandicapped students. *Social mainstreaming* is implemented when school staff structure the learning environment so that handicapped and nonhandicapped students have opportunities to interact socially. *Instructional mainstreaming* occurs when students with special needs and nonhandicapped peers receive their academic instruction in the same setting.

Factors Contributing to the Impetus for Mainstreaming

Several factors contribute to the impetus for mainstreaming. These factors include normalization, deinstitutionalization, advocacy, litigation, legislation, and research.

NORMALIZATION.   The mainstreaming movement has its roots in the principle of *normalization,* a concept first formulated in Scandinavia (Kugel & Wolfensberger, 1969) and later brought to the United States (Wolfensberger, 1972). The normalization principle seeks to provide social interactions and experiences that parallel those of society to adults and children with disabilities (Nirje, 1969). Thus, the philosophy of mainstreaming rests on the principle that educational, housing, employment, social, and leisure opportunities for individuals with handicapping conditions should resemble as closely as possible the patterns, opportunities, and activities enjoyed by their nonhandicapped peers (Haring & McCormick, 1986).

Individuals with disabilities enjoy many of the social and leisure activities that other members of society enjoy. (Photo: Paul Conklin/Monkmeyer Press Photo Service)

The normalization principle serves as a guide to the delivery of services to individuals who are mentally retarded. Bruininks and Warfield (1978) noted that professionals and agencies can adhere to the normalization principle in the delivery of services by

- Planning and managing for services that require attention to normative cultural patterns
- Allowing retarded persons to experience normal routines of the day (e.g., dressing, eating in normal-sized groups) and normal routines of the life cycle (e.g., activities appropriate to one's age) that generally accompany increasing maturity
- Respecting choices and desires, and providing normal economic and civic privileges
- Providing education, training, care, and residential living in facilities of normal size and appearance

  • Using generic services whenever possible, rather than separate ones.
    (pp. 191–192)

DEINSTITUTIONALIZATION.   The normalization principle has contributed to the movement toward *deinstitutionalization.* The deinstitutionalization movement advocates eliminating large institutions for
individuals with handicapping conditions, placing them in smaller,
community-based group homes and independent living arrangements.
While the deinstitutionalization movement has encountered some resistance from local communities and suffers from a lack of funding, many
examples of its successful implementation exist.

ADVOCACY GROUPS.   The rise of organizations, called *advocacy
groups,* for parents and professionals also contributed to the mainstream-
ing movement. Parental groups such as the National Association for
Retarded Citizens (formerly the Association for Retarded Children), the
United Cerebral Palsy Association, and the Association for Children with
Learning Disabilities provided a voice for parents and others interested

Institutional settings can isolate individuals with disabilities from society.
(Photo: Alan Carey/The Image Works)

in finding and developing services for individuals with handicapping conditions. In addition to promoting public awareness of issues related to individuals with disabilities, these organizations lobbied state and federal legislators and brought litigation on behalf of individuals with disabilities. Similarly, professional organizations, such as the Council for Exceptional Children, united professionals and advocated improving services to individuals with special needs. As public awareness heightened and the needs of individuals with handicaps were recognized, the number of parental, professional, and advocacy groups increased. In the early 1980s, the power of these groups was displayed when they united to form a coalition to prevent the Reagan administration from attempting to appeal or dilute PL94–142 (Cartwright, Cartwright, & Ward, 1985). A listing of some of these groups is presented in Appendix A.

LITIGATION.   The movement toward mainstreaming was aided by legislation and litigation supporting the need for free, appropriate public education for children with handicaps in the least restrictive environment (Cartwright, Cartwright, & Ward, 1985). The precedent for much of the special education-related litigation and legislation was established by the *Brown v. Board of Education* case in 1954 (Gearheart, Weishahn, & Gearheart, 1988). The decision in this landmark case determined that segregating students in schools based on race, even if other educational variables appear to be equal, is unconstitutional (Zirkel, 1978). This precedent of "separate but equal is not equal" served as the underlying argument in suits brought by parents to ensure that their children with handicapping conditions received a free, appropriate public education.

In the class-action suit, *Pennsylvania Association for Retarded Children (PARC) v. Commonwealth of Pennsylvania,* PARC represented children with mental retardation. The suit questioned provisions of the Pennsylvania School Code that could be used to exclude children who are mentally retarded from school, and another provision that established education and training for these children in a segregated setting. In a consent-agreement approved by the court, the Commonwealth of Pennsylvania agreed that all children who are mentally retarded have a right to a free public education. While the *PARC* case resulted in a consent-agreement between two parties, *Mills v. Board of Education of the District of Columbia* was decided by a judge based on constitutional grounds. The *Mills* case extended the right to a free public education to all children with handicapping conditions.

Several cases dealing with the education of students from minority backgrounds also had an impact on the mainstreaming movement. In *Hobson v. Hansen* (1967), it was ruled that the practice of tracking was unconstitutional and should be abolished because it segregated students based on race and/or economic disadvantage. Other cases (for example, *Diana v. State Board of Education* and *Larry P. v. Riles*) dealing with nondiscriminatory testing changed evaluation procedures used to place minority students in special education programs. These cases are reviewed in Chapter 9.

LEGISLATION.   These cases provided a background that helped shape several Congressional acts, the primary focus of which was to integrate individuals with disabilities into the mainstream of society. In 1973, Congress passed the Vocational Rehabilitation Act (PL93-112), which served as a civil rights law for individuals with handicaps. Section 504 of this legislation forbids discrimination against the disabled in education, employment, housing, and access to public programs and facilities. Section 504 also requires institutions to make architectural modifications that increase physical accessibility to their buildings. Two years later, Congress passed the Education for All Handicapped Children Act of 1975 (PL94-142). The major provisions of PL94-142 mandate that

1. All children with disabilities, regardless of the nature and severity of their handicap, must be provided with a free appropriate public education.
2. Each child with a disability will have an Individual Educational Program (IEP) that is based on and tailored to address the child's unique learning needs.
3. Children with disabilities will be educated in the least restrictive environment with their nonhandicapped peers, to the maximum extent appropriate.
4. Students with disabilities must have access to all areas of school participation.
5. Children with disabilities and their families are guaranteed rights with respect to nondiscriminatory testing, confidentiality, and due process.

In 1986, Congress passed PL99-457, which extends many of the rights and safeguards of PL94-142 to handicapped children, ages birth to five years. PL99-457 encourages the delivery of early intervention services and includes provisions for establishing a child find system to identify eligible infants, toddlers, and preschoolers; conducting public awareness activities; training personnel; delivering related services; and developing an *Individualized Family Service Plan* (IFSP).

The IFSP, developed by a multidisciplinary team and the child's parents, details the early intervention services necessary to meet the developmental needs of eligible children. Eligible services, provided at no cost to families unless federal or state law requires payments by parents, include special education class placement, speech and language therapy, occupational and physical therapy, family training and counseling, case management, and some medical and health services. Similar in scope to PL94–142's IEP, and IFSP must include

- a statement of the child's present level of development;
- a statement of the family's strengths with respect to promoting the development of the child;
- a statement of the anticipated outcomes for the child and family to be achieved by the program;
- a listing of the criteria, techniques, and timelines for evaluating progress;
- a statement of the early education services and their intensity and frequency that will be delivered in order to meet the child's and the family's unique needs;
- the anticipated dates for initiating services and their duration;
- the name of the individual who will serve as the case manager and coordinate the implementation of the plan; and
- procedures for promoting the transition from early intervention into preschool.

The IFSP must be evaluated annually, and reviewed every six months, or more often if necessary.

EFFICACY STUDIES.   The reports of *efficacy studies* examining the value of special education services in the mid- to late sixties also provided impetus for mainstreaming (Dunn, 1968; Goldstein, Moss, & Jordan, 1965). In a classic review, Dunn (1968) argued that special education classes for students with mild handicaps were unjustifiable in that they served as a form of homogeneous grouping and tracking. He supported this argument by citing the efficacy studies that showed students with mild handicaps "made as much or more progress in the regular grades as they do in special classes," (p. 8) as well as studies that showed labeling has a negative impact on self-concept and teacher expectations for success in school.

Goldstein, Moss, and Jordan (1965) examined the effectiveness of carefully designed, "ideal" special education and regular education placements on student performance. They found no differences between the two placements on arithmetic performance, and a slight difference on reading performance in favor of regular class placement. These findings led the researchers to the conclusion that regular class placements are a better educational alternative for mildly handicapped students.

Several researchers have raised questions about the conclusions of the efficacy studies (Gottlieb, Alter, & Gottlieb, 1983; Hallahan, Keller, Mc-

Kinney, Lloyd, & Bryan, 1988; Tindal, 1985). They note that the efficacy studies often failed to assign students to different classes randomly; are dated in that they compared settings that used methods no longer comparable to practices used in regular and special education settings today; focused on physical placements rather than educational practices within these settings; and did not support regular education placements over special education placements for students with mild handicaps.

REGULAR EDUCATION INITIATIVE.   As a result of the efficacy studies and concern about the large number of students being labeled as handicapped, some educators have proposed the *Regular Education Initiative (REI)*, which calls for the restructuring of the relationship between regular, special, remedial, and compensatory education programs (Wang, Reynolds, & Walberg, 1986; Will, 1986). Proponents of the REI argue that the current educational service delivery system for students with mild handicaps is inefficient, costly, and fragmented by numerous "pull-out" programs (such as special education, migrant education, Chapter 1 programs, and the like), and that students with mild handicaps should receive their education in regular education classes. They endorse the establishment of a partnership between regular and special education that results in a coordinated educational delivery system based on empirically validated practices.

The REI also seeks to provide funds to support experimental trials of "more integrated forms of education for students who are unjustifiably segregated in separate programs" (Wang, Reynolds, & Walberg, 1986, p. 28). Others have criticized the validity of the REI by arguing that it is based on faulty assumptions (Kauffman, Gerber, & Semmel, 1988); represents policy advocacy rather than policy analysis (McKinney & Hocutt, 1988); and lacks an adequate research base (Hallahan, et al., 1988).

Arguments for Mainstreaming

While the concept of mainstreaming is not new, the debate about its advantages and disadvantages continues. Proponents of mainstreaming support it because it

- minimizes the deleterious effects of labelling;
- allows students with disabilities and their nonhandicapped peers the opportunity to learn from and interact with each other;
- prepares students with disabilities for their careers and lives in a setting that is more representative of society;
- promotes the academic and social development of students with disabilities;

- fosters the development of an understanding and appreciation of individual differences;
- is consistent with the moral and ethical values of our culture;
- provides for the delivery of services to nonhandicapped, "at risk" students without stigmatizing them; and
- infuses the skills of special educators into the school and curriculum.

Others attack special class placements as providing handicapped students with a "watered down" curriculum that focuses on practical knowledge, social skills, and emotional adjustment rather than academic skills (Guskin & Spicker, 1968). Advocates of mainstreaming also question the over-reliance on standardized tests to label students as disabled, which results in a disproportionate number of minority students being isolated in special education classes (Mercer, 1973).

Arguments against Mainstreaming

However, others argue against mainstreaming because they believe that

- regular educators are not trained to work with students with disabilities;
- students with disabilities will require excessive amounts of teacher time, thereby impeding the progress of nonhandicapped students;
- regular educators and nonhandicapped students have negative attitudes toward students with disabilities, which will result in the isolation and stigmatization of those students in the regular education milieu;
- regular education is not structured to accommodate the needs of students with disabilities;
- students with disabilities will be denied services and specialized instruction, and will fall further behind their nonhandicapped peers;
- emphasis on the excellence in education movement will create greater discrepancies between students with disabilities and their nonhandicapped peers; and
- research has not clearly established the efficacy of the mainstreamed setting.

Others believe that special class placement is best for students with handicapping conditions because it will protect them from the harmful effects of repeated failures that they will experience in the regular education setting.

Mainstreaming Research

Studies Supporting the Efficacy of Mainstreaming

Research on the efficacy of mainstreaming has reported mixed results (Caparulo & Zigler, 1983; Carlberg & Kavale, 1980; Polloway, 1984). The results of the mainstreaming studies should be interpreted with some caution, however (MacMillan & Semmel, 1977; Reynolds & Birch, 1988). Because of the difficulties of conducting comparative field investigations in education (for example, ensuring equal resources, equivalent students, teachers, and definitions of mainstreaming), it is not possible to conclude unequivocally that the results of these studies are correct (Reynolds & Birch, 1988). The relative newness of mainstreaming as an educational alternative and the recent changes and improvements in special education services also make mainstreaming a difficult concept to study empirically.

Several researchers have found that mainstreaming has promoted educational as well as social growth in students with disabilities (Guerin & Szatlocky, 1974; Haring & Krug, 1975; Macy & Carter, 1978; Madden & Slavin, 1983; Wang & Birch, 1984b). In carefully controlled studies, Calhoun and Elliot (1977) and Leinhardt (1980) found that randomly selected students with mild handicaps placed in mainstreamed settings showed significantly greater gains in achievement than did their counterparts who were educated in self-contained, special education classes. In reviewing the comparative effectiveness of mainstreamed placements on social outcomes, Madden and Slavin (1983) found that "for outcomes as self-derogation, and self-concept, classroom behavior, and attitudes toward school, regular class placement with adequate supports typically is superior to full-time special class placement" (p. 536).

Wang, Anderson, and Bram (1985) performed a meta-analysis of fifty studies comparing regular and special education placements. The subjects of these studies included approximately 3,400 students with various types of handicapping conditions and grade-level placements ranging from preschool to high school. The results across all types of handicapping conditions indicated not only that the academic and social performance of students with special needs in mainstreamed settings were superior to those students educated in special classes, but also that the students who were mainstreamed on a full-time basis performed better than their peers who were mainstreamed on a part-time basis.

Reynolds and Birch (1988) reviewed several non-data-based reports on mainstreaming programs. They concluded that mainstreaming was a successful alternative, as evidenced by the positive reactions of teachers, parents, and students; the decrease in the number of students referred for special education services; and the increase in consultation services provided to regular educators. They also noted that many of the problems associated with the implementation of mainstreaming were resolved.

The Adaptive Learning Environments Model

One successful mainstreaming program is the Adaptive Learning Environments Model (ALEM), developed at the University of Pittsburgh (Wang & Birch, 1984a, 1984b). ALEM is a full-time mainstreaming program that assists educators in adapting the instructional setting to accommodate the needs of special education students in the regular classroom. The program is designed to describe students in terms of their specific instructional needs rather than by categorical labels, and provides for early identification of learning needs through an ongoing assessment of the students' progress in relation to the program's curriculum. Individualized instructional programs are developed based on the students' strengths and weaknesses, and students are encouraged to assume control of their learning (Wang & Birch, 1984b).

Research shows that ALEM can be implemented in a variety of inner-city, suburban, and rural settings to facilitate student achievement (Wang & Birch, 1984a). Furthermore, a comparison between ALEM and a traditional resource room approach indicated that ALEM was superior in promoting interactions between students with disabilities and their peers and teachers, improving basic academic skills and increasing the positive attitudes of students (Wang & Birch, 1984b).

However, concerns about the ALEM findings have been raised (Anderegg & Vergason, 1988; Fuchs & Fuchs, 1988). Critics of the ALEM note that the studies examining its efficacy contain a variety of methodological limitations. These limitations include failing to provide descriptive information on program and student characteristics; using a small number of students; failing to provide data to verify the extent to which the ALEM procedures were implemented in the classes; and using inappropriate statistical data analysis procedures (Hallahan, et al., 1988; Fuchs & Fuchs, 1988).

Studies Questioning the Efficacy of Mainstreaming

While some researchers have found no differences between students placed in special education classes and those educated in regular education classes (Gottlieb & Budoff, 1976; Walker, 1974), others have found that mainstreaming has not been an effective educational alternative for students with disabilities (Budoff & Gottlieb, 1973; Gottlieb, 1981; Gresham, 1982). Carlberg and Kavale (1980) performed an analysis of special education versus mainstream placements, and found that students labeled learning disabled, behaviorally disordered, and emotionally disturbed performed better in special classes. The results of several studies indicate that students with IQs between 70 to 75 who do not receive supportive services in the regular education setting perform better in structured special education classes (Goldstein, Moss, & Jordan, 1965; Myers, 1976). In related research, others have found that special needs students in mainstreamed settings tend to be less popular (Bryan & Bryan, 1978; Gottlieb & Budoff, 1973; Siperstein, Bopp, & Bak, 1978).

Gresham (1982) reviewed the social skills literature and concluded that mainstreaming was a misguided approach because it was predicated on three premises that have not been empirically validated: that mainstreaming will result in increased social interaction between mainstreamed students and their nonhandicapped peers; that mainstreaming will result in increased acceptance of mainstreamed students by their peers; and that mainstreamed students will learn appropriate behavior through exposure to positive peer models in the regular education setting. Similarly, in reviewing the studies on mainstreamed placements for educable mentally retarded (EMR) students, Gottlieb (1981) determined that mainstreaming was not fulfilling its promise.

Resolving the Discrepancy in the Mainstreaming Research

Leinhardt and Pallay (1982) reviewed the literature contrasting special and regular education placements for students with special needs. They found successful examples of all types of placement alternatives for students with mild handicaps. They resolved the discrepancy in the existing studies by concluding that

> the most significant point of view is that setting is not an important determinant of child or program success. When effective practices are used, then the mildly handicapped benefit. Therefore educators should focus less on debates of setting, and more on issues of finding and implementing sound educational processes. For moral and social reasons, the least restrictive environment is preferable, and this review indicates that most of the valuable practices can be implemented in either resource rooms or regular education settings [p. 574].

Another explanation for these contradictory findings may lie in the variation of mainstreaming policies and their implementation from one school district to another (Gresham, 1982; Zigler & Muenchow, 1979). Others attribute the inconsistency of findings concerning mainstreaming to the failure of schools to change their programs to facilitate the mainstreaming of students with disabilities (Bogdan, 1983; Stainback, Stainback, Courtnage, & Jaben, 1985). Zigler and Muenchow (1979) noted that because many school districts do not have clear guidelines for mainstreaming, their programs often become the least expensive rather than the least restrictive alternative for exceptional students. Similarly, Gresham (1982) criticized local and state education personnel for their failure to develop workable guidelines for mainstreaming.

Several studies have examined the mainstreaming procedures of school districts (Bogdan, 1983; Salend, Brooks, & Salend, 1987). Wang, Anderson, and Bram (1985) examined the program features that appear to be related to effective mainstreaming. They noted that the important mainstream program characteristics included use of

- ongoing assessment of student performance
- adaptive instructional techniques and materials;
- individualized instruction
- student self-management strategies
- peer tutoring
- consultation and instructional teaming.

Salend, Brooks, and Salend (1987) surveyed educators responsible for coordinating their school districts' mainstreaming programs to determine the extent to which their programs incorporated the factors that contribute to successful mainstreaming programs. They concluded that while districts have acknowledged a commitment to the philosophy of mainstreaming, few of the districts surveyed had systematic and viable procedures to ensure its implementation. Furthermore, they reported that the implementation of mainstreaming appears to be based on informal networks between regular and special educators within individual schools, rather than on established policies. These results are consistent with the findings of Bogdan (1983), who examined the mainstreaming policies of numerous school districts and found that few adaptations had been made to ensure the successful implementation of mainstreaming programs.

A Model for Mainstreaming

In light of these findings and the continued commitment to mainstreaming as the preferred educational alternative for students with disabilities, this book is intended to provide educators with a model for implementing effective mainstreaming (see Figure 1.4). The design of the model is

FIGURE 1.4. A Model for Mainstreaming.

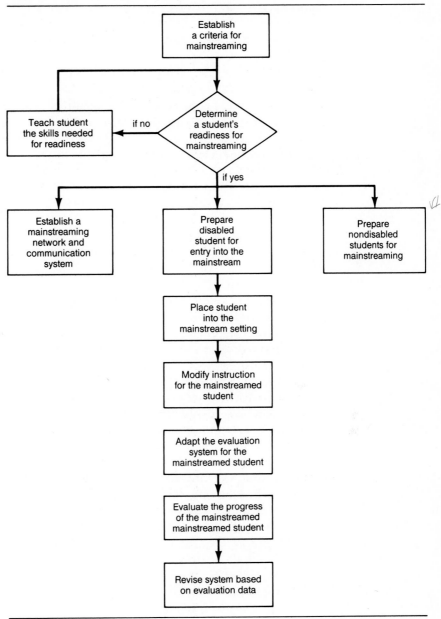

based on the mainstreaming literature and will offer educators specific procedures for successfully mainstreaming students with disabilities. The model and the book's chapters are outlined and briefly discussed below; each step is discussed in greater detail in the chapters that constitute this book.

CHAPTER 2: ESTABLISHING CRITERIA FOR MAINSTREAMING

The initial step in the model is to establish criteria for mainstreaming. The criteria delineate the academic, behavioral, and social skills a student needs to be successful in the mainstreamed setting, and should be employed by multidisciplinary placement teams to determine a student's readiness for mainstreaming. Chapter 2 of this book reviews characteristics of handicapping conditions, provides specific criteria and competency-based procedures that educators can consider in determining the readiness for mainstreaming of elementary and secondary-level students with disabilities, and delineates the roles and composition of the multidisciplinary placement team. Cautions in using the criteria also are examined.

CHAPTER 3: PREPARING STUDENTS WITH DISABILITIES FOR MAINSTREAMING

If the multidisciplinary placement team decides that a student is to be mainstreamed, then the regular and special education teachers should prepare the student for the transition to the mainstreamed setting. Similarly, students who lack the skills to be mainstreamed should be trained to increase their readiness for mainstreaming. Chapter 3 assists educators in helping students with disabilities make the transition from special to regular education settings. Guidelines are presented for preparing the student to deal with the critical factors that affect student performance in the regular classroom, such as instructional format and materials, curricular demands, teaching and learning style, behavioral expectations, evaluation techniques, physical design, and student support services. Strategies for teaching the skills necessary for success in mainstreamed settings and promoting the generalization of these skills are presented.

CHAPTER 4: PREPARING NONHANDICAPPED STUDENTS FOR MAINSTREAMING

Since the mainstreaming concept is based on the social and instructional interactions between nonhandicapped students and those who have disabilities, nonhandicapped students also will need to be prepared for the entry of students with disabilities into the mainstream. Chapter 4 provides educators with specific strategies for assessing attitudes toward students with handicapping conditions, teaching about handicapping conditions, and promoting positive attitudes toward the handicapped. Specific attitude change strategies, including films, disability simulations, an introduction to successful individuals with handicapping conditions, books about the handicapped, group discussions, guest speakers, hypothetical examples, and other commercially produced materials concerning the handicapped individuals are outlined. Additionally, strategies are detailed that promote an environment of acceptance and understanding of cultural diversity in the classroom.

CHAPTER 5: PROMOTING COMMUNICATION TO FOSTER THE MAINSTREAMING PROCESS

An essential factor in the success of any mainstreaming program is communication between regular and special educators, ancillary support personnel, and parents. Therefore, a network of support and ongoing communication between professionals and parents should be established to share information. Chapter 5 offers guidelines for promoting such a network and ensuring communication, cooperation, and congruence among educators, parents, and community agencies. Consultation strategies, guidelines for establishing congruence in the delivery of the students' educational program, agendas for information sharing, and models for involving parents are highlighted.

CHAPTER 6: MODIFYING INSTRUCTION FOR MAINSTREAMED STUDENTS

If students with disabilities are to be successful in the mainstream, regular classroom teachers must make modifications in their instructional programs to accommodate the needs of these students. Chapter 6 presents a wide variety of instructional modifications that can be used across content areas; teachers can make these modifications to facilitate the mainstreamed student's academic and social performance. Additionally, strategies consistent with emerging teacher-effectiveness data are reviewed, as are adaptive devices and other technology that can assist individuals with disabilities. Guidelines are presented for designing the classroom environment for mainstreamed students and dealing with behavior problems.

CHAPTER 7: MODIFYING CONTENT AREA INSTRUCTION

Chapter 7 offers guidelines for making adaptations for mainstreamed students that are unique to the specific content areas. Specific strategies for adapting instruction in reading, mathematics, science, social studies, writing, handwriting, and spelling are presented.

CHAPTER 8: ADAPTING GRADING AND TESTING FOR MAINSTREAMED STUDENTS

In addition to modifying the instructional environment, educators also may find it necessary to adapt their evaluation procedures to adequately assess the skills of mainstreamed students. Chapter 8 deals with a variety of methods for adapting formal standardized and informal teacher-made tests. Specific techniques to consider in constructing teacher-made tests that optimize the performance of mainstreamed students are discussed, as is the use of computer technology. Additionally, guidelines for employing alternative grading procedures and teaching test-taking skills are offered.

CHAPTER 9: EVALUATING THE PROGRESS OF MAINSTREAMED STUDENTS

To ensure that the student continues to benefit academically, socially, and behaviorally, the student's progress in the mainstream should be examined periodically. Information concerning the student's progress can be used to validate existing services or assist educators in revising, deleting, or adding services to facilitate the mainstreaming process. Follow-up evaluation also can provide educators with data to evaluate their mainstreaming policies and procedures. Chapter 9 offers educators guidelines for monitoring the progress of students with disabilities who have been placed in mainstream settings, with special attention paid to students from multicultural backgrounds. Specific guidelines for obtaining follow-up data using standardized tests, curriculum-based assessments, and minimum competency testing as well as informal strategies are reviewed. Procedures for soliciting follow-up information from educators, parents, and mainstreamed students are also discussed.

References

Anderegg, M. L., & Vergason, G. A. (1988). An analysis of one of the cornerstones of the regular education initiative. *Focus on Exceptional Children, 20*(6), 1–7.

Blackhurst, A. E., & Berdine, W. H. (1981). *An introduction to special education.* Boston: Little, Brown and Company.

Bogdan, R. (1983). A closer look at mainstreaming. *Educational Forum, 47,* 425–434.

Bruininks, R. H., & Warfield, G. (1978). The mentally retarded. In E. L. Meyen (Ed.), *Exceptional children and youth: An introduction* (pp. 162–216). Denver: Love Publishing.

Bryan, T. S., & Bryan, J. H. (1978). Social interactions of learning disabled children. *Learning Disabilities Quarterly, 1,* 33–38.

Budoff, M., & Gottlieb, J. (1976). Special class EMR children mainstreamed: A study of an aptitude (learning potential) X treatment interaction. *American Journal of Mental Deficiency, 81,* 1–11.

Calhoun, G., & Elliot, R. (1977). Self-concept and academic achievement of educable retarded and emotionally disturbed pupils. *Exceptional Children, 44,* 379–380.

Caparulo, B., & Zigler, E. (1983). The effects of mainstreaming on success expectancy and imitation in mildly retarded students. *Peabody Journal of Education, 60,* 85–98.

Carlberg, C., & Kavale, K. (1980). The efficacy of special versus regular placements for exceptional children: A meta-analysis. *Journal of Special Education, 14,* 295–309.

Cartwright, G. P., Cartwright, C. A., & Ward, M. E. (1985). *Educating special learners.* Belmont, Calif.: Wadsworth.

Danielson, L. C., & Bellamy, G. T. (1989). State variation in placement of children with handicaps in segregated environments. *Exceptional Children, 55,* 448–455.

Deno, E. (1970). Special education as developmental capital. *Exceptional Children, 37,* 229–237.

Dunn, L. M. (1968). Special education for the mildly retarded—is much of it justifiable? *Exceptional Children, 35,* 5–22.

Fuchs, D., & Fuchs, L. S. (1988). Evaluation of the adaptive learning environments model. *Exceptional Children, 55,* 115–127.

Gearheart, B. R., & Weishahn, M. W, & Gearheart, C. J. (1988). *The handicapped child in the regular classroom (4th ed.).* Columbus: Charles E. Merrill.

Goldstein, H., Moss, J., & Jordan, L. (1965). *The efficacy of special class training on the development of mentally retarded children* (U.S. Office of Education Cooperative Project No. 619). Urbana: University of Illinois Press.

Gottlieb, J. (1981). Mainstreaming: Fulfilling the promise? *American Journal of Mental Deficiency, 86,* 115–126.

Gottlieb, J., Alter, M., & Gottlieb, B. W. (1983). Mainstreaming mentally retarded children. In J. L. Matson & J. A. Mulich (Eds.) *Handbook of mental retardation* (pp. 67–77). New York: Pergamon.

Gottlieb, J., & Budoff, M. (1973). Social acceptability of retarded children in nongraded schools differing in architecture. *American Journal of Mental Deficiency, 78,* 15–19.

Greer, J. V. (1988). No more noses to the glass. *Exceptional Children, 54,* 294–296.

Gresham, F. (1982). Misguided mainstreaming: The case for social skills training with handicapped children. *Exceptional Children, 48,* 422–433.

Guerin, G. R., & Szatlocky, K. (1974). Integration programs for the mildly retarded. *Exceptional Children, 41,* 173–179.

Guskin, S. L., & Spicker, H. H. (1968). Educational research in mental retardation. In N. R. Ellis (Ed.), *International review of research in mental retardation (Vol. 3).* (pp. 217–278). New York: Academic Press.

Hallahan, D. P., Keller, C. E., McKinney, J. D., Lloyd, J. W., & Bryan, T. (1988). Examining the research base of the regular education initiative:

Efficacy studies and the adaptive learning environments model. *Journal of Learning Disabilities, 21,* 29–34, 55.

Haring, N. G., & Krug, D. A. (1975). Placement in regular programs: Procedures and results. *Exceptional Children, 41,* 413–417.

Haring, N. G., & McCormick, L. (1986). *Exceptional children and youth. (4th).* Columbus: Charles E. Merrill.

Kauffman, J. M., Gerber, M. M., & Semmel, M. I. (1988). Arguable assumptions underlying the regular education initiative. *Journal of Learning Disabilities, 21,* 6–11.

Kaufman, M., Gottlieb, J., Agard, J., & Kukic, M. (1975). Mainstreaming: Toward an explanation of the concept. In E. Meyen, G. Vergason, & R. Whelan (Eds.), *Alternatives for teaching exceptional children.* (pp. 35–54). Denver: Love Publishing.

Kugel, R. B., & Wolfensberger, W. (1969). *Changing patterns in residential services for the mentally retarded.* Washington, D.C.: President's Committee on Mental Retardation.

Leinhardt, G. (1980). Transition rooms: Promoting maturation or reducing education? *Journal of Educational Psychology, 72,* 55–61.

Leinhardt, G., & Pallay, A. (1982). Restrictive educational settings: Exile or haven? *Review of Educational Research, 52,* 557–578.

Lewis, R. B., & Doorlag, D. H. (1987). *Teaching special students in the mainstream. (2nd ed.).* Columbus: Charles E. Merrill.

MacMillan, D. L., & Semmel, M. I. (1977). Evaluation of mainstreaming programs. *Focus on Exceptional Children, 9,* 1–14.

Macy, D. J., & Carter, J. L. (1978). Comparison of a mainstream and self-contained special education program. *Journal of Special Education, 12,* 303–313.

Madden, N., & Slavin, R. (1983). Mainstreaming students with mild handicaps: Academic and social outcomes. *Review of Educational Research, 53,* 519–569.

McKinney, J. D., & Hocutt, A. M. (1988). The need for policy analysis in evaluating the regular education initiative. *Journal of Learning Disabilities, 21,* 12–18.

Mercer, J. R. (1973). *Labeling the mentally retarded.* Berkeley: University of California Press.

Myers, J. K. (1976). *The special day school placement for high IQ and low EMR pupils.* Paper presented at the annual meeting of the Council for Exceptional Children, Chicago (ERIC Document Reproduction Services No. ED 125 197).

Nirje, B. (1969). The normalization principle and its human management implications. In R. B. Kugel & W. Wolfensberger (*Eds.*), *Changing patterns in residential services for the mentally retarded.* (pp. 231–240). Washington, D.C.: U. S. Government Printing Office.

Polloway, E. (1984). The integration of mildly retarded students into the schools: A historical review. *Remedial and Special Education, 5,* 18–28.

Reynolds, M. C., & Birch, J. W. (1988). *Adaptive mainstreaming: A primer for teachers and principals (3rd ed.),* New York: Longman.

Salend, S. J., Brooks, L., & Salend, S. (1987). Identifying school districts' policies for implementing mainstreaming. *The Pointer, 32*, 34-37.

Schultz, J. B., and Turnbull, A. P. (1983). *Mainstreaming Handicapped Students* (2nd ed.), Boston: Allyn and Bacon.

Siperstein, G., Bopp, M., & Bak, J. (1978). Social status of learning disabled children. *Journal of Learning Disabilities, 11*, 98-102.

Stainback, W., Stainback, S., Courtnage, L., & Jaben, T. (1985). Facilitating mainstreaming by modifying the mainstream. *Exceptional Children, 52*, 144-152.

Stephens, T. M., Blackhurst, A. E., & Magliocca, L. A. (1982). *Teaching mainstreamed students.* New York: John Wiley & Sons.

Tindal, G. (1985). Investigating the effectiveness of special education: An analysis of methodology. *Journal of Learning Disabilities, 18*, 101-112.

Tucker, J. A. (1989). Less required energy: A response to Danielson and Bellamy. *Exceptional Children, 55*, 456-458.

United States Department of Education. (1988). *Tenth annual report to Congress on the implementation of the Education of the Handicapped Act.* Washington, D.C.: Author.

Walker, V. S. (1974). The efficacy of the resource room for educating retarded children. *Exceptional Children, 40*, 288-289.

Wang, M. C., Anderson, K. A., & Bram, P. J. (1985). *Toward an empirical data base on mainstreaming: A research synthesis of program implementation and effects.* Pittsburgh: Learning Research and Development Center, University of Pittsburgh.

Wang, M. C., & Birch, J. W. (1984a). Effective special education in regular classes. *Exceptional Children, 50*, 391-398.

Wang, M. C., & Birch, J. W. (1984b). Comparison of a full-time mainstreaming program and a resource room approach. *Exceptional Children, 51*, 33-40.

Wang, M. C., Reynolds, M. C., & Walberg, H. J. (1986). Rethinking special education. *Educational Leadership, 44*(1), 26-31.

Wilcox, B., & Sailor, W. (1982). Service delivery issues: Integrated educational systems. In B. Wilcox & R. York (Eds.), *Quality education for the severely handicapped* (pp. 277-302). Falls Church, Va: Quality Handicrafted Books.

Will, M. C. (1986). Educationing children with learning problems: A shared responsibility. *Exceptional Children, 52*, 411-415.

Wolfensberger, W. (1972). *The principle of normalization in human services.* Toronto: National Institute on Mental Retardation.

Zigler, E. & Muenchow, S. (1979). Mainstreaming: The proof is in the implementation. *American Psychologist, 34*, 993-996.

Zirkel, P. A. (1978). *A digest of Supreme Court decisions affecting education.* Bloomington, Ind.: Phi Delta Kappa.

CHAPTER 2

Establishing Criteria for Mainstreaming

(Photo: Alan Carey/The Image Works)

Educators make many important decisions concerning the educational needs of students with disabilities. These decisions include assessing the effectiveness of prereferral strategies, determining a student's eligibility for special education, placing the student in appropriate educational environments, identifying educational and related service needs in order to assist teachers and parents in developing and implementing a student's Individualized Educational Program (IEP), and determining a student's readiness for mainstreaming. This chapter provides information to help educators make these important decisions. Specifically, the chapter outlines the roles and responsibilities of the multidisciplinary team and its members, reviews information on the characteristics of specific handicapping conditions, describes the use of a competency-based approach to mainstreaming, and examines some of the issues in determining the readiness for mainstreaming of students from multicultural backgrounds.

Roles and Responsibilities of the Multidisciplinary Team

Prior to congressional enactment of the Education for All Handicapped Children Act of 1975 (PL94–142), many educational decisions concerning a student's special education needs were typically made by the school psychologist. However, PL94–142 requires that a team of professionals and parents determine a student's eligibility for special education classes and the types of related services necessary to meet student needs and help the student benefit from special education. Although the makeup of the multidisciplinary team varies depending on the needs of the student in question and the decisions to be made (Hart, 1977), the team may be composed of individuals with training in regular education, special education, administration, school psychology, speech and language therapy, vocational education, physical therapy, occupational therapy, counseling, social work, and medicine (Golightly, 1987). In addition to these professionals, the team also should include a parent and, when appropriate, the student. For students with specific cultural or language needs, individuals who have experience with the student or an expertise in the specialized area should be a part of the team. For example, in determining the needs of limited English-proficient students, the team should be expanded to include a bilingual educator; a migrant educator also should be asked to join a multidisciplinary team reviewing the educational placement of a migrant student (Salend, in press).

The School Administrator

The building principal or the special education coordinator usually serves as the chairperson of the multidisciplinary team. The chairperson is responsible for coordinating meetings and delivery of services to students and their families. The chairperson also ensures that all legal guidelines for due process, parental involvement, assessment, and confidentiality are followed (Pasanella, 1980). Through their leadership and support, principals can foster a tone of acceptance and commitment to the concept of mainstreaming. For example, scheduling time for regular and special educators to meet and planning in-service programs to prepare teachers to work with mainstreamed students can create a positive environment that can facilitate the success of mainstreaming.

The Regular Educator

It is critical that the multidisciplinary team include a regular educator (Lewis & Doorlag, 1987). Regular educators who have experience working with the student can offer information on the student's strengths and weaknesses, as well as data on the effectiveness of specific instructional approaches. In deciding on a mainstreamed placement, regular educators can provide team members with a perspective on the academic and social rigors of the regular education classroom. Involving the regular educator in the process also can allay the fears of the regular classroom teachers and foster their commitment to the success of the mainstreaming placement.

The Special Educator

Another vital member of the multidisciplinary team is the special educator, who can assist the multidisciplinary team in developing an Individualized Educational Program (IEP) by providing data concerning the student's academic and social skills, readiness for mainstreaming, and reactions to instructional techniques and materials. The special educator can offer information on the special education placement options within the school district. When a student is going to be mainstreamed, the special educator can consult with regular classroom teachers concerning instructional modifications, grading alternatives, prosthetic devices, and peer acceptance of the mainstreamed student. The special education teacher also assumes the primary responsibility for preparing the student for entry into the mainstream.

The School Psychologist

An important member of the multidisciplinary team is the school psychologist. In many instances, teams are chaired by school psychologists because of their training and expertise in the administration and interpretation of standardized tests. In addition to carrying out test-related tasks, school psychologists also collect data on students by observing them in their classrooms and interviewing other professionals who work with the students. Many school psychologists are trained as consultants to assist classroom teachers in designing, implementing, and evaluating prereferral interventions and behavior management systems (Zins, Curtis, Graden, & Ponti, 1988). Occasionally, school psychologists provide counseling to parents and students (Gloeckler & Simpson, 1988).

To minimize the time demands on school psychologists, some school districts employ an educational diagnostician. Although diagnosticians can perform many of the roles of school psychologists, they are not trained to administer many psychological and intelligence tests.

The Speech and Language Clinician

Information on the speech and language abilities of students can be provided by the speech and language clinician. Although these professionals have historically delivered services to remediate articulation problems, voice, and fluency disorders, their responsibilities have been expanded to include students with language problems. They also offer teachers assistance in fostering the communication skills of students within the classroom environment.

The Social Worker

The social worker is a liaison between the home, the school, and community agencies. In terms of the home–school relationship, the social worker counsels students and families, obtains information to assess the effect of the student's home life on school performance, and assists families during emergencies. In addition, the social worker can be instrumental in helping families obtain services from community agencies, and can contact agencies concerning the needs of the student and parents, as well as the impact of services on the family.

Speech/Language clinicians help students develop their communication skills.
(Photo: Irene Boyer: Monkmeyer Press Photo Service)

The Guidance Counselor

Although more likely to work with secondary-level students, the guidance counselor can assist mainstreamed students at all levels. The counselor can provide the multidisciplinary team with insights concerning the student's social and emotional development, including self-concept, attitudes toward school, and social interactions with others. In schools that don't have a social worker, the counselor may be the professional responsible for contacting parents and community agencies that provide services to the student and the family.

Frequently, counselors are given the responsibility of coordinating, assessing, and monitoring the mainstreamed student's program, as well as reporting the progress of the program to members of the team. The guidance counselor also may deliver counseling services to students and parents. For example, during the initial transition period, the mainstreamed student may need counseling to make the social and emotional adjustment to the regular education setting.

The Bilingual Educator

Many students come from backgrounds where English is not the dominant language spoken; they will require the services of a bilingual educator (Baca & Cervantes, 1984). Bilingual special education offers students specialized instruction in their primary language while helping them gain skill in English. Bilingual education also fulfills the sociocultural and psychological needs of limited English-proficient (LEP) students. Toward these ends, the bilingual educator performs a variety of roles, including

- teaching curriculum areas using two languages;
- using the student's native language to teach reading;
- teaching English as a second language;
- helping students develop a positive self-concept;
- instilling in students a sense of pride in their culture;
- emphasizing positive attitudes toward cultural diversity;
- assisting in the assessment of students from multicultural backgrounds;
- helping determine an appropriate placement for LEP students;
- developing an instructional program that meets the needs of LEP students;
- evaluating the progress of LEP students; and
- helping parents become involved in their child's education (Plata & Santos, 1981).

The Migrant Educator

To address the educational needs of migrant students, the federal government funds migrant education programs through the states. Typically, when a migrant family moves to a new area, it is certified as being eligible for migrant status and services by a recruiter from a local migrant education agency. After a family has been identified as migrant-eligible, a migrant educator is often charged with the responsibility of assisting the family in enrolling the children in school. The migrant educator also contacts local agencies, organizations, businesses, and other community resources that can provide assistance to migrant families.

Once the migrant students are in school, the migrant educator often gives them supplementary individualized instruction in small groups. The migrant educator is available to assist regular and special education personnel in meeting the unique needs of migrant students, to train parents, and to serve as a liaison between migrant parents and the school. Migrant educators often perform a variety of other roles, including acting as interpreters for parents; ensuring that students receive proper medical, dental, and health-related services; providing transportation for families; and offering bilingual instruction, career education, and training in English as a second language.

The Vocational Educator

As part of the multidisciplinary team, the vocational educator offers valuable information concerning the mainstreamed student's work, career experiences, and potential. Vocational educators are responsible for providing students with vocational and career education experiences, which require vocational educators to collaborate with families and employers within the community (Brolin, 1982). Vocational education seeks to provide work experience and training to prepare students for specific careers. Specific vocational education services include:

- assessing students' job skills, aptitudes, and interests;
- developing specific work-related skills and behaviors;
- offering job counseling;
- providing students with information and exposure to various jobs through work experiences and job tryouts;
- helping students find jobs; and
- serving as a job coach.

In addition, career education focuses on developing awareness, attitudes, habits, interests, and skills relative to employment options (Kokaska & Brolin, 1985). Brolin (1978) has developed a life-centered career education curriculum of 103 subcompetencies within the domains of daily living skills, personal-social skills, and occupational guidance and preparation that can provide career education to mainstreamed students.

Physicians and Nurses

PL94–142 established the need for greater involvement of medical and health-related personnel in the education of students with special needs (Guralnick, 1982). Levine (1982) noted that physicians can aid the multidisciplinary team by performing diagnostic tests to assess the student's physical development, sensory abilities, medical problems, and central nervous system functioning; providing an understanding of nutrition, allergies, chronic illnesses, and somatic symptoms; planning and monitoring the effectiveness of medical interventions; and discussing the potential side effects of drug interventions.

Some students may require the services of a medical specialist, who can meet the specific medical and physical needs of students by providing diagnostic and treatment services within their areas of specialization. For example, an *ophthalmologist*—a physician who specializes in the treatment of conditions affecting the eyes—can provide information and assistance to students with specific visual impairments. Students with hearing impairments may need the medical services of an *otologist,* a physician with an expertise in treating auditory disorders. Other specialists who can help students include psychiatrists, neurologists, orthopedic surgeons, and ear, eye, nose, and throat specialists. Although they are not physicians, optometrists and audiologists can assist in the assessment and treatment of students with visual and hearing impairments, respectively.

Because physicians are costly, many medical-related services may be provided by school nurses, who can screen students for sensory and physical problems; treat some illnesses; offer explanations of medical records; monitor the effects of pharmacological interventions; teach students specific health-care skills; offer training in nutrition, dental care, and other health-related skills; check the fit, maintenance, and functioning of prosthetic and adaptive devices; and help parents obtain medical and dental services.

The Physical and Occupational Therapist

Students with fine and gross motor problems may require the services of physical and occupational therapists. These therapists can be a source of valuable information as part of the multidisciplinary team. The physical therapist usually focuses on the assessment and training of the lower extremities and large muscles, while the occupational therapist deals with the upper extremities and fine motor abilities (Gearheart, Weishahn, & Gearheart, 1988). The physical therapist helps students strengthen muscles, improve posture, and increase motor function and range (Gloeckler & Simpson, 1988). The occupational therapist works with students to prevent, restore, or adapt to impaired or lost motor functions, and to develop the necessary fine motor skills to perform everyday independent tasks. In addition to providing direct services to students, the physical therapist is a consultant to teachers, nurses, and adaptive physical

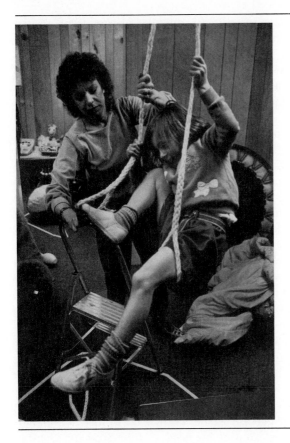

Physical therapists focus on the assessment and training of the lower extremities and large muscles. (Photo: Mark Antman/The Image Works)

educators who are responsible for implementing the therapy program. For students with impaired motor functions, occupational and physical therapists can offer recommendations concerning the use of adaptive equipment, as well as suggestions for adapting materials and classroom environments (Haring & McCormick, 1986).

Prereferral Strategies

While many referrals for special education placement are made by regular educators, referrals also may be made by parents, support personnel, administrators, physicians, significant individuals in the student's life, and the student. Most students referred for testing are placed in special education in the category in which they were referred.

Many school districts have instituted some type of prereferral system through the multidisciplinary team or a teacher assistance team to reduce the number of special education placements (Chalfant, Pysh, & Moultrie, 1979). In *a prereferral system,* a team of educators provides assistance to regular classroom teachers prior to considering a referral for a special education placement (Graden, Casey, & Christenson, 1985; Hayek, 1987). The team helps the regular education teacher devise and implement interventions to keep the student in the regular classroom. Possible interventions include behavior management systems, curricular and testing modifications, and instructional strategies adaptations. The effectiveness of these interventions is assessed before formally evaluating the student for placement in special education. If the interventions are effective, the student remains in the regular classroom. If they are not effective, a formal evaluation is conducted.

Prereferral interventions have been successful in reducing the number of students placed in special education. Graden, Casey, and Bonstrom (1985) implemented a prereferral system that resulted in a decline in the number of students tested for and placed in special education. Chalfant, Pysh, and Moultrie (1979) found that a prereferral system reduced the percentage of students subsequently referred for special education placement to 37 per cent of the students referred to the preferral team. Gilmer (1985) reported that prereferral interventions were successful in helping teachers keep students in the regular classroom in 62 per cent of the cases. In addition to decreasing special education placements, prereferral systems provide data to assist placement teams in determining appropriate special education services; increase teacher knowledge of instructional alternatives; and help teachers examine the needs of their students (Schram & Semmel, 1984).

Eligibility for Special Education

When prereferral strategies are not effective, the multidisciplinary placement team determines if a student is eligible for special education placement based on a variety of standardized and informal assessment procedures (see Chapter 9). Although problems with labeling students have been noted (Ysseldyke & Algozzine, 1982), state and federal funding formulas require the use of labels and definitions. However, educators must realize that no two students are alike, and, therefore, each educational program must be based on individual needs rather than on a label (Haring & McCormick, 1986).

Students with special needs are categorized as mildly handicapped, sensory impaired, physically handicapped, and severely handicapped.

Students with mild handicaps make up the largest percentage of students with disabilities, and include students labeled learning-disabled, sensory-impaired, educable mentally retarded, mildly behaviorally disordered, and speech- and language-impaired. *Students with sensory impairments* are those who have specific sensory disabilities, including hearing and visual impairments. *Students with physical disabilities* have a variety of unique physical needs, and include students who are orthopedically impaired or health-impaired. Individuals who are deaf-blind, multihandicapped, seriously emotionally disturbed, or profoundly retarded are said to be *severely handicapped*.

Students with Learning Disabilities

The largest group of mildly handicapped students are those classified as *learning-disabled*. In addition to the term learning disabilities, these students also may be referred to as having perceptual problems, minimal brain dysfunction, hyperactivity, attention deficits, information processing problems, dyslexia, and developmental aphasia. The federal government estimates that approximately 5 per cent of the students in our nation's schools are learning-disabled (United States Department of Education, 1988). However, some school districts report estimates as high as 20 per cent of their school population (Tucker, Stevens, & Ysseldyke, 1983). The fact is that between 1978 and 1987, the number of students identified as having learning disabilities has increased by approximately one million (United States Department of Education, 1988).

The variation in the estimates of students with learning disabilities is related to the vagueness of the definitions of a learning disability as well as to differences in the assessment procedures used to identify students. Additionally, the comparative social acceptability of the learning disabilities label has led many school districts to categorize low-achieving students and other mildly handicapped students as learning-disabled (Mercer, 1986). Although several definitions of the term learning disabilities have been proposed (Hammill, Leigh, McNutt & Larsen, 1981; Wallace & McLoughlin, 1979), most definitions of learning disabilities include students exhibiting a discrepancy between their intellectual ability and their academic achievement and exclude students whose learning problems are due to a sensory or motor handicap; mental retardation; emotional disturbance; or environmental, cultural, or economic factors. The United States Office of Education's (USOE) (1977) defines a specific learning disability as

> a disorder in one or more of the basic psychological processes involved in understanding or in using language, spoken or written, which may man-

ifest itself in an imperfect ability to listen, think, speak, read, write, spell, or to do mathematical calculations. The term includes such conditions as perceptual handicaps, brain injury, minimal brain dysfunction, dyslexia, and developmental aphasia. The term does not include children who have learning problems which are primarily the result of visual, hearing or motor handicaps, of mental retardation, or emotional disturbance, or of environmental, cultural, or economic disadvantage.

Just as the definitions and estimates of students with learning disabilities vary, the explanations of the causes of learning disabilities also vary. Some researchers believe that the etiology of learning disabilities is brain dysfunction. Initially, proponents of the brain dysfunction cause of learning disabilities focused on research to differentiate students with learning disabilities from their peers on the basis of hard and soft signs of neurological impairments (Gottesman, Croen, & Rotkin, 1982; Myklebust & Boshes, 1969). The results of these studies, however, were unclear as neurological irregularities were present in both learning-disabled and non-learning-disabled students. Although some researchers continue to identify neurological factors that distinguish individuals with learning disabilities (Ahn et al., 1980), many are now examining the relationship between learning disabilities and the hemispheric differences of the brain (Galaburda, 1983; Harness, Epstein, & Gordon, 1984).

Research also has been conducted to examine the role of heredity as a cause of learning disabilities. Studies show the learning problems often are common to several family members (Decker & DeFries, 1980). Similarly, other studies support the finding that twins who have the same genetic makeup (identical twins) are more likely to have similar learning patterns than twins who do not have the same genetic makeup (fraternal twins) (Hermann, 1959). However, the results of these studies fail to take into account environmental factors such as economic status, cultural and linguistic differences, educational experience, and family interaction and child-rearing practices that can affect the ability to learn (Argulewicz, 1983; Coles, 1980; Kavale, 1980).

Characteristics of Students with Learning Disabilities

Because of the wide range of characteristics associated with learning disabilities, these students present many enigmas for educators. Despite the presumption that students with learning disabilities have normal or above normal intelligence, they often fail to perform academic tasks at a level commensurate with their potential or equal to their peers. This discrepant performance usually results in problems with reading, writing, spelling, and mathematics.

The characteristics and behaviors of individual students labeled learning-disabled vary; many learning-disabled students evidence problems in a variety of areas. These difficulties may manifest themselves in learning, language, perceptual, motor, social, and behavioral problems.

LEARNING PROBLEMS.   Many learning-disabled students have memory and attention problems that hinder their ability to master academic content (Hallahan & Kauffman, 1982; Weener & Senf, 1982). Studies indicate that the performance of students with learning disabilities on school-related academic tasks lags behind their non-learning-disabled peers (Bryan, Pearl, Donahue, Bryan, & Pflaum, 1983) and that this gap increases with age (Cone, Wilson, Bradley, & Reese, 1985). Although most students with learning disabilities have reading problems, they may be proficient in some content areas but experience difficulties in others. Students with learning disabilities also tend to use inefficient and ineffective strategies for learning (Alley & Deshler, 1979; Torgesen, 1977). For example, Wong (1982) noted that learning-disabled students often fail to use appropriate metacognitive strategies to complete a task.

LANGUAGE PROBLEMS.   Language disorders are another common characteristic of many learning-disabled students (Mercer, 1986). Many educators believe that the language problems experienced by learning-disabled students contribute to their difficulties in reading and acquiring information in the content areas (Wiig & Semel, 1984).

PERCEPTUAL AND MOTOR PROBLEMS.   Even though it appears that their senses are not impaired, many students with learning disabilities may experience difficulties recognizing, discriminating, and interpreting visual and auditory stimuli (Gearheart, Weishahn, & Gearheart, 1988; Morsink, 1981). For example, some students with learning disabilities may experience difficulty discriminating shapes and letters, copying from the blackboard, following multiple step directions, associating sounds with letters, paying attention to relevant stimuli, and working on a task for a sustained period of time. While some educators consider perception as an underlying factor in learning, others question its importance (Arter & Jenkins, 1979).

Students with learning disabilities also may have deficits in their gross and fine motor skills (Mercer, 1986). Gross motor deficits include awkward gaits, clumsiness, and an inability to catch or kick balls, skip, and follow a rhythmic sequence of movements. Fine motor problems include difficulty cutting, pasting, drawing, and holding a pencil. Another motor problem found in some learning-disabled students is hyperactivity, which results in constant movement and difficulty staying seated (Myers & Hammill, 1982).

SOCIAL AND BEHAVIORAL PROBLEMS.   Students with learning disabilities may have social and behavioral problems (Wallace & McLoughlin, 1979) and may show signs of poor self-concept, task avoidance, social withdrawal, frustration, and anxiety (Mercer, 1986). Research also indicates that the poor social perception of learning-disabled students results in students having difficulties relating to their peers (Bryan, 1977; Gresham & Reschly, 1986).

Another social-emotional trait often associated with learning-disabled students is *learned helplessness* or the inability to establish a locus of control. As a result, students with learning disabilities often are unable to attribute to themselves their own success or failure. While many individuals believe their success and failure is related to their efforts and ability, students with learning disabilities exhibit a learned helplessness—they attribute academic success to factors beyond their control (Pearl, Bryan, & Donahue, 1980).

Students With Mental Retardation

Along with the significant increase in the number of students classified as learning-disabled, there has been a decrease in the number of students classified as mentally retarded (Polloway & Smith, 1983; Reschly, 1988). During the last ten years, the number of students with mental retardation has decreased by 20 per cent (United States Department of Education, 1988). Currently, these students comprise 1.68 per cent of the preschool and school-aged students in the United States (United States Department of Education, 1988). The USOE (1977) defines students who are mentally retarded as having

significantly subaverage general intellectual functioning existing concurrently with deficits in adaptive behavior and manifested during the developmental period, which adversely affects a child's educational performance.

The causes of mental retardation can be categorized as biomedical and social-environmental (Lynch, 1988). Biomedical causes include genetic and chromosomal disorders, infectious diseases (e.g., congenital rubella, meningitis), gestational and obstetric disorders (e.g., prematurity, Rh incompatibility, lack of oxygen, perinatal injury), environmental hazards (for example, lead poisoning, fetal alcohol syndrome, head injuries), and neurocutaneous syndromes (Moore, 1982). However, biomedical factors account for the documented cause in only 20 to 30 per cent of the cases (Garber & McInerney, 1982).

The predominant cause of mental retardation, particularly mild retardation, is thought to be social-environmental factors. Social-environmental factors that can affect a student's intellectual functioning and adaptive behavior performance include socioeconomic status, parenting style, health care, and nutrition and educational opportunities.

Depending on the degree of mental retardation, students may be classified as mildly, moderately, or severely/profoundly mentally handicapped. Students with *mild retardation* make up approximately 85 per cent of the total number of students with mental retardation (Gajria & Hughes, 1988). Their IQs range from above 50 to below 75 and they exhibit many of the behaviors of their learning-disabled counterparts. However, while learning-disabled students show an uneven learning profile with strengths and weaknesses in the different areas, students who are mildly retarded typically show a low learning profile in all areas.

Research indicates that students with mild retardation have difficulty learning material because of problems in

- paying attention to a task for an extended period of time
- attending to the important aspects of a task
- transferring and generalizing skills learned to new situations
- acquiring information through incidental learning
- remembering information that has just been taught
- using and understanding language
- thinking abstractly (Espin & Deno, 1988)

These problems often result in school performance that is significantly behind their nonretarded peers. The frustration of repeated school failure may in turn lead to low self-esteem, an inability to work independently, and an expectancy of failure (Espin & Deno, 1988). Additionally, many students with mild retardation have poor social skills that hinder their ability to interact with their peers (Strain & Shores, 1977).

Students with *moderate retardation* have IQ scores that range from 30 to 50 and compose between 6 to 10 per cent of the individuals with mental retardation (Gajria & Hughes, 1988). Their performance levels tend to be slightly below the performance levels of students with mild retardation. Educational programs for students with moderate retardation often focus on the development of communication, vocational, daily living, and functional academic skills. As a result of these programs, many individuals with moderate retardation often learn basic reading and math skills and usually are employed and live independently in the community (Espin & Deno, 1988).

Students with *severe and profound retardation* have IQ scores below 30 and account for 4 per cent of the individuals with mental retardation (Gajria & Hughes, 1988). These individuals may engage in inappropriate behavior such as tantrums, headbanging, attacks against others, pica, stereotypic and self-injurious behavior (Espin & Deno, 1988). Additionally, many of these students may have unique physical and health needs (Westling, 1986). Educational programs for these students help them learn appropriate behavior, develop functional living and communication skills, and obtain employment in a supervised work setting. Even though these students are often educated in self-contained classrooms or specialized schools, successful programs to integrate them into the mainstream of the school exist (Stainback & Stainback, 1988).

Students with Emotional and Behavioral Disorders

Several different terms are used to refer to students with emotional and behavior problems. These terms include emotionally disturbed, behaviorally disordered, conduct disordered, and socially maladjusted (Cartwright, Cartwright, & Ward, 1985). These students make up 1 per cent of the preschool and school-aged population (Jordan & Zantal-Weiner, 1987) with males significantly outnumbering females (Mendelsohn & Jennings, 1986). Students with behavioral disorders tend to be identified as they enter the middle grades (Morse, Cutler, & Fink, 1964). The USOE (1977) defines a seriously emotionally disturbed student as:

1. Exhibiting one or more of the following characteristics over a long period of time and to a marked degree, which adversely affects educational performance:
   a. An inability to learn which cannot be explained by intellectual, sensory, or health factors;
   b. An inability to build or maintain satisfactory interpersonal relationships with peers and teachers;
   c. Inappropriate types of behavior or feelings under normal circumstances;
   d. A general pervasive mood of unhappiness or depression or
   e. A tendency to develop physical symptoms or fears associated with personal or school problems.
2. The term includes children who are schizophrenic or autistic. The term does not include children who are socially maladjusted, unless it is determined that they are seriously emotionally disturbed.

Several biological and environmental factors appear to affect an individual's behavior (Doorlag, 1988). Biological variables such as genetic, neurological, biochemical, and nutritional factors can contribute to a behavior disorder (Nicol & Erlenmeyer-Kimling, 1986). While biologi-

cal factors are thought to make an individual more vulnerable to behavior disorders (Thomas & Chess, 1984), environmental factors such
as parent-child interaction, cultural background, and school experience
also can influence the development of a behavior disorder (Hallahan &
Kauffman, 1988).

Regardless of the term used, these students are often categorized as
mildly or severely disturbed depending upon their behaviors and the nature of their condition. Students who are _mildly disturbed_ may resemble
learning-disabled and mildly retarded students in terms of their academic
and social needs (McCoy & Prehm, 1987). While the intellectual abilities of students with mild behavior disorders varies, many have IQ scores
in the low average range (Hallahan & Kauffman, 1988). Their classroom
behavior is often characterized by learning problems that cause poor academic performance and deficient social skills (Lewis & Doorlag, 1987).
They may exhibit high rates of inappropriate behavior such as tem-
per tantrums, hitting and fighting with others, cursing, destruction of
property, distractibility, attention seeking, and hyperactivity. They exhibit low rates of appropriate behavior such as attending to a task, working independently, interacting with peers, following rules and directions
(Cullinan & Epstein, 1986; Quay, 1979).

Students considered _severely emotionally disturbed_ exhibit many deviant behaviors over a period of time. These students may exhibit cognitive, perceptual, speech and language deficits. They also may lack daily
living skills, engage in self-stimulatory and self-mutilatory behaviors,
harm others, and fail to respond to others (Hallahan & Kauffman, 1988).

Students with Speech/Language Impairments

A growing number of students with special needs have _speech and
language impairments._ Approximately 3 per cent of preschool and
school-aged children have been identified as having a speech or language impairment (Jordan & Zantal-Wiener, 1987). Most students with
speech and language impairments are identified when they are between
the ages of five and 14 (Swift, 1988). A student with a speech/language
impairment has

> a communication disorder, such as stuttering, impaired articulation, a
> language impairment, or a voice impairment that adversely affects a child's
> educational performance (USOE, 1977).

These students have receptive and expressive language disorders that
hinder their performance in the classroom. _Receptive language_ refers to
the ability to understand spoken language. Students with receptive lan-

guage problems may have difficulty following directions and benefitting from material presented orally.

Expressive language relates to the ability to express one's ideas in words and sentences. Students with expressive language disorders may be reluctant to participate in verbal activities that can have a negative effect on their academic performance and their social-emotional development. Expressive language disorders include articulation, voice, and fluency disorders. Students with articulation disorders comprise approximately 75 per cent of the students with communication disorders (Swift, 1988). Articulation problems include omissions (for example, the student says "ird" instead of "bird"), substitutions (the student says "wove" instead of "love"), distortions (the student may distort a sound so that it sounds like another sound), and additions (the student says "ruhace" for "race").

Students with voice disorders are approximately 6 per cent of the school-age students identified as speech/language impaired (Moore, 1986). Voice disorders relate to deviations in the pitch, volume, and quality of sounds produced. Breathiness, hoarseness, harshness, as well as problems in resonation are all indications of possible voice quality disorders.

Fluency disorders, which relate to the rate and rhythm of an individual's speech, account for 3 per cent of the communication disorders (Swift, 1988). Although stuttering is the most prevalent type of fluency disorder, cluttering which involves talking in a rapid, disorganized manner that is difficult to understand, is another type of fluency disorder (Hallahan & Kauffman, 1988).

Speech and language disorders may be caused by biological and environmental factors. Nervous system dysfunctions can impair speech production and language functions, while structural deviations (for example, cleft palates, loss of teeth) and obstructions in the nasal passages can cause disorders in speech production (Swift, 1988). Although it is difficult to identify the cause of most communication disorders, environmental factors such as vocal misuse, inappropriate language models, lack of language stimulation, and emotional trauma may also contribute to a speech or language impairment.

Taylor (1986) noted that speech and language abilities can be affected by race, ethnic background, socio-economic status, educational experience, geographical area, gender, peers, context, and exposure to language. Therefore, since students from various ethnic backgrounds and geographic regions may have limited experience with English or speak with a different dialect, educators should exercise caution in identifying these students as speech/language impaired. In fact, many of these students may have already mastered a language or dialect that has many sophisticated structures and rules (Bernthal & Bankson, 1988), and may be quite adept at code switching (Kirk & Gallagher, 1989).

Students with Physical and Health Needs

Students with *physical impairments* and/or health related problems compose 1 per cent of our nation's preschool and school-aged students (Jordan & Zantal-Wiener, 1987). The USOE (1977) recognizes two types of students with physical disabilities : orthopedically impaired and other health impaired. *Orthopedically impaired* students are defined as having

> A severe orthopedic impairment which adversely affects a child's educational performance. The term includes impairments caused by congenital anomaly (e.g., clubfoot, absence of some member, etc.), impairments caused by disease (e.g., poliomyelitis, bone tuberculosis, etc.), and impairments from other causes (e.g., cerebral palsy, amputations, and fractures or burns which cause contractures) [USOE, 1977].

Other health impaired is defined as

> (i) having an autistic condition which is manifested by severe communication and other developmental and educational problems; or (ii) having limited strength, vitality, or alertness, due to chronic or acute health problems such as a heart condition, tuberculosis, rheumatic fever, nephritis, asthma, sickle cell anemia, hemophilia, epilepsy, lead poisoning, leukemia, or diabetes, which adversely affects a child's educational performance [Federal Register, 34, July 1, 1985].

In addition to their physical and medical needs, some of these students may have concomitant handicapping conditions such as learning disabilities, communication disorders, and mental retardation (Bigge & Sirvis, 1986).

Because of the wide range of conditions included in this category, it is difficult to generalize its specific characteristics. As a group, students with physical and health conditions tend to have IQ scores within the normal range. Although their IQ scores tend to be skewed toward the lower side of the IQ curve, many individuals with severe physical disabilities have above average IQ scores (Brady, 1988). However, their academic performance may be negatively affected by irregular school attendance caused by their need for medical care. In terms of social/emotional development, students with physical disabilities appear to be at-risk for developing dependent behavior patterns (Brady, 1988). They also have a lower self-concept and higher anxiety level than their nondisabled peers (Harvey & Greenway, 1984).

Students with Hearing Impairments

Students with hearing impairments constitute about 5 per cent of the school-aged population (Heward & Orlansky, 1988). This category includes deaf and hard-of-hearing students. Students are considered *deaf* when they have

> a hearing impairment which is so severe that the child is impaired in processing linguistic information through hearing, with or without amplification, which adversely affects educational performance [USOE, 1977].

Hard of hearing is defined as:

> a hearing impairment, whether permanent or fluctuating, which adversely affects a child's educational performance but which is not included under the definition of "deaf" [USOE, 1977].

Approximately 0.2 per cent of the school-aged students have a *severe or profound hearing disorder* (Hoemann & Briga, 1981). While students with severe hearing impairments are usually identified and provided with special services, only about 20 per cent of the hard-of-hearing students are receiving special services (Berg, 1986).

Trybus (1985) identified the primary causes of hearing impairments as heredity, maternal rubella, prenatal and perinatal complications, meningitis, and childhood diseases and injuries. However, the etiology of hearing impairments cannot be determined in approximately 20 per cent of the cases (Moores, 1982).

A hearing loss can be *unilateral* (affecting one ear) or *bilateral* (affecting both ears), and may be categorized according to the type and degree of hearing loss (Gearheart, Weishahn, & Gearheart, 1988). There are two types of hearing losses: conductive and sensorineural (Lowenbraun & Thompson, 1986). *Conductive hearing losses* are impairments in the transmission of sound from the outer ear to the middle ear. Some conductive hearing losses can be corrected by surgery, while others can be minimized by use of a hearing aid. *Sensorineural losses* are caused by damage within the inner ear and affect the conversion of sound waves into electrical impulses. Sensorineural losses tend to be permanent; they are not as amenable to correction through surgery or the use of a hearing aid. Both types of hearing losses may affect the student's academic performance, speech/language development, and social skills.

The degree of hearing loss is assessed by giving the student an audiometric evaluation which provides a measure of the intensity and frequency of sound that the student can hear. The intensity of the sound is defined in terms of decibel levels (db); the frequency is measured in hertz (hz). Based on the audiometric evaluation, the hearing loss is classified from mild to profound.

Some hearing disorders may not be detected before children enter school. Many students with hearing losses are identified by their teachers. A student with a hearing loss may

- have difficulty following directions and paying attention to auditory stimuli;
- articulate poorly;
- ask the speaker or peers to repeat statements or instructions;
- avoid oral activities;
- rely heavily on gestures;
- turn up the volume when listening to audiovisual aids such as televisions, radios, and cassette recorders; and
- cock the head to one side (Gearheart, Weishahn, & Gearheart, 1988; Green, 1981).

If a hearing loss is suspected, the student should be referred to the school nurse or physician for an audiometric evaluation.

The intellectual abilities of students with hearing impairments parallel the intellectual capacity of students with hearing. However, the concomitant communication problems in learning an oral language system associated with hearing disorders can create an experiential and informational deficit that hinders the intellectual functioning and academic performance of such students (Moores & Maestas y Moores, 1988). Research indicates that students with hearing impairments perform below their intellectual potential on traditional standardized tests measuring academic achievement (Moores & Maestas y Moores, 1988).

Difficulties in communication also can affect the social/emotional development of students with hearing impairments; they may have difficulty establishing friendships, and exhibit shyness and withdrawn behavior (Loeb & Sarigiani, 1986).

Students with Visual Impairments

Students with visual impairments that require special services make up about 0.1 per cent of the school-aged population (Hallahan & Kauffman, 1988). Definitions and types of visual impairments vary; however, the USOE (1977) defines a *visual handicap* as

> A visual impairment which, even with correction, adversely affects a child's educational performance. The term includes both partially seeing and blind children.

Hereditary is the major cause of visual impairments. Other factors include infectious diseases, poisoning, diabetes, tumors, and prenatal complications. Aging has become a primary cause of blindness in the elderly.

Barraga (1983) identified three types of individuals with visual impairments: blind, low vision, and visually limited. *Blind individuals* have no vision or limited light perception. Individuals who have *low vision* can see objects that are close by but have difficulty seeing things at a distance. Individuals who are *visually limited* need aids or special lighting to see under normal conditions.

Most definitions of a visual impairment measure vision in terms of *acuity,* which is assessed through use of a Snellen Chart. The Snellen Chart provides a measure of the clarity of an individual's vision by comparing the individual's vision to that of a person with normal vision. For example, a visual acuity of 20/100 means that the individual can read a letter or symbol at 20 feet that a person with normal vision could read at 100 feet.

In addition to acuity, visual functioning and efficiency also are important (Barraga, 1983). *Visual efficiency* describes the ease, comfort, and time in which an individual can perform visual tasks; *visual functioning* relates to the ways individuals use the vision they possess (Barraga, 1983). Students who are visually impaired should be encouraged to increase their visual efficiency and functioning.

As a group, individuals with visual impairments have IQ scores within the normal range. However, their cognitive and language development may be limited by their inability to obtain and abstract visual information from the environment (Terzieff, 1988). For example, students with visual impairments may have problems learning spatial concepts. Their language may be characterized by the use of verbalisms, or words or phrases inconsistent with one's sensory experiences (Cutsworth, 1951). Additionally, because of limited mobility, the motor development of some students with visual impairments may be delayed.

In terms of academic achievement, students with visual impairments may lag behind their sighted peers in learning abstract concepts during the middle school years. However, as they enter high school, their ability to understand these abstract concepts improves significantly (Terzieff, 1988). If isolated from peers, students with visual impairments may lack appropriate socialization skills and develop a poor self-image.

Since visual impairments can hinder a student's cognitive, language, motor and social development (Lowenfeld, 1971), early detection of visual impairments is important. Some common indications of visual problems arise when the student:

- holds reading material close to the eyes;
- has difficulty seeing things from a distance;
- blinks, squints, and rubs the eyes or tilts the head frequently;
- covers or closes one eye;
- has frequent swollen eyelids and inflamed or watery eyes; and
- exhibits irregular eye movements (National Society to Prevent Blindness, 1977)

Educators who suspect a visual problem should refer the student to the school nurse or physician.

Individualized Education Program (IEP)

If the multidisciplinary team decides that a student's needs require the provision of special education services, the team—in concert with the student's teachers, parents, and, whenever possible, the student—also determines which educational services a student should receive. While the teacher usually assumes a leadership role in designing this plan, called the Individualized Educational Program (IEP), in many states the multidisciplinary team provides information that assists in writing the student's IEP. The IEP includes:

- a statement of the student's present level of functioning;
- a list of annual goals and the short-term objectives relating to these goals;
- a projection concerning the initiation of services as well as the anticipated duration of the services;
- a determination of the special education services that will be provided to the student, as well as the necessary related services that the student will need to benefit from the provision of special education services; and
- an evaluation procedure, including objective criteria and a timeline for determining the student's progress in mastering the IEP's short-term objectives on at least an annual basis.

In addition, the IEP should contain a determination of the extent to which a student should be placed in the regular education program. A sample IEP is presented in Figure 2.1.

FIGURE 2.1.   A Part of an Individualized Education Plan.

Name: Jack S.   **Sex:** Male   **Grade of Reference Group:** 4th

Date of Birth: 12/25/78   **Chronological Age:** 10-3

Address: 1776 Main Street, New Cliff, NY   **Telephone:**

Parent, Guardian, Surrogate Name: Agnes and Harry S.

Current Educational Placement: Self-contained special education class with part-time in regular class

Dominant Language:
- Student: English
- Home: English

Recommendation for Placement: Regular education class and one hour of resource room per day.

Percentage of time in the Regular Education Program: 83%

Rationale for Placement: Standardized assessment and curriculum-based assessment results indicate that Jack possesses the skills to perform in the regular classroom. However, he will need one hour a day of resource room instruction to support regular classroom instruction in the content areas and help him to make the transition to the regular classroom setting.

Related Services: Jack will require no related services. He needs no adaptive devices or specialized transportation.

Alternative Testing Techniques: Major unit tests in the content areas will be administered by the resource room teacher, who will read test directions when Jack experiences difficulty. Time limits will be waived.

Alternative Grading Systems: A mastery-level grading system will be employed.

Present Level of Functioning (Math): Performance on the *Keymath* and teacher-made, criterion-referenced tests indicate that Jack has mastered addition, subtraction, and multiplication facts and operations. However, he has not mastered division facts and operations.

Long-Term Goal: To improve division facts and operations.

Short-Term Objectives:
1. Given 40 problems with no remainders using one-digit dividends and one-digit divisors, Jack will write the correct answer to each problem within two minutes with no more than two errors.
2. Given 40 problems with no remainders, using two-digit dividends with zero in the ones column and one-digit divisors, Jack will write the correct answer to each problem within three minutes with no more than two errors.
3. Given 40 problems with no remainders, using three-digit dividends with zero in the ones and tens columns and one-digit divisors, Jack will write the correct answer to each problem within three minutes with no more than two errors.
4. Given 40 problems with no remainders, using two-digit dividends and one-digit divisors, Jack will write the correct answer to each problem within three minutes with no more than two errors.

FIGURE 2.1. *(continued)*

5. Given 40 problems with remainders, using one-digit dividends and one-digit divisors, Jack will write the correct answer to each problem within three and one half minutes with no more than two errors.

Evaluation Criteria: Daily timed probes will be employed. When Jack demonstrates mastery of an objective on three consecutive probes, the next objective will be taught. Jack will check his answers using a talking calculator and graph his performance daily.

Timelines:
Date IEP is effective: 1/25/89
Date IEP will be reviewed: 5/18/89

Multidisciplinary Team:

Name	Position	Signature
Ms. Agnes S.	Parent	_____
Mr. Harry S.	Parent	_____
Ms. Kris Doecharm	Principal	_____
Mr. Terry Feaster	Special Education Teacher	_____
Ms. Danielle Doyle	Fourth-Grade Teacher	_____
Mr. John Walker	Resource Room Teacher	_____

Readiness for Mainstreaming

Not every student will be ready for full-time placement in the regular classroom setting (Lewis & Doorlag, 1987). Some students may need part-time resource room assistance to supplement regular education instruction; the educational needs of other students might best be met in self-contained classrooms or specialized programs. Although the multidisciplinary placement team also is responsible for determining a student's readiness for mainstreaming, very few districts have established procedures for determining a student's readiness for entry into the mainstream (Gresham, 1982; Palmer, 1980). Salend, Brooks, and Salend (1985) surveyed school administrators concerning their districts' mainstreaming policies and found that 90 per cent of them did not have a procedure for determining student readiness for mainstreamed placement. Gresham (1982) also addressed the need for explicit guidelines for determining mainstreaming readiness by noting that most districts have interpreted the least restrictive environment concept ". . . to mean that most, if not all handicapped children should be mainstreamed" (p. 430).

A Competency-Based Approach to Mainstreaming

Salend and Lutz (1984) and Hundert (1982) have proposed that the effectiveness of mainstreaming can be increased by employing *a competency-based approach toward mainstreaming*, which necessitates that school districts identify behaviors that are requisite for success in regular education settings, and set minimum standards of acceptability. Placement teams can then assess student readiness for mainstreaming by determining mastery of the identified competencies within the standards of acceptability. Performance within the acceptable levels would suggest that a candidate is ready for mainstreaming.

For students lacking the necessary skills to be mainstreamed, the competencies can form the objectives of a training program to increase their readiness for mainstreaming in the future. Thus, the competencies can provide educators with a framework of objectives in which to teach, so that the student's ability to be mainstreamed successfully is increased. These objectives could then be incorporated into the student's IEP.

The competencies also may facilitate continuous communication between regular and special educators. Initially, placement teams may use the competencies to provide regular educators with relevant data to document the readiness of students to enter the mainstream. This documentation can help allay the concerns of regular classroom teachers by assuring them that students possess the skills to perform in the regular classroom. Next, the teacher can employ the competencies as a checklist for ongoing evaluation of student progress in the regular classroom. Areas of weakness identified by the ongoing evaluation then can be remediated by cooperative interactions between regular and special education teachers.

Social Skill Competencies

Several researchers have begun to identify the competencies that contribute to success in regular education programs. Wilkes, Bireley, and Schultz (1979) surveyed educators concerning the importance of forty-one academic and social criteria in deciding on an elementary-level student's readiness for placement in a mainstreamed setting. They concluded that a student's behavior was considered more important than academic performance in determining a student's readiness for mainstreaming. Other social skills they found to be important for success in mainstreamed settings included the ability to interact with the teacher and peers, and to work independently.

Similarly, Salend and Lutz (1984) surveyed elementary-level regular and special education teachers to identify the social skill competencies these teachers felt a mainstreamed student should possess to be successful in the regular classroom. The teachers surveyed rated seventeen social skills as critical for success in the mainstream. These skills related to the social skill areas of interacting positively with others, obeying class rules, and displaying proper work habits; they are presented in Figure 2.2.

Furthermore, differences were found between intermediate-level (third grade through sixth grade) and primary-level (kindergarten through second grade) teachers, with the behavioral demands of intermediate-level settings being more rigorous than the behavioral expectations in primary-level settings. The results suggest that classroom behaviors such as handraising, working independently, sitting in seats, and lining up are more important for success in intermediate-level classrooms than they are in primary-level classrooms. Therefore, in placing students in mainstreamed settings, placement teams should consider differences

FIGURE 2.2.   Elementary-Level Social Skill Competencies.

Each competency is preceded by the competency stem, *To function effectively in elementary-level regular education settings, mainstreamed students should be able to*

1. follow directions.
2. ask for help when it's appropriate.
3. begin an assignment after the teacher gives it to the class.
4. demonstrate an adequate attention span.
5. obey class rules.
6. try to complete a task before giving up.
7. refrain from speaking when others are talking.
8. work well with others.
9. respect the feelings of others.
10. refrain from cursing and swearing.
11. avoid getting in fights with others.
12. play cooperatively with others.
13. respect the property of others.
14. share materials and property with others.
15. refrain from stealing others' property.
16. attend class regularly.
17. tell the truth.

Source: S. J. Salend and J. G. Lutz, *Journal of Learning Disabilities* (1984).

in the social skill requirements that are a function of variations in grade-level placements.

Salend and Salend (1986) examined the social skill competencies necessary for successful performance in secondary mainstreamed settings. Although some similarities arose between responses of elementary- and secondary-level educators, the findings indicated that there is a more stringent attitude at the secondary level concerning classroom decorum and behavioral expectations. Whereas the elementary-level educators rated seventeen skills as very important (Salend & Lutz, 1984), the secondary-level educators identified twenty-nine skills as very important. These twenty-nine social skills are presented in Figure 2.3. A discrepancy also was noted between the responses of the junior high school educators and the high school educators, with junior high educators being more stringent than their high school counterparts.

MEASURING MASTERY OF THE SOCIAL SKILL COMPETENCIES. Placement teams can measure the student's mastery of the social competencies in a variety of ways. Data on the student's social competence can be collected by having one of the placement team members observe the student in his or her current classroom setting and sharing the results of the observation with other team members in an anecdotal report. The observation can provide information in a variety of areas, but it should be focused on the competencies the placement team is interested in measuring. Cartwright and Cartwright (1974) suggest several guidelines for conducting an observation that the placement team should follow, such as

- selecting an individual to serve as the observer;
- identifying the behaviors that will be observed;
- delineating the setting(s) of the observation(s);
- determining when the observation(s) will be conducted; and
- deciding on a method for recording the observation(s).

DEFINING BEHAVIOR. First, the team should select the social skill competencies that will be helpful in making the decision concerning a student's readiness for mainstreaming. Next, these competencies should be operationally defined in observable and measurable terms. For example, the social skill of *demonstrates adequate attention* could be clearly defined as *eyes on the teacher or an instructional object, whichever is appropriate for the learning environment.*

CHOOSING A RECORDING SYSTEM. After the behavior has been operationally defined, an appropriate recording strategy should be selected and implemented during a day that is typical and representative. The

FIGURE 2.3.   Secondary-Level Social Skill Competencies.

Each competency is preceded by the competency stem, *To function effectively in secondary-level regular education settings, mainstreamed students should be able to*

1. attend class regularly.
2. refrain from stealing others' property.
3. obey class rules.
4. follow directions.
5. respect the property of others.
6. refrain from cutting classes.
7. avoid getting in fights with others.
8. respect adults.
9. tell the truth.
10. bring the necessary materials to class.
11. refrain from cheating on tests.
12. try to complete a task before giving up.
13. ask for help when it is appropriate.
14. complete homework.
15. refrain from cursing and swearing.
16. demonstrate an adequate attention span.
17. refrain from speaking when others are talking.
18. display proper health and hygiene habits.
19. communicate their needs.
20. remember more than one oral direction at a time.
21. exhibit appropriate behavior in large group settings.
22. begin an assignment after the teacher gives it to the class.
23. be aware of the effects of their behavior on others.
24. complete work on time.
25. refrain from boastful comments concerning inappropriate behaviors.
26. respect the feelings of others.
27. seek teacher permission before speaking.
28. avoid distractions.
29. work well with others.

Source: S. J. Salend and S. M. Salend, *Journal of Learning Disabilities* (1986).

recording system selected should relate to the nature or the behavior being observed. Examples of recording systems are presented in Figure 2.4.

EVENT RECORDING.   If the behavior to be observed has a discrete beginning and ending and occurs for brief, uniform time periods, *event recording* is an appropriate choice (Koorland, Monda, & Vail, 1988). In event recording, the observer counts the number of behaviors that occurred during the observation period (see Figure 2.4a). For example, a teacher could use event recording to count the number of times a student calls out during a thirty-minute teacher-directed activity. Data collected using event recording is displayed as either a frequency (number of times it occurred) or a rate (number of times it occurred per length of observation).

Teachers often use an inexpensive grocery, stitch, or golf counter to assist in event recording. If a mechanical counter is not available, marks can be made on a pad, index card, blackboard, or piece of paper taped

FIGURE 2.4.   Examples of Observational Recording Strategies.

Date	Length of Sessions	Number of Events
9/11	30 minutes	卌
9/15	30 minutes	卌 卌 l
9/20	30 minutes	l l l

(a) Event Recording of Call-outs

Date	Occurrence Number	Time Start	End	Total Duration
5/8	1	9:20	9:25	5 minutes
	2	9:27	9:30	3 minutes
5/9	1	10:01	10:03	2 minutes
	2	10:05	10:06	1 minute
	3	10:10	10:14	4 minutes

(b) Duration Recording of Out-of-seat Behavior

15 Sec	15 Sec	15 Sec	15 Sec
+	−	−	+
+	+	−	−
+	−	−	−
−	+	+	+
+	+	−	+

(c) Interval Recording of On-task Behavior

to the wrist. Some teachers use a transfer system where they place small objects (for example, poker chips or paper clips) in one pocket, and transfer one of the objects to another pocket each time the behavior occurs. The number of objects transferred to the second pocket gives an accurate measure of the behavior.

DURATION OR LATENCY RECORDING. If time is an important factor of the observed behavior, an appropriate recording strategy would be either duration or latency recording. *Duration recording* involves the observer recording the length of time a behavior lasts (see Figure 2.4b). *Latency recording,* on the other hand, is used to determine the length of time it takes an individual to begin a task after receiving instructions or a request from the teacher. For example, if a teacher was interested in finding out how much time a student spends out of his or her seat during a twenty-five-minute independent seatwork period, duration recording would be used. However, if a teacher wanted to assess how long it took a student to begin an assignment after the directions were presented, latency recording would be employed. Both of these recording systems can be presented as the total length of time or as a duration average. Duration recording data also can be summarized as a percentage of time in which the student engaged in the behavior by dividing the length of time the behavior occurs by the length of the observation period, then multiplying by 100.

INTERVAL RECORDING OR TIME SAMPLING. *Interval recording,* or *time sampling,* is another method that can be used to record behaviors. When using interval recording, the observer divides the observation period into equal intervals and records whether or not the behavior occurred during each of the intervals, with a plus (+) indicating occurrence and a minus (−) indicating nonoccurrence of the behavior. In interval recording systems, the intervals usually do not exceed thirty seconds, while the intervals in time sampling are usually defined in terms of minutes (Alberto & Troutman, 1986). A + does not indicate how many times the behavior occurred in that interval, but only that the behavior did occur. Therefore, this system is scored as the percentage of intervals in which the behavior has occurred, rather than as a frequency.

The percentage of intervals in which a behavior occurred is calculated by dividing the number of intervals in which the behavior occurred by the total number of intervals in the observation period, then multiplying by 100. For example, a teacher might use an interval recording system to measure on-task behavior. After defining the behavior, the teacher would divide the observation period into intervals and construct a corresponding interval score sheet (see Figure 2.4c). Using the score sheet, the teacher would record whether the student was on-task or not for each interval. The teacher would then divide the number of intervals in which the behavior occurred by the number of total intervals to determine the percentage of intervals in which the student was on-task.

There are three types of interval/time sampling recording systems: whole, partial, and momentary. In *whole interval recording,* the behavior must occur continuously during the entire interval for it to be scored as an occurrence. In *partial interval recording,* the observer records an occurrence of the behavior if the behavior was exhibited at least once during the interval. In *momentary interval recording,* the observer checks to see if the behavior is occurring only toward the end of the interval.

ANECDOTAL RECORDS. An *anecdotal record,* also referred to as *continuous recording,* is often an appropriate method of reporting the results of the observation. An anecdotal record is a narrative of the events that took place during the observation. Wright (1967) offers several suggestions for writing narrative anecdotal reports, including

- describing the activities, design, individuals, and their relationships to the setting in which the observation was conducted;
- reporting in observable terms all verbal and nonverbal behaviors of the targeted student, as well as the responses of others to these behaviors;
- avoiding interpretations; and
- providing an indication of the sequence and duration of events.

A sample anecdotal record is presented in Figure 2.5. Alberto and Troutman (1986) suggest that educators analyze data collected in an anecdotal report by responding to the following questions:

1. What are the behaviors that can be described as inappropriate?
2. Is this behavior occurring frequently, or has a unique occurrence been identified?
3. Can reinforcement or punishment be identified?
4. Is there a pattern to these consequences?
5. Can antecedents to the behavior be identified?
6. Is there a pattern that can be identified for certain events or stimuli (antecedents) that consistently precede the behavior's occurrence? (p. 100.)

CHECKLISTS AND RATING SCALES. Placement teams also can use checklists and rating scales to assess student performance with respect to the competencies. After the checklist is developed, individuals familiar with the student can be asked to rate the student on each item. To ensure that the rating is accurate, the ratings should be performed by a variety of individuals in different settings.

FIGURE 2.5.   Sample Anecdotal Report.

The observation of Jack took place on the school playground during a fifteen-minute recess period. The playground is made up of an open space area for group games and an area with typical playground equipment of swings, a jungle gym, and two slides. During the first five minutes of the observation, Jack played by himself on a swing with no interactions with his peers, who were also swinging or waiting for a turn. One of the waiting students asked Jack for a turn on the swing. Jack ignored the request, neither slowing down the swing, making eye contact, or verbally responding to the student. The teacher's aide then intervened, asking Jack to finish his ride so others could have a turn. Jack responded by jumping off the swing in mid-flight and loudly cursing at the aide. The aide then removed Jack from the playground.

THE SBS INVENTORY OF TEACHER SOCIAL BEHAVIOR STANDARDS AND EXPECTATIONS

One such rating scale that has been developed is the *SBS Inventory of Teacher Social Behavior Standards and Expectations,* or simply the *SBS Inventory* (Walker & Rankin, 1983). The SBS Inventory has three sections designed to aid educators in determining the behavioral demands of the regular classroom setting. Part 1 asks teachers to rate as *critical, desirable,* or *unimportant* fifty-six prosocial behaviors of children. Similarly, in Part 2, teachers rate the acceptability of fifty-one inappropriate behaviors using the choices of *unacceptable, tolerated,* or *acceptable.* In Part 3, teachers determine which skills from Parts 1 and 2 are important for the student to master to be successful in the mainstreamed setting. Examples of items from Parts 1 and 2 of the SBS are presented in Figure 2.6.

PEER REFERENCING.   Once the student's behavior has been recorded, it can be compared to the levels of the same behavior in the regular classroom through *peer referencing* (Brulle, Barton, & Repp, 1984; Deno, 1985), whereby data on the performance of students in the regular classroom are collected by recording the behavior of randomly selected students. These data then provide a normative baseline for assessing the mainstreaming candidate's performance in relation to nonhandicapped peers. Germann and Tindal (1985) provide a formula that educators can use to calculate the discrepancy between the behavioral rates of the mainstreaming candidate and the nonhandicapped classroom peers. In this formula, the median rate of the nonhandicapped students as well as the mainstreaming candidate's rate of behavior are computed and then compared by dividing the lower number into the higher number.

In interpreting these data, placement teams should consider the variations in performance that may be a function of the setting and the

FIGURE 2.6.   Sample Items from the SBS Inventory.

Sample Item from Part 1			
	Critical	*Desirable*	*Unimportant*
Child is flexible and can adjust to different instructional situations.	( )	( )	( )

Sample Item from Part 2			
	Unacceptable	*Tolerated*	*Acceptable*
Child disturbs or disrupts the activities of others.	( )	( )	( )

activity. For example, the estimates of on-task behavior for regular elementary classes average 70 per cent and 85 per cent during seatwork and teacher-directed activities, respectively, while mildly handicapped students in special education classes tend to be on-task during seatwork and teacher-directed activities approximately 60 per cent and 90 per cent of the time, respectively (Wilson, 1987).

Academic Competencies

In addition to social skills, mainstreamed students should have the academic skills necessary to benefit from regular classroom instructional programs (Conway & Gow, 1988). Therefore, placement teams also should consider the student's mastery of the requisite academic skills in determining a student's readiness for mainstreaming. Wilkes, Bireley, and Schultz (1979) reported that a sample group of school psychologists, regular classroom teachers, learning disabilities teachers, and supervisors of programs for the learning-disabled identified eight skills that were important for academic success in the regular classroom. These skills include the ability to

- recognize familiar words;
- write and read with no reversals;
- express oneself in writing;
- comprehend and use speech;
- read at the appropriate level and have requisite math skills;

- follow oral and written directions;
- retain general concepts; and
- handle the academic demands of the class.

Lowenthal (1987) believes that mainstreamed students should be able to use regular classroom textbooks, perform at a consistent and appropriate level of speed and accuracy on assignments, and demonstrate an ability to complete assignments. Schumaker, Deshler, Alley, and Warner (1983) noted that secondary students must be able to adjust to a bigger school with a larger student body, new and more difficult content areas taught by different teachers, and a greater emphasis on displaying independent behaviors.

The curriculum of the class in which the student will be placed can serve as a guide for assessing a student's readiness for the academic rigors of the mainstreamed setting. However, standardized tests may be of limited value in providing placement teams with data to make this decision (Palmer, 1980). Because of differences in content, conditions, environmental surroundings, and motivational factors, the student's performance on standardized tests may be markedly different from performance in the mainstreamed setting (Bortner & Birch, 1970). Therefore, placement teams should examine some recent criterion-referenced curriculum-based assessment data of the student's academic skills and compare the student's performance to the skills and objectives outlined in the classroom's curriculum.

Brulle, Barton, & Repp (1984) suggest that educators examine how the student performs on simple academic tasks that are typical in the mainstreamed setting, such as homework assignments, tests, worksheets, and instructional materials. Furthermore, information on the student relative to the mainstream curriculum can be gathered through a meeting of the sending special education teacher and the receiving regular education teacher; they should review the student's record with respect to the curriculum. The special educator should complete a checklist rating the student's mastery of the objectives that comprise the curriculum of the mainstreamed setting.

Since a major vehicle of instruction in most classrooms is a textbook, mainstreamed students must master the ability to obtain information from a text. Therefore, it is important that mainstreamed students possess the reading skills needed to acquire information from the textbook and other instructional materials used in the classroom. Educators can determine this ability by examining the readability of the textbooks and instructional materials employed in the classes in which the student will be mainstreamed. The student's reading ability should then be compared with the readability levels of the materials in terms of independent, instructional, and frustration levels.

READABILITY FORMULAS.   There are more than fifty readability formulas that can be used to assess textbooks' ranges of readability (Idol, 1988; Schuyler, 1982). Readability formulas provide a measure of the reading level students need to comprehend textbook material (Vaca, Vaca, & Gove, 1987). The readability levels of print materials are usually determined by analyzing the writing style of the author according to semantic and syntactic complexity. *Semantic and syntactic complexity* is often defined in terms of sentence length, the number of syllables in words, and the level of vocabulary.

Educators should exercise caution in using readability formulas to assess the reading levels of texts because problems have been reported (Harris & Sipay, 1985). Armbruster and Anderson (1988) noted that readability formulas fail to account for readers' experiential, cognitive, emotional, motivational, and linguistic backgrounds. Davison (1984) suggests that educators assess the readability of a textbook in terms of clauses used, background information, interrelationship between topics, and the perspective of the author. Educators also can supplement readability formulas by carefully examining and evaluating textbooks in terms of their understandability, usability, and interestability (Vaca, Vaca, & Gove, 1987). Excellent checklists for assessing these aspects of textbooks are available (Clewell & Clifton, 1983; Irwin & Davis, 1980).

The regular education instructional environment may be different from that of special education (Salend & Viglianti, 1982). Therefore, placement teams should consider the student's ability to acquire, retain, and demonstrate mastery of the material presented in the regular classroom. For example, a regular education teacher is more likely than a special education teacher to use a lecture format for delivering material, a homework assignment for practicing and reviewing material, and a written test for evaluating mastery. Mainstreamed students may need to master several learning strategies in order to be efficient and successful learners in the regular classroom (Robinson, Trefz–Braxdale, & Colson, 1988). The multidisciplinary team should consider the student's ability to pay attention to information presented verbally, take notes, prepare reports, write book reports, give oral presentations, understand the language and terminology used in the class and in the discipline, use instructional materials such as reference books and dictionaries, record assignments, complete homework on time, participate in class discussions, seek clarification, react positively to feedback, and take tests (Kokoszka & Drye, 1981; Link, 1980).

Cautions in Using the Competencies

Multidisciplinary placement teams should be aware of several caveats when using the competencies. First, placement teams should not expect each mainstreaming candidate to master all of the social and academic competencies. Such an expectation would be unfair and would severely limit the number of mainstreamed students. Rather, educators should view the competencies as flexible tools for examining the individual's strengths and weaknesses and potential for success in the mainstreamed setting.

Second, because the competencies may differ from district to district, school to school, grade to grade, and class to class, placement teams should consider the unique characteristics of their schools in establishing their own specific mainstreaming competencies and corresponding minimum standards of acceptability. Therefore, while the competencies presented in this chapter can serve as a springboard for assisting teams in delineating a list of mainstreaming competencies, school districts should solicit information from their staffs to develop a list of competencies. These lists can guide placement teams in determining a student's readiness for mainstreaming, as well as establish the minimum expectations for mastery.

Cultural Conflict

Our schools—and, therefore, the academic and social competencies—are based on the Anglo culture (Almanza & Mosley, 1980; Gonzalez, 1974). It is important that educators be aware of potential cultural bias when using the competencies. Because cultures differ in their views, philosophies, values, styles, and languages (Hilliard, 1980), employing the competencies with students not raised in the dominant culture can result in a cultural conflict (Aragon, 1974; Trueba, 1983). Research indicates that the cultural values of Hispanic-Americans (Brischetto & Arciniega, 1980; Pediatric Research and Training Center, 1988), Native Americans (Pepper, 1976), and Asian-Americans (Leung, 1988; Morrow, 1987) differ from the perspectives of Anglo-Americans. These divergent views are summarized in Figure 2.7, and can result in differences in the behaviors and achievement levels of students from these cultures (Morrow, 1987).

Hoover and Collier (1985) noted that the behavior of some students from non-Anglo backgrounds may be related to their cultural norms and customs. For example, a Mexican-American student may appear to be passive, withdrawn, and uninterested in the teacher's questions during an observation period. The observer and the teacher may interpret this behavior as evidence of the student's immaturity. However, it may be an indication of the child's respect for the adult, an authority figure (Ramirez & Price–Williams, 1974). This can be desirable behavior in the Mexican-American culture, where parents emphasize respect for authority as well as strong family ties and strict sex role differentiations

(Ramirez & Casteneda, 1974). The cultural conflict that many students from diverse backgrounds experience may be particularly prevalent during acculturation, when the student is trying to adapt to the new culture (Hoover & Collier, 1986). The framework for contrasting the differences

FIGURE 2.7. Comparison of Asian–American, Hispanic–American, Native–American, and Anglo–American Perspectives.

Asian–American	Hispanic–American	Native–American	Anglo–American
Emphasis on cooperation	Emphasis on sharing and working as a group	Emphasis on working as a group	Emphasis on competition
Subjugate desires and needs to family; family is basis for society	Family unit is important; needs of community supersede needs of individual	Family unit is important	Stress independent behavior
Teachers and parents are highly respected; avoid eye contact with respected individuals	Parents and elders are highly respected	Wisdom of age and experience is respected	Teachers and adults are not automatically respected; make eye contact with respected individuals
Quiet/nonverbal; confrontations with issues and problems are avoided	Interact assertively and stand up for self	Quiet/nonverbal; express self and ideas through actions	People express themselves and attempt to impress others through speech
Humility is valued	Humility is valued	Excellence is related to the contribution to group, not personal glory	Status based on achievement
Time is not critical	Time is not critical	Time is not critical	Punctuality is important
Live on day-to-day basis	Live in the present	Live in the present	Plan for the future
Man lives in harmony with nature	One's condition in life is accepted without question	People conform to nature	Man attempts to dominate nature
Dissociate from others outside of the culture	Depend on extended families and neighbors for support	Depend on extended families and others within culture for support	Seek support and assistance outside the family

Source: Adapted from Brischetto and Arciniega (1980), Leung (1988), Morrow (1987), Pediatric Research and Training Center (1988), Pepper (1976).

between the Anglo and non-Anglo culture may be useful in understanding certain cognitive styles and associated behaviors in students, but educators should exercise caution in generalizing a specific behavior for any cultural group.

English Proficiency

Another concern in applying the competencies with many students from multicultural backgrounds is their English proficiency. Since the language of instruction and social interaction in the regular classroom milieu is English, placement teams need to examine the student's *basic interpersonal communication skills (BICS)* and *cognitive academic language proficiency (CALP)*. Because BICS can be learned within two years (Cummins, 1981), many students may have mastered the language skills necessary to guide them in developing relationships with others. However, they may still lack the cognitive academic language proficiency to partake successfully in the regular education academic program. Research indicates that students receiving instruction in English may take up to seven years to acquire cognitive academic language proficiency (Cummins, 1981).

In light of the unique needs and experiences of students from multicultural backgrounds, placement team members should exercise some caution in employing the competencies with these students. In determining the appropriateness of the competencies for these students, placement teams should consider

1. Has the student had sufficient time to adjust to the new culture?
2. Has the student had prior experiences similar to those of students from the dominant culture?
3. What sociocultural factors associated with the student's cultural background might affect the student's behavior and achievement?
4. What are the effects of the student's family on school performance?
5. How does the student's cultural background affect interactions with others?
6. How do the student's language skills affect performance?

Summary

Decisions concerning a student's eligibility for special education, as well as the related services necessary to meet these needs, are made by a multidisciplinary team of parents and professionals. The composition of the multidisciplinary team varies depending on the needs of the student, and may include professionals with training in regular education, special education, educational administration, school psychology, speech and language therapy, vocational education, physical and occupational therapy, counseling, social work, and medicine. Multidisciplinary teams also are responsible for determining a student's readiness for mainstreaming. Placement teams can assess student readiness for mainstreaming by determining mastery of district-wide social and academic competencies with respect to established levels of adequate performance.

References

Ahn, H., Prichep, L., John, E. R., Baird, H., Trepetin, M., & Kaye, H. (1980). Developmental equations reflect brain dysfunctions. *Science, 210*(12), 1259–1262.

Alberto, P. A., & Troutman, A. C. (1986). *Applied behavior analysis for teachers (2nd ed.).* Columbus: Charles E. Merrill.

Alley, G., & Deshler, D. (1979). *Teaching the learning disabled adolescent.* Denver: Love Publishing.

Almanza, H. P., & Mosley, W. J. (1980). Curriculum adaptations and modifications for culturally diverse handicapped children. *Exceptional Children, 46*, 608–613.

Aragon, J. (1974). Cultural conflict and cultural diversity in education. In L. A. Bransford, L. Baca, & K. Lane (Eds.), *Cultural diversity and the exceptional child* (pp. 24–31). Reston, Va: The Council for Exceptional Children.

Armbruster, B. B., & Anderson, T. H. (1988). On selecting "considerate" content area textbooks. *Remedial and Special Education, 9*(1), 47–52.

Argulewicz, E. N. (1983). Effects of ethnic membership, socioeconomic status, and home language on LD, EMR, and EH placements. *Learning Disability Quarterly, 6*, 195–200.

Arter, J. A., & Jenkins, J. R. (1979). Differential diagnosis-prescriptive teaching: A critical appraisal. *Review of Educational Research, 49*, 517–555.

Baca, L. M., & Cervantes, H. T. (1984). *The bilingual special education interface.* St. Louis: Times Mirror/Mosby.

Barraga, N. C. (1983). *Visual handicaps and learning.* Austin, Tex.: Exceptional Resources.

Berg, F. S. (1986). Characteristics of the target population. In F. S. Berg, J. C. Blair, S. H. Viehweg, & A. Wilson-Vlotman (Eds.), *Educational audiology for the hard of hearing child* (pp. 1–24). Orlando: Grune & Stratton.

Bernthal, J., & Bankson, N. (1988). *Articulation and phonology disorders (2nd ed.).* Englewood Cliffs, N.J.: Prentice-Hall.

Bigge, J. L., & Sirvis, B. (1986). Physical and health impairments. In N. G. Haring & L. McCormick (Eds.), *Exceptional children and youth (4th ed.)* (pp. 313–354). Columbus: Charles E. Merrill.

Bortner, M., & Birch, H. (1970). Cognitive capacity and cognitive competence. *American Journal of Mental Deficiency, 74,* 735-744.

Brady, R. C. (1988). Physical and health handicaps. In E. W. Lynch & R. B. Lewis (Eds.), *Exceptional children and adults: An introduction to special education* (pp. 136-179). Boston: Scott, Foresman and Company.

Brischetto, R., & Arciniega, T. (1980). Examining the examiners: A look at educators' perspectives on the Chicano student. In M. Cotera & L. Hufford (Eds.), *Bridging two cultures: Multidisciplinary readings in bilingual bicultural education* (pp. 145-167). Austin, Tex.: National Educational Laboratory Publishers.

Brolin, D. (1978). *Life-centered career education: A competency-based approach.* Reston, Va.: Council for Exceptional Children.

Brolin, D. (1982). Life-centered career education for exceptional children. *Focus on Exceptional Children, 14*(7), 1-15.

Brulle, A. R., Barton, L. E., & Repp, A. C. (1984). Evaluating LRE decisions through social comparison. *Journal of Learning Disabillities, 17,* 462-466.

Bryan, T. H. (1977). Learning disabled children's comprehension of nonverbal communication. *Journal of Learning Disabilities, 10,* 501-506.

Bryan, T. H., Pearl, R., Donahue, M., Bryan, J. H., & Pflaum, S. (1983). The Chicago institute for the study of learning disabilities. *Exceptional Educational Quarterly, 4*(1), 1-22.

Cartwright, C. A., & Cartwright, G. P. (1974). *Developing observational skills.* New York: McGraw-Hill.

Cartwright, G. P., Cartwright, C. A., & Ward, M. E. (1985). *Educating special learners.* Belmont, Calif.: Wadsworth.

Chalfant, J. C., Pysh, M. V., & Moultrie, R. (1979). Teacher assistance teams: A model for building problem solving. *Learning Disability Quarterly, 2,* 85-95.

Clewell, S. F., & Clifton, A. M. (1983). Examining your textbook for comprehensibility. *Journal of Reading, 27,* 314-321.

Coles, G. S. (1980). Evaluation of genetic explanations of reading and learning problems. *Journal of Special Education, 14,* 365-383.

Cone, T. E., Wilson, L. R., Bradley, C. M., & Reese, J. H. (1985). Characteristics of LD students in Iowa: An empirical investigation. *Learning Disability Quarterly, 8,* 211-220.

Conway, R. N. F., & Gow, L. (1988). Mainstreaming special students with mild handicaps through group instruction. *Remedial and Special Education, 9*(5), 34-41.

Cullinan, D., & Epstein, M. H. (1986). Behavior disorders. In H. G. Haring & L. McCormick (Eds.), *Exceptional children and youth (4th ed.).* (pp. 161-200). Columbus: Charles E. Merrill.

Cummins, J. (1981). Four misconceptions about the language proficiency in bilingual children. *Journal of the National Association of Bilingual Education, 5,*(3), 31-45.

Cutsworth, T. (1951). *The blind in school and society. (2nd ed.).* New York: American Foundation for the Blind.

Davison, A. (1984). Readability—Appraising text difficulty. In R. C. Anderson,

J. Osborn, & R. J. Tierney (Eds.), *Learning to read in American schools* (pp. 121–140). Hillsdale, N.J.: Erlbaum.

Decker, S. N., & DeFries, J. C. (1980). Cognitive abilities in families of reading-disabled children. *Journal of Learning Disabilities, 13,* 517–522.

Deno, S. L. (1985). Curriculum-based assessment: The emerging alternative. *Exceptional Children, 52,* 219–232.

Doorlag, D. H. (1988). Behavior disorders. In E. W. Lynch & R. B. Lewis (Eds.), *Exceptional children and adults: An introduction to special education* (pp. 407–455). Boston: Scott, Foresman & Company.

Espin, C. A., & Deno, S. L. (1988). Characteristics of individuals with mental retardation. In P. J. Schloss, C. A. Hughes, & M. A. Smith (Eds.). *Mental retardation: Community transition* (pp. 35–55). Boston: College-Hill.

Federal Register. (1985, July 1). Washington, D.C.: U.S. Government Printing Office.

Gajria, M., & Hughes, C. A. (1988). Introduction to mental retardation. In P. J. Schloss, C. A. Hughes, & M. A. Smith (Eds.) *Mental retardation: Community transition* (pp. 35–55). Boston: College-Hill.

Galaburda, A. (1983). Developmental dyslexia: Current anatomical research. *Annals of Dyslexia, 33,* 41–51.

Garber, H. L., & McInerney, M. (1982). Sociobehavioral factors in mental retardation. In P. Cegelka & H. Prehm (Eds.) *Mental retardation: From categories to people* (pp. 111–145). Columbus: Charles E. Merrill.

Gearheart, B. R., Weishahn, M. W., & Gearheart, C. J. (1988). *The exceptional student in the regular classroom (4th ed.).* Columbus: Charles E. Merrill.

Germann, G. & Tindal, G. (1985). An application of curriculum-based assessment: The use of direct and repeated measurement. *Exceptional Children, 52,* 244–265.

Gilmer, J. F. (1985). *Factors related to the success and failure of teacher assistance teams in elementary schools.* Unpublished doctoral dissertation, University of Arizona, Tucson.

Gloeckler, T., & Simpson, C. (1988). *Exceptional students in regular classrooms: Challenges, services, and methods.* Mountain View, Calif.: Mayfield.

Golightly, C. J. (1987). Transdisciplinary training: A step in special education teacher preparation. *Teacher Education and Special Education, 10*(3), 126–130.

Gonzalez, G. (1974). Language, culture, and exceptional children. In L.A. Bransford, L. Baca, & K. Lane (Eds.), *Cultural diversity and the exceptional child* (pp. 2–11). Reston, Va.: The Council for Exceptional Children.

Gottesman, R. L., Croen, L. G., & Rotkin, L. G. (1982). Urban second grade children: A profile of good and poor readers. *Journal of Learning Disabilities, 15,* 268–272.

Graden, J. L., Casey, A., & Bonstrom, O. (1985). Implementing a prereferral system: Part 2. The data. *Exceptional Children, 51,* 487–496.

Graden, J. L., Casey, A., & Christenson, S. L. (1985). Implementing a prereferral intervention system: Part 1. The model. *Exceptional Children, 51,* 377–384.

Green, W. W. (1981). Hearing disorders. In A. E. Blackhurst & W. H. Berdine (Eds.), *An introduction to special education* (pp. 154–205). Boston: Little, Brown and Company.

Gresham, F. M. (1982). Misguided mainstreaming: The case for social skills training with handicapped children. *Exceptional Children, 48,* 422–433.

Gresham, F. M., & Reschly, D. J. (1986). Social skill deficits and low peer acceptance of mainstreamed learning disabled children. *Learning Disability Quarterly, 9,* 23–32.

Guralnick, M. J. (1982). Pediatrics, special education, and handicapped children: New relationships. *Exceptional Children, 48,* 294–295.

Hallahan, D. P., & Kauffman, J. M. (1982). *Exceptional children: Introduction to special education (2nd ed.).* Englewood Cliffs, N.J.: Prentice-Hall.

Hallahan, D. P., & Kauffman, J. M. (1988). *Exceptional children: Introduction to special education (4th ed.).* Englewood Cliffs: Prentice-Hall.

Hammill, D. D., Leigh, J. E., McNutt, G., & Larsen, S. C. (1981). A new definition of learning disabilities. *Learning Disability Quarterly, 4,* 336–342.

Haring, N. G., & McCormick, L. (1986). *Exceptional children and youth (4th ed.).* Columbus: Charles E. Merrill.

Harness, B., Epstein, R., & Gordon, H. (1984). Cognitive profile of children referred to a clinic for reading disabilities. *Journal of Learning Disabilities, 17*(5), 346.

Harris, A. J., & Sipay, E. R. (1985). *How to increase reading ability: A guide to developmental and remedial methods (8th ed.).* New York: Longman.

Hart, V. (1977). The use of many disciplines with severely and profoundly handicapped. In E. Sontag, J. Smith, & N. Certo (Eds.), *Educational programming for the severely and profoundly handicapped.* Reston, Va.: Division of Mental Retardation, The Council for Exceptional Children.

Harvey, D., & Greenway, A. (1984). The self-concept of physically handicapped children and their non-handicapped siblings: An empirical investigation. *Journal of Child Psychology and Psychiatry, 25,* 273–284.

Hayek, R. A. (1987). The teacher assistance team: A pre-referral support system. *Focus on Exceptional Children, 20*(1), 1–7.

Hermann, K. (1959). *Reading disability: A medical study of word-blindness and related handicaps.* Springfield, Ill.: Charles C. Thomas.

Heward, W. L., & Orlansky, M. D. (1988). *Exceptional children (3rd ed.).* Columbus: Charles E. Merrill.

Hilliard, A. G. (1980). Cultural diversity and special education. *Exceptional Children, 46,* 584–588.

Hoemann, H. W., & Briga, J. S. (1981). Hearing impairments. In J. M. Kauffman and D. P. Hallahan (Eds.) *Handbook of special education.* Englewood Cliffs, N.J.: Prentice-Hall.

Hoover, J. J., & Collier, C. (1986). *Classroom management through curricular adaptations: Educating minority handicapped students.* Lindale, Tex.: Hamilton.

Hoover, J. J., & Collier, C. (1985). Referring culturally different children: Sociocultural considerations. *Academic Therapy, 20,* 503–509.

Hundert, J. (1982). Some considerations of planning the integration of handicapped children into the mainstream. *Journal of Learning Disabilities, 15*, 73–80.

Idol, L. (1988). Johnny can't read: Does the fault lie with the book, the teacher, or Johnny? *Remedial and Special Education, 9*(1), 8–25.

Irwin, J. W., & Davis, C. A. (1980). Assessing readability: The checklist approach. *Journal of Reading, 24*, 124–130.

Jordan, J. B., & Zantal-Wiener, K. (1987). *1987 special education yearbook.* Reston, Va.: The Council for Exceptional Children.

Kavale, K. A. (1980). Learning disability and cultural-economic disadvantage: The case for a relationship. *Learning Disability Quarterly, 3*(3), 97–112.

Kirk, S. A., & Gallagher, J. J. (1989). *Educating exceptional children (6th ed.).* Boston: Houghton Mifflin.

Kokaska, C., & Brolin, D. (1985). *Career education for handicapped individuals (2nd ed.).* Columbus: Charles E. Merrill.

Kokoszka, R., & Drye, J. (1981). Toward the least restrictive environment: High school L.D. students. *Journal of Learning Disabilities, 14*, 22–23.

Koorland, M. A., Monda, L. E., & Vail, C. O. (1988). Recording behavior with ease. *Teaching Exceptional Children, 21*, 59–61.

Leung, E. K. (1988). Cultural and acculturational commonalities and diversities among Asian Americans: Identification and programming considerations. In A. A. Ortiz & B. A. Ramirez (Eds.), *Schools and the culturally diverse exceptional student: Promising practices and future directions.* Reston, Va.: Council for Exceptional Children.

Lewis, R. B., & Doorlag, D. H. (1987). *Teaching special students in the mainstream (2nd ed.).* Columbus: Charles E. Merrill.

Levine, M. D. (1982). The child with school problems: An analysis of physician participation. *Exceptional Children, 48*, 296–305.

Link, D. (1980). *Essential learning skills and the low achieving student at the secondary level: A rating of the importance of 24 academic abilities.* Unpublished master's thesis. University of Kansas, Lawrence.

Loeb, R., & Sarigiani, P. (1986). The impact of hearing impairments on self-perceptions of children. *The Volta Review, 88*(2), 89–100.

Lowenbraun, S., & Thompson, M. D. (1986). Hearing impairments. In N. G. Haring & L. McCormick (Eds.), *Exceptional children and youth (4th ed.)* (pp. 357–396). Columbus: Charles E. Merrill.

Lowenfeld, B. (1971). *Our blind children.* Springfield, Ill.: Charles C. Thomas.

Lowenthal, B. (1987). Mainstreaming—Ready or not. *Academic Therapy, 22*, 393–397.

Lynch, E. W. (1988). Mental retardation. In E. W. Lynch & R. B. Lewis (Eds.), *Exceptional children and adults* (pp. 96–135). Boston: Scott, Foresman and Company.

Mendelsohn, S. R., & Jennings, K. D. (1986). Characteristics of emotionally disturbed children referred for special education assessment. *Child Psychiatry and Human Development, 16*, 154–170.

McCoy, K. M., & Prehm, H. J. (1987). *Teaching mainstreamed students: Methods and techniques.* Denver: Love Publishing.

Mercer, C. D. (1986). Learning disabilities. In N. G. Haring & L. McCormick (Eds.), *Exceptional children and youth (4th ed.)* (pp. 119–160). Columbus: Charles E. Merrill.

Mercer, J. R. (1973). *Labelling the mentally retarded.* Berkeley: University of California Press.

Moore, B. C. (1982). Biomedical factors in mental retardation. In P. Cegelka & H. Prehm (Eds.), *Mental retardation: From categories to people* (pp. 76–110). Columbus: Charles E. Merrill.

Moore, P. (1986). Voice disorders. In G.H. Shames & E.H. Wiig (Eds.) *Human communication disorders (2nd ed.)* (pp. 183–229). Columbus: Charles E. Merrill.

Moores, D. (1982). *Educating the deaf: Psychology, principles, practices (2nd ed.).* Boston: Houghton Mifflin.

Moores, D. F., & Maestas y Moores, J. (1988). Hearing disorders. In E. W. Lynch & R. B. Lewis (Eds.), *Exceptional children and adults: An introduction to special education* (pp. 276–317). Boston: Scott, Foresman and Company.

Morrow, R. D. (1987). Cultural differences—Be aware. *Academic Therapy, 23,* 143–149.

Morse, W. C., Cutler, R. L., & Fink, A. H. (1964). *Public school classes for the emotionally handicapped: A research analysis.* Washington, D.C.: Council for Exceptional Children.

Morsink, C. V. (1981). *Learning disabilities.* In A. E. Blackhurst & W. H. Berdine (Eds.), *An introduction to special education* (pp. 354–390). Boston: Little, Brown, and Company.

Myers, P. I., & Hammill, D. D. (1982). *Learning disabilities: Basic concepts, assessment practices, and instructional strategies.* Austin, Tex.: Pro-Ed.

Myklebust, H. R., & Boshes, B. (1969). *Minimal brain damage in children.* Washington, D.C.: Neurological and Sensory Disease Control Program, Department of Health, Education, and Welfare.

National Society for the Prevention of Blindness (1977). *Signs of possible eye trouble in children.* New York: Author.

Nicol, S. E., & Erlenmeyer-Kimling, L. (1986). Genetic factors in psychopathology: Implications for prevention. In B. A. Edelstein & L. Michelson (Eds.), *Handbook of prevention.* New York: Plenum.

Palmer, D. J. (1980). Factors to be considered in placing handicapped children in regular education classes. *Journal of School Psychology, 18,* 163–171.

Pasanella, J. (1980). A team approach to educational decision making. *Exceptional Teacher, 1,* 1–2, 8–9.

Pearl, R., Bryan, T., & Donahue, M. (1980). Learning disabled children's attributions for success and failure. *Learning Disabilities Quarterly, 3,* 3–9.

Pediatric Research and Training Center (1988). *An introduction to cultural sensitivity: Working with Puerto Rican families in early childhood special education.* Farmington, Conn.: Author.

Pepper, F. C. (1976). Teaching the American Indian child in mainstream settings. In R. L. Jones (Ed.), *Mainstreaming and the minority child* (pp. 133–158). Reston, Va.: The Council for Exceptional Children.

Plata, M., & Santos, S. L. (1981). Bilingual education: A challenge for the future. *Teaching Exceptional Children,* 97–100.

Polloway, E. A., & Smith, J. D. (1983). Changes in mild mental retardation: Population, programs, and perspectives. *Exceptional Children, 50,* 149–159.

Quay, H. C. (1979). In H. C. Quay & J. S. Werry (Eds.), *Psychopathological disorders of childhood (2nd ed.)*. New York: John Wiley.

Ramirez, M., & Casteneda, A. (1974). *Cultural democracy, bicognitive development, and education*. New York: Academic Press.

Ramirez, M., & Price-Williams, D. (1974). Cognitive styles in children: Two Mexican communities. *Inter-American Journal of Psychology, 8,* 93–100.

Reschly, D. J. (1988). Minority MMR overrepresentation and special education reform. *Exceptional Children, 54,* 316–323.

Robinson, S. M., Trefz-Braxdale, C., & Colson, S. E. (1988). Preparing dysfunctional learners to enter junior high school: A transitional curriculum. In E. L. Meyen, G. A. Vergason, & R. J. Whelan (Eds.), *Effective instructional strategies for exceptional children* (pp. 243–258). Denver: Love.

Salend, S. J. (in press). *A migrant education guide for special educators. Teaching Exceptional Children.*

Salend, S. J., Brooks, L., & Salend, S. (1987). Identifying School Districts' Policies for Implementing Mainstreaming. *The Pointer, 32,* 34–37.

Salend, S. J., & Lutz, J. G. (1984). Mainstreaming or mainlining: A competency-based approach to mainstreaming. *Journal of Learning Disabilities, 17,* 27–29.

Salend, S. J., & Salend, S. M. (1986). Competencies for mainstreaming secondary-level learning disabled students. *Journal of Learning Disabilities, 19,* 91–94.

Salend, S. J., & Viglianti, D. (1982). Preparing secondary students for the mainstream. *Teaching Exceptional Children, 14,* 137–140.

Schram, L., & Semmel, M. I. (1984). *Problem-solving teams in California: Appropriate responses by school site staff to students who are difficult to teach and manage.* Santa Barbara: University of California, Graduate School of Education (ERIC Document Reproduction Service No. ED 255 485).

Schumaker, J. B., Deshler, D. D., Alley, G. R., & Warner, M. M. (1983). Toward the development of an intervention model for learning disabled adolescents: The University of Kansas. *Exceptional Education Quarterly, 4,* 45–74.

Schuyler, M. R. (1982). A readability formula program for use on microcomputers. *Journal of Reading, 25,* 560–591.

Stainback, S., & Stainback, W. (1988). Educating students with severe disabilities. *Teaching Exceptional Children, 21,* 16–19.

Stephens, T. M., Blackhurst, A. E., & Magliocca, L. A. (1982). *Teaching mainstreamed students.* New York: John Wiley & Sons.

Strain, P. S., & Shores, R. E. (1977). Social reciprocity: A review of research and educational implications. *Exceptional Children, 43,* 526–530.

Swift, C. A. (1988). Communication disorders. In E. W. Lynch & R. B. Lewis (Eds.), *Exceptional children and adults: An introduction to special education* (pp. 318–351). Boston: Scott, Foresman and Company.

Taylor, O. (1986). Language differences. In G. Shames & E. Wiig, (Eds.), *Human communication disorders (2nd ed.)*. Columbus: Charles E. Merrill.

Terzieff, I. S. (1988). *Visual impairments.* In E. W. Lynch & R. B. Lewis (Eds.), *Exceptional children and adults: An introduction to special education* (pp. 227–275). Boston: Scott, Foresman and Company.

Thomas, A., & Chess, S. (1984). Genesis and evolution of behavioral disorders: From infancy to early adult life. *American Journal of Psychiatry, 141,* 1–9.

Torgesen, J. K. (1977). The role of nonspecific factors in the task performance of learning disabled children: A theoretical assessment. *Journal of Learning Disabilities, 10,* 27–34.

Trueba, H. T. (1983). Adjustment problems of Mexican and Mexican-American students: An anthropological study. *Learning Disability Quarterly, 6,* 395–415.

Trybus, R. (1985). *Today's hearing impaired children and youth: A demographic and academic profile.* Washington, D.C.: Gallaudet Research Institute.

Tucker, J., Stevens, L. J., & Ysseldyke, J. E. (1983). Learning disabilities: The experts speak out. *Journal of Learning Disabilities, 16,* 6–14.

United States Office of Education. (1977, August 23). Implementation of Part B of the Education of the Handicapped Act. *Federal Register, 42,* 42474–42518.

United States Department of Education (1988). *Tenth annual report to Congress on the implementation of Public Law 94–142: The Education of All Handicapped Children Act.* Washington, D.C.: U.S. Government Printing Office.

Vaca, J. L., Vaca, R. T., & Gove, M. K. (1987). *Reading and learning to read.* Boston: Little, Brown and Company.

Walker, H. M., & Rankin, R. (1983). Assessing the behavioral expectations and demands of less restrictive settings. *School Psychology Review, 12,* 274–284.

Wallace, G., & McLoughlin, J. A. (1979). *Learning disabilities: Concepts and characteristics (2nd ed.).* Columbus; Charles E. Merrill.

Weener, R. D., & Senf, G. M. (1982). Learning disabilities. In H. E. Mitzel (Ed.), *Encyclopedia of educational research (5th ed.).* New York: The Free Press.

Westling, D. L. (1986). *Introduction to mental retardation.* Englewood, N.J.: Prentice-Hall.

Wiig, E. H., & Semel, E. M. (1984). *Language assessment and intervention for the learning disabled (2nd ed.).* Columbus: Charles E. Merrill.

Wilkes, H. H., Bireley, J. K., & Schultz, J. J. (1979). Criteria for mainstreaming the learning disabled into the regular classes. *Journal of Learning Disabilities, 12,* 251–256.

Wilson, R. (1987). Direct observation of academic learning time. *Teaching Exceptional Children, 20,* 13–17.

Wong, B. Y. L. (1982). Understanding learning disabled students' reading problems: Contributions from cognitive psychology. *Topics in Learning and Learning Disabilities, 1,* 43–50.

Wright, H. F. (1967). *Recording and analyzing child behavior.* New York: Harper & Row.

Ysseldyke, J. E., & Algozzine, B. (1982). *Critical issues in special and remedial education.* Boston: Houghton Mifflin.

Zins, J. E., Curtis, M. J., Graden, J. L., & Ponti, C. R. (1988). *Helping students succeed in the regular classroom.* San Francisco: Jossey-Bass.

CHAPTER 3

Preparing Students
with Disabilities
for Mainstreaming

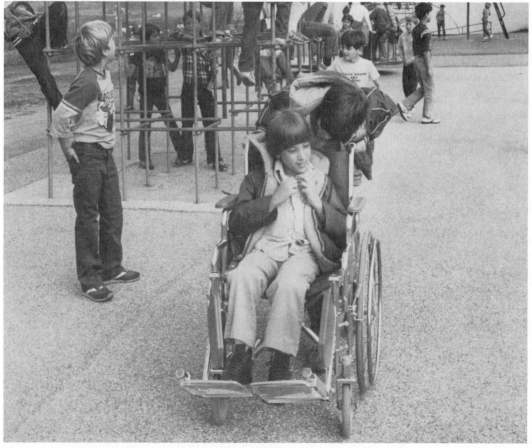

(Photo: David Strickler/Monkmeyer Press Photo Service)

Beginnings are difficult. Mainstreaming means a new beginning for students with disabilities. Students moving from a self-contained classroom to the regular class setting within the same school must learn to adjust to different instructional formats, curriculum demands, teaching styles, behavioral expectations, physical designs, and student socialization patterns. For example, a student is much more likely to receive individualized instruction in a special education class than in a regular education class, and therefore may encounter difficulties in moving from one setting to another (Rose, Lesson, & Gottlieb, 1982). Similarly, students moving from a special day school to an integrated program within the community's public school system will encounter new rules, extracurricular activities, and personnel. Thus, learning the rules and schoolwide procedures prior to entering the new school can help avoid a potentially confusing and troublesome adjustment to the new school. It is essential, then, that the student be prepared for entry into the mainstream after the placement team has decided a student is ready to make the change (Hundert, 1982; Lowenthal, 1987).

This chapter offers a framework based on Anderson–Inman's (1986) transenvironmental programming model for preparing students to function successfully in mainstreamed settings. Specifically, the chapter provides guidelines for teaching students to use a variety of strategies for obtaining information from regular classroom textbooks, listening to information from teachers and peers, taking notes from lectures and textbooks, remembering specific information, working independently, and developing appropriate social, language, and behavioral skills. Additionally, strategies for promoting the generalization of skills to mainstreamed settings and moving students from special day schools to public schools are presented.

Transenvironmental Programming

Anderson–Inman's (1986) four-step transenvironmental programming model can serve as an excellent framework for planning and delivering a program to prepare students with disabilities for mainstreamed settings. The four steps in the model are environmental assessment, intervention and preparation, generalization to, and evaluation in the target environment. *Environmental assessment* involves determining the content of the training program by identifying the skills that facilitate success in the regular classroom. In the *intervention and preparation phase,* the objectives identified in the environmental assessment are taught to students using a variety of instructional strategies. After the students have learned the skills, the next two steps are to *promote and evaluate* use of the skills in the regular classroom. Each step necessitates the communication between special and regular educators.

Determining the Content of the Transitional Program

The orientation program developed from the environmental assessment should teach mainstreamed students about their new class placement and make their adjustment as easy as possible. The teacher should establish the content of the orientation program by analyzing the critical environmental features of the new learning environment. Salend and Viglianti (1982) have provided educators with a useful format to identify the dimensions of classrooms that affect student performance, including

* instructional materials and support personnel;
* presentation of subject matter;
* learner response variables;
* student evaluation;
* classroom management;
* social interactions; and
* physical design.

An educator can complete the form presented in Figure 3.1, observing a variety of variables related to the mainstreamed setting. Although educators can obtain most of the information to complete the form by observing the future learning environment, they can acquire some background material by meeting with regular classroom teachers. Educators also should assess additional characteristics of the regular program, such as routines in the cafeteria and at assemblies, movement between classes, and expectations in physical education, art, and music classes.

The academic as well as behavioral objectives of the orientation program also can parallel the school's competencies for mainstreaming (see Chapter 2). Thus, prior to placing a student in the mainstream, educators can use the criteria to prepare these students for transition into the regular classroom by teaching them the skills they will need so that they are fully integrated into the instructional and social framework of the new class (Salend & Salend, 1986). Similarly, for those students lacking the necessary skills for mainstreaming, the competencies can form the objectives of a training program to increase their readiness for mainstreaming (Salend & Lutz, 1984).

The determination of the content and sequence of the transitional program should be the shared responsibility of the regular and special educators. Wood and Miederhoff (1989) have developed a checklist that can

FIGURE 3.1. Classroom Variables Analysis Form.

Teacher: _____   **Subject:** _____
Grade: _____   **Date:** _____
Teacher Completing the Observation: _____

**A. INSTRUCTIONAL MATERIALS AND
SUPPORT PERSONNEL**

1. What textbooks are used in the class?
   What are the grade levels of the texts?

2. What supplementary materials are used
   in the class? What are the grade levels
   of the supplementary materials?

3. What types of media are frequently
   used in the classroom?

   _____television

   _____films

   _____filmstrips

   _____slides

   _____overhead projector

   _____record player

   _____audio tapes

   _____others (please list)

   _____

   _____

   _____

4. What type(s) of support personnel are
   available in the classroom? How often
   are they available?

   _____aide

   _____volunteer

   _____peer tutor

   _____others (please list)

   _____

   _____

   _____

B. PRESENTATION OF SUBJECT MATTER

1. How often does the
   teacher . . .   *% of time*

   a. lecture?   _____

   b. use the blackboard?   _____

   c. use individualized   _____
      instruction?

   d. use small group   _____
      instruction?

   e. use large group   _____
      instruction?

   f. use individual centers?   _____

   g. others (please list)   _____

   _____   _____

   _____   _____

   _____   _____

FIGURE 3.1. (*continued*)

2. What is the language and vocabulary level used by the teacher?

2. How are grades determined?

C. LEARNER RESPONSE VARIABLES

3. What types of tests are given?

1. How often is the student required to . . .   % of time

_____essay

a. take notes?   _____

_____true/false

b. copy from the board?   _____

_____multiple choice

c. read aloud in class?   _____

_____matching

d. do independent work?   _____

_____completion

e. participate in class?   _____

_____oral

f. others (please list)   _____

_____simple recall

_____ _____

_____fill in

_____ _____

_____other

_____ _____

4. Does the teacher assign homework?

a. What type?

2. In what ways can a student request assistance in the classroom?

b. How much?

c. How often?

3. How are directions given to students? How many directions are given at one time?

5. Does the teacher assign special projects or extra-credit work? Please explain.

D. STUDENT EVALUATION

E. CLASSROOM MANAGEMENT

1. How often and in what ways does the teacher evaluate student progress?

1. Does the teacher have a management system? Briefly describe it.

FIGURE 3.1.   *(continued)*

2. What are the stated rules in the classroom?

3. What are the unstated rules in the classroom?

4. What are the consequences of following the rules? What are the consequences of not following the rules?

5. In what ways and how often does the teacher reinforce the students?

6. Does the teacher follow any special routines? What are they?

c. interests?

d. acceptance of individual differences?

e. other unique relevant characteristics? Please list.

3. What are the students' attitudes toward the handicapped?

4. What is the language and vocabulary level of the students?

5. What personality variables does the teacher exhibit that seem to affect the class?

F. SOCIAL INTERACTIONS

1. How often are student interactions . . .   *% of time*

   a. individualistic?   _____

   b. cooperative?   _____

   c. competitive?   _____

2. What are the student norms in this class concerning . . .

   a. dress?

   b. appearance?

G. PHYSICAL DESIGN

1. What, if any, architectural barriers are in the classroom?

2. How does the design affect the students' . . .

   a. academic performance?

   b. social interactions?

Source: S. J. Salend and D. Viglianti, *Teaching Exceptional Children* (February 1982): 138–139.

help regular and special education teachers plan the student's transition from special education to mainstreamed settings. The program should be individualized to address the skills of the mainstreamed student as well as the characteristics of the regular education milieu. Some students may need instruction in numerous transitional skills; others may require training in a limited number of areas. In planning the preparation program, educators also may need to prioritize the skills to be taught and identify which skills will be taught prior to and after the student has been placed into the mainstreamed setting.

Some schools have included a nonhandicapped peer on the placement team to assist in identifying the content that should comprise the transitional program (McNeil, Thousand, & Bove, 1989). The student member of the team can provide input in such areas as books and materials needed, social interaction patterns, class routines, and student dress.

Teaching Transitional Skills

Once educators have determined the objectives of the training program, they should implement the orientation program. The objectives should be specified in the student's IEP, and instruction should begin prior to the student's placement in the mainstream. Once the student is placed in the mainstream, special education teachers should continue to monitor them, teaching new and reviewing old transitional skills as necessary.

Learning Strategies

Much of the content of the training program may include learning strategies. *Learning strategies* are "techniques, principles, or rules that will facilitate the acquisition, manipulation, integration, storage, and retrieval of information across situations and settings" (Alley & Deshler, 1979, p. 13). Rather than teaching a specific content area, learning strategies help students learn how to learn. For example, DISSECT, a word-identification learning strategy, can be taught to students to help them determine the meaning of unknown words (Lenz, Deshler, Schumaker, & Beals, 1984). The steps in DISSECT are

D = Discover the context
I = Isolate the prefix
S = Separate the suffix
S = Say the stem
E = Examine the stem using the rules of twos and threes:

If a stem or part of the stem begins with a vowel, divide off the first two letters; if it begins with a consonant, divide off the first three letters

C = Check with someone

T = Try the dictionary (Ellis & Lenz, 1987, p. 101).

In determining if a specific learning strategy should be included in the transitional program, educators should consider:

- Is the strategy critical for success in the regular classroom?
- Is the strategy required in multiple settings?
- Does the strategy enable the student to solve problems independently? (Crank & Keimig, 1988).

Alley and Deshler (1979) and Clark, Deshler, Schumaker, Alley, and Warner (1984) provide a model for teaching learning strategies that educators can employ to prepare mainstreamed learners for the rigors of the regular classroom. The model includes

- allowing students to perform a task without instruction to assess the student's skill level;
- assisting students in realizing the problems associated with their current strategy;
- explaining the new strategy and its advantages as compared to the old strategy;
- demonstrating the strategy for students;
- teaching students to verbally rehearse the strategy;
- providing the students with the opportunities to practice the strategies with materials written at their level, then with materials used in the regular classroom setting;
- offering feedback on the student's use of the strategy; and
- post-testing students to ensure mastery of the strategy.

Specific guidelines for implementing these steps and promoting generalization in the use of the strategy are available (Ellis, Lenz, & Sarbornie, 1987).

Preteaching

Anderson–Inman (1986) suggests that mainstreamed students can be prepared for the academic expectations of the regular classroom through preteaching. Preteaching entails the special educator employing the curriculum, teaching style, and instructional format of the regular classroom in the special education classroom. The transitional program should introduce the student to the content of the regular education curriculum, as well as to the instructional formats (commercially produced instructional programs, media, or software) that are employed in the mainstreamed setting. Therefore, as part of the transitional program, special educators should obtain and review the objectives, sequence, learning activities, and other relevant parts of the regular education curriculum. Similarly, a meeting with the regular education teachers should be convened to determine the skills that are currently covered in the curriculum, as well as the assignments and materials they use to teach these skills.

Using Regular Classroom Textbooks

Prior to being mainstreamed, the student should be exposed to the textbooks and instructional materials used in the regular classroom. In addition to using the textbook as part of the instructional program in the special education setting, special educators can prepare students to use the text by carefully analyzing several dimensions, such as content, method of presentation, supplementary materials, and format (Burnette, 1987). Teachers should examine the vocabulary and concept development that students will need to use the book, and teach students how to identify and define these terms. For example, the teacher and the student can review chapters from the book, selecting key terms and concepts that they can define by using the book's glossary or another resource, such as a dictionary or an encyclopedia. When the student demonstrates proficiency at this task, he or she should be encouraged to perform the steps without teacher assistance.

An understanding of the organization of textbooks can assist students in effectively and efficiently comprehending the information presented (Meyer, Brandt, & Bluth, 1979). Because information is presented in a similar fashion from chapter to chapter in a textbook, reviewing the textbook's organization also can help students. This task can be accomplished by reviewing and explaining the functions and interrelationships among the book's components (the table of contents, glossary, index, and appendices) and the elements of the textbook's chapters (titles, objectives, abstracts, headings, summary, study guides, follow-up questions, references, and alternative learning activities). Because students will be working with several books that may have different formats, students should be exposed to the components of different books they will be using (Gleason, 1988).

In teaching about a textbook, it may be helpful to teach students the strategies that the author(s) employ to present content (Spargo, 1977). Vaca, Vaca, and Gove (1987) suggest that students should receive instruction to help them identify five patterns typically used by authors: enumeration, time order, comparison-contrast, cause-effect, and problem solution. These strategies are often repeated throughout the book, so students can be taught to analyze a book by examining the numbering (*1, 2, 3*), lettering (*a, b, c*), or word (*first, second, third*) system used to show the relative importance of information as well as the order of ideas; the typographic signs (boldfacing, underlining, color cuing, and boxing) employed to highlight critical information; and the word signals that indicate the equal importance of information (*furthermore, likewise*), elaboration (*moreover*), rebuttals and clarification (*nevertheless, however, but*), cause and effect (*therefore, consequently*), and termination (*finally, in conclusion*) (Spargo, 1977).

Meyer (1984) offers a six-step procedure for teaching students to identify and use the organization of a textbook. These six steps are

- discussing with students relationships in everyday situations;
- explaining how relationships are established and how information is organized in textbooks;
- teaching the key words that indicate relationships;
- questioning students to show how information is interrelated;
- teaching students to ask questions that identify relationships; and
- offering time for practice.

Orienting the student to the sequence, repetition, and length of the material presented in the text's chapters also can be helpful. Similarly, an examination of the directions given and objectives specified, as well as the in-text and end-of-chapter assignments and evaluation, can help students benefit from the book. For example, the student—under the direction of the teacher—can be shown the relationship between the objectives, content, and study questions in a chapter. Then the student can be asked to predict some study questions based on the objectives.

Many textbooks are accompanied by supplemental materials, such as student activity worksheets and overviews. Therefore, students should receive some training in completing the activity worksheets and interpreting information presented in graphic displays. Archer (1988) suggests that teachers can help students learn to complete end-of-chapter questions by training them to

- read each question carefully to determine what is being asked;
- convert appropriate parts of the question into part of the answer;

- identify the paragraphs of the chapter that relate to the question;
- locate the answer to the question by reading the chapter; and
- write the answer to the question.

Learning to look for highlighted information that is usually italicized or boldfaced also can help students identify main points that often contain answers to study questions.

Visual Aids

Additionally, textbooks provide information in the form of graphs, charts, tables, and other illustrations. Pauk (1984) suggests that teachers can show students how to gain information from visual displays by previewing the graphics to obtain a general idea of their purpose; reading the title, captions, and headings to determine relevant information about the graphics; identifying the units of measurement; and relating and generalizing graphical information to the text. Barry, cited in Ellis and Lenz (1987), developed the *Reading Visual Aids Strategy (RVAS)* to assist students in gaining information from graphic presentations. The strategy involves

R = Read the written material until you are referred to a visual
    aid or until the material is not making sense

V = View the visual aid using CLUE

    C = Clarify the stated facts in the written material

    L = Locate the main ideas (global) and details (specific parts)

    U = Uncover the signal words (look for captions or words in the
    visual aid)

    E = Examine the logic (Does what you "read" make sense with
    what you read in the material?)

A = Ask yourself about the relationship between the visual aid and the
    written material using FUR

    F = Ask how the visual aid and
    the written material "Fit" together

    U = Ask how the visual aid can help you "Understand" the
    written material

    R = Ask how the visual aid can help you "Remember" the
    written material

S = Summarize the most important information (Ellis & Lenz, 1987,
    p. 98)

Text Comprehension Strategies

Because many mainstreamed students may have difficulty reading the textbooks used in the regular education setting, teachers will need to train them in comprehension skills. Many text comprehension strategies require students to identify the main ideas of the reading selections. However, mainstreamed students may need training in finding the main idea (Baumann, 1982). Teachers can foster an understanding of main ideas by

- having students select the best title for short and then longer selections;
- discussing how to identify the main idea in a paragraph;
- assigning students the task of writing headlines for passages and newspaper articles;
- teaching students the relationship between headings, subheadings, topic sentences, and main ideas; and
- encouraging students to focus on information presented in introductory and summary paragraphs (Harris & Sipay, 1985).

Because the main idea of a paragraph is usually embedded in the topic sentence, teachers should train students to identify the topic sentence by locating the initial sentence of the paragraph. However, sometimes the topic sentence is located in the midpoints and endpoints of the paragraph, so students also should learn to identify main points by looking for repetitions of the same word or words throughout the paragraph (Crank & Keimig, 1988).

Anderson–Inman (1986) suggests several steps for teaching textbook comprehension skills to mainstreamed students. These steps are

- prioritize with the student the textbooks to be used;
- with the regular classroom teacher, discuss and analyze the textbooks to determine the most important comprehension skills needed;
- employ appropriate instructional materials and strategies to teach the necessary skills; and
- provide training in the skill with the textbooks the student will be using in the regular classroom.

Several strategies that teachers can employ to overcome difficulties in acquiring information from print materials are available; they are described below.

SURVEYING.   *Surveying* a reading assignment from the textbook can facilitate understanding of the content of the passage. The *SQ3R tech-*

nique can assist students in surveying reading material (Robinson, 1969). The steps in the SQ3R are

1. *Survey.* When surveying, the reader looks for clues to the content of information presented in the chapter. In surveying, the reader should
   a. examine the title of the chapters and try to anticipate what information will be presented;
   b. read the first paragraph to try to determine the objectives of the chapter;
   c. review the headings and subheadings to identify main points;
   d. analyze visual aids to determine relevant supporting information and related details; and
   e. read the final paragraph to summarize main points.
2. *Question.* Questioning helps the reader to continue to identify important content. Students can formulate questions by restating headings and subsection titles as questions as well as basing them on their own reactions to the material.
3. *Read.* Reading enables the learner to examine the section more closely and to answer the questions posed in the questioning phase.
4. *Recite.* Reciting assists the student in recalling the information for further use. In this step, students should be encouraged to study the information they have just covered.
5. *Review.* Reviewing also aids the student in remembering the content of the book. This task can be accomplished by having the students prepare an oral or written summary of the main topics presented in the section.

Bradstad and Stumpf (1987) provide excellent guidelines for training students to learn each step involved in the use of SQ3R.

MULTIPASS.   A modified version of SQ3R that has been employed successfully by students with learning disabilities is *Multipass* (Schumaker, Deshler, Denton, Alley, Clark, & Warner, 1982). The Multipass technique encourages students to review the content of a reading selection three times. The first pass is called the *survey pass*. This pass orients the reader to the structure and organization of the selection. In making the first pass, the student previews the material by examining the chapter title, introductory and summary paragraphs, headings, visual displays, and organization of the chapter. The survey pass is concluded with the student paraphrasing the content of the selection.

The second review, called the *size-up pass,* is designed to help the student identify the critical content to be learned from the chapter. The student reads the chapter questions; those that the student can answer after the initial pass are delineated by a checkmark. The student then surveys the material to locate the answers to those questions that do not have checkmarks by paying attention to cues, phrasing cued information as a question, skimming paragraphs to determine the answers, and paraphrasing the answer and all the material that can be remembered.

In the final pass, referred to as the *sort-out pass,* students once more read the selection and answer the accompanying questions. Again, a checkmark is placed as the student completes a question and moves on until all questions are answered.

Other similar techniques, such as SOS (Schumaker, et al., 1983), PANORAMA (Edwards, 1973), OK5R (Pauk, 1984), and PQST (Pauk, 1984), also can be employed to help students comprehend material.

SELF-QUESTIONING.   Several *self-questioning procedures* have been effective in promoting comprehension skills (Reetz & Crank, 1988; Wong & Jones, 1982). Wong and Jones (1982) increased the comprehension abilities of students with learning disabilities by training them to use a self-questioning technique that involved determining the reasons for studying the passage, identifying the main idea or ideas with an underline, generating a question associated with each main idea and writing it in the margin, finding the answer to the question and writing it in the margin, and reviewing all the questions and answers. Similarly, an adapted version of self-questioning, whereby students paraphrase the main idea and identify essential details after underlining the main idea, also was successful in promoting the comprehension skills of students with learning disabilities (Wong, Wong, Perry, & Sawatsky, 1986).

Another self-questioning technique was developed and evaluated at the Institute for Research in Learning Disabilities at the University of Kansas (Clark, Deshler, Schumaker, Alley, & Warner, 1984). In applying this procedure to written material, students are taught to compose and give symbols for who, what, where, when, and why questions; and find and denote the correct answers to the questions by placing the corresponding symbol in the correct location of the text.

Reetz and Crank (1988) propose another type of self-questioning strategy. In this technique, students read a part or title of a section and devise questions based on what they've read; continue reading the rest of the section to find the answer to their questions; and repeat the answers to their questions to ensure retention. Upon completion of the self-questioning phase, the teacher checks the students' comprehension of the material.

Cohen, et al. (1973) propose using a main-idea questioning strategy to facilitate text comprehension. This questioning strategy requires students to identify the main point of a paragraph and phrase it as a question, the answer to which summarizes the relevant information presented in the selection. Cohen and her colleagues provide excellent activities for teaching students how to generate questions.

PARAPHRASING.   Another learning strategy that can help students acquire information from print materials is *paraphrasing* (Herr, 1988). Schumaker, Denton, and Deshler (1984) found that teaching students with learning disabilities to paraphrase significantly improved their correct responses to grade-level comprehension questions. Paraphrasing requires the student to read a section of text, ask questions about the section to determine the main idea and corresponding relevant information, and paraphrase the responses to these questions in their own words. Paraphrased statements should be communicated in a complete sentence; be correct and logical; provide new and useful information; and be stated in the student's words.

SCANNING.   *Scanning* abilities can help students learn to respond quickly to review and preview questions in textbooks. To help students develop scanning skills, teachers should demonstrate how to search out and interpret key content, such as graphic displays, titles, headings, introductory and summary paragraphs, and italicized information.

OUTLINING.   Students can gain information from textbooks by learning to outline chapters. *Outlining* allows students to identify, sequence, and group main and secondary points so that they can better understand what they've read. In developing an outline, students should learn to use a separate outline for each topic, delineate essential parts of a topic using Roman numbers, present subtopics by subdividing each main heading using capital letters, and group information within a subdivision in a sequence using numbers (Fisher, 1967), as shown in Figure 3.2. Spargo

FIGURE 3.2.   Sample Outlining Format.

     I. Main Point
      A. Subtopic
      B. Subtopic
   II. Main Point
      A. Subtopic
        1. Supporting information
        2. Supporting information
        3. Supporting information

(1977) offers an outline format in which the left-hand margin contains all the main points with a brief explanation. Students record and easily review supporting information relative to each main point as an indented subheading. Teachers can train students to outline by having students complete a teacher-generated, partially completed outline (Roe, Stodt, & Burns, 1983). As students become successful at this technique, the teacher can decrease involvement in creating the outline information as the student takes over the task.

SUMMARIZATION.   Another approach to teaching text comprehension skills that has recently been found to be effective for students with disabilities is *summarization* (Gajria, 1988; McNeil & Donant, 1982). Brown, Campione, and Day (1981) and Gajria (1988) identified several basic rules students can employ in summarizing text. These rules include

- identify and group main points;
- eliminate information that is repeated;
- find the topic sentence;
- devise topic sentences for paragraphs that are missing one; and
- delete phrases and sentences that fail to present new or relevant information.

PARAGRAPH RESTATEMENTS.   Another form of summarization that students can learn is *paragraph restatements,* which Jenkins, Heliotis, Stein, and Haynes (1987) found significantly improved students' reading comprehension of narrative passages. Paragraph restatements help students actively process reading material by encouraging them to devise original sentences that summarize the main points of the reading selection. The sentences should include the fewest words possible, and can be written on the text, recorded as notes on a separate sheet, or constructed mentally. Jenkins, Heliotis, Stein, and Haynes (1987) provide guidelines for teaching students to use this technique.

CRITICAL THINKING MAPS.   *Critical thinking maps* can help students interpret and comprehend textbook information. Idol (1987) improved the skills of students with reading comprehension problems by teaching them to use a critical thinking map. Students complete the map during or after reading the selection by listing

- the main point(s) of the selection;
- the important facts, actions, examples, events, or steps that lead to and support the main point(s);

- their interpretations, opinions, and prior knowledge with respect to the content of the chapter, as well as additional viewpoints of the author;
- their conclusions concerning the information presented; and
- the relationship between the information presented and events and issues in society and their lives.

GUIDED PROBING. Idol–Maestas (1985) increased students' comprehension on factual, sequential, and inferential questions by teaching them to apply a *guided probe technique* called *TELLS Fact or Fiction.* The TELLS Fact or Fiction procedure involves:

T	*Title*	What is the title? Does it give a clue as to what the story is about?
E	*Examine*	Look through each page of the story. Skim for clues.
L	*Look*	Look for important words. Talk about what they mean.
L	*Look*	Look for hard words. Practice saying them and talk about what they mean.
S	*Setting*	What is the setting of the story? When did it take place? Where did it take place?
	Fact or Fiction	Is it a true story (Fact) or is this a pretend story (fiction)? (Idol-Maestas, 1985, p. 246).

After implementing the guided probe, students read the selection and answer corresponding comprehension questions.

VISUAL IMAGERY. Some students may be able to improve their reading comprehension skills by using *visual imagery* (Clark, et al., 1984). Visual imagery necessitates that the student read the section of the book, create an image for every sentence read, contrast each new image with the prior image, and evaluate the images to make sure they are complete. Rose, Cundick, and Higbee (1983) improved the text comprehension skills of students with learning disabilities by using a visual imagery strategy that taught them to "pause after reading a few sentences, close their eyes, and make pictures of a movie in their mind about what they had read." (p. 353)

VERBAL REHEARSAL. Another strategy, *verbal rehearsal,* can improve students' text comprehension skills (Rose, Cundick, & Higbee, 1983). Verbal rehearsal involves students pausing after reading several sentences to themselves, then verbalizing to themselves the selection's content. Initially, teachers can cue students to engage in verbal rehearsal by placing red dots at various places in the selection.

COMBINING TECHNIQUES. Masters and Mori (1986) propose a model for comprehending written material that has elements of several of the techniques presented. Their model encourages students to approach a reading assignment as follows:

1. Examine the book, article, or handout carefully before starting to read. See how it is organized, look over the introductory section, examine pictures, read the table of contents, and any summary statements at the conclusion of the material.

2. If the material is divided by sections, examine each and get a general idea of how everything flows together. Then keep the organization as a whole in mind.

3. On the first reading, don't attempt to remember anything. Just read it rapidly. This gives a general idea of what the material contains.

4. Read the material for detail and hard-to-understand passages last.

5. Write on the reading material. When possible, students should make their own headings, write notes in the margins, and underline important information. Students should be taught to underline the topic sentence, make a star next to unique details, and put a question mark next to things they question or don't understand. (p. 142)

Note Taking from Textbooks

Proper note-taking skills while reading textbooks can be an invaluable aid for students acquiring information. A good way of teaching students to take notes from their textbooks is to set up a margin, about two inches from the left side of the paper, into which they can jot questions based on the information presented in the chapter as well as examine chapter subheadings and discussion and study questions. Students should use this column to list vocabulary words and their definitions. They should use the rest of the page to record answers to the identified questions and critical information from the chapter.

If allowed by the school, highlighting information in a textbook can increase the student's ability to comprehend, evaluate, and remember information (Spargo, 1977). This form of note taking can help the student identify parts of a chapter that are critical for class sessions and assist in studying for exams. Adler (1969), Pauk (1984), and Spargo (1977) recommend that, in highlighting information from written material, the student should be taught to

- be selective;
- employ a double underline system to identify relevant main points, and a single underline to denote supporting statements;
- summarize information from visual displays by writing a brief synopsis in the margin;

- delineate important sections with brackets;
- use a symbol to identify essential facts (*) or information that needs further clarification (?);
- number items presented in a list or series;
- write abbreviations in the margins to identify definitions (*def.*) or content relating to visual displays (*vis.*);
- indicate a similar point has already been made by placing vertical lines in the margin;
- circle key terminology; and
- record reactions and questions in the margins.

Examples of these guidelines for highlighting are presented in Figure 3.3.

Listening Skills

Students in elementary and secondary regular education classrooms spend much of their school day listening. For example, Gearheart and Weishahn (1984) estimated that students spend 66 per cent of their school time engaged in listening activities. Good listening skills help students follow oral directions and receive information from teachers and their peers. However, many students may initially lack the necessary listening skills to participate fully in the regular education program (Loban, 1976). Consequently, an orientation program for mainstreamed students should promote the development of listening skills. Research indicates that listening skills can be taught to a wide range of students using a variety of strategies (Alley & Deshler, 1979). Several of these strategies are described below.

Paraphrasing

Students can be taught to receive and follow directions by learning to *paraphrase* oral information (Wallace & Kauffman, 1986). Paraphrasing requires students to receive the information, then convert it into words that they can understand. Paraphrasing skills can be taught by asking students to paraphrase directions, assignment instructions, or peer comments. As students improve their paraphrasing skills, the complexity of the verbal message should be increased to match the levels used in the regular classroom.

FIGURE 3.3. Guidelines for Highlighting Textbook Information.

Explanation and Description	Symbols, Markings, and Notations
1. Use double lines under words or phrases to signify main ideas.	Radiation can produce mutations . . .
2. Use single lines under words or phrases to signify supporting material.	comes from cosmic rays . . .
3. Mark small circled numbers near the initial word of an underlined group of words to indicate a series of arguments, facts, ideas—either main or supporting.	Conditions change . . . ① rocks rise . . . ② some sink . . . ③ the sea dashes . . . ④ strong winds . . .
4. Rather than underlining a group of three or more important lines, use a vertical bracket in the margin.	⎡ had known . . . ⎢ who gave . . . ⎢ the time . . . ⎣ of time . . .
5. Use one asterisk in the margin to indicate ideas of special importance, and two for ideas of unusual importance. Reserve three asterisks for principles and high-level generalizations.	*When a nuclear blast is . . . **People quite close to the . . . ***The main cause of mutations . . .
6. Circle key words and terms.	The ⟨genes⟩ are the . . .
7. Box words of enumeration and transition.	⟦fourth,⟧ the lack of supplies . . . ⟦furthermore,⟧ the shortage . . .
8. Place a question mark in the margin opposite lines you do not understand as a reminder to ask the instructor for clarification.	⎧ The latest . . . ? ⎨ cold period . . . ⎩ about 1,000,000 . . . Even today . . .
9. If you disagree with a statement, indicate that in the margin.	Disagree ⎰ Life became . . . ⎱ on land only . . . 340 million years . . .
10. Use the top and bottom margins of a page to record ideas of your own that are prompted by what you read.	Why not use carbon dating? ⋯⋯⋯⋯⋯ Check on reference of fossils found in Tennessee stone quarry.
11. On sheets of paper that are smaller than the pages of the book, write longer thoughts or summaries; then insert them between the pages.	Fossils Plants : 500,000,000 years old Insects : 260,000,000 " " Bees : 100,000,000 " " True fish : 330,000,000 " " Amphibians : 300,000,000 " . Reptiles : 300,000,000 " " Birds : 150,000,000 " "
12. Even though you have underlined the important ideas and supporting materials, still jot brief cues in the side margins.	Adapt — · · · · · · · · · · · fossil — · · · · · · · · · · · layer — · · · · · · · · · · ·

Source: W. Pauk, *How to Study in College* (Boston: Houghton Mifflin, 1984), p. 192. Reprinted by permission of the publisher.

Questioning

Students will need to ask questions to help clarify information missed during a verbal presentation. Therefore, students should be taught the appropriate times to ask questions; the correct ways to ask questions; and the value of meeting with the teacher after class to discuss material (Alley & Deshler, 1979).

Using Cues

Both nonverbal and verbal cues can aid listening skills (Alley & Deshler, 1979). *Nonverbal cues,* such as eye contact and gestures, as well as being aware of the reactions of others in the audience, are skills that can increase a student's ability to gain verbal information. For example, if a student observes others in the class looking intently at the teacher, it should indicate the need to listen carefully to the teacher's comments. Similarly, students should be taught how to respond to *verbal cues,* such as pacing, inflection, and loudness. Additionally, students should learn the words and statements that teachers use to highlight and organize key points. Alley and Deshler (1979) suggest that teachers use the videocassette recorder to teach these skills because it allows students to experience different speaking styles, and can be stopped and replayed to demonstrate key points.

Screening

An efficient listener knows how to distinguish relevant from nonessential points of a verbal presentation. Mainstreamed students can learn to *screen* information by listening for phrases that suggest critical information (*This is important, Do you understand?, I want you to remember this*). Alley and Deshler (1979) noted that teachers can use several activities to help students identify main points:

1. Have the student listen to a short selection and suggest a title.
2. Tell a short story and have students summarize it in one sentence.
3. Give three statements, one containing a main idea and two containing subordinate ideas. Have students identify each statement.
4. Have students listen to a class presentation on videotape and identify the main ideas. In the beginning, students should be presented with a worksheet from which they can choose the main idea. Students should discuss why each of the other choices is not a main idea (too general, too specific, irrelevant, or inaccurate). (pp. 295-296)

TQLR

Tonjes and Zintz (1981) recommend the *TQLR technique:* students are taught to listen by tuning in, questioning, listening, and reviewing. *Tuning in* involves being ready to listen, alertly focused on what the speaker is saying. *Questioning* involves asking oneself questions based on the speaker's statements to determine the meaning and direction of the message. *Reviewing* entails conducting a mental review at the end of the presentation to remember key points.

Cue Cards

Gloeckler and Simpson (1988) suggest that students' listening skills can be enhanced by use of a cue card that lists the guidelines for listening. For example, a cue card can remind students to

1. Keep alert.
2. Be quiet.
3. Don't be distracted by others or noises.
4. Don't touch or play with objects.
5. Concentrate on what the teacher and students are saying.
6. Avoid daydreaming or thinking about other things.

The cue card can be placed in the student's notebook or taped to the student's desk to serve as a prompt.

Listening Materials

A variety of instructional materials that help teach listening skills have been developed for elementary and secondary students (Robinson & Smith, 1983). These materials are designed to teach a variety of listening skills, including discriminating and attending to auditory stimuli; using memory strategies, such as visualization, rehearsal, and grouping; following directions; determining sequence, main ideas, and details of verbally presented content; identifying supporting information; and making inferences and predicting outcomes.

Listening to Lectures

Many secondary-level mainstreamed students will need to develop their listening skills to improve their ability to obtain information from lectures. Masters and Mori (1986) offer the following strategies that students can use to maintain their attention during oral presentations. These strategies include encouraging students to

1. Take notes.
2. Draw small simple pictures that provide a general explanation of the content that is presented.
3. Try to anticipate what will be said next.
4. Actively employ memory strategies during the presentation.
5. Restate the main idea to yourself during the presentation and try to tie in the related or supporting points.
6. Formulate questions and ask them either during or immediately after the presentation. (p. 130)

Lecture Note-Taking Skills

Because information in the regular education setting is often conveyed through large-group presentation or lecture, mainstreamed students should have the skills to record information for later use. There are many ways to record information. The type of note-taking strategy selected depends on the content being presented. Therefore, students should be taught to match their note-taking strategy to the material. One way to determine which strategy to employ is to teach the student to identify words and phrases that indicate the type of note-taking technique to use. For example, terms such as *in comparison, whereas,* and *on the other hand* indicate that information is being contrasted or compared.

Bradstad and Stumpf (1987) present key terminology that students should be taught in learning the type of note-taking technique to employ. A *chart method* of note taking is used when the speaker is contrasting information, such as a discussion of the advantages and disadvantages of using a certain type of note-taking system. When information is presented according to the date of occurrence, the student should learn to use a *time-line approach* to note taking, whereby students make a horizontal line across the page and record the events and dates in sequence. If content of the lecture is presented in steps, then an appropriate note-taking method is listing the steps in *numerical* fashion. Examples of these three note-taking systems are presented in Figure 3.4.

Note-taking skills also can be facilitated by teaching students to use symbols to represent phrases and relationships. For example, the symbol = can be used to indicate a relationship between two concepts.

Another note-taking system that some students may prefer is the 2-5-1 format (Learning Resource Center, n.d.). In this system, students divide the page into three columns. In the first column, which should be

FIGURE 3.4.   Three Methods of Note Taking.

Chart Method

	Hamilton	*Jefferson*
Cabinet Position	Secretary of the Treasury	Secretary of State
Political Party	Federalist	Republican
Constitutional	Supported England	Supported France

Timeline Method

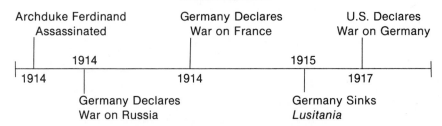

Step-Wise Method

The three principles underlying Roosevelt's "Good Neighbor" Policy:
1. Non-interference in affairs of independent countries
2. Concern for economic policies of Latin American countries
3. Establishment of Inter-American cooperation

two inches wide, students summarize concepts presented in class. In the second column, five inches wide, they list the critical points offered by the teacher. In the last column, one inch wide, students can reflect and expand on the ideas discussed. Saski, Swicegood, and Carter (1983) provide additional information on other note-taking formats.

Students can improve their note-taking skills by engaging in several behaviors before, during, and after the lecture (Bradstad & Stumpf, 1987). Before the lecture, students should read the corresponding material that has been assigned, review notes from previous classes, anticipate the material the teacher will cover in class, have the necessary materials and writing utensils, and organize the pages into two columns, one on the left for checking comprehension and the other on the right for recording notes. During the lecture, students should pay attention and avoid being distracted by extraneous stimuli, listen to and watch for verbal and nonverbal cues from the speaker and the audience, write legibly, jot down only critical points and essential details, and use a variety of note-taking techniques, depending on the content being presented. Following the lecture, students should add any missing words, incomplete thoughts, or original ideas; summarize the main points using a note-shrink technique that involves surveying the notes, identifying and highlighting main points, and listing these points in the quiz column; review their notes; and assess their mastery of the content. Sometimes, students should rewrite notes after the class; doing so allows them to organize and easily review their notes (Adler, 1969).

Other note-taking skills can be helpful to the student, such as learning to select a seat near the speaker and to realize the importance of bringing writing utensils, notebooks, and a tape recorder if necessary (Masters & Mori, 1986). A number of researchers, including Bradstad and Stumpf (1987), Learning Resource Center (n.d.), and Spargo (1977), stress other note-taking skills that should be taught to students:

- skipping a line to indicate transitions between material;
- recording notes in their own words;
- indenting to indicate main points and establish a structure to the notes;
- marking important or missed information with a symbol;
- jotting down a key word or leaving a blank when there is not enough time to record a whole thought;
- asking the teacher or a peer to provide missed information immediately after the class is completed;
- delineating and labeling the student's thoughts and peer comments from those of the teacher;
- recording the teacher's examples to clarify information;
- listening for key phrases that indicate important information and transitions from one point to another;
- highlighting points the speaker emphasizes;
- listing the name or content area of the class, page number, and date on each page to ensure continuity;
- writing complete statements rather than unconnected words or phrases; and
- indicating an overlap between the textbook and the teacher's comments.

To help students study for tests, they should record in their class notes the length of time spent on a topic, and highlight information the teacher says might appear on the next test (Adler, 1969).

Abbreviations can help students take complete notes quickly. Pauk (1984) has identified several rules for using abbreviations and symbols in note taking. However, abbreviations should be used with caution; their overuse can result in notes that are hard to decipher.

Teachers can teach appropriate note-taking skills through modeling. For example, the teacher and student can listen to a tape of a lecture from a mainstreamed class. The teacher can take notes, using the appropriate note-taking skills, while the student observes the process. To make sure the student understands the different techniques and when to apply them, the teacher can stop the tape and review with the student why certain information was not taken down and why a specific format was used. As the student's skills improve, the teacher and the student can take notes in the regular classroom. The teacher's and student's notes can then be compared, emphasizing the critical factors that make for good note taking.

Memory Skills

Because mainstreamed students also need to retain large, diverse amounts of information, developing memory skills will be helpful. One strategy for increasing retention of information is *rehearsal* (Levin & Allen, 1976). Rehearsal involves the student repeating essential facts that have just been presented. However, since rehearsal requires concentration, it should only be implemented after class or when the teacher is not presenting additional information. Since research indicates that reviewing material is a significant factor in remembering content, students should be taught to engage in frequent and spaced reviews of material after it is presented, rather than trying to memorize large amounts of information at once (Bragstad & Stumpf, 1987).

Categorization

Memory of specific information can be increased by teaching students to *categorize* information (Pauk, 1984). Thus, rather than trying to memorize a series of facts or a list of terms individually, students should try to cluster them before memorizing. For example, when attempting to memorize the names of all the states in the United States, students could categorize them according to geographic location, then memorize each geographical cluster. Additionally, since research shows that the items at the beginning and end of a list are more readily remembered, students should give careful attention to learning items from the middle of the list.

Chunking

Studies indicate that the average individual's memory span is approximately seven "bits" of content (Miller, 1956). Because the size of these bits doesn't appear to affect memory, it is recommended that students memorize information by creating seven broad areas, supplementing these areas with additional bits of information. This information can then be recalled by associating it with the broad areas (Pauk, 1984).

Mental Visualization

Some students' memory skills may be enhanced by practicing *mental visualization* (Paivio, 1971), a technique in which they conjure up a mental, visual display of the content to be remembered. Later, students recall the mental picture to try to prompt their memory. *Visual rehearsal,* where students repeatedly review visual images, also can enhance memory (Ellis & Lenz, 1987).

Mnemonics

Students also can learn to improve their memory skills by using *mnemonics,* which aid memory by providing the learner with visual or word-related aids that facilitate retrieval of information. For example, students can be taught to memorize a list of items that go together by remembering a word or sentence, the letters of which represent the first letters and sequence of each item to be remembered. The colors of the spectrum, for instance, can be taught using the mnemonic *Roy G. Biv,* a name composed of the first letter of each color of the light spectrum. In devising word or sentence mnemonics, students should be taught to determine the key word in each item that will trigger memory of the main point; record the first letter of the words so identified; and compose an easy-to-remember word or sentence from the letters identified (Pauk, 1984). If there is an order to the items to be remembered, it should be reflected in the mnemonic. Nagel, Schumaker, and Deshler (1986) have developed a learning strategy for teaching students to use mnemonics.

Narrative Chaining

A similar memory aid that some students find effective is *narrative chaining,* a technique in which students devise a story that includes the items to be remembered. Bragstad and Stumpf (1987) offer a use of this technique for remembering the biological classification system:

> The *kingdom* was in chaos, so the knights sharpened their weapons. "File 'em!" (*phylum*) they were directed. The peasant *class* had revolted and the knights were to impose *order*. Every *family,* even those containing geniuses (*genus*), was to be investigated to eradicate traitors from the *species*. (p. 57)

Teachers should teach students to apply several guidelines that are associated with successful mnemonic devices. Masters and Mori (1986) identify these guidelines as

1. Always encourage the students to make up their own images and/or pictures as they will be more powerful than any the teacher might impose.
2. Images that are linked should use the "HEAR" rule, which includes the following:

   Humor—images should be created that are humorous to their creator.

   Exaggeration—enlarging the size or proportion of the pictures will add a unique quality to the image.

   Action—make the image perform movements such as flying, hopping, or crawling when they do not normally do so.

   Ridiculous—create images that are unusual or nonsensical.
3. When possible add the dimension of sound, taste, smell, and touch to the images.
4. When memorizing a list of more than four objects it is best to break the items into "chunks" of three. (p. 116)

Independent Work Skills

Although students may be able to receive frequent teacher assistance in smaller special education classes, the number of students in regular education classes may limit the assistance mainstreamed students receive from their teachers. Therefore, an important skill for student success in the regular classroom is the ability to work independently. Teachers should use a gradual approach to teaching students to work without teacher assistance (Cohen & de Bettencourt, 1988). Initially, teachers should require students to work without assistance for short periods of time. As students are able to work independently for a specific interval, the length of the interval should be increased until it approaches the amount of time regular classroom students work independently.

A *job card* can help students learn to function independently (Cohen & de Bettencourt, 1988). The job card structures the students' performance of each task by having them determine the materials needed to do the assignment, the best ways to obtain the necessary materials, the appropriate location in which to complete the assignment, the amount of time allocated to finish the task, and the procedures for handing in their work and finishing assignments early (Cohen & de Bettencourt, 1988).

Writing Assignments

Regular classroom students are expected to complete many written assignments. In addition to evaluating content and writing skills, teachers often grade these assignments based on appearance. Therefore, mainstreamed students should be taught to hand in neat assignments that follow the format the teacher requires. The *HOW technique,* outlined below, provides students with a structure for producing papers that fit the expectations of the teacher (Archer 1988). Archer outlines the HOW technique as

How should your paper look?

H = Heading
1. Name
2. Date
3. Subject
4. Page number if needed

O = Organized
1. On the front side of the paper
2. Left margin
3. Right margin
4. At least one blank line at the top
5. At least one blank line at the bottom
6. Good spacing

W = Written neatly
1. Words or numbers on the line
2. Words or numbers written neatly
3. Neat erasing and crossing out. (p. 56)

SEATWORK.   Mainstreamed students also will be required to complete many seatwork assignments. In addition to working within the time frame established by the teacher, students will need to develop the skills to complete the assignment successfully. Archer (1988) has proposed a model for training students to complete seatwork. The steps in the model are

Step 1. Plan it.

    Read the directions and circle the words that tell you what to do.

    Get out the material you need.

    Tell yourself what to do.

Step 2. Complete it.

    Do all items.

    If you can't do an item, go ahead or ask for help.

    Use HOW.

Step 3. Check it.

    Did you do everything?

    Did you get the right answers?

    Did you proofread?

Step 4. Turn it in. (p. 56)

PROOFREADING.   Proofreading skills also can help maximize the mainstreamed student's performance on writing tasks. Students should be taught to review their written products to check for misspelled words, sentence fragments, and errors in punctuation, capitalization, and grammar. To strengthen their students' proofreading skills, teachers can show them how to review their products and identify all spelling errors, check that capital letters are used to begin all sentences and proper nouns, include punctuation marks at appropriate places and at the end of sentences, and ensure that paragraphs are indented (Tompkins & Friend, 1988). One strategy that trains students to use these proofreading skills in a systematic way is *COPS* (Schumaker, Nolan, & Deshler, 1985). In the COPS procedure, students learn to proofread their papers by checking the capitalization, overall appearance, punctuation, and spelling. Other strategies, such as DEFENDS and WRITER, employ COPS to monitor the quality of written language products (Ellis & Lenz, 1987).

Students' proofreading skills can be strengthened by employing proofreader's marks as they review their papers (Tompkins & Friend, 1988). Teachers can train students to use these marks by teaching students the system, and modeling its use when giving feedback on written assignments. Teachers should give students a handout of editing symbols paired with examples of their use, as shown in Figure 3.5 (Whitt, Paul, & Reynolds, 1988).

Organizational Skills

NOTEBOOKS.   In most regular classrooms, students take notes and record information in their notebooks. Therefore, mainstreamed students should be taught to maintain a notebook according to the specifications

EDITING SYMBOLS

Mark	Explanation	Example
◯	Circle words that are spelled incorrectly.	My freind and I went to the zoo last Sunday.
/	Change a capital letter to a small letter.	Mary and Jim watched Television for one hour.
≡	Change a small letter to a capital letter.	bob loves the way I play horn.
∧	Add letters, words, or sentences.	My friend lives in the ∧ brick house next door.
⊙	Add a period.	My dog, Frisky, and I are private detectives⊙
ℓ	Take out letters, words, or punctuation.	Last summer Bob went and flew an airplane in Alaska.
⁁	Add a comma.	Bob visited Alaska⁁ Ohio⁁ and Florida.

FIGURE 3.5. Editing Symbols Form. Source: J. Whitt, P. V. Paul, and C. J. Reynolds, *Teaching Exceptional Children, Vol 20,* (Reston, VA: Council for Exceptional Children, 1988), p. 38. Reprinted by permission of the publisher.

of the regular education teacher(s). For secondary students, this procedure often entails use of a three-ring looseleaf binder divided by subject, and a writing utensils pouch (Archer, 1988). An 8½-by-11-inch binder allows duplicated materials to be inserted easily. Elementary-level students usually need training in using two folders; one for in-class work and the other for work that goes home (Archer, 1988). When notebooks become crowded, students should remove the oldest notes and place them in a separate notebook or folder.

Students need to learn to use an assignment notebook. Usually, the assignment notebook can be a small pad, which can be kept in the binder or the pencil pouch, on which they can record homework assignments. Students should be trained to list assignments in the notebook, including textbook page numbers, dates the assignments are due, and relevant information needed to complete the task (Reetz & Crank, 1988).

ASSIGNMENT LOGS. Shields and Heron (1989) suggest that students learn to use an assignment log to keep track of assignments. They propose a log that consists of two pocket folders with built-in space to store assignment sheets that contain the name of the assignment, a description of the assignment, the date the assignment was given and is due, and a place for a parent's signature. When assignments are given to students, they complete the information on the assignment sheet and place it into the pocket folder labeled *To Be Completed*. Upon completing the assignment, the assignment sheet is updated (signed by the parent) and put in the *Completed Work* pocket folder.

TIME MANAGEMENT.   Students also learn how to keep track of the numerous activities that make up life in the mainstreamed setting by maintaining a monthly calendar onto which teachers can train students to list their homework, exams, long-term assignments, and classroom and school activities (Archer, 1988). Students also should be trained to look at the calendar every day to determine daily activities and plan for long-term projects.

In addition to the monthly calendar, students can increase their productivity by charting their daily schedules. The daily chart could include a listing of the time of day and the activity that should and did occur during that time period (Reetz & Crank, 1988). Students also should be taught to review the daily schedule at different times during the day to ensure that they are following the schedule (Masters & Mori, 1986). Initially, teachers can guide students in planning the schedules. However, as students develop skill in planning and following the schedule, they should be encouraged to plan their own schedules and determine the obstacles they encounter in successfully following those schedules (Alley & Deshler, 1979). In developing their schedules, students should be encouraged to

- consider and allot time for all types of activities;
- allocate a sufficient amount of time to study for each class;
- divide study time into several short study periods rather than one lengthy study period;
- prioritize school tasks based on due dates, importance of task, and time demands;
- schedule time for relaxation; and
- reward studying by planning other activities (Mercer & Mercer, 1985; Pauk, 1984).

Pauk (1984) proposes the use of a time reminder system that combines elements of the monthly calendar and the daily schedule systems. The time reminder system requires the student to record all essential daily and long-term activities on a 3-by-5-inch index card.

Another valuable planning system is the assignment-oriented weekly schedule, which helps students determine a schedule for completing weekly assignments (Pauk, 1984). In stage one, students list their weekly assignments, including subject area, approximate length of time needed to complete the assignment, and the due dates. They use this information in stage two to develop a weekly schedule, allotting time from each part of the day to work on assignments. Figure 3.6 presents a sample assignment-oriented weekly schedule.

ESTABLISHING PRIORITIES.   Students' use of time can be improved by learning how to establish priorities. Lakein (1973) has developed an ABC system that students can learn to accomplish this goal. The ABC system requires students to list all the critical activities that need to be accomplished; assign each task a value, with A, B, and C indicating high, medium, and low values, respectively; rank-order items given the same letter value, using a numbering system (A-1, A-2); and complete the activities according to the established priorities.

FIGURE 3.6.   Sample Weekly Assignment Schedule.

Subject	Assignment	Estimated Time	Date due	Time due
Electronics	Chap. V – 32 pp. – Read	2 hr.	Mon. 13th	8:00
English	Paper to write	18 hr.	Mon. 20th	9:00
Math	Problems on pp. 110–111	3 hr.	Tues. 14th	10:00
Industrial Safety	Make shop layouts	8 hr.	Fri. 17th	11:00
Graphics	Drawing of TV components	6 hr	Fri. 17th	1:00
Electronics	Chap. VI – 40 pp. – Read	2 ½ hr.	Wed. 22nd	8:00

Day	Assignment	Morning	Afternoon	Evening
Sun.	Electronics – Read Chap. V English – Find a topic			7:30 – 9:30 9:30 –10:30
Mon.	English – Gather notes Math – Problems		2:00 – 6:00	7:00 – 10:00
Tues.	English – Gather notes Industrial Safety	8:00 –10:00	3:00 – 6:00	7:00 –10:00
Wed.	English – First draft Graphics		2:00 – 6:00	7:00 – 10:00
Thurs.	Industrial Safety English – Paper Graphics	8:00 – 10:00	3:00 – 6:00	7:00 – 10:00
Fri.	English – Final Copy Electronics		2:00 – 6:00	7:00 – 9:30
Sat.				

Source: W. Pauk, *How to Study in College*. Boston: Houghton Mifflin, 1984), p. 46. Reprinted by permission of the publisher.

HOMEWORK.   One instructional strategy that regular classroom teachers may employ more often than special educators do is homework. Since mainstreamed students are likely to encounter more frequent and greater amounts of homework in the regular classroom, special educators can prepare students for regular education placements by approximating the homework demands of the mainstreamed milieu in their classrooms (Salend & Schliff, 1988). Thus, if the regular classroom teacher requires forty-five minutes of homework four days a week, the special education teacher can assign the same amount of homework in the special education setting.

Students' ability to complete their homework also can be enhanced by reviewing some helpful hints. Teachers can review such appropriate homework habits as choosing a distraction-free place, scheduling and budgeting time, organizing materials, knowing how to use resources, seeking assistance from others when necessary, and asking questions to make sure students understand the directions and expectations of a homework assignment (Salend & Schliff, in press). Teachers should teach mainstreamed students to organize their homework by recording assignments on notepads and transporting homework to and from school in separate folders, as well as using folders as a regular place to store homework assignments before and after they are completed. Similarly, students should be taught to review their skill at receiving the directions for homework assignments by checking with a peer.

LIBRARY SKILLS.   Mainstreamed students will need certain library skills to be successful in the regular classroom (Mastropieri & Scruggs, 1987). Students should be taught the type of information that can be obtained, as well as how to locate information in reference sources that are used by students in the mainstreamed setting (dictionary, encyclopedia, and thesaurus). For example, students should learn that the dictionary can assist them in defining, spelling, and pronouncing words. Similarly, instruction in how to use the dictionary should include looking up words alphabetically, using the guide words that indicate the first and last words located on a page, and selecting the correct meaning of a word (Spargo, 1977). Students should be introduced to the library, including how to use the card catalogue and the Dewey Decimal System.

Social Skills

Peer Relationships

Many students with disabilities may exhibit behaviors that result in social rejection by their nonhandicapped peers (Sarbonie & Kauffman, 1985). Because a major goal of mainstreaming is the social integration of students with disabilities, mainstreamed students need to be taught appropriate behaviors for establishing and maintaining positive peer relationships. Therefore, mainstreamed students needing social skill training should be taught to employ some of the behaviors that result in peer acceptance (Hollinger, 1987), such as using praise, social greetings, and affection to positively reinforce others (Masters & Furman, 1981); seeking to enter a group by using low-key techniques, such as standing around a group and waiting to be asked to play rather than commenting on the group's activities or members (Dodge, Schlundt, Schoken, & Delugach, 1983); initiating social interactions at appropriate times, such as playground time rather than during seatwork (Dodge, Coie, & Brakke, 1982); engaging in nonaggressive behaviors (French & Wass, 1985); and demonstrating prosocial behaviors (Hollinger, 1987).

Social Skills Training Programs

Commercial programs to teach social skills are available. One such program, which was designed to prepare students for the classroom behaviors and the peer relationships that they will encounter in the mainstreamed setting, is *A Curriculum for Children's Effective Peer and Teacher Skills* (ACCEPTS) (Walker, McConnell, Holmes, Todis, Walker, & Golden, 1983). ACCEPTS uses a variety of techniques, such as direct instruction, modeling, and repeated practice, to teach appropriate social skills. Field test results of ACCEPTS indicate that it has been effective in increasing classroom on-task behavior and social interactions on the playground. Carter and Sugai (1988) list other instructional programs that can help teach social skills to mainstreamed students (see Figure 3.7).

Language Skills

Since the language that guides social interactions and instruction in the classroom is English, many students from multicultural backgrounds will need to receive instruction to develop the necessary *basic interpersonal communication skills* (BICS) and *cognitive academic language proficiency skills* (CALP) to be successful in the mainstreamed setting. Observing the mainstreamed students' interaction patterns in a variety of settings (such as recess, the cafeteria, or after-school activities) can help teachers determine the appropriate BICS and social skills that students need to learn to interact with their peers. These skills can then be taught by providing students with the opportunities to use and practice these skills. Furthermore, BICS and other social skills can be taught to students via a variety of strategies that provide students with experiences

FIGURE 3.7.   List of Social Skills Curricula.

- Goldstein, A.P., Sprafkin, R.P., Gershaw, M.J., & Klein, P. (1980). *Skill-streaming the adolescent: A structured learning approach to teaching prosocial skills.* Champaign, IL: Research Press.
- Jackson, J.F., Jackson, D.A., & Monroe, C. (1983). *Getting along with others: Teaching social effectiveness to children.* Champaign, IL: Research Press.
- McGinnis, E., & Goldstein, A.P. (1984). *Skillstreaming the elementary school child: A guide for teaching prosocial skills.* Champaign, IL: Research Press.
- Spence, S. (1981). *Social skills training with children and adolescents: A counselor's manual.* Windsor, Berks, London: NFER—Nelson Publishing Company.
- Stephens, T.M. (1978). *Social skills in the classroom.* Columbus, OH: Cedar Press.
- Waksman, S.A., & Messmer, C.L. (1985). *Assertive behavior: A program for teaching social skills to children and adolescents.* Portland, OR: Enrichment Press.
- Walker, H.M., McConnell, S., Holmes, D., Todis, B., Walker, J., & Golden, N. (1983). *The Walker social skills curriculum: The ACCEPTS program.* Austin, TX: ProEd.
- Wilkinson, J., & Canter, S. (1982). *Social skills training manual: Assessment, program design, and management of training.* New York: Wiley.

Source: J. Carter and G. Sugai, *Teaching Exceptional Children*, Vol. 20 (Reston, Virginia: Council for Exceptional Children, 1988), p. 68. Reprinted by permission of the publisher.

in the language and settings that structure social interactions. Some of these strategies are described below.

Modeling

Modeling allows students to view appropriate examples of social interaction patterns. For example, the mainstreamed student can observe other students in the mainstreamed setting during a social interaction activity, or view a video of such an activity. The teacher can then review the observation with the student, emphasizing language, behaviors, and cues that promote social interactions—specifically, strategies and language for initiating and maintaining social interactions.

Teachers can also introduce peers into the self-contained classroom to serve as models to stimulate the development of language and social skills (Carter & Sugai, 1988). These students can be matched with mainstreamed students during socialization activities, providing the mainstreamed students with exemplars who they can imitate.

Role Playing

Students can develop BICS and social skills through *role playing* social interaction situations (Hoover & Collier, 1986). Where possible, the role play should take place in the environmental milieu in which the behavior is to be implemented. Following the role play, teachers should give students corrective feedback concerning their performances.

Prompting

Teachers can employ *prompting* to help students learn relevant cues that can assist them in engaging in appropriate interpersonal skills (Carter & Sugai, 1988). In prompting, the student is taught to use environmental stimuli to acquire new skills. For example, in promoting the use of BICS on the playground, the student and the teacher can visit the playground, identify stimuli, and discuss how these stimuli can promote socialization. Specifically, playground equipment, such as a slide, can prompt such statements as *Do you want to play?*, *This is fun,* and *Is it my turn?*.

Coaching

Carter and Sugai (1988) suggest *coaching* to guide students in recognizing appropriate behaviors and when to exhibit them. They describe a coaching technique to teach students how to engage in conversation in various settings; the teacher coaches students to verbalize and follow the rules for conversations in that setting.

Scripting

Since much of the dialogue that makes up daily social conversation is predictable and often redundant, teachers can show students the language and structure of social interactions through *scripts* that outline conversations that might occur in a specific environmental setting (Gaylord-Ross & Haring, 1987). For example, a typical conversation at lunchtime can be scripted to include questions and responses relating to the day's events (*How are you doing today?*), menus (*Are you buying lunch today? What type of sandwich do you have?*), and school or class events (*Are you going to the game after school?*). Gaylord-Ross and Haring (1987) suggest guidelines for scripting, which include identifying the topics, sequence, structure, and language of the script through considering the cultural and environmental setting in which the interaction will occur; observing typical, naturally occurring interactions and interviewing peer participants to determine verbalizations and topics that are reflective of the ecology of the interaction; teaching students the script and how to expand on it; and providing opportunities to practice in the setting where the script will be used.

The strategies for teaching BICS also can be employed in teaching CALP. CALP can be facilitated through providing students with techniques for understanding the instructional terminology used in the mainstreamed setting. Students can maintain words and concepts used in classroom discussions, textbooks, and assignments in a word file for retrieval as needed (Alley & Deshler, 1979).

For quick retrieval, the file should be organized alphabetically or by content area. As the student demonstrates mastery of specific terminology, those terms can be deleted or moved to an inactive section of the file. The student can also maintain a record of key words and concepts by using the *divided page method* (Bragstad & Stumpf, 1987). Students divide a page into three columns. In column one, the student lists the term, phrase, or concept. The context in which the term is used is presented in column two, and the word is defined concisely in the third column. Students can then keep a separate list for each new chapter or by subject area. These methods of listing difficult terminology can be adapted for students from multicultural backgrounds by recording information in their dominant language. For example, the dominant language equivalents of words and phrases can be included in a word list or sections of the divided page.

Behavioral Skills

An important part of success in the regular classroom is the ability to demonstrate the requisite behavioral skills (Wilkes, Bireley, & Schultz, 1979). Because students with disabilities often engage in inappropriate behaviors (Alberto & Troutman, 1986), they may need instruction in how to comply with the behavioral expectations of the regular classroom teacher's management system. Although many special educators use a management system based on the delivery of frequent, systematic reinforcement, many regular education teachers view techniques based on behavioral principles as difficult to implement within the confines of the regular classroom (Lovitt, 1975). Therefore, students who are being prepared for entry into a regular education setting should be weaned from any specialized management systems used in the special education setting and taught to respond under the management system employed in the mainstreamed setting, or to use self-management strategies. For example, rather than using a token reinforcement system, a soon-to-be mainstreamed student can be taught to monitor his or her "talking out" via a self-management technique.

Self-Management

Self-management strategies teach students how to monitor and control their behavior. These strategies can be used unobtrusively in a variety of settings to encourage development of appropriate behavior and promote independence (Alberto & Troutman, 1986). Self-management strategies are superior to management by adults in that they promote consistency, increase motivation and awareness, don't require a large communication network, and can be applied in settings in which adults are not available (Kazdin, 1975). Several self-management strategies are described below.

SELF-RECORDING.   *Self-recording techniques* have been successful in modifying a variety of classroom behaviors, including staying seated, talking out, time on-task, and aggression toward others (Alberto & Troutman, 1986). Because self-recording strategies are often effective in maintaining behaviors that have been learned via externally managed systems (O'Leary & Dubey, 1979), they are particularly appropriate for promoting the transition from special to regular education settings. Self-recording involves student monitoring of specific behaviors by measuring them using a data-collection system such as event recording, duration recording, permanent product or time-sampling (see Chapter 2 for an explanation of these strategies). For example, Broden, Hall, and Mitts (1971) taught a student to increase her on-task behavior during a lecture class by placing a + in a box when she paid attention for several minutes, and a − if she was off-task. Sample self-recording systems are presented in Figure 3.8.

Teachers can help strengthen the student's ability to monitor behavior by using a *countoon* (Jones & Jones, 1986), a recording sheet that includes a visual depiction of the behavior being recorded and space for students to record each occurrence of the behavior. Countoons can increase student awareness and motivation by providing the student with a visual display depicting the behavior, as well as an area in which to record behavior. For example, a countoon for in-seat behavior would include a drawing of a student sitting in a chair with a box under the chair for recording.

SELF-REINFORCEMENT.   Because the effects of self-recording can be short term, educators also should consider using *self-reinforcement* (O'Leary & Dubey, 1979). In self-reinforcement, the student is taught to evaluate her or his behavior, then deliver reinforcement if it is appropriate. Rhode, Morgan, and Young (1983) found that a self-reinforcement

FIGURE 3.8.   Self-Recording Examples.

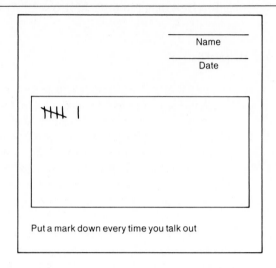

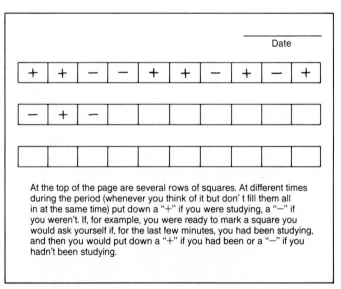

Source: M. Broden, R. V. Hall, and B. Mitts. *Journal of Applied Behavior Analysis,*
1971, 4, 193, 496. Copyright 1971 by the Society for The Experimental Analysis of Behavior, Inc.

system was successful in transferring behavior from a special education
to a regular education classroom. Since the reinforcers available in the
regular classroom may be different from those of the special education
setting, the reinforcers used in self-reinforcement should be consistent
with those available in the regular classroom.

SELF-MANAGED, FREE-TOKEN, RESPONSE-COST SYSTEM. One system that combines elements of self-recording and self-reinforcement has been successfully employed by mainstreamed students in regular classrooms. It is called the *student-managed, free-token, response-cost system* (Salend, Tintle, & Balber, 1988). In this system, students are given an index card with a fixed number of symbols on it. The symbols represent the number of inappropriate behaviors the student can exhibit before losing the agreed-upon reinforcement. Each time an inappropriate behavior occurs, the student crosses out one of the symbols on the index card. If there are any symbols remaining at the end of the class time, the student receives the agreed-upon reinforcement.

SELF-EVALUATION. A self-management system that has been used to promote appropriate behavior in the regular classroom is *self-evaluation* (Rhode, Morgan, & Young, 1983), in which students are taught to evaluate their in-class behavior using a rating scale. For example, Smith, Young, West, Morgan, & Rhode (1988) had students rate their on-task and disruptive behavior using a 0-to-5-point (unacceptable to excellent) rating scale. Students earned points, which they exchanged for reinforcers based on their behavior and accuracy in rating their behavior.

SELF-INSTRUCTION. Another effective self-management technique is *self-instruction* (Burron & Bucher, 1978), which teaches students to solve problems by verbalizing to themselves the questions and responses necessary to identify problems (*What am I being asked to do?*), generate potential solutions (*What are the ways to do it?*), evaluate solutions (*What is the best way?*), and implement appropriate solutions (*Did I do it?*) and determine if the solutions were effective (*Did it work?*). (Mastropieri & Scruggs, 1987). Students are usually taught to employ self-instruction by

- observing the teacher performing and verbalizing the steps in a task;
- performing the task under the guidance of the teacher;
- executing and verbalizing the task without guidance from the teacher;
- whispering while performing the task; and
- implementing the task by covertly verbalizing the steps (Meichenbaum & Goodman, 1971).

Students' ability to use self-instruction can be fostered by *cuing cards* (Palkes, Stewart, & Kahana, 1968), index cards with visual stimuli depicting self-instruction steps for following directions (stop, look, listen, and think). These cards are placed on the students' desk to guide them in self-instruction.

Teaching Self-Management Skills

To implement self-management strategies successfully, students will need to receive some instruction. Salend (1983) has developed a six-step model for teaching students the specifics of a self-managed program, including the behavior to be changed and the intervention. The steps in the model are

1. *Explanation.* The need for rules in general and, in particular, the need for a rule related to the target behavior are explained to the student.
2. *Identification.* The target behavior is identified and its effect on the student and others is discussed.
3. *Demonstration.* The teacher demonstrates examples and nonexamples of the target behavior. While the demonstration is occurring, the teacher accentuates and verbalizes the observable, salient features that characterize the behavior to be changed.
4. *Differentiation.* The teacher presents examples and nonexamples of the target behavior, and the student decides whether or not the target behavior did occur. As the student becomes proficient in differentiating the behavior, the teacher increases the difficulty of the task by presenting incidents that require finer discriminations and having students present examples and nonexamples of the target behavior.
5. *Role playing.* The student and the teacher role-play the intervention in the environmental milieu where it will be implemented. Following the role play, the teacher provides feedback to the student concerning her or his use of the system.
6. *Assessment.* The student's mastery of the intervention is assessed. Assessment questions should relate to the following areas: the target behavior, the rationale for the behavior change, the daily and weekly goals, the data recording system, the environmental conditions in which the system will be in effect, the consequences of appropriate and inappropriate behavior, and the roles of the student and the teacher.

Promoting Generalization

Once a transitional skill has been learned in the special education setting, educators should take steps to promote *generalization,* which ensures the transfer of training to the mainstreamed setting (Anderson–Inman, 1986). Transfer of training to other settings does not occur spontaneously; educators must have a systematic plan for the generalization of behavior (Stokes & Baer, 1977). In planning a generalization program for mainstreamed students, teachers must consider students' abilities as well as the nature of the regular classroom, including academic content, activities, and the teaching style (Vaughn, Bos, & Lund, 1986).

Goodman (1979) suggests that teachers can promote generalization by *approximating the new environment*—in other words, by training the mainstreamed student to perform under the conditions and expectations that they will encounter in the regular classroom. This goal can be achieved by introducing dimensions of the regular classroom into the special education classroom and providing students with the opportunity to experience sufficient exemplars (Stokes & Baer, 1977).

For example, if the regular classroom situation requires students to do vocabulary homework by defining words on Mondays, using words in sentences on Tuesdays, and spelling words on Wednesdays, then the special education teacher should strive for the same work demands in the special education setting. Similarly, a student who will be placed in the regular classroom should be trained to perform under the natural contingencies that are available in the mainstreamed milieu.

Teachers can use several generalization strategies to prepare students for the demands of the mainstreamed setting, including changing reinforcement, cues, materials, response set, dimensions of the stimulus, settings, and teachers (Vaughn, Bos, & Lund, 1986). Descriptions and examples of these generalization techniques are presented in Figure 3.9.

Teachers also can seek to promote transfer of training by

- encouraging students to try the new techniques in additional settings;
- discussing with students other milieus in which they could employ the strategy;
- identifying with students similarities and differences between settings;
- role-playing the use of the strategy in other situations;
- requesting that regular education teachers assist students in using the strategy;
- establishing with students an understanding of the link between the strategy and improved performance in the mainstreamed setting; and
- allowing students time to review use of strategies periodically (Gleason, 1988).

Once the skill has been mastered in the special education setting, the student should be provided the opportunity to practice it in the regular education classroom.

Generalization also can be fostered by employing components of the orientation program in the regular classroom (Alberto & Trout-

FIGURE 3.9.   Transfer of Training Techniques.

Change Reinforcement

Description/Methods	*Examples*
Vary amount, power, and type of reinforcers.	
• Fade amount of reinforcement.	• Reduce frequency of reinforcement from completion of each assignment to completion of day's assignments.
• Decrease power of reinforcer from tangible reinforcers to verbal praise.	• Limit use of stars/stickers and add more specific statements, e.g., "Hey, you did a really good job in your math book today."
• Increase power of reinforcer when changing to mainstreamed setting.	• Give points in regular classroom although not needed in resource room.
• Use same reinforcers in different settings.	• Encourage all teachers working with student to use the same reinforcement program.

Change Cues

Description/Methods	*Examples*
Vary instructions systematically.	
• Use alternate/parallel directions.	• Use variations of cue, e.g., "Find the . . ."; "Give me the . . ."; "Point to the . . ."
• Change directions.	• Change length and vocabulary of directions to better represent the directions given in the regular classroom, e.g., "Open your book to page 42 and do the problems in set A."
	• Move from real objects to miniature objects.
• Use photograph.	• Use actual photograph of object or situation.
• Use picture to represent object.	• Move from object/photograph to picture of object or situation.
• Use line drawing or symbol representation.	• Use drawings from workbooks to represent objects or situations.
• Use varying print forms.	• Vary lower and upper case letters; vary print by using manuscript, boldface, primary type.
	• Move from manuscript to cursive.

Change Materials

Description/Methods	*Examples*
Vary materials within task.	
• Change medium.	• Use unlined paper, lined paper; change size of lines; change color of paper.
	• Use various writing instruments such as markers, pencil, pen, typewriter.
• Change media.	• Use materials such as films, microcomputers, filmstrips to present skills/concepts.
	• Provide opportunity for student to phase into mainstream.

FIGURE 3.9.   *(continued)*

Change Response Set

Description/Methods	*Examples*
Vary mode of responding.	
• Change how student is to respond.	• Ask child to write answers rather than always responding orally.
	• Teach student to respond to a variety of question types such as multiple choice, true/false, short answer.
• Change time allowed for responding.	• Decrease time allowed to complete math facts.

Change Some Dimension(s) of the Stimulus

Description/Methods	*Examples*
Vary the stimulus systematically.	
• Use single stimulus and change size, color, shape.	• Teach colors by changing the size, shape, and shade of "orange" objects.
• Add to number of distractors.	• Teach sight words by increasing number of words from which child is to choose.
• Use concrete (real) object.	• Introduce rhyming words by using real objects.
• Use toy or miniature representation.	• Use miniature objects when real objects are impractical.

Change Setting(s)

Description/Methods	*Examples*
Vary instructional work space.	
• Move from more structured to less structured work arrangements.	• Move one-to-one teaching to different areas within classroom.
	• Provide opportunity for independent work.
	• Move from one-to-one instruction to small-group format.
	• Provide opportunity for student to interact in large group.

Change Teachers

Description/Methods	*Examples*
Vary instructors.	
• Assign child to work with different teacher.	• Select tasks so that child has opportunities to work with instructional aide, peer tutor, volunteer, regular classroom teacher, and parents.

Source: S. Vaughn, C. S. Bos, and K. A. Lund, *Teaching Exceptional Children*, Vol. 18 (Reston, Virginia: Council for Exceptional Children, 1986), p. 177–178. Reprinted by the permission of the publisher.

man, 1986). Students can be instrumental in ensuring that elements of the training program are transferred to the regular education setting (Anderson–Inman, 1986). For example, a list developed in the resource room of difficult terms used in the regular classroom and their meanings can be brought into the mainstreamed setting to assist students. Because many of the learning strategies students employ follow a sequence of discrete steps, cue cards (Ellis, Lenz, & Sabornie, 1987) or self-monitoring checklists can guide and monitor students' use of these strategies in the regular classroom. For example, the student can be given a cue card listing the steps in the strategy, or be taught to complete a checklist that presents the skills the student should demonstrate when implementing a specific strategy in the regular classroom. The specifics of the checklist should be individualized for each student. Figure 3.10 presents a sample checklist relating to the use of SQ3R.

Media can be a vehicle for promoting the transfer of skills. Videocassette recordings can show mainstreamed students many key elements of the regular classroom. For example, a typical instructional session in a regular classroom setting can be recorded and shown to students to orient them to their new classroom. Teachers can then view the cassette with the mainstreamed students, pointing out and discussing the critical elements of the classroom environment. In addition to introducing the student to the routines and expectations of the mainstreamed setting, the video can stimulate a discussion of any questions and concerns the students may have about the new setting. Similarly, videocassettes can help teach learning strategies by simulating the regular classroom. For example, a student's note-taking skills under the conditions of the reg-

FIGURE 3.10. Monitoring Checklist for SQ3R.

STEPS	YES	NO
1. Did I survey the chapter?	_____	_____
a. headings and titles	_____	_____
b. first paragraph	_____	_____
c. visual aids	_____	_____
d. summary paragraphs	_____	_____
2. Have I made questions?	_____	_____
3. Did I read the selection?	_____	_____
4. Did I recite the main points?	_____	_____
5. Did I produce a summary of the main points?	_____	_____

ular education setting can be simulated by having the student watch a videotaped lecture in the regular classroom and take notes.

Classroom Procedures

As students move from special education to regular education settings, they will need to be taught the procedures and routines of the mainstreamed classroom. So, before the students are placed in the mainstream, they should be introduced to several aspects of the regular classroom milieu. The orientation should include an explanation of the class rules, jobs, and special events, as well as class routines, such as lunch count, homework, attendance, and the like (Kansas–National Education Association, 1984). The class schedule should be reviewed, and necessary materials and supplies for specific classes should be identified. Teachers should explain the procedures for storing materials; using learning centers, media, materials and other equipment; working on seatwork activities and in small groups; obtaining assistance; handing in completed assignments; seeking permission to leave the room; and making transitions to activities and classes (Everston, Emmer, Clements, Sanford, & Worsham, 1989). They should also conduct a tour of the classroom to acquaint students with the design of the room and instructional materials. Once students are moved into regular education classrooms, classmates can be peer helpers to assist them in learning about the class and school routines, schedules, rules, instructional materials, and facilities (Goodman, 1979).

Get-Acquainted Activities

Once a student is placed in the mainstreamed setting, teachers should use ice-breaking activities to acquaint mainstreamed students with their peers (Salend & Schobel, 1981). Salend and Schobel (1981) and Schniedewind and Davidson (1988) outline a variety of cooperative activities that teachers can use to introduce new students to the group and give all students a common experience on which to build future friendships.

Movement from Special Day Schools

Students and classes moving from special day schools to self-contained classrooms within a local school district building also will require a transitional program to prepare them for entry into their new school. Salend

(1981) noted that such a transitional program should introduce students to the new school's personnel and their roles; physical design, including the location of the cafeteria, gymnasium, and auditorium; rules and procedures; and extracurricular activities. For example, if students learn the location and the rules of the school cafeteria before the first day in school, they can avoid a potentially confusing and troublesome situation. Teachers can orient new students to the new setting by giving them a map of the school with key areas and suggested routes highlighted, assigning a reliable peer to help the new student learn how to get around the school, and color coding the student's schedule (Gillet, 1986).

Goodman (1979) has developed a model for integrating students from specialized schools to schools within their community. The model involves

1. *Deciding on placement.* Initially, educators determine the appropriate community school placement based on location, attitudes of school personnel, availability of services, and student needs.

2. *Approximating the new environment.* Educators in the special school help students adjust to the new placement by attempting to replicate the demands, conditions, and strategies of the new setting.

3. *Leveling academic skills.* Students are prepared for the academic requirements of the new setting, and transitions to the new placement's textbooks, instructional materials, and assignments are established.

4. *Building skills in the new school.* Staff from the special school setting meet with teachers, administrators, and support personnel from the new school to discuss strategies that have been successfully employed with the students.

5. *Visiting the school.* Students tour the new school.

6. *Starting with small units of time.* Initially, some students may attend the new setting for a brief period of time to help them gradually adjust to the new placement. As students feel comfortable in the new setting, the length of time in the new school increases until the student spends the whole school day in the new setting.

7. *Accompanying the child.* A staff member from the sending school may first accompany the student to the new school to serve as a resource for the student and the staff.

8. *Structuring social acceptance.* Teachers in the new setting structure the environment to promote the social acceptance of the new students by locating their work area near class leaders or assigning them an important class job.

9. *Opening lines of communication.* Communication systems between personnel from the sending and receiving schools are established on an ongoing basis.

10. *Scheduling follow-up.* As part of the communication system, teachers should gather for follow-up meetings to discuss the students' progress and resolve areas of conflict.

School Administrators: A Special Role

School administrators can be instrumental in orienting and welcoming students in self-contained classes to their new school. Principals can help assimilate students into the new school by referring to the class as they would any other class, by room number or teacher's name; acknowledging the classes' achievements over the intercom system; having the class design a class symbol, such as a flag; ensuring that the class participates in all school-wide activities; giving the class a guided tour of the school; encouraging students to participate in clubs and organizations; having the class run a school contest or conduct a school poll; and assigning school jobs to the entire class or class members (Salend, 1979).

Summary

Regular and special education settings often differ in instructional format, curriculum demands, language used to present content, teaching style, instructional materials, behavioral expectations, physical design, and student socialization patterns. If the transition from special to regular education is to be successful, the mainstreamed student must be prepared for the demands of the regular education classroom. The transitional program should include assessment, instruction, and generalization training in use of textbooks; text comprehension strategies; and note-taking, listening, memory, independent work, organizational, library, social, language, and behavioral skills. Similarly, students should be weaned from the specialized strategies employed in the special education setting. Students moving from special schools to community-based settings also will need a transitional program to orient them to their new placement.

References

Adler, M. (1969). *How to mark a book.* In F.L. Christ (Ed.), *SR/SE resource book* (pp. 41–45) Chicago: Science Research Associates.

Alberto, P. A., & Troutman, A. C. (1986). *Applied behavior analysis for teachers (2nd ed.).* Columbus: Charles E. Merrill.

Alley, G., & Deshler, D. (1979). *Teaching the learning disabled adolescent: Strategies and methods.* Denver: Love Publishing.

Anderson-Inman, L. (1986). Bridging the gap: Student-centered strategies for promoting the transfer of learning. *Exceptional Children, 52,* 562–572.

Archer, A. L. (1988). Strategies for responding to information. *Teaching Exceptional Children, 20,* 55–57.

Baumann, J. F. (1982). Research on children's main idea comprehension: A problem of ecological validity. *Reading Psychology, 3,* 167–177.

Bragstad, B. J., & Stumpf, S. M. (1987). *A guide book for teaching study skills and motivation (2nd ed.).* Boston: Allyn & Bacon.

Broden, M., Hall, R. V., & Mitts, B. (1971). The effects of self-recording on the classroom behavior of two eighth-grade students. *Journal of Applied Behavior Analysis, 4,* 191–199.

Brown, A. L., Campione, J. C., & Day, J. D. (1981). Learning to learn: On training students to learn from texts. *Educational Researcher, 10,* 14–21.

Burnette, J. (1987). *Adapting instructional materials for mainstreamed students.* Reston, Va.: The Council for Exceptional Children.

Burron, D., & Bucher, B. (1978). Self-instructions as discriminative cues for rule-breaking or rule-following. *Journal of Experimental Psychology, 26,* 46–57.

Carter, J., & Sugai, G. (1988). Teaching social skills. *Teaching Exceptional Children, 20,* 68–71.

Clark, F., Deshler, D., Schumaker, J., Alley, G., & Warner, M. (1984). Visual imagery and self-questioning: Strategies to improve comprehension of written material. *Journal of Learning Disabilities, 17*(3), 145–149.

Cohen, R., King, W., Knudsvig, G. P., Markel, G., Patten, D., Shtogren, J., & Wilhelm, R. W. (1973). *Quest: Academic skills program.* New York: Harcourt Brace Jovanovich.

Cohen, S., and de Bettencourt, L. (1988). Teaching children to be independent learners: A step-by-step strategy. In E. L. Meyen, G. A. Vergason, & R. J. Whelan (Eds.), *Effective instructional strategies for exceptional children.* Denver: Love Publishing.

Crank, J. N., & Keimig, J. (1988). *Learning strategies assessment for secondary students.* Paper presented at the Council for Exceptional Children's 66th International Convention. Washington, D.C., March 28–April 1.

Dodge, K. A., Coie, J. D., & Brakke, N. P. (1982). Behavior patterns of socially rejected and neglected preadolescents: The roles of social approach and aggression. *Journal of Abnormal Psychology, 10,* 389–410.

Dodge, K. A., Schlundt, D. C., Schoken, I., & Delugach, J. D. (1983). Social competence and children's social status: The role of peer group entry strategies. *Merrill-Palmer Quarterly, 29,* 309–326.

Edwards, P. (1973). Panorama: A study technique. *Journal of Reading, 17,* 132–135.

Ellis, E. S., & Lenz, B. K. (1987). A component analysis of effective learning strategies for LD students. *Learning Disabilities Focus, 2,* 94–107.

Ellis, E. S., Lenz, B. K., & Sabornie, E. J. (1987). Generalization and adaptation of learning strategies to natural environments: Part 2: Research into practice. *Remedial and Special Education, 8*(2), 6–23.

Everston, C. M., Emmer, E. T., Clements, B. S., Sanford, J. P., & Worsham, M. E. (1989). *Classroom management for elementary teachers (2nd ed.).* Englewood Cliffs, N.J.: Prentice Hall.

Fisher, J. A. (1967). *Learning and study skills: A guide to independent learning.* Des Moines: Drake University Reading and Study Skills Clinic.

French, C. D., & Wass, G. A. (1985). Behavior problems of peer-neglected and peer-rejected elementary aged children: Parent and teacher perspectives. *Child Development, 56,* 246–252.

Gajria, M. (1988). *Effects of a summarization technique on the text comprehension skills of learning disabled students.* Unpublished doctoral dissertation, Pennsylvania State University.

Gaylord-Ross, R., & Haring, T. (1987). Social interaction research for adolescents with severe handicaps. *Behavioral Disorders, 12,* 264–275.

Gearheart, B. R., & Weishahn, M. W. (1984). *The exceptional student in the regular classroom.* St. Louis: Mosby.

Gillet, P. (1986). Mainstreaming techniques for LD students. *Academic Therapy, 21,* 389–399.

Gleason, M. M. (1988). Study skills. *Teaching Exceptional Children, 20,* 52–53.

Gloeckler, T., & Simpson, C. (1988). *Exceptional students in regular classrooms: Challenges, services, and methods.* Mountain View, Calif.: Mayfield.

Goodman, G. (1979). From residential treatment to community based education: A model for reintegration. *Education and Training of the Mentally Retarded, 14*(2), 95–100.

Harris, A. J., & Sipay, E. R. (1985). *How to increase reading ability: A guide to developmental and remedial methods (8th ed.).* New York: Longman.

Herr, C. (1988). Strategies for gaining information. *Teaching Exceptional Children, 20,* 53–55.

Hollinger, J. D. (1987). Social skills for behaviorally disordered children as preparation for mainstreaming: Theory, practice, and new directions. *Remedial Education and Special Education, 8,* 17–27.

Hoover, J. J., & Collier, C. (1986). *Classroom management through curricular adaptations: Educating minority handicapped students.* Lindale, Tex.: Hamilton.

Hundert, J. (1982). Some considerations of planning the integration of handicapped students into the mainstream. *Journal of Learning Disabilities, 15,* 73–80.

Idol, L. (1987). A critical thinking map to improve content area comprehension of poor readers. *Remedial and Special Education, 8*(4), 28–40.

Idol-Maestas, L. (1985). Getting ready to read: Guided probing for poor comprehenders. *Learning Disability Quarterly, 8,* 243–254.

Jenkins, J. R., Heliotis, J. D., Stein, M. L., & Haynes, M. C. (1987). Improving reading comprehension by using paragraph restatements. *Exceptional Children, 54,* 54–59.

Jones, F. J., & Jones, L. S. (1986). *Comprehensive classroom management: Creating positive learning environments.* Boston: Allyn & Bacon.

Kansas–National Education Association. (1984). Shape the future as a teacher: A manual for beginning teachers. In S. Fenner (Ed.), *Student teaching and special education* (pp. 4–9). Guilford, Conn.: Special Learning Corporation.

Kazdin, A. E. (1975). *Behavior modification in applied settings.* Homewood, Ill.: Dorsey.

Lakein, A. (1973). *How to get control of your time and your life.* New York: New American Library.

Learning Resource Center. (n.d.) *Study skills handouts.* New Paltz: Learning Resource Center, State University of New York.

Lenz, B. K., Deshler, D. D., Schumaker, J. B., & Beals, V. C. (1984). *The word identification strategy.* Lawrence: The University of Kansas.

Levin, J. R., & Allen, V. L. (1976). *Cognitive learning in children: Theories and strategies:* New York: Academic Press.

Loban, W. (1976). *Language development: Kindergarten through grade twelve (Research Report #18).* Urbana: National Council of Teachers of English.

Lovitt, T. C. (1975). Operant conditioning techniques for children with learning disabilities. In S. A. Kirk & J. M. McCarthy (Eds.), *Learning disabilities: Selected ACLD papers* (pp. 248–254). Boston: Houghton Mifflin.

Lowenthal, B. (1987). Mainstreaming—Ready or not. *Academic Therapy, 22,* 393–397.

Masters, J. C., & Furman, W. (1981). Popularity, individual friendship selection, and specific peer interaction among children. *Developmental Psychology, 17,* 344–350.

Masters, L. F., & Mori, A. A. (1986). *Teaching secondary students with mild learning and behavior problems: Methods, materials, strategies.* Rockville, Md.: Aspen.

Mastropieri, M. A., & Scruggs, T. E. (1987). *Effective instruction for special education.* Boston: College-Hill.

McNeil, J., & Donant, L. (1982). Summarization strategy for improving reading comprehension. In J. Niles and L. A. Harris (Eds.), *New inquiries in reading: Research and instruction* (pp. 215–219). Rochester, N.Y.: National Reading Conference.

McNeil, M., Thousand, J., & Bove, M. (1989, April). *The powers of partnerships: Adults and children collaborating in education.* Paper presented at the meeting of the Council for Exceptional Children, San Francisco.

Meichenbaum, D. H., & Goodman, J. (1971). Training impulsive children to talk to themselves: A means of developing self-control. *Journal of Abnormal Psychology, 77,* 115–126.

Mercer, C. D., & Mercer, A. R. (1985). *Teaching students with learning problems (2nd ed.).* Columbus: Charles E. Merrill.

Meyer, B. J. F. (1984). Organizational aspects of text: Effects of reading comprehension and applications for the classroom. In J. Flood (Ed.), *Promoting reading comprehension* (pp. 113–138). Newark, Del.: International Reading Assoc.

Meyer, B. J. F., Brandt, D., & Bluth, G. (1979). Use of top-level structure in text: Key for reading comprehension of ninth-grade students. *Reading Research Quarterly, 16,* 72–103.

Miller, G. A. (1956). The magical number seven, plus or minus two: Some limits on our capacity for processing information. *Psychological Review, 63,* 81–97.

Nagel, D. R., Schumaker, J. B., & Deshler, D. D. (1986). *The FIRST-Letter mnemonic strategy.* Lawrence: University of Kansas for Research in Learning Disabilities.

O'Leary, S. G., & Dubey, D. R. (1979). Applications of self-control procedures by children: A review. *Journal of Applied Behavior Analysis, 12,* 449–465.

Paivio, A. (1971). *Imagery and verbal processes.* New York: Rinehart and Winston.

Palkes, H., Stewart, M., & Kahana, K. (1968). Porteus maze performance of hyperactive boys after training in self-directed verbal commands. *Child Development, 39,* 817–826.

Pauk, W. (1984). *How to study in college.* Boston: Houghton Mifflin.

Reetz, L. J., & Crank, J. (1988). Include time management and learning strategies in the ED curriculum. *Perceptions, 23*(2), 26–27.

Rhode, G., Morgan, D. P., & Young, K. R. (1983). Generalization and maintenance of treatment gains for behaviorally disordered handicapped students from resource rooms to regular classrooms using self-evaluation procedures. *Journal of Applied Behavior Analysis, 16,* 171–188.

Robinson, F. P. (1969). Survey Q3R method of reading. In F.L. Christ *SR/SE resource book* (pp. 35–40). New York: Harper Brothers.

Robinson, S., & Smith, D. D. (1983). Listening skills: Teaching learning disabled students to be better listeners. In E. L. Meyen, G. A. Vergason, & R. J. Whelan (Eds.), *Promising practices for exceptional children: Curriculum practices* (pp. 143–166). Denver: Love Publishing.

Roe, B. D., Stodt, B. D., & Burns, P. C. (1983). *Secondary school reading instruction: The content areas (2nd ed.).* Boston: Houghton Mifflin.

Rose, M. C., Cundick, B. P., & Higbee, K. L. (1983). Verbal rehearsal and visual imagery: Mnemonic aids for learning disabled children. *Journal of Learning Disabilities, 16,* 352–354.

Rose, T. L., Lesson, E. I., & Gottlieb, J. (1982). A discussion of transfer of training in mainstreaming programs. *Journal of Learning Disabilities, 15,* 162–165.

Salend, S. J. (1979). New kids in school. *Instructor, 89,* 142.

Salend, S. J. (1981). The treasure hunt game: A strategy for assimilating new students into the mainstream of the school culture. *Education Unlimited, 3,* 40–42.

Salend, S. J. (1983). Guidelines for explaining target behaviors to students. *Elementary School Guidance and Counseling, 18,* 88–93.

Salend, S. J., & Lutz, G. (1984). Mainstreaming or mainlining?: A competency-based approach to mainstreaming. *Journal of Learning Disabilities, 17,* 27–29.

Salend, S. J., & Salend, S. M. (1986). Competencies for mainstreaming secondary learning disabled students. *Journal of Learning Disabilities, 19,* 91–94.

Salend, S. J., & Schliff, J. (1988). The many dimensions of homework. *Academic Therapy, 23,* 397–404.

Salend, S. J., & Schliff, J. (in press). An examination of the homework practices of teachers of the learning disabled. *Journal of Learning Disabilities.*

Salend, S. J., & Schobel, J. (1981). Getting the mainstreamed into the mainstream. *Early Years,* 66–67.

Salend, S. J., Tintle, L., & Balber, H. (1988). Effects of a student-managed response-cost system on the behavior of two mainstreamed students. *Elementary School Journal. 89,* 89–97.

Salend, S. J., & Viglianti, D. (1982). Preparing secondary students for the mainstream. *Teaching Exceptional Children, 14,* 137–140.

Sabornie, E. J., & Kauffman, J. M. (1985). Regular classroom sociometric status of behaviorally disordered adolescents. *Behavioral Disorders,* 268–274.

Saski, J., Swicegood, P., & Carter, J. (1983). Notetaking formats for learning disabled adolescents. *Learning Disability Quarterly, 6,* 265–272.

Schniedewind, N. & Davidson E. (1987). *Cooperative Learning: Cooperative Lives.* Dubuque: William C. Brown.

Schumaker, J. B., Denton, P. H., & Deshler, D. D. (1984). *The paraphrasing strategy.* Lawrence: University of Kansas.

Schumaker, J. B., Deshler, D. D., Alley, G. R., & Warner, M. M. (1983). Toward the development of an intervention model for learning disabled adolescents: The University of Kansas Institute. *Exceptional Education Quarterly, 4,* 45–74.

Schumaker, J. B., Deshler, D. D., Denton, P. H., Alley, G. R., Clark, F. L., & Warner, M. M. (1982). Multipass: A learning strategy for improving reading comprehension. *Learning Disability Quarterly, 5,* 295–304.

Schumaker, J. B., Nolan, S. M., & Deshler, D. (1985). *Learning strategies curriculum: The error monitoring strategy.* Lawrence: University of Kansas.

Shields, J. M., & Heron, T. E. (1989). Teaching organizational skills to students with learning disabilities. *Teaching Exceptional Children, 21,* 8–13.

Smith, D. J., Young, K. R., West, R. P., Morgan, D. P., & Rhode, G. (1988). Reducing the disruptive behavior of junior high school students: A classroom self-management procedure. *Behavioral Disorders, 13,* 231–239.

Spargo, E. (1977). *The now student: Reading and study skills.* Jamestown, R.I.: Jamestown.

Stokes, T. F., & Baer, D. M. (1977). Am implicit technology of generalization. *Journal of Applied Behavior Analysis, 10,* 349–369.

Tompkins, G. E., & Friend, M. (1988). After your students write: What next? *Teaching Exceptional Children, 20,* 4–9.

Tonjes, M. J., & Zintz, M. V. (1981). *Teaching reading/thinking/study skills in content classrooms.* Dubuque: William C. Brown.

Vaca, J. L., Vaca, R. T., & Gove, M. K. (1987). *Reading and learning to read.* Boston: Little, Brown and Co.

Vaughn, S., Bos, C. S., & Lund, K. A. (1986). . . . But they can do it in my room: Strategies for promoting generalization. *Teaching Exceptional Children, 18,* 176–180.

Walker, H. M., McConnell, S., Holmes, D., Walker, J., & Golden, N. (1983). *The Walker social skills curriculum: The ACCEPTS program.* Austin, Tex.: ProEd.

Walker, H. M., McConnell, S., Walker, J. L., Clarke, J. Y., Todis, B., Cohen, G., & Rankin, R. (1983). Initial Analysis of the ACCEPTS Curriculum: Efficacy of Instructional and Behavior Management Procedures for Improving the Social Adjustment of Handicapped Children. *Analysis and Intervention in Developmental Disabilities, 3,* 105–127.

Wallace, G., & Kauffman, J. M. (1986). *Teaching students with learning and behavior problems.* Columbus: Charles E. Merrill.

Whitt, J., Paul, P. V., & Reynolds, C. J. (1988). Motivate reluctant learning disabled writers. *Teaching Exceptional Children, 20,* 36–39.

Wilkes, H. H., Bireley, J. K., & Schultz, J. J. (1979). Criteria for mainstreaming the learning disabled child into the regular classes. *Journal of Learning Disabilities, 12,* 46–51.

Wood, J. W., & Miederhoff, J. W. (1989). Bridging the gap. *Teaching Exceptional Children, 21,* 66–68.

Wong, B. Y. L., & Jones, W. (1982). Increasing metacomprehension in learning disabled and normally achieving students through self-questioning training. *Learning Disability Quarterly, 5,* 228–240.

Wong, B. Y. L., Wong, R., Perry, N., & Sawatsky, D. (1986). The efficacy of a self-questioning summarization strategy for use by underachievers and learning disabled adolescents in social studies. *Learning Disabilities Focus, 2,* 20–35.

CHAPTER 4

Preparing Nonhandicapped Students for Mainstreaming

(Photo: E & F Bernstein Photos/Peter Arnold, Inc.)

Nonhandicapped students can play a significant role in determining the success or failure of mainstreaming (Gottlieb, 1980; Westervelt & McKinney, 1980). When nonhandicapped students interact positively with their handicapped peers and aid them in adjusting to and functioning in the mainstream by serving as role models, peer tutors, and friends (Salend, 1984), the mainstreaming process can go smoothly. Nonhandicapped students can be instrumental in implementing adaptations, such as peer tutoring or note taking, that can help mainstreamed students perform successfully in the regular classroom.

However, the ability and willingness of nonhandicapped students to aid their mainstreamed peers may be influenced by their attitudes toward people with disabilities. This chapter reviews the research on peer attitudes toward individuals with disabilities as well as suggestions for assessing attitudes. The chapter also provides strategies for promoting positive attitudes toward individuals with disabilities and an acceptance of cultural diversity within the classroom setting.

Research on Peer Attitudes Toward Individuals with Disabilities

While some studies suggest that nonhandicapped students view students with disabilities positively (Perlmutter, Crocker, Corday, & Garstecki, 1983; Prillaman, 1981; Randolph & Harrington, 1981), the majority of studies indicate nonhandicapped students demonstrate negative attitudes toward their peers with disabilities (Horne, 1985). Several studies suggest that mainstreamed students are rejected by or less accepted than their regular education peers (Gerber, 1977; Goodman, Gottlieb, & Harrison, 1972). These unfavorable attitudes can have a negative impact on mainstreamed students' goals and school achievement (Glick, 1969; Ide, Parkerson, Haertel, & Walberg, 1981), social-emotional adjustment (Hansell, 1981), in-class behavior (Horne & Powers, 1983), and attitudes toward school and self (Horne, 1985).

Several variables may influence perceptions of individuals with disabilities (Horne, 1985). While nonhandicapped students hold less than favorable attitudes to students with all types of handicapping conditions, they tend to be more accepting of students with sensory and physical disabilities and less accepting of students with learning and emotional problems (Horne, 1985; Miller, Hagan, & Armstrong, 1980). Monroe and Howe (1971) found that students with disabilities from higher socioeconomic status backgrounds are viewed more positively by their classmates than low socioeconomic status students with handicapping conditions. Bryan (1974) and Scranton and Ryckman (1979) reported that females labeled learning-disabled were more likely to be rejected by their peers than were males labeled learning-disabled. However, female nonhandicapped students tend to hold more favorable attitudes toward individuals with disabilities than do their male counterparts (Sandberg, 1982; Voeltz, 1980). Generally, older students possess less favorable attitudes toward individuals with disabilities than do younger students (Simpson, 1980).

A number of factors contribute to children's negative attitudes toward individuals with disabilities. Many child-rearing practices limit interactions between nonhandicapped children and their peers with disabilities (Horne, 1985). Attitudes toward the disabled also are shaped by the media, which, unfortunately, tend to portray individuals with disabilities in a negative manner. Donaldson (1981) analyzed eighty-five randomly selected thirty-minute segments of prime-time television shows and found few individuals with handicapping conditions represented. She further noted that when they *are* on television, they are often portrayed in a negative role. Similarly, Weinberg and Santana (1978) found that disabled characters in comic books are often presented as evil.

Assessing Attitudes Toward the Disabled

Before employing an attitude change strategy, educators should assess their students' attitudes toward disabled peers, as well as their understanding and knowledge of handicapping conditions. If the assessment reveals that students have accepting attitudes toward mainstreamed students, teachers can forego implementing activities to modify attitudes toward individuals with disabilties; in this case, these activities may serve to point out differences the students either have not discovered or considered important. However, if the assessment indicates that mainstreamed students are being isolated and segregated, educators should implement a training program to prepare nonhandicapped students for the entry of students with disabilities into their classes.

Observation

Direct observation of interactions between mainstreamed and nonhandicapped students can be an excellent way of assessing attitudes (Horne, 1985). For example, Dunlop, Stoneman, and Cantrell (1980) examined the relationship between disabled and nonhandicapped preschoolers by observing their play and classroom interactions, and Marotz–Ray (1985) used an observational recording system to record the peer interaction skills of mainstreamed students.

Because interactions occur in a variety of settings, teachers should examine the interaction patterns of their students in locations other than the classroom, such as the lunchroom and the playground. In observing interactions, teachers should consider these questions:

- How often are mainstreamed and nonhandicapped students interacting with each other?
- What is the nature of these interactions?
- Who is initiating the interactions?
- How many nonhandicapped students are interacting with their mainstreamed peers?
- What events seem to promote interactions?
- What events seem to limit interactions?
- Do the mainstreamed students possess the requisite skills to interact with their nonhandicapped peers?
- What are the outcomes of these interactions?

Teachers can obtain data relative to these factors by using an observational recording system. Keep in mind that it is difficult to measure attitudes in a reliable and valid manner; direct observation yields information on behavior that may or may not be related to attitudes. Teachers can also gather information on the extent to which mainstreamed students are accepted by their peers from parents, special education teachers, guidance counselors, and lunchroom and playground aides.

Sociometric Measures

The most widely used technique for measuring peer acceptance of students with disabilities is sociometric measurement (Horne, 1981). One sociometric strategy that many educators employ to assess peer relationships is peer nomination, in which students complete a *sociogram* (Asher & Taylor, 1981). A sociogram is a technique for assessing classroom interaction patterns and students' preferences for social relationships by asking students to identify the peers with whom they would like to do a social activity (Cartwright & Cartwright, 1974; Gronlund, 1976). Results of the sociogram can determine the extent to which mainstreamed students are being integrated into the social fabric of the classroom. In addition to providing data on the acceptance of mainstreamed students, sociograms can offer educators information that can assist them in identifying students in need of improved socialization skills and grouping students for instructional purposes (Wallace & Larsen, 1978).

The first step in implementing a sociogram is to devise questions. Teachers should consider the following when devising questions:

- What kind of information do I want to gather?
- What do I suspect about the classroom interactions?
- What are the ways students segregate themselves from others?
- What are the ways students show they like each other?
- What skills do the most popular students have?
- What skills do the least popular students lack?

Because it is important to obtain information on the classes' stars and isolates, teachers should include both acceptance and rejection questions. Questions should be phrased in language the students can understand. To ensure confidentiality, students should be assigned numbers, and each question should begin with the stem, "Write down the numbers of the students . . ." Sample questions that can constitute a sociogram are presented in Figure 4.1.

After formulating the questions, teachers should construct a handout listing each student's name and number. To make scoring easier, teachers should assign numbers based on the variables they are interested in measuring. For example, if teachers want to examine interactions between mainstreamed and nonhandicapped students, then mainstreamed students can be assigned even numbers and nonhandicapped students odd numbers. To ensure confidentiality, teachers should explain to students the importance of using numbers rather than names. Teachers also should review with students the list of names. Teachers can help students who cannot read the names on the list by administering the sociogram to them individually, having them raise their hands to obtain teacher assistance, putting numbers on each student's back, and creating a bulletin board that has the students' pictures and numbers.

Initially, teachers must make students understand the concept of the sociogram. Teachers can introduce the sociogram to the class by providing practice sessions where students demonstrate mastery of the concept by responding to nonsense questions. For example, teachers can offer students practice by asking them to list the numbers of all the students in the class who are wearing sneakers, whose first name begins with an S, or whose hair color is red.

Scoring sociograms allows teachers to develop a graphic picture of the classroom interactions by graphing each question separately, arranging the students' numbers in a circular design on a piece of paper, then drawing lines indicating choices from number to number to represent

FIGURE 4.1. Sample Sociogram Questions.

1. Write down the numbers of three students whom you would like to sit next to on the next school trip.
2. Write down the numbers of three students whom you would not like to sit with during lunch.
3. Write down the numbers of three students whom you would like to play with during recess.
4. Write down the numbers of three students whom you would like to invite to your birthday party.

the students' responses (Wallace & Larsen, 1978). A solid line indicates a negative choice, while a broken line denotes a positive choice. In examining the graphic, teachers should attempt to identify students who are rejected, isolated, or accepted. Rejected students are those who receive several negative choices, while students who receive several positive choices are considered accepted. Students that are not selected as either positive or negative choices are considered isolated. If mainstreamed students are rated as rejected or isolated, a program to increase social interactions should be initiated.

The sociogram can be adapted to assess attitudes toward individuals with disabilities. Instead of rating classroom peers, students can answer sociogram questions by rating pictorials depicting students with different types of disabilities. The use of pictures makes this strategy especially viable for assessing the attitudes of young children toward the disabled.

Several structured sociometric rating procedures have been developed for educators. These techniques provide educators with specific questions to ask students, and standardized procedures to follow when administering the sociometric procedure. For example, *How I Feel Toward Others* (Agard, Veldman, Kaufman, & Semmel, 1978) is a fixed-choice sociometric rating scale where each class member rates every other class member as "likes very much" (friend), "all right" (feels neutral toward), "don't like" (does not want as a friend), or "don't know." Other structured sociometric rating scales include the Peer Acceptance Scale (Bruininks, Rynders, & Gross, 1974) and the Ohio Social Acceptance Scale (Lorber, 1973).

Attitude Change Assessment Instruments

Several instruments have been developed to assess attitudes toward individuals with disabilities. Yuker, Block, and Young (1970) developed the

Attitudes Toward Disabled Persons (ATDP) Scale to measure attitudes toward individuals with disabilities. The ATDP comprises thirty statements about individuals with disabilities (for example, *Disabled persons are often unfriendly*) that students rate on a Likert-type scale, from *strongly agree* to *strongly disagree*. High scores on the scale are indicative of positive attitudes; low scores suggest that respondents have a negative view of individuals with disabilities. Since the language used in the ATDP can be confusing to students (Falty, 1965), teachers should provide time to answer students' questions and explain the meaning of certain statements. Teachers can adapt the scale by simplifying the language and phrasing items in a true-false format (Lindsey & Frith, 1983). An adapted form of the ATDP is the Attitudes Toward Handicapped Individuals, which contains only twenty items and uses the term *handicapped* in place of *disabled* (Lazar, Gensley, and Orpet, 1971).

Another assessment instrument that has been used to measure students' attitudes toward the handicapped is the *Personal Attribute Inventory for Children,* or *PAIC* (Parish, Ohlsen, & Parish, 1978). The PAIC is an alphabetically arranged adjective checklist consisting of twenty-four negative and twenty-four positive adjectives. The students are asked to select fifteen adjectives that best describe students with disabilities. The scores are computed in terms of the total number of negative adjectives chosen (Parish & Taylor, 1978).

Bagley and Greene (1981) developed the *Peers' Attitudes Toward the Handicapped Scale (PATHS)* to assess the attitudes of students in grades four through eight toward students with various handicapping conditions. Students read thirty statements describing a student with a physical, behavioral, or learning handicap and a problem that the student is experiencing. Then they determine where the student depicted in the description should work. Choices include *Work with Me in My Group, Work in Another Group, Work in No Group, Work Outside of Class,* or *Stay at Home.*

Esposito and Peach (1983) and Esposito and Reed (1986) used the *Primary Student Survey of Handicapped Persons (PSSHP)* to assess the attitudes of young children and nonreaders. The PSSHP contains six questions, which are administered to each child orally to minimize the need for reading and writing. The six questions are

1. Tell me everything you know about a handicapped person.
2. Do you like handicapped people?
3. Do you have any handicapped friends?
4. Can you get sick playing with handicapped people?
5. Are you afraid of handicapped people?
6. Do you think that handicapped people seem a lot different from you?

Each of the student's responses can be recorded verbatim by the examiner or on audiocassette and later transcribed onto a score sheet. Negative responses are scored 0, neutral responses are scored 1, and positive responses receive 2. The PSSHP manual contains guidelines for rating student responses and information on PSSHP's technical adequacy.

Another instrument for measuring attitudes toward individuals with disabilities is the *ST. Joseph Curriculum-Based Attitude Scale (STJCBAS)* (Fielder & Simpson, 1987). This attitude measurement scale is made up of twenty-five items that are rated on a six-point Likert scale, from *very much like me* to *very much unlike me*. Higher scores suggest more propitious attitudes toward individuals with disabilities.

Several attitude assessment instruments employ pictures of disabled and nonhandicapped students to sample attitudes toward the former. Picture-oriented attitude scales are especially appropriate for assessing the attitudes of young students and students from multicultural backgrounds (Chigier & Chigier, 1968; Jones & Sisk, 1967). Richardson, Goodman, Hastorf, and Dornbusch (1961) assessed students' attitudes by having them rank a series of drawings depicting male and female, black, Puerto Rican, and white students who are nonhandicapped; have a leg brace and use crutches; use a wheelchair; and have only one hand. Billings (1963) developed a two-step procedure that uses pictures to measure attitudes toward the disabled. Initially, students view a picture, then write a story about the child in the picture. In the second step, students again write a story, but this time they are told that the child in the picture has a disability.

The *Scale for Children's Attitudes Toward Exceptionalities (SCATE)* uses graphics to measure students' attitudes toward the disabled (Miller, Hagan, & Armstrong, 1980; Miller, Richey, & Lammers, 1983). Students read a narrative depicting a student with disabilities and view a graphic of disabled and nonhandicapped students. Teachers then assess attitudes by asking students to predict the responses of the disabled and nonhandicapped students to situations involving social distance (being in a group with a disabled student), friendship (desire to be friends with a disabled student) and subordination-superordination (acceptance of disabled students in leadership roles) (Miller & Loukellis, 1982).

Other attitude assessment techniques include The Perception of Closeness Scale (Horne, 1981), Disability Social Distance Scale (Tringo, 1970), Mental Retardation Attitude Inventory (Harth, 1971), and Attitudes to Blindness Scale (Marsh & Friedman, 1972).

Pretest on Handicapping Conditions

Teachers can assess nonhandicapped students' knowledge of handicapping conditions via a pretest that queries the students' understanding of different handicapping conditions (*What does it mean to be learning-disabled?*); stereotypic views of individuals with disabilities (*True or false: People in wheelchairs are retarded*); needs of individuals with different disabilities (*What are three things that you would have difficulty doing if you were blind?*); ways to interact with and assist (if necessary) individuals with disabilities (*If you were hearing-impaired,*

FIGURE 4.2. Quiz on Disabilities.

YES ☐ NO ☐ NOT SURE ☐	1. Is a person with a disability usually sick?
YES ☐ NO ☐ NOT SURE ☐	2. Can a person who is blind go to the store?
YES ☐ NO ☐ NOT SURE ☐	3. If someone can't talk, do you think he's retarded?
YES ☐ NO ☐ NOT SURE ☐	4. Were people with disabilities born that way?
YES ☐ NO ☐ NOT SURE ☐	5. Do you feel sorry for someone who is disabled?
YES ☐ NO ☐ NOT SURE ☐	6. Can blind people hear the same as other people?
YES ☐ NO ☐ NOT SURE ☐	7. If a person is retarded, does it mean that he/she will never grow up?
YES ☐ NO ☐ NOT SURE ☐	8. Are all deaf people alike?
YES ☐ NO ☐ NOT SURE ☐	9. Can a person in a wheelchair be a teacher?
YES ☐ NO ☐ NOT SURE ☐	10. Do all children have a right to go to your school?

Source: E. Barnes, C. Berrigan, and D. Biklen, *What's the Difference? Teaching Positive Attitudes Toward People with Disabilities* (Syracuse, N.Y.: Human Policy Press, 1978), p. 5. Reprinted by permission of the publisher.

FIGURE 4.3.   Student Drawing Depicting a Disabled Individual.

how would you want others to treat you?); and devices and aids designed to assist individuals with disabilities (*What is a device that a student with one arm could use?*). A sample quiz on disabilities developed by Barnes, Berrigan and Biklen (1978) is presented in Figure 4.2.

Students' Drawings

Students' acceptance and knowledge of handicapping conditions can be revealed in the ways they depict and describe individuals with disabilities. Therefore, having students draw a picture of a scene depicting individuals with disabilities can be a valuable way of assessing their attitudes. To obtain an accurate assessment of the students' feelings, teachers should ask students to write a story explaining the picture.

For example, examine the picture in Figure 4.3. How would you rate the attitude of the student who drew this picture toward the disabled? An initial assessment of the drawing may suggest that the student possesses a negative attitude. However, when the story accompanying this picture is included, the student's attitude is much clearer: The student explained the picture by stating, "Disabled people are almost always made fun of. This picture shows a handicapped person crying because of the way other people laugh at him. Put yourself in his position."

Attitude Change Strategies

When nonhandicapped students possess negative attitudes toward the disabled, teachers can foster positive attitudes through a variety of *attitude change strategies* (Conway & Gow, 1988; Donaldson, 1980). An essential factor in the success of attitude change strategies is the establishment of an *equal status relationship* between disabled and nonhandicapped individuals. Donaldson (1980) defined equal status relationships as ". . . those in which the handicapped individual is approximately the same age as the nondisabled person and/or is approximately equal in social, educational, or vocational status (p. 505)." To be successful, attitude change strategies should provide nonhandicapped individuals with information that counters their stereotypic views toward and decreases their feelings of uneasiness about the disabled (Donaldson, 1980). Additionally, effective attitude change strategies give nonhandicapped individuals a structured experience with their disabled peers (Donaldson, 1980). Several attitude change strategies that have been successful in modifying attitudes toward the disabled follow. These activities have four goals:

1. to provide information about disabilities;
2. to increase the comfort level with people who have disabilities;
3. to foster empathy with disabled people; and
4. to facilitate accepting behavior toward people with disabilities. (Barnes, Berrigan & Biklen, 1978, p. 19)

In choosing an attitude change strategy, teachers should evaluate each strategy using the guidelines presented in Figure 4.4.

Simulations

One unique way to teach positive attitudes toward individuals with disabilities is through *disability simulations* (Barnes, Berrigan, & Biklen, 1978; Hochman, 1980; Ward, Arkell, Dahl, & Wise, 1979), which teach

FIGURE 4.4.   Attitude Change Strategy Checklist.

Several attitude change strategies exist. Teachers can determine the appropriate strategy to use in the classroom by evaluating the strategy in terms of

- Is the strategy appropriate for my students?
- What skills do I need to implement the strategy? Do I have these skills?
- What resources will I need to implement the strategy? Do I have these resources?
- Does the strategy teach critical information about individuals with disabilities?
- Does the strategy present positive, nonstereotypic examples of individuals with disabilities?
- Does the strategy provide for an equal status relationship between the nonhandicapped and the disabled?
- Does the strategy offer students a structured experience in which to learn about individuals with disabilities?
- Does the strategy facilitate follow-up activities and additional opportunities for learning?

nonhandicapped students about conditions by providing them with experiences that give them an idea of how it feels to have a disability. In addition to introducing students to the problems encountered by individuals with disabilities, Wright (1978) recommends that simulations also expose students to methods of adaptation that individuals with disabilities use. Jones, Sowell, Jones, and Butler (1981) found that a training program including simulations to sensitize nonhandicapped students to the needs and experiences of those who are disabled led to an increase in positive attitudes toward the disabled. Clore and Jeffrey (1972) noted that attitude change via disability simulations were long-lasting, especially when the simulation allowed nonhandicapped students to view the reactions of other nonhandicapped individuals.

When using disability simulations, teachers should follow the activities with group discussions to provide additional information concerning such issues as causes, severity, and feelings (Popp, 1983). For example, teachers can stimulate a follow-up discussion by having students respond to a series of questions that require students to examine the simulation experience. Similarly, to help students examine their reactions to simulations, teachers can have students write about their experience (Jones, Sowell, Jones, & Butler, 1981). A variety of simulations across disabilities and sample corresponding follow-up questions follow (Bookbinder, 1978; Glazzard, 1979; Hochman, 1980; Israelson, 1980; Popp, 1983; Ward, Arkell, Dahl, & Wise, 1979).

VISUAL IMPAIRMENT SIMULATIONS. *Activity:* Blindfold students and seat them at a desk. Give them an empty cup and a pitcher of water. Have them fill the cup with water. Because other students may be observing the activity, use a see-through plastic cup.

Follow-up Questions:

1. How did you approach the task?

2. How did you know when to stop?

3. What other activities would be difficult to do if you couldn't see?

Activity: Set up an obstacle course using several chairs and desks. Group students into pairs, one blindfolded and the other not blindfolded. Starting at the beginning of the obstacle course, the blindfolded student must find the chair at the end of the obstacle course, without touching any of the obstacles, by following directions given by the peer who is not blindfolded.

Follow-up Questions:

1. What was it like to give directions? to receive directions?

2. What other senses did you use? How did they help you?

3. How does a visually impaired person move around without knocking into things?

Activity: Have students wear blindfolds during part of the school day. Blindfold one student and assign another student to serve as a helper to follow the blindfolded student around the room and building. Periodically, have the helper and the blindfolded student change roles. Structure the activity so that students must move around in the classroom, eat a meal, go to the bathroom, and move to other classes. Have the blindfolded student complete a form with the helper only providing verbal assistance.

Follow-up Questions:

1. What problems did you have during the activity? observe as a helper?

2. What did you do that helped you perform the activities without seeing? What did the helper do to help you perform the activities?

3. What changes could be made to assist students who can't see in school? at home?

HEARING IMPAIRMENT SIMULATIONS.   *Activity:* Give students a new pair of ear plugs and have them wear them for several hours during the school day. Try to structure the school day so that they have a variety of experiences that require listening and talking, such as following directions for class assignments, ordering lunch in the cafeteria, attending an assembly program in the auditorium, and hearing a message over the loudspeaker system.

Follow-up Questions:

1. What problems did you experience? How did these problems affect you?
2. What strategies did you use to help you understand what was being said?

Activity: Give directions to students by mouthing the words. The students must try to determine the directions by reading your lips.

Follow-up Questions:

1. What were you being asked to do?
2. What problems did you have in lip reading?

Activity: Show a movie or video without the sound. Ask students questions that can only be answered by having heard the sound. Show the same film or video again with the sound and have students respond to the same questions.

Follow-up Questions:

1. How did your answers differ?
2. What information did you use to answer the questions the first time you viewed the video?

PHYSICAL DISABILITIES SIMULATIONS.   *Activity:* Put a dowel rod in the joints of the students' elbows while their arms are positioned behind their backs. First, give the students a comb and have them attempt to comb their hair. Then untie their shoes and ask them to tie them.

Activity: Place stockings or rubber wash gloves on the students' hands and have them put together a puzzle, sort small objects, or draw a picture.

Activity: Place a splint on the back of each finger on the student's writing hand or a bandage on the student's dominant hand. Have the student perform classroom activities that require the use of that hand, including eating, writing, cutting, drawing, and pouring.

Follow-up Questions:

1. Were you successful at combing your hair? tying your shoes? doing the puzzle? sorting? drawing? eating? writing?

2. What other activities would you have difficulty doing if you had limited use of your hands?

3. Are there any strategies or devices that could help you perform the tasks?

Activity: Place a low balance beam on a gym mat. Have the student spin around ten times and then try to walk across the balance beam. (To prevent injury to students, it is essential that the floor surface be cushioned where this activity is being performed.)

Activity: Tape rulers and sandbags to students' legs and assign tasks that require them to move around the room.

Follow-up Questions:

1. What happened? Were you able to walk across the balance beam?

2. How would it feel if walking was that difficult for you all the time?

3. How could you play with someone who couldn't walk?

Activity: Place students in wheelchairs and have them maneuver around the classroom and the school. Structure the activity so that students attempt to drink from a water fountain, write on the blackboard, make a phone call, go to the bathroom, and transfer themselves onto a toilet. Because of the potential architectural barriers in the school, have a same-sex peer assist and observe the students as they travel around the school in their wheelchairs.

Follow-up Questions:

1. Did you encounter any problems in maneuvering around the school?

2. How would you feel if you couldn't go to the bathroom alone because you use a wheelchair?

3. What were the reactions of other students who saw you in the wheelchair? How did their reactions make you feel?

4. What are some barriers that would make it hard for a wheelchair-bound person to move around on a street? in a store?

5. What modifications can make it easier for wheelchair-bound individuals to maneuver in schools? streets? stores? homes?

SPEECH IMPAIRMENT SIMULATIONS. *Activity:* Assign students to dyads. Have one student try to communicate messages to the other by using physical gestures only, talking without moving their tongues, and using a communication board.

Follow-up Questions:

1. Were you able to communicate the message to your partner?

2. What strategies did you use to communicate the message?

3. How did you understand the message your partner was trying to give?

4. How did it feel to try to understand the speaker?

5. If you had difficulty talking, how would you want others to talk to you?

6. How would you feel if you talked like that all the time?

LEARNING DISABILITIES SIMULATIONS.   *Activity:* Place a mirror and a sheet of paper on the students' desks so that they can see the reflection of the paper in the mirror. Have the students write a sentence and read a paragraph while looking in the mirror. Then have the students try to do the same tasks without looking in the mirror. Compare their ability to do the tasks under the two different conditions.

Follow-up Questions:

1. What problems did you experience writing and reading while looking in the mirror?

2. How did it feel to have difficulty writing and reading?

3. What other tasks would be hard if you saw this way all the time?

Successful Individuals with Disabilities

Many famous, highly successful individuals had some type of handicapping condition. Lessons on these individuals' achievements and how they overcame their disabilities can help nonhandicapped students see individuals with disabilities in a more positive light (Lazar, Gensley, & Orpet, 1971). Lazar, Gensley, and Orpet (1971) found that they could promote positive attitudes toward the disabled by delivering an attitude change program that included exposure to a unit on individuals with disabilities who have made a significant contribution to society.

One effective way to introduce nonhandicapped students to the achievements of individuals with disabilities is through a matching activity, in which students are given a list of famous disabled athletes, writers, musicians, politicians, and historical figures, and are required to match the individual to his or her disability. This activity can be followed by a discussion of the individuals' lives, including the factors that helped them overcome their disabilities. A sample matching activity is provided in Figure 4.5.

Book reports on the lives of famous disabled individuals can be a valuable activity to introduce nonhandicapped students to the achievements of many individuals with disabilities (Lewis & Doorlag, 1987), such as Thomas Edison, Nelson Rockefeller, Albert Einstein, Woodrow Wilson, Hans Christian Andersen, Leonardo Da Vinci, or Bruce Jenner. Discussions and reports should focus attention on how these historical figures were able to develop as individuals and adjust to their disability (Simpson, 1980). The report could include:

- the nature of the handicap and how it occurred;
- how the handicap affected the person's education, home life, friends, and job;
- what problems were encountered as a result of the handicap;
- the accomplishments, contributions, goals, and future hopes of that person. (Research for Better Schools, 1978, p. 25)

Aaron, Phillips, & Larsen (1988) have done some interesting research that can help guide students' reports. Teachers can assign students the

FIGURE 4.5.   Sample Disabled Individuals Matching Test.

In the space provided next to each individual's name, indicate the letter of the disability they possess(ed).

Individual	Disability
_____ Franklin Roosevelt, U.S. President	a. blind
_____ Ludwig van Beethoven, composer	b. deaf–blind
_____ Wilma Rudolph, Olympic gold medalist	c. paralyzed in both legs
_____ Helen Keller, author	d. speech impediment
_____ Winston Churchill, British Prime Minister	e. reading and writing disability
_____ Albert Einstein, mathematician	f. deaf
_____ Stevie Wonder, musician	g. childhood polio
_____ Jim Abbott, major league pitcher	h. born without a hand

task of writing about a friend or relative who is disabled, or a research report on the causes of different disabilities (Barnes, Berrigan, & Biklen, 1978).

Group Discussion

Providing students with the opportunity to discuss issues related to students with disabilities can be an effective attitude change strategy (Gottlieb, 1980). Gottlieb (1980), found that a structured group discussion resulted in a significant improvement in the attitudes of nonhandicapped students toward disabled peers. In his treatment, Gottlieb showed students a short videotape of a boy with mental retardation in a variety of settings. After viewing the video, an adult led a small group discussion that addressed the following questions:

1. Why do you think the boy is retarded?
2. How do you think he feels?
3. How do the children in his class treat him?
4. Do you think he has many friends?
5. How do you think he would be treated if he were in your class? (p. 109)

Since Siperstein, Bak, and Gottlieb (1977) found that an unstructured group discussion can have a negative effect on students' perceptions of the disabled, teachers should carefully structure the discussion so that it relates to specific questions and highlights positive features about individuals with disabilities. The success of this technique can be enhanced by the teacher or nonhandicapped peers modeling positive responses and attitudes toward the disabled (Donaldson & Martinson, 1977). When using group discussion, teachers should create an open environment that allows students to ask questions and explore and examine their feelings.

Films and Books About Disabilities

A number of films and videos depicting the lives of individuals with handicapping conditions are available (Barnes, Berrigan, & Biklen, 1978; Research for Better Schools, 1978). Westervelt and McKinney (1980) found that viewing a film about a disabled student led to an increase in the nonhandicapped students' attraction to a wheelchair-bound classmate. However, because the attitude change via the film was short-lived, Westervelt and McKinney suggest the pairing of films with other attitude change strategies, such as group discussions or listening to a guest speaker.

Books about disabilities can promote positive attitudes toward individuals with disabilities (Greenbaum, Varas, & Markel, 1980; Litton, Banbury, & Harris, 1980). Leung (1980) examined the efficacy of a literature program consisting of ten short stories and discussions concerning individuals with disabilities on the social acceptance of mainstreamed students. The findings indicated that the number of positive and neutral interactions between mainstreamed students and their regular classroom teachers and peers increased, while the number of negative interactions involving mainstreamed students decreased. In addition, nonhandicapped students possessed more propitious attitudes toward individuals with disabilities. The sociometric ratings of mainstreamed students remained unchanged; regular classroom teachers held high opinions of the program.

Litton, Banbury, and Harris (1980) have compiled a helpful list of books about disabilities by age and grade level. Similarly, Gropper and Schuster (1981), Froschl, Colon, Rubin, and Sprung (1984) and Slapin, Lessing, and Belkind (1987) have identified and rated children's books about disabilities. In choosing appropriate books to use with nonhandicapped students, teachers should consider several factors, including:

- Is the language and style of the book appropriate?
- Is the book factually correct and realistic?
- Is the disabled individual depicted in the book shown in a variety of situations and settings?
- Does the book portray disabled individuals as positive, competent, and independent?
- Are disabled individuals depicted as multidimensional, having ideas and feelings that are not associated with their disability?
- Does the book introduce readers to the adaptations and devices individuals with certain disabilities need?
- Does the book allow readers to develop an equal status relationship and learn about the similarities and differences between disabled and nonhandicapped individuals?
- Do the illustrations facilitate discussion and the sharing of information?
- Will the book stimulate questions and discussions about disabled people? (Moe, 1980; Slapin, Lessing, & Belkind, 1987).

Salend and Moe (1983) compared the effects of two situations: in one, students were exposed only to books about disabilities by listening to a teacher reading them. In the second, the teacher read the books to the students and highlighted the main points to be learned about individuals with disabilities through discussion, simulations, and explanations. The results suggested that while the books-only condition did not lead to a significant change in student attitudes, the books-and-activities condition did. Figure 4.6 lists books about disabilities and corresponding activities to highlight critical content to be learned about individuals with disabilities.

Older students can be introduced to the disabled via literature. *The Handicapped in Literature: A Psychosocial Perspective* (Bowers, 1980) includes selections from H.G. Wells, Carson McCullers, Somer-

FIGURE 4.6.   Sample Activities for Children's Books About Handicapping Conditions.

Wolf, B. *Don't Feel Sorry for Paul.* Philadelphia: J. B. Lippincott, 1974.

This story introduces the reader to the active life of a boy with a physical disability by focusing on his home and school activities.

Activity:

1. After reading page seven to the class, ask: How long does it take to get dressed in the morning? Note the variance in their responses.
2. Simulate Paul's condition by having the students put on their coats using both arms, and then using one arm. Time both attempts and compare them.
3. On page six, the students are introduced to prosthetic devices. Tell them a prosthesis is a device that helps someone do something that they normally couldn't do. Review with them examples of prosthetic devices such as eyeglasses, crutches, eating utensils, pens, and rulers. Ask them to identify some things that they can't do and what devices they use to overcome these things.
4. After reading page eighteen, ask the students:
   a. Is it right to be more demanding of Paul than other children?
   b. Should Paul be treated differently?
   c. Would you want to be treated differently?
5. After reading page twenty, have the students try to shell peanuts wearing winter gloves. Ask them:
   a. What jobs could Paul do?
   b. What jobs would be difficult for Paul?
6. After reading page thirty-three, ask the students to identify the ways it might be an advantage to having only one real arm or leg (possible responses might include *you only have to wash one hand before dinner,* or *you only need one winter glove*).
7. After reading page forty-five, ask the students what things Paul might have difficulty doing in school.
8. After completing the book, ask the students
   a. How is Paul like you?
   b. How is Paul different from you?

FIGURE 4.6.   *Continued*

Tobias, T. *Easy or Hard? That's a Good Question.* Chicago: Children's Press, 1977.

This book makes the point that we are all similar in some ways and different in other ways, and that some things are easy for some people and hard for others.

1. Before reading the book, ask the students to identify two things that are easy and two things that are hard for them to do.
2. Divide the class in half, with one side of the room labeled the easy side and the other side the hard side. After reading each easy or hard sequence in the book, have students indicate whether the behavior or task mentioned in the book is easy or hard for them by moving to the easy or hard side of the classroom. Note the similarities and differences between their responses.
3. After completing the book, ask students to share the two things they felt were easy and hard to do. Again, note similarities and differences in their responses.
4. Discuss with the students how abilities and disabilities affect the ease with which one can perform a task by asking them to identify what things would be easy or hard if they
   • had a reading problem;
   • were in a wheelchair;
   • couldn't hold a pencil;
   • couldn't see;
   • couldn't hear; and
   • didn't understand English.
   Ask students to analyze their performance of a task with and without a simulated disability.
5. Conclude the discussion of the book by asking students, "If you knew someone who found something hard, what could you do to show that person that you understand that some things are hard?"

---

set Maugham, and Kurt Vonnegut; *The Exceptional Child Through Literature* (Landau, Epstein & Stone, 1978) contains short stories by Joyce Carol Oates, John Steinbeck, and Alfred Kazin. Both can give students insights into the experiences and feelings of disabled individuals. Follow-up questions to guide the discussion are included with both books. Landau, Epstein, and Stone (1978) offer a bibliography of adult books dealing with disabled individuals. Guidelines for using folktales to promote a greater understanding of individuals with disabilities also are available (Barnes, Berrigan, & Biklen, 1978).

Instructional Materials

A drawback in the use of simulations, children's books, and other attitude change strategies is the time it takes teachers to prepare the activities. Teachers can minimize the time required to plan attitude change activities by using commercially developed instructional materials for teaching nonhandicapped students about their disabled peers. These programs usually include a variety of activities, materials necessary to implement the activities, and a teacher's manual. For example, Froschl, Colon, Rubin, and Sprung (1984) have developed a curriculum for teaching preschoolers about the various disabilities, while Barnes, Berrigan, and Biklen (1978) have identified numerous activities for use with elementary and secondary students. A list of other commercially available programs is presented in Figure 4.7.

Teachers can promote the acceptance of individuals with disabilities by introducing several materials in their classrooms. Posters and pho-

Books about other children with disabilities can promote positive attitudes and information sharing. (Photo: Ann-Marie Mott)

FIGURE 4.7.   Commercially Developed Attitude Change Materials.

Accepting Individual Differences. Developmental Learning Materials, 7440 Natchez Ave., Niles IL 60648

  Disabilities: Mentally retarded, learning disabled, visually impaired, hearing impaired, motor impaired.

  This kit contains four large flip books, an audiocassette, and four booklets. It is suitable for grades K-6.

Approaches to Mainstreaming. Teacher Resources, 50 Pond Park Rd., Hingham MA 02043

  This kit is designed to help regular teachers with classroom organization, management, selecting and adapting materials, and modifying and evaluating instructional characteristics of exceptional children and individual differences. The kit contains four filmstrips, audiocassettes, and guides that include an audioscript, discussion questions, extension activities, and a bibliography.

Be My Friend. Canadian Council on Children and Youth, 323 Chapel, Ottawa, Ontario KIN 722

  Disabilities: Physically handicapped, hearing impaired, speech impaired, visually impaired, mentally retarded

  Stories, games, and illustrations are included in this coloring book for grades 2–3.

Everybody Counts! A Workshop Manual to Increase Awareness of Handicapped People, M.J. Ward, R.N. Arkell, H.G. Dahl, and J.H. Wise. The Council for Exceptional Children, 1920 Association Dr., Reston VA 22091

  Disabilities: Covers all disabilities

  This workshop is designed as an initial experiential learning strategy to assist groups toward a fuller understanding of the needs and desires of disabled individuals. It includes a discussion guide for 25 simulation activities that allow participants to feel what it is like to be disabled. Included are an 80 page manual and a cassette tape.

Feeling Free. Human Policy Press, P.O. Box 127, Syracuse NY 13210

  Disabilities: Visually impaired, hearing impaired, physical and health impaired, mentally retarded, learning disabled

  Suitable for grades 3–10, this kit contains children's books, educational guides, and six posters.

Getting Through: A Guide to Better Understanding of the Hearing Impaired. Zenith Radio Co., 6501 W. Grand Ave., Chicago IL 60635

  Suitable for all grade levels, this record contains simulated hearing loss activities and hints on how to make communication easier.

Hello Everybody. Opportunities for Learning, Inc., 8950 Lurline Ave., Dept 79, Chatsworth CA 91311

  Disabilities: Physically handicapped, learning disabled, emotionally disturbed, mentally retarded

  This kit, which is suitable for grades 4–12, contains eight lessons of approximately 15 minutes each, accompanied by a filmstrip and cassette tape. Also included is a teaching guide.

I'm Just Like You: Mainstreaming the Handicapped. Opportunities for Learning, 8950 Lurline Ave., Dept. 79, Chatsworth CA 91311

  Disabilities: Physically handicapped, emotionally disturbed, learning disabled, mentally retarded

  Suitable for grades K-12, this kit contains two filmstrips and cassettes.

Keep on Walking. National Foundation—March of Dimes, 1275 Mamaroneck Ave., White Plains NY 10605

  Disabilities: Physically handicapped

  This 16 mm. film about the adaptation to life of a boy born without any arms is suitable for all grade levels.

FIGURE 4.7. *Continued*

Kids Come in Special Flavors. The Kids Come in Special Flavors Co., P.O. Box 562, Dayton OH 45405

Disabilities: Learning disabled, hearing impaired, mentally retarded, visually impaired, cerebral palsy, spina bifida

This kit, which is suitable for grades K-12, contains a book of simulation activities, a cassette, and materials for simulation activities.

My New Friend Series. Eye Gate Media, Jamaica NY 11435

Disabilities: Hearing impaired, visually impaired, physically handicapped, mentally retarded

This kit contains four filmstrips and cassettes.

Special Friends. Listen and Learn Co., 13366 Pescadero Rd., LaHonda CA 94020

Disabilities: Physically handicapped, learning disabled, emotionally disturbed, visually impaired, hearing impaired, mentally retarded

This kit, which is suitable for grades K-3, contains eight lessons of approximately 15 minutes each, accompanied by filmstrips, cassette tape, and a teaching guide.

What Is a Handicap? BFA Educational Media, 2211 Michigan Ave., Santa Monica CA 90404

Disabilities: Orthopedically handicapped, communication disordered, hearing impaired, emotionally disturbed, multiply handicapped

This kit, which is suitable for grades 4-6, contains six duplicating masters, four cassette tapes, and four filmstrips.

Source: F. W. Litton, M. M. Banbury, and K. Harris, *Teaching Exceptional Children,* Vol. 13 (Reston, Virginia: Council for Exceptional Children, 1980), p. 40–41. Reprinted by permission of the publisher.

tographs depicting disabled individuals in typical situations can stimulate discussions and decorate the walls of the room. *Feeling Free Posters,* a resource material that includes three color posters of individuals with disabilities, is available from

Human Policy Press
P.O. Box 127
Syracuse, NY 13210

Resource Photos for Mainstreaming, an adult and children's series of black-and-white photographs depicting disabled individuals in a variety of situations, can be purchased from

Women's Action Alliance, Inc.
370 Lexington Avenue
New York, NY 10017

Puppets, dolls, and stuffed animals that have disabilities can be used to teach students about disabilities. *New Friends* provides educators with three make-your-own patterns to follow in creating multiracial dolls that depict individuals with disabilities. The dolls can introduce students to various disabilities and the adaptive equipment that disabled individuals employ (Froschl, Colon, Rubin, & Sprung, 1984). The doll patterns are available from

Chapel Hill Training Outreach Project
Lincoln Center, Merritt Hill Road
Chapel Hill, NC 27514

Similarly, *Special Friends,* stuffed animals with disabilities (for instance, an elephant who uses a hearing aid), can be obtained for use in the classroom by contacting

Pediatric Projects, Inc.
P.O. Box 1880
Santa Monica, CA 90406

Kids on the Block presents information about a range of disabilities through puppet shows that portray life-size puppets of disabled children in real-life situations. The vignettes encourage the audience to explore their feelings toward the disabled and ask questions concerning individuals with specific disabilities. Additional information on *Kids on the Block* groups in local areas can be obtained by contacting:

Kids on the Block
9385-C Gerwig Lane
Columbia, MD 21046

A series of books for children based on the *Kids on the Block* puppets has been developed (Aiello & Shulman, 1988).

Information on Disabilities and Characteristics

Fielder and Simpson (1987) found that either a categorical or noncategorical curriculum concerning information related to individuals with disabilities could promote positive attitudes toward their disabled peers. The categorical curriculum focused on categories of exceptionality, and included a review of standard definitions, characteristics, and causes for each of the handicapping conditions (learning disabilities, mental handicaps, visual and hearing impairments, and so on). The noncategorical curriculum examined the problems with labeling, an understanding of the use of language to describe individuals, an acceptance of individual differences, a review of the benefits of acceptance and integration of disabled individuals, and the need for self-advocacy, advocacy, and independence.

Acceptance of Individual Differences

Teaching students to accept and appreciate the value of individual differences also can facilitate the acceptance of individuals with disabilities (Simpson, 1980). Individual differences instruction should seek to promote the belief that individuals with disabilities are more similar to than different from nonhandicapped individuals, as well as facilitate an understanding of one's strengths and weaknesses, likes and dislikes.

The Smallest Minority: Adapted Regular Education Social Studies Curricula for Understanding and Integrating Severely Disabled Students is a curriculum program that teaches nondisabled students about the needs and feelings of disabled students and the value of individual differences. The Smallest Minority Curriculum is divided into three levels: lower elementary, upper elementary, and secondary grades. *The Lower Elementary Grades: Understanding Self and Others* (Brown, Hemphill, & Voeltz, 1982), designed for K-3 students, introduces them to similarities and differences among all people, to prostheses, and to adaptive methods of communicating. *The Upper Elementary Grades: Understanding Prejudice* (Brown, Fruehling, & Hemphill, 1982), which targets students in grades 4-6, examines the effects of prejudice and focuses on group dynamics. *The Secondary Grades (7–12): Understanding Alienation* (Hemphill, Zukas, & Brown, 1982) explores the effects of physical and programmatic barriers on the alienation of disabled individuals. Additional activities for infusing an understanding of disabled students into the curriculum are available in *Special Alternatives: A Learning System for Generating Unique Solutions to Problems of Special Education in Integrated Settings* (Fruehling, Hemphill, Brown, & Zukas, 1981).

Adaptive Device Instruction

Many mainstreamed students require devices, aids, materials, and appliances to function successfully in the mainstreamed setting. These aids include talking books, hearing aids, speech synthesizers, wheelchairs, and Braille. A program to prepare nonhandicapped students for the entry of these students into the mainstream should introduce them to these aids and devices (Aiello, 1979; Bookbinder, 1978). Wherever possible, it would be best for the mainstreamed students to introduce and explain the aids and devices they use. Nonhandicapped students should be shown the devices and allowed to touch and experiment with them. For example, a student with a hearing impairment could explain the parts and maintenance of the hearing aid, then have students use a hearing aid for a brief period of time. If mainstreamed students do not feel comfortable showcasing and explaining the aids they use, a professional—a physical therapist, special education teacher, or guidance counselor—or parent can do so.

Alternative communication systems, such as Braille, sign language and fingerspelling, can be introduced to students in a variety of ways that simultaneously promote academic skills. Teachers can teach students the manual alphabet, then have them practice their spelling skills by spelling them manually. Teachers can include hand signs for numbers as part of a math assignment. For example, rather than writing the numbers of a division computation on the board, teachers can present the numbers using numerical hand signs. Basic signs can be introduced to students and used by teachers to give directions for assignments. Students who have learned Braille can be assigned the task of reading Braille books, and writing their names or compositions in Braille.

Aiello (1979) proposed that adaptive devices can be introduced to non-handicapped students through a center approach, in which adaptive devices can be obtained from a variety of sources and placed in a central location in the classroom. Students can then experiment with and explore the devices at different times during the school day.

Guest Speakers

An attitude change strategy that provides nonhandicapped students with direct exposure to individuals with disabilities is inviting to class guest speakers who have disabilities (Bookbinder, 1978; Froschl, Colon, Rubin, & Sprung, 1984). Teachers can find potential guest speakers by contacting local community agencies, parent groups, special education teachers, and special education schools. Although many potential speakers may be available, teachers should meet with them beforehand to determine their appropriateness for talking to students.

When selecting a guest speaker (Bookbinder, 1978), teachers should consider these issues:

- Is the individual comfortable with his or her disability?
- Does the individual have an independent lifestyle?
- Does the individual have a range of experiences to share with students?
- Does the individual represent a positive role model for students?
- Does the individual have the skills to talk to students at a language level they can understand?
- Does the individual possess a sense of humor and warmth that will appeal to students?
- Can the individual deal with the questions your students may ask?

Once speakers have been selected, teachers should meet with them to help plan their presentations (Bookbinder, 1978). Speakers may want to address such topics as problems they encounter now as well as those they experienced when they were the students' age; school experiences; hobbies and interests; family; jobs; a typical day; future plans; causes of their disability; ways to prevent their disability (if possible); adaptations they need; ways of interacting with others; and adaptive devices they use. Speakers should be encouraged to use short anecdotes and humorous stories that portray positive examples of their lifestyles.

To assist speakers in tailoring their remarks to students, teachers should provide speakers with background information about the class (age level, grade level, and exposure to and understanding of disabilities) and possible questions students may ask. Before each speaker comes to class, teachers should have students identify the questions they have about the disability to be discussed, so that they can be shared with the speaker. Because some students may hesitate to ask questions, the teacher can help overcome their reluctance by initially asking the speaker some questions the students previously identified.

Reverse Mainstreaming

McCann, Semmel, and Nevin (1985) suggest that increased acceptance of students with disabilities can be promoted through *reverse mainstreaming,* which can take the form of visits to special education classes to perform a function, such as serving as a peer tutor. These reverse mainstreaming activities can lessen the stigma that is often related to placement in special education classes by promoting a greater understanding of their purpose and function. Reverse mainstreaming can also provide opportunities for friendships that can carry over into the regular classroom setting.

Hypothetical Examples

Most attitude change strategies attempt to promote propitious attitudes toward individuals with disabilities by exposing nonhandicapped students to positive, nonstereotypic examples of disabled persons (Salend, 1984). However, while they are often successful in changing attitudes toward individuals with disabilities, these examples frequently fail to teach nonhandicapped students the skills needed to interact with their mainstreamed peers (Tymitz–Wolf, 1982). Furthermore, nonhandicapped students experiencing these attitude change strategies can develop well-meaning but overly sympathetic behaviors toward their mainstreamed peers (Donaldson, 1980b; Putcamp, 1954). Specifically, nonhandicapped students may assist disabled students when they don't need assistance, or make unnecessary exceptions for mainstreamed students. These superfluous modifications can limit the development of independence in mainstreamed students (Wolfensberger, 1972), as well as inhibit the fostering of constructive, equal-status relationships between mainstreamed and nonhandicapped students (Donaldson, 1980a; Johnson & Johnson, 1980).

One cognitive-based attitude change strategy that sensitizes nonhandicapped students in when and how to aid their mainstreamed peers is to present hypothetical examples that illustrate the problems mainstreamed students are likely to encounter in the regular classroom (Salend & Knops, 1984). After the hypothetical examples are presented, students discuss them and brainstorm possible solutions. For example, the following hypothetical example can be presented to the class:

During class discussions, Jack a student with a hearing impairment, has difficulty understanding what we are talking about and knowing who is talking. What can we do so that Jack will understand better?

Following a discussion of this scenario, students can problem-solve solutions, such as allowing Jack to leave his work area so that he can read lips, or having a peer point to speakers to indicate changes in the flow of the conversation. Other sample hypothetical examples that can be presented to students are presented in Figure 4.8.

FIGURE 4.8.   Sample Hypothetical Examples.

1. The class is having a spelling bee. Jack, a student with a hearing impairment, is a good speller, but is having difficulty hearing the spelling words. What could be done?

2. The class is returning from physical education class and is getting drinks at the water fountain. Lee, a wheelchair-bound student, is thirsty, but cannot reach the fountain. What could be done?

3. Nydia, a student with a visual impairment, uses large print and Braille. Because these books are heavy and cumbersome, she has difficulty carrying them during class changes. What could be done?

4. As part of social studies class, students are required to take notes from lectures. Some of the students have difficulty taking notes. What could be done?

5. While the class is playing kickball during recess, Stacy, a student with a leg brace, is not included in the game. What could be done?

Salend and Knops (1984) examined the effectiveness of hypothetical examples and found them to be easy-to-use, effective strategies for promoting positive attitudes toward the disabled. They found that the positive effects of the treatment conditions were maintained at a three-week follow-up assessment. Salend (1983) has developed a six-step model for generating and implementing hypothetical examples in the classroom. These steps are described below.

STEP 1   DETERMINING STUDENTS' STRENGTHS AND WEAKNESSES
Initially, teachers should determine the strengths, weaknesses, and unique needs of mainstreamed students in order to determine the areas in which they will need assistance, as well as those areas in which students will not require help from others. For example, a wheelchair-bound student may excel in academic areas but have difficulty maneuvering through lunch lines and playing movement games on the playground during recess.

STEP 2   SPECIFYING THE ENVIRONMENTAL DEMANDS
An analysis of the total classroom environment in relation to students' handicapping conditions can help teachers pinpoint problem areas. Classroom variables that teachers should analyze to determine the needs of mainstreamed students can be identified by addressing the following issues:

1. What social and academic activities are difficult for students?
2. How does the presentation of the material affect the students' performance?
3. How does the response mode of the material affect the students' performance?
4. Do students require specialized materials or specific academic adaptations? What are they?
5. Do students have difficulty with social interactions? (If so, describe these difficulties.)
6. Does the class follow any special routines? What are they?
7. Are there any architectural barriers that affect the students' performance? What are they?

STEP 3   IDENTIFYING PROBLEM AREAS
Based on information gathered in Steps 1 and 2, teachers can specify the content of the hypothetical examples, which should relate to existing discrepancies between the mainstreamed students' unique needs and the characteristics and demands of the regular classroom.

STEP 4   PHRASING PROBLEM AREAS AS HYPOTHETICAL EXAMPLES

Problem areas identified in Step 3 should be translated into hypothetical examples, which should be stated so that information about the problem areas is presented, phrased in language that is consistent with the age and grade level of the class, and posed as a question.

STEP 5   PRESENTING THE HYPOTHETICAL EXAMPLES

When presenting the hypothetical examples to classes, teachers should describe and explain the purpose of the activity. To train students in the process, it may be helpful for teachers to present hypotheticals and model possible solutions.

Teachers should assume the role of facilitator, encouraging students to respond in an honest, positive way. Pity and other responses that would produce an overdependence can be discouraged by including some examples that portray situations where students with disabilities will not need assistance. Introducing the activity by presenting examples that relate to generic problems that any class member might experience (for example, students who are picked last in games, or name calling) can establish an open, positive environment for brainstorming realistic solutions.

STEP 6   BRAINSTORMING SOLUTIONS

During this phase, students discuss the hypothetical examples, and identify and evaluate possible solutions. Teachers should guide the discussion and provide additional information concerning the disability in each example. The class can evaluate all potential solutions by examining each solution with respect to the following concerns:

1. Is the solution complete and understandable?

2. Does the proposed solution actually solve the problem?

3. How many individuals are needed to implement the solution?

4. How much time is needed to implement the solution?

5. What are the environmental consequences of the solution?

6. Is the solution consistent with class rules? school rules?

7. How will the solution affect the student portrayed in the example?

Professional Organizations

Numerous organizations provide information to assist individuals with disabilities. Many of these organizations also provide resources that teachers can include as part of a training program to promote positive reactions to disabled individuals. Appendix A lists some of these organizations.

Promoting Acceptance of Cultural Diversity

Mainstreamed students from multicultural backgrounds may be particularly vulnerable to isolation from their regular education peers. Interactions with their peers may be minimized as a result of both their disability and their unique set of cultural experiences. Many regular education students may view multicultural students as different, and limit their interactions with them because of their unique language, clothes, and customs (Lewis & Doorlag, 1987). Teachers can help students overcome these attitudes by teaching them about the different culture and the value of cultural diversity (Garcia, 1978; Chinn & McCormick, 1986; Schniedewind & Davidson, 1983).

Teachers can create an environment of acceptance and understanding of cultural diversity via a variety of strategies that can sensitize students to different cultures. These strategies include

- sharing information about the teacher's cultural backgrounds;
- asking students and their parents to discuss the unique characteristics of their cultures;
- discussing the similarities and differences among cultures, including music, foods, customs, holidays, and languages;
- making cultural artifacts from different cultures;
- listening to music from different cultures and learning ethnic songs in music class;
- teaching students words, phrases, and songs in other languages;
- constructing bulletin boards that introduce students to a multicultural perspective—for example, a new bulletin board related to a different culture each month;
- making a class calendar that recognizes the holidays and customs of all cultures—for example, the Iroquois celebration of the maple in early spring, which includes singing and dancing;
- celebrating holidays that are common to several cultures in a way that recognizes each culture's customs;
- planning multicultural lunches, where students and their parents work together to cook multi-ethnic dishes, and compiling a class cookbook of these recipes;

- developing a mural that has elements of many cultures;
- taking field trips that introduce students to the lifestyles of different cultures;
- showing movies and videos that highlight aspects of different cultures;
- reading ethnic folktales to students;
- teaching students ethnic games to play during recess; and
- decorating the room with pictures and symbols that offer a multicultural perspective. (Chinn & McCormick, 1986; Garcia, 1978; Schniedewind & Davidson, 1983)

Mack (1988) has identified several activities that teachers can use to promote an awareness of the cultures of blacks, Hispanics, Asian/Pacific Islanders, and Native Americans.

Because frequent changes in schools can result in isolation from peers, migrant students also may benefit from activities that teach their peers about cultural diversity and the migrant lifestyle (Salend, in press). Teachers can introduce students to the value and importance of the work of migrants by having migrant students and their parents discuss their experiences and the places where they have lived; developing a map that traces the path of migrant families; establishing a pen-pal system where full-year students write to their migrant classmates who are traveling around the country; discussing the importance of migrant workers to our society; and planting and harvesting a class garden.

Teachers also can incorporate an acceptance of cultural diversity into their curricula. They should carefully examine textbooks and other materials for inclusion of minority individuals and the roles they played in the specific content area. In examining books, teachers should consider:

- Is the language of the book free of cultural and sexual biases?
- Are individuals from multicultural backgrounds portrayed in a positive, nonstereotypic way?
- Does the book recognize and include the contributions of individuals from minority backgrounds?
- Does the book offer examples that depict individuals from multicultural backgrounds in a variety of situations and settings?
- In what proportion are individuals from different ethnic groups shown in pictures and illustrations? (Schniedewind & Davidson, 1983)

Teachers can supplement the texts they use to ensure that the contributions of members of different ethnic groups are infused into the content areas (Garcia, 1978). For example, celebrating holidays in recognition of the accomplishments of black scientists in science class or Hispanic poets in English class can teach students about the contributions of those ethnic groups (Schniedewind & Davidson, 1983). Additionally, students can be assigned to read books about different cultures, including biographies of minority group members who have made significant contributions to society. Teachers can obtain additional information on books and curriculum materials that promote an acceptance of cultural diversity by contacting

Council on Interracial Books for Children
1841 Broadway
New York, NY 10023
(212) 757-5339

An important aspect of learning about cultural diversity is learning about discrimination and its deleterious effects (Schniedewind & Davidson, 1983). Teachers can help students learn about discrimination by having students experience it. For example, teachers can group students according to some arbitrary trait (hair color, eye color, or type of clothing), and then treat groups in different ways in terms of rules, assignments, compliments, grading procedures, privileges, homework, and class jobs. Similarly, teachers can show students what it means to be discriminated against by assigning several groups the same task, but giving groups vastly different resources to complete the task. The differential performance of the groups becomes related to resources rather than ability (Schniedewind & Davidson, 1983). Following these activities, teachers and students can discuss the effects of discrimination on individuals.

Class Cohesiveness

Acceptance of multicultural students can be fostered by activities that promote a sense of class cohesiveness. These group activities facilitate acceptance by creating a class identity that recognizes the unique contributions of each class member. A list of activities that educators have used to promote class cohesiveness (Canfield & Wells, 1976) is provided in Figure 4.9.

Name Calling

Mainstreamed students, particularly those from multicultural backgrounds, may be the target of name calling. While mainstreamed students can learn to ignore name calling, this technique often results in the name callers escalating their ridicule (Salend & Schobel, 1981). Teachers

FIGURE 4.9.   Activities to Promote a Sense of Class Cohesiveness.

1. Create a class scrapbook that includes the work or recognition of everyone in the class.
2. Make a class mural by having each student complete a part of the mural.
3. Construct a class tree. Each branch of the tree can contain a picture of a student or work produced by a student.
4. Compile a "Who's Who" in the class book. Each child can have a page in the book devoted to interests, achievements, and so on.
5. Leave space in the room for a "Proud Of" bulletin board, where students can hang up work of which they are proud.
6. Set up a tutoring center. Students can advertise something that they can teach to others in the class.
7. Include student's names as spelling words.
8. Have a "class applause" session, where the whole class acknowledges the accomplishments or improvements of individual classmates.
9. Publish a class newspaper with each student in the class contributing a piece or drawing during the school year.

Additional guidelines for implementing these and other activities can be obtained by consulting Canfield, J., and Wells, H. C. *100 Ways to Enhance Self-Concept in the Classroom*. Englewood Cliffs, New Jersey: Prentice-Hall, 1976.

can discipline name callers, but this method of dealing with the problem emphasizes the negative, and usually has only temporary results.

A positive approach to name calling involves implementing a series of activities to teach students the importance, meaning, derivation, and function of names as well as the negative effects of calling others names (Salend & Schobel, 1981). These activities could include:

1. Have the students explore the derivation of names by identifying how they received their names. While the responses will be varied (named after their relatives, famous individuals, or parents' favorite names), teachers should emphasize the similarities in how students received their names.

2. Instruct students about the meaning of names in different cultures. For example, in Anglo cultures, an individual's first name was historically related to a personality trait (for instance, Ann means *full of grace*), while last names were related to an individual's profession. Review with students how different cultures select names for their children. Assign students the task of researching the meaning of their names. Follow up this lesson by having students pick names they would like to have if they were from the various cultures dis-

cussed. Additionally, students can be asked to identify a futuristic name by responding to, "If I lived on the planet Nimrollia in the year 3001, my name would be . . ."

3. Play the Jim Croce song "I Got a Name" and discuss the importance of names to people and families. Discuss with the students how the names of slaves and immigrants were changed.

4. Emphasize the importance of unique names by having students pretend they all have the same name (such as Jean Doe) for a period of time. During this time period, conduct activities that require students to refer to each other by name. After the activities are completed, discuss the confusion that results when everyone has the same name.

5. Have the students write poems about their names. For example, students can compose a poem depicting their names in relation to the five senses by completing the following:

If I could see my name it would look like _____ .

If I could smell my name it would smell like _____ .

If I could feel my name it would feel like _____ .

If I could hear my name it would sound like _____ .

If I could taste my name it would taste like _____ .

6. Play the record "The Name Game" by Shirley Ellis and highlight the auditory and syllabic differences in names by having the students collectively perform the name game on each student's name.

7. Have the students make an art project related to their names by folding a piece of paper in half and writing their names on the face of the paper. Students then produce a design by cutting from the open edge at the top the outer outline of the letters. Students can then compare their designs and discuss the configurative differences.

8. Have students identify a variety of names that students are called. Then discuss the effect of these names on students and have them respond to the following:

• Do you have any nicknames? How do they make you feel? What other names have you been called in your lifetime?

• What are the names that make you feel good—that make you feel proud or self-confident?

• What are the names that make you feel bad—that make you lose your self-confidence?

• What would a classroom be like if everyone had a nickname that made him or her feel bad?

• What would a classroom be like if everyone had a nickname that made him or her feel good and self-confident? (Canfield & Wells, 1976, p. 103).

- What would a classroom be like if everyone had a nickname that made him or her feel good and self-confident? (Canfield & Wells, 1976, p. 103).

9. Have students think of a name-calling incident in which they were involved. Ask the students to share their incident with the class.

10. Assign small groups of students to develop and present a role play on name calling. After each role play, have the class discuss the different responses to the situations role-played.

11. Construct a book of names, with each student in the class having a page that includes the student's name, derivation and meaning of the name, futuristic name, favorite nickname, and name poem. (Barnes, Berrigan, & Biklen, 1978; Salend & Schobel, 1981; Schniedewind & Davidson, 1983).

Peer Support Committees

Some teachers have instituted peer support committees to address classroom social interaction problems and promote peer acceptance of mainstreamed students and students from multicultural backgrounds (DiMeo, Ryan, & Defanti, 1989). Peer support committees are charged with the responsibility of ensuring that all students are valued and accepted as contributing members in the class. The peer support committee identifies problems individual class members or the class as a whole are experiencing and devises strategies to alleviate these problems. Typically, the membership on the committee is rotated so that each member of the class has an opportunity to serve.

Summary

Mainstreaming is based on the premise that placing students with disabilities with their peers will create increased positive social interactions. However, the prior experiences and negative attitudes of nonhandicapped students can limit the number and nature of these interactions. Attitude change strategies found to be effective in fostering positive attitudes toward individuals with disabilities include disability simulations, films and children's books about the disabled, commercially produced materials, hypothetical examples, guest speakers, group discussion, information on handicapping conditions, individual differences and adaptive device instruction, reverse mainstreaming, and knowledge about successful disabled individuals. A program to prepare nonhandicapped students to accept their disabled peers also may include training in accepting cultural diversity, dealing with name-calling, and using peer support committees.

References

Aaron, P. G., Phillips, S., & Larsen, S. (1988). Specific reading disability in historically famous persons. *Journal of Learning Disabilities, 21,* 523–538.

Agard, J. A., Veldman, D. J., Kaufman, M. J., & Semmel, M. I. (1978). *How I feel toward others: An instrument of the PRIME instrument battery.* Baltimore: University Park Press.

Aiello, B. (1979). Hey, what's it like to be handicapped? *Education Unlimited, 1,* 28–31.

Aiello, B., & Shulman, J. (1988). *The kids on the block book series.* Frederick, Md.: Twenty-First Century Books.

Asher, S. R., & Taylor, A. R. (1981). Social outcomes of mainstreaming: Sociometric assessment and beyond. *Exceptional Education Quarterly, 1,* 13–30.

Bagley, M. T., & Greene, J. F. (1981). *Peer attitudes toward the handicapped scale.* Austin, Tex.: Pro-Ed.

Barnes, E., Berrigan, C., & Biklen, D. (1978). *What's the difference? Teaching positive attitudes toward people with disabilities.* Syracuse: Human Policy Press

Benavides, A. (1980). Cultural awareness training for exceptional teachers. *Teaching Exceptional Children, 13,* 8–11.

Billings, H. K. (1963). An exploratory study of the attitudes of non-crippled children toward crippled children in three selected elementary schools. *Journal of Experimental Education, 31,* 381–387.

Bookbinder, S. R. (1978). *Mainstreaming: What every child should know about disabilities.* Boston: Exceptional Parent Press.

Bowers, E. M. (1980). *The handicapped in literature: A psychosocial perspective.* Denver: Love Publishing.

Brown, S., Fruehling, R., & Hemphill, N. J. (1982). *The smallest minority: Adapted regular education social studies curricula for understanding and integrating severely disabled students. Upper elementary grades: Understanding prejudice.* Honolulu: University of Hawaii/Manoa, Hawaii Integration Project.

Brown, S., Hemphill, N. J., & Voeltz, L. (1982). *The smallest minority: Adapted regular education social studies curricula for understanding and integrating severely disabled students. Lower elementary grades: Understanding self and others.* Honolulu: University of Hawaii/Manoa, Hawaii Integration Project.

Bruininks, R. H., Rynders, J. E., & Gross, J. C. (1974). Social acceptance of mildly retarded pupils in resource rooms and regular classes. *American Journal of Mental Deficiency, 78,* 377–383.

Bryan, T. H. (1974). Peer popularity of learning disabled children. *Journal of Learning Disabilities, 7,* 621–625.

Canfield, J., & Wells, H. C. (1976). *100 ways to enhance self-concept in the classroom.* Englewood Cliffs, N.J.: Prentice-Hall.

Cartwright, C. A., & Cartwright, G. P. (1974). *Developing observational skills.* New York: McGraw-Hill.

Chigier, E., & Chigier, M. (1968). Attitudes to disability of children in the multi-cultural society of Israel. *Journal of Health and Social Behavior, 9,* 310–317.

Chinn, P. C., & McCormick, L. (1986). Cultural diversity and exceptionality. In N. G. Haring & L. McCormick, (Eds.), *Exceptional Children and Youth (4th ed.)* (pp. 95–117). Columbus: Charles E. Merrill.

Clore, G. L., & Jeffrey, K. M. (1972). Emotional roleplaying, attitude change and attraction toward a disabled person. *Journal of Personality and School Psychology, 23,* 105–111.

Conway, R. N. F., & Gow, L. (1988). Mainstreaming special students with mild handicaps through group instruction. *Remedial and Special Education, 9*(5), 34–41.

DiMeo, J., Ryan, L., & Defanti, A. (1989, April). *Activating collective expertise through collaborative consultation: Classroom alternatives support teams.* Paper presented at the meeting of the Council for Exceptional Children, San Francisco.

Donaldson, J. (1980). Changing attitudes toward handicapped persons: A review and analysis or research. *Exceptional Children, 46,* 504–516.

Donaldson, J. (1981). The visibility and image of handicapped people on television. *Exceptional Children, 47,* 413–416.

Donaldson, J., & Martinson, M. C. (1977). Modifying attitudes toward physically disabled persons. *Exceptional Children, 43,* 337–341.

Dunlap, K. H., Stoneman, Z., and Cantrell, M. H. (1980). Social interaction of exceptional and other children in a mainstreamed preschool classroom. *Exceptional Children, 47,* 132–141.

Esposito, B., & Peach, W. (1983). Changing attitudes of preschool children toward handicapped persons. *Exceptional Children, 49,* 361–363.

Esposito, B. G., & Reed, T. M. (1986). The effects of contact with handicapped persons on young children's attitudes. *Exceptional Children, 53,* 224–229.

Falty, J. E. (1965). *Attitudes toward physical disability in Costa Rica and their determinants: A pilot study.* Unpublished dissertation, Michigan State University.

Fielder, C. R., & Simpson, R. L. (1987). Modifying attitudes of nonhandicapped high school students toward handicapped peers. *Exceptional Children, 53,* 342–349.

Froschl, M., Colon, L., Rubin, E., & Sprung, B. (1984). *Including all of us: An early childhood curriculum about disability.* New York: Educational Equity Concepts.

Fruehling, R., Hemphill, N. J., Brown, S., & Zukas, D. (1981). *Special alternatives: A learning system for generating unique solutions to problems of special education in integrated settings.* Honolulu: University of Hawaii/Manoa, Hawaii Integration Project.

Garcia, R. L. (1978). *Fostering a pluralistic society through multi-ethnic education.* Bloomington, Ind.: Phi Delta Kappa Educational Foundation.

Gerber, M. (1977). Awareness of handicapping conditions and sociometric status in an integrated pre-school setting. *Mental Retardation, 15,* 24–25.

Glazzard, P. (1979). Simulation of handicaps as a teaching strategy for pre-service and in-service training. *Teaching Exceptional Children, 11,* 101–104.

Glick, O. (1969). Person-group relationships and the effect of group properties on academic achievement in the classroom. *Psychology in the Schools, 1,* 197–203.

Goodman, H., Gottlieb, J., & Harrison, R. H. (1972). Social acceptance of EMRs integrated into a non-graded elementary school. *American Journal of Mental Deficiency, 76,* 412–417.

Gottlieb, J. (1980). Improving attitudes toward retarded children by using group discussion. *Exceptional Children, 47,* 106–11.

Greenbaum, J., Varas, M., & Markel, G. (1980). Using books about handicapped children. *The Reading Teacher, 33,* 416–419.

Gronlund, N. E. (1976). *Measurement and evaluation in teaching.* New York: Macmillan.

Gropper, N., & Schuster, A. (1981, Winter-Spring). Separate is not equal: Intended and implicit messages about the disabled in children's literature. *Equal Play,* 5–9.

Hansell, S. (1981). Ego development and peer friendship networks. *Sociology of Education, 54,* 51–63.

Harth, R. (1971). Attitudes toward minority groups as a construct in assessing attitudes toward the mentally retarded. *Education and Training of the Mentally Retarded, 6,* 142–147.

Hemphill, N. J., Zukas, D., & Brown, S. (1982). *The smallest minority: Adapted regular education social studies curricula for understanding and integrating severely disabled students. The secondary grades: Understanding alienation.* Honolulu: University of Hawaii/Manoa, Hawaii Integration Project.

Hochman, B. (1980). *Simulation activities handout.* Bethlehem, Pa.: Project STREAM.

Horne, M. D. (1981). *Assessment of classroom status: Using the perception of social closeness scale.* ERIC Document Reproduction Service No. 200 616.

Horne, M. D. (1985). *Attitudes toward handicapped students: Professional, peer, and parent reactions.* Hillsdale, N.J.: Lawrence Erlbaum Associates.

Horne, M. D., & Powers, J. E. (1983). Teacher's ratings of aggression and students' own perceived status. *Psychological Reports, 53,* 275–278.

Ide, J. K., Parkerson, J., Haertel, G. D., & Walberg, H. J. (1981). Peer group influence on educational outcomes: A quantitative synthesis. *Journal of Educational Psychology, 73,* 472–484.

Israelson, J. (1980). I'm special too—A classroom program promotes understanding and acceptance of handicaps. *Teaching Exceptional Children, 13,* 35–38.

Johnson, D. W., & Johnson, R. T. (1980). Integrating handicapped students into the mainstream. *Exceptional Children, 47,* 90–98.

Jones, R. L., & Sisk, D. A. (1967). Early perceptions of orthopedic disability. *Exceptional Children, 34,* 551–556.

Jones, T. W., Sowell, V. M., Jones, J. K., & Butler, G. (1981). Changing children's perceptions of handicapped people. *Exceptional Children, 47,* 365–368.

Landau, E. D., Epstein, S. E., & Stone, A. P. (1978). *The exceptional child through literature.* Englewood Cliffs, N.J.: Prentice-Hall.

Lazar, A. L., Gensley, J. T., & Orpet, R. E. (1971). Changing attitudes of young mentally gifted children toward handicapped persons. *Exceptional Children, 37,* 600–602.

Leung, E. K. (1980). Evaluation of a children's literature program designed to facilitate the social integration of handicapped children into regular elementary classrooms. Doctoral dissertation, The Ohio State University. *Dissertation Abstracts, 40,* 4528–A.

Lewis, R. B., & Doorlag, D. H. (1987). *Teaching special students in the mainstream.* Columbus: Charles E. Merrill.

Lindsey, J. D., & Frith, G. H. (1983). The effects of nonhandicapped students' personal characteristics on their attitude toward handicapped peers. *Journal for Special Educators, 20,* 64–69.

Litton, F. W., Banbury, M. M., & Harris, K. (1980). Materials for educating handicapped students about their handicapped peers. *Teaching Exceptional Children, 13,* 39–43.

Lorber, N. M. (1973). Measuring the character of children's peer relations using the Ohio social acceptance scale. *California Journal of Educational Research, 24,* 71–77.

Mack, C. (1988). Celebrate cultural diversity. *Teaching Exceptional Children, 21,* 40–43.

Marotz-Ray, B. (1985). Measuring the social position of the mainstreamed handicapped child. *Exceptional Children, 52,* 57–62.

Marsh, V., & Friedman, R. (1972). Changing public attitudes toward blindness. *Exceptional Children, 38,* 426–428.

McCann, S. K., Semmel, M. I., & Nevin, A. (1985). Reverse mainstreaming: Nonhandicapped students in special education classrooms. *Remedial and Special Education, 6,* 13–19.

Miller, M., Hagan, M., & Armstrong, S. (1980). Non-handicapped students' attitudes as assessment variables. *Diagnostique, 5,* 20–25.

Miller, M., & Loukellis, I. (1982, April). *Assessment of rural elementary students' attitudes toward the handicapped.* Paper presented at the meeting of the Council for Exceptional Children, Houston.

Miller, M., Richey, D. D., & Lammers, C. A. (1983). Analysis of gifted students' attitudes toward the handicapped. *The Journal for Special Educators, 19,* 14–21.

Moe, L. (1980). *Guidelines for evaluating books about individuals with handicaps.* Bethlehem, Pa.: Project STREAM.

Monroe, J. D., & Howe, C. E. (1971). The effects of integration and social class on the acceptance of retarded adolescents. *Education and Training of the Mentally Retarded, 6,* 20–24.

Parish, T. S., Ohlsen, R. L., & Parish, J. G. (1978). A look at mainstreaming in light of children's attitudes toward the handicapped. *Perceptual and Motor Skills, 46,* 1019–1021.

Parish, T. S., & Taylor, J. (1978). The Personal Attribute Inventory for Children: A report on its validity and reliability as a self-concept scale. *Educational and Psychological Measurement, 38,* 565–569.

Perlmutter, B. F., Crocker, J., Corday, D., & Garstecki, D. (1983). Sociometric status and related personality characteristics of mainstreamed learning disabled adolescents. *Learning Disability Quarterly, 6,* 20–30.

Popp, R. A. (1983). Learning about disabilities. *Teaching Exceptional Children, 15,* 78–81.

Prillaman, D. (1981). Acceptance of learning disabled students in the mainstream environment: A failure to replicate. *Journal of Learning Disabilities, 14,* 344–368.

Putcamp, R. (1954, May). Glass George. *Instructor,* p. 39.

Randolph, A. H., & Harrington, R. M. (1981). Fifth graders' projected responses to physically handicapped classmate. *Elementary School Guidance and Counseling, 16,* 31–35.

Research for Better Schools. (1978). *Clarification of PL 94–142 for the classroom teacher.* Philadelphia: Author.

Richardson, S. A., Goodman, N., Hastorf, A. H., & Dornbusch, S. M. (1961). Cultural uniformity in reaction to physical disabilities. *American Sociological Review, 26,* 241–247.

Salend, S. J. (1983). Using hypothetical examples to sensitize nonhandicapped students to their handicapped peers. *The School Counselor, 30,* 306–310.

Salend, S. J. (1984). Factors contributing to the development of successful mainstreaming programs. *Exceptional Children, 50,* 409–416.

Salend, S. J. (in press). A migrant education guide for special educators. *Teaching Exceptional Children.*

Salend, S. J., & Knops, B. (1984). Hypothetical examples: A cognitive approach to changing attitudes toward the handicapped. *The Elementary School Journal, 85,* 229–236.

Salend, S. J., & Moe, L. (1983). Modifying nonhandicapped students' attitudes toward their handicapped peers through children's literature. *Journal for Special Educators, 19,* 22–28.

Salend, S. J., & Schobel, J. (1981). Coping with namecalling in the mainstreamed setting. *Education Unlimited, 3,* 36–37.

Sandburg, L. D. (1982). Attitudes of nonhandicapped elementary school students toward schoolaged trainable mentally retarded students. *Education and Training of the Mentally Retarded, 17,* 30–34.

Schniedewind, N., & Davidson, E. (1983). *Open minds to equality: A sourcebook of learning activities to promote race, sex, class and age equity.* Englewood, N.J.: Prentice-Hall.

Scranton, T. R., & Ryckman, D. B. (1979). Sociometric status of learning disabled children in integrative programs. *Journal of Learning Disabilities, 12,* 49–54.

Simpson, R. L. (1980). Modifying the attitudes of regular class students toward the handicapped. *Focus on Exceptional Children, 13*(3), 1–11.

Siperstein, G. N., Bak, J. J., & Gottlieb, J. (1977). Effects of group discussion on children's attitudes toward handicapped peers. *The Journal of Educational Research, 70,* 131–134.

Slapin, B., Lessing, J., & Belkind, E. (1987). *Books without bias: A guide to evaluating children's literature for handicapism.* Berkeley: KIDS Project.

Tringo, J. L. (1970). The hierarchy of preference toward disability groups. *Journal of Special Education, 4,* 295–306.

Tymitz-Wolf, B. L. (1982). Extending the scope of inservice training for mainstreaming effectiveness. *Teacher Education and Special Education, 5,* 17–23.

Voeltz, L. M. (1980). Children's attitudes toward handicapped peers. *American Journal of Mental Deficiency, 84,* 455–464.

Wallace, G., & Larsen, S. C. (1978). *Educational assessment of learning problems: Testing for teaching.* Boston: Allyn and Bacon.

Ward, M. J., Arkell, R. N., Dahl, H. G., & Wise, J. H. (1979). *Everybody counts! A workshop manual to increase awareness of handicapped persons.* Reston, Va.: Council for Exceptional Children.

Weinberg, N., & Santana, R. (1978). Comic books: Champions of the disabled stereotype. *Rehabilitation Literature, 39,* 327–331.

Westervelt, V. D., & McKinney, J. D. (1980). Effects of a film on nonhandicapped children's attitudes toward handicapped children. *Exceptional Children, 46,* 294–296.

Wolfensberger, W. (1972). *The normalization principle in human service systems.* Toronto: National Institute of Mental Retardation.

Wright, B. (1978). The coping framework and attitude change: A guide to constructive role-playing. *Rehabilitation Psychology, 25,* 177–183.

Yuker, H., Block, J., & Young, J. (1970). *The measurement of attitudes toward disabled persons.* Albertson, N.Y.: Human Resources Center.

Promoting Communication to Foster the Mainstreaming Process

(Photo: Alan Carey/The Image Works)

Successful mainstreaming depends on an ongoing process of good communication and cooperation among educators, parents, and community resources (Hundert, 1982). Mainstreaming means that educational programming for students with disabilities, once the sole domain of special education, is now a shared responsibility (Conway & Gow, 1988). Research suggests that the success of mainstreaming is often dependent on the quality of communication and support among educators, other professionals, and parents (Miller & Sabatino, 1978).

This chapter provides guidelines for establishing a network of professionals based on communication and congruence. Specifically, the chapter presents strategies for promoting communication between regular and special educators, encouraging the involvement of families, and using community resources and professional and parent organizations.

Establishing a Network of Communication

One method for establishing ongoing communication is through the development of an interdisciplinary network of educators, parents, and community resources. This network will work cooperatively to provide appropriate services to students with disabilities and their families (Cobb, 1978). The network can facilitate mainstreaming by establishing a problem-solving team approach that is based on communication and mutual obligation. The purposes of the network are to expand the range of services available to mainstreamed students and their teachers, share the responsibility for mainstreaming, and coordinate the services provided to students and their families by the schools and the community. For mainstreamed students, the network can consist of regular and special educators, administrators, ancillary support personnel, paraprofessionals, volunteers, parents, local community resources, and professional and parent organizations, as shown in Figure 5.1 (Taylor & Salend, 1983). The components of the network vary depending on the needs of mainstreamed students and their families. For example, a network for a student with a physical disability might be expanded to include medical and health professionals, such as physicians, nurses, and physical therapists.

Communicating Between Regular and Special Education Teachers

Successful mainstreaming will require that regular and special educators work together closely throughout the process, determining a stu-

FIGURE 5.1.   Sample Mainstreaming Network.

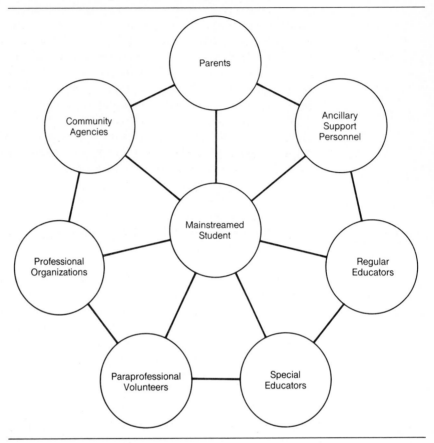

dent's readiness for mainstreaming; preparing students for entry into the mainstream; implementing attitude change strategies with nonhandicapped students; designing remedial instruction that parallels and supports regular education instruction; planning and implementing instructional, testing, and grading modifications; obtaining supportive services for mainstreamed students and their families; maintaining communication with parents and other members of the mainstreaming network; and evaluating student progress in the mainstream. For example, special and regular education teachers may jointly adapt a content-area test for a mainstreamed student, with the special education paraprofessional administering the test in the resource room.

Communication and cooperation among educators should be initiated with the decision to mainstream a student into a specific classroom (Goodman, 1979). Special and regular educators should work together to plan an orientation and instructional program for main-

streamed students. Prior to mainstreaming, special educators should provide regular educators with information concerning a student's academic achievement, social development, supplementary support services, medical needs, adaptive devices, and preparedness for entering the mainstream (Salend & Hankee, 1981). Safran and Safran (1985) suggest that the initial communication between special and regular educators should clarify goals and achievement expectations, identify appropriate materials, delineate adapted instructional techniques, determine assignment modifications, plan for supportive instruction in the resource room, and establish grading options. For students with sensory impairments, the regular classroom teacher should receive information concerning the nature of the sensory loss as well as the amount of residual hearing or vision (Gearheart, Weishahn, & Gearheart, 1988). In the case of students with hearing impairments, teachers also should be informed of the student's communication abilities and needs, and have an opportunity to meet with the student to establish a relationship.

One method of communicating necessary information to the regular educator is the *pre-entry questionnaire* (Salend & Hankee, 1981), a written record of a special educator's responses to a series of questions and items concerning a mainstreamed student's performance in the special education setting. The completed questionnaire is sent to the regular education teacher at least two weeks before the mainstreamed student's entry into the regular education class. A sample pre-entry questionnaire is presented in Figure 5.2.

Consultation

Collaborative efforts between regular and special educators should extend beyond the mainstreamed student's initial placement into the mainstream (Salend, 1984). Specifically, special educators should provide follow-up supportive services (Miller & Sabatino, 1978), such as *consultation* (West & Cannon, 1988). Consultation is an indirect service delivery system to improve the quality of instruction for students with disabilities educated in regular education settings (West & Idol, 1987). Idol, Paolucci–Whitcomb, and Nevin (1986) define consultation as

> an interactive process that enables people with diverse expertise to generate creative solutions to mutually defined problems. The outcome is enhanced, altered and produces solutions that are different from those that the individual team members would produce independently. The major outcome of collaborative consultation is to provide comprehensive and effective programs for students with special needs within the most appropriate context, thereby enabling them to achieve maximum constructive interaction with their nonhandicapped peers. (p. 1)

FIGURE 5.2.   Sample Pre-Entry Questionnaire.

1. What are the student's academic strengths?

2. What are the student's academic weaknesses?

3. What approaches and materials have been effective with the student?

4. What approaches and materials have not been effective with the student?

5. What instructional modifications does the student require?

6. What remedial activities are appropriate for use with the student?

7. What social and behavioral skills does the student possess?

8. What social and behavioral skills does the student lack?

9. What are the student's hobbies and interests?

10. In what school clubs or extracurricular activities does/could the student participate?

11. How does the student get along with his or her peers?

12. How does the student feel about his or her disability?

13. What school personnel and community agencies will be working with the student? What services will they provide?

14. To what extent will the student's parents be involved in the mainstreaming process?

15. What communication system will be used to communicate between professionals? with parents?

16. What adaptive devices or medications does the student require?

17. Has the student been prepared for entry into the mainstream?

Often, the consultation follows a triadic model in which the consultant, usually the special educator or an ancillary support personnel member (a school psychologist, speech and language therapist, or physical therapist), assists the consultee, usually the regular education teacher, who has primary responsibility for serving the student (Zins, Curtis, Graden & Ponti, 1988). Thus, the goals of consultation are to remediate problems and provide the consultee with improved knowledge and skills to deal with similar situations in the future.

Consultation differs in several ways from an expert approach to assisting teachers. These differences are summarized in Figure 5.3. In consultation, rather than supervising the consultee, the consultee has an equal-status relationship with the consultant. However, based on prior experience, regular classroom teachers may view their roles as passive referral agents (Salend & Salend, 1984). Therefore, early in the consultation process, consultants and consultees will need to clarify and agree upon their respective roles. Typically, consultees provide a knowledge of the scope and sequence of the curriculum, child development, and instruc-

tional procedures for large groups, while consultants offer a knowledge of behavior management, assessment, and instructional strategies and adaptations (West & Idol, 1987). Mutual clarification and understanding of roles can foster the establishment of a good relationship (Rodin & Janis, 1979), increased motivation (McClelland, 1977), and greater adherence to recommended interventions (Kasl, 1975).

The use of consultation has benefitted students, teachers, and educational systems (Zins, Curtis, Graden, & Ponti, 1988). In terms of impact on students, consultation has led to a decrease in inappropriate behavior (Idol–Maestas, 1981), an increase in academic proficiency over an extended period of time (Jackson, Cleveland, & Merenda, 1975), and an

FIGURE 5.3. Comparison of Consultation and Expert Systems.

	Relationship Style	
Dimension	*Collaborative*	*Expert/ Authoritative*
Objectives/goals	Resolve presenting problem and improve consultee skills	Resolve presenting problem
Target of behavior change	Client and consultee	Client
Relationship	Equal partners	Superior/subordinate
Person responsible		
for client	Consultee	Consultee
for intervention development	Consultant and consultee	Consultant
Consultee involvement in problem solving	Extensive	Minimal
Amount of information generated about problem situation	Usually extensive	Minimal to extensive
Number of alternatives generated	Usually multiple	Often one
Assumption about consultee's involvement	Wants to be involved in problem solving	Wants consultant to solve problem
Time involved	Usually greater	Usually less
Person with problem-solving expertise	Consultant and consultee	Consultant

Source: J. E. Zins, M. J. Curtis, S. G. Graden, and C. R. Ponti. *Helping Students Succeed in the Regular Classroom* (San Francisco: Jossey-Bass, Inc., 1988). Reprinted by permission of the publisher.

improvement in the academic and social performance of nontargeted students (Jason & Ferone, 1978). With respect to teachers, consultation has led to an increase in their acquisition of teaching skills (Gutkin, 1980), positive attitudes toward serving students with learning and behavioral problems (Gutkin, Singer, & Brown, 1980), and knowledge and understanding of at-risk students (Curtis & Watson, 1980). System-wide, consultation has resulted in a decrease in the number of students referred and tested for special education services (Ponti, Zins, & Graden, 1988).

COUNTERING RESISTANCE TO CONSULTATION. Despite its effectiveness, teachers may be resistant to the use of consultation. Friend and Bauwens (1988) identified four sources of resistance to consultation: maintenance of the status quo, failure and frustration, professional pride, and varying perceptions of the process. They suggest that consultants can overcome this resistance by enlisting the support of administrators, involving classroom teachers in the whole process, providing incentives for teachers to participate, sharing data on the effectiveness of consultation, designing interventions that are consistent with the teacher's style, providing nonjudgmental feedback, and establishing a trusting relationship.

The effectiveness of the consultation process can be enhanced by the consultant's display of *referent power,* an individual's ability to be liked, admired, and respected by others (Martin, 1978). Referent power is found in professionals who can develop a sense of empathy and rapport with others. Suggestions from a consultant who possesses referent power are more likely to be accepted than suggestions from consultants who are disliked or coercive. Consultants can increase their referent power by: interacting with teachers in noninstructional or social settings, such as the teacher's lounge (Martin, 1978); emphasizing similarities in beliefs, attitudes, and values (Rodin & Janis, 1979); displaying a positive attitude (Rodin & Janis, 1979); showing respect for the consultee's profession and expertise (Hughes & Falk, 1981); listening actively (Hughes & Falk, 1981); maintaining a nonauthoritarian, supportive attitude (Hughes & Falk, 1981); limiting the use of jargon (Dorr, 1977); and soliciting the support of influential school personnel (Salend & Salend, 1984).

STEPS IN CONSULTATION. Bergan (1977) identified the steps in effective consultation as problem identification, problem analysis, plan implementation, and plan evaluation.

Problem Identification. The initial step in the consultation process
is to identify the problem by meeting with the regular education
teacher and/or observing the student in the mainstreamed setting.
Factors to consider in identifying the problem include the curricu-

lum, physical environment of the room, instructional strategies, teaching styles, peer relationships, student ability levels, family, and school-wide policies and procedures (Zins, Curtis, Graden & Ponti, 1988). Although teachers may want to focus on several problem areas at once, consultants should encourage the team to work on one behavior at a time. If it is necessary to consider more than one problem, then it may be advisable to set priorities and select the most critical problems to work on first (Salend & Salend, 1984).

Once the problem has been identified and agreed upon by the consultant and consultee, it should be clearly defined in observable terms. For example, if the consultant and consultee agree that the problem is inappropriate student comments during formal instruction and the goal is to decrease them, then the terms "inappropriate student comments" and "formal instruction" must to be defined by their observable characteristics. Examples and nonexamples of the problem behavior can be presented by the consultant to check whether or not the consultee can discriminate between them. The definition should include a statement of the student's current level of performance as well as a statement of the student's desired level of performance relative to the identified problem (Zins, Curtis, Graden & Ponti, 1988).

During this stage of the process, consultants also should determine if prospective settings, behaviors, and individuals are amenable to the consultation process (Pinkerton, Miller, & Martin, 1974). If it is evident that the problem cannot be ameliorated by consultation, consultants should attempt to divorce themselves from the process and refer the teacher to other school or community services that are designed to alleviate the problem (Salend & Salend, 1984).

Problem Analysis. In the second phase of the consultation process, consultants and consultees analyze the critical environmental features that appear to be related to the student's identified problem. Analyzing these aspects of the classroom will help in planning the intervention strategies. Classroom variables that may need to be examined include student behaviors, antecedents to and consequences of student behaviors, teacher behaviors, instructional format, classroom physical design, scheduling, peer socialization patterns, and unique classroom characteristics. To analyze these various components of the problem, educators should address the following issues:

1. What social and academic behaviors are difficult for the student(s)?

2. Which antecedent and consequence events seem to affect student behavior?
3. How does the teacher's behavior and style affect student performance?
4. Which teacher management strategies appear to be effective? ineffective? Why?
5. What objects, events, or individuals could serve as potential positive reinforcers?
6. How do the presentation and response modes of the classroom material affect student performance?
7. How does the physical design of the classroom affect student performance? the teacher's management system?
8. What unique characteristics of the classroom milieu appear to be affecting the student's and teacher's behaviors?

Plan Implementation. Information gathered during the problem analysis stage should help educators plan and select appropriate interventions to be implemented. During this step, consultants and teachers should decide on an appropriate intervention strategy that addresses the identified problem as well as the concerns and context of the classroom (Salend, Tintle, & Balber, 1988). The consultant and consultee will share their expertise in devising the intervention; ultimately, however, the consultee will determine whether a specific strategy or modification will be implemented. Therefore, when designing interventions, consultant and consultee should consider such factors as practicality, effectiveness, effects on others, time demands, cost, and ease of implementation (Zins, Curtis, Graden & Ponti, 1988).

Once the intervention has been selected, its specifics should be outlined. To acquire the skills necessary to implement the intervention, teachers should observe the consultant modeling the correct use of the strategy. Additionally, role-playing the intervention can be a valuable technique for helping consultees successfully master its implementation. For example, the consultant can display examples and nonexamples of the desired behavior while the teacher tries to implement the intervention. The intervention can then be modified based on the consultee's performance in the role play.

The agreement between the consultant and the consultee also can be assessed by discussing the specifics of the intervention plan. For example, if the intervention is a positive reinforcement system to increase the student's interactions with peers, then educators can discuss:

1. What are the observable features that make up the behavior to be changed?
2. What are the daily and weekly goals of the intervention?
3. How will the change in behavior be measured?
4. What are the environmental conditions under which the program will be in effect?
5. What are the consequences of appropriate behavior? inappropriate behavior?
6. What reinforcers will be used? How frequently will they be delivered?
7. What is the teacher's role in the plan?
8. What is the consultant's role in the plan?

Plan Evaluation. Once the intervention has been implemented, periodic checks on its effectiveness should occur. Data on the effectiveness of the intervention in promoting changes in student performance can be obtained through direct observation recording techniques, curriculum-based assessments, and analysis of student work samples.

In addition to monitoring student performance, teachers should plan follow-up evaluation to examine the implementation of the intervention and identify any problem areas that need change. Teachers may not change their behaviors as intended (Breyer & Allen, 1975), or may display behavior changes that go beyond the treatment conditions (Chadwick & Day, 1971). For example, a teacher may forget to check a mainstreamed student's seatwork at specific intervals as agreed.

Consultant feedback can enhance the teacher's ability to implement the program. Feedback should be an ongoing, interactive process focused on the intervention plan rather than on the individuals involved. To be helpful, feedback should be

- based on observations rather than inferences and judgments;
- designed for sharing of ideas and information as well as exploring alternatives;
- offered as valuable information for the receiver, not as a release for the provider; and
- delivered at the appropriate time and place.

Teacher skill in implementing the intervention also can be fostered by positively reinforcing compliance with the intervention. This can take the form of graphing data to demonstrate success, praising the teacher, and sharing positive results with parents and other professionals. En-

couraging teachers to present the results of successful consultations at school-wide or district-wide faculty meetings also can reinforce competence and solicit participation of other educators in need of consultation services.

Promoting Congruence

A goal of the mainstreaming communication system and network should be to ensure *congruence* (Allington & Broikou, 1988), the relationship among the curriculum, learning goals, instructional materials, and strategies of the regular classroom and the supportive services programs. A congruent program is one in which supportive service personnel (special educators, reading specialists, speech and language therapists, and bilingual and migrant educators) serving mainstreamed students deliver a cohesive educational program based on common assessment results, goals, objectives, instructional strategies, and materials.

However, rather than providing a program where the instruction in the remedial setting parallels the regular core curriculum, many special education and supportive service personnel deliver fragmented educational programs based on divergent and conflicting curricula and instructional approaches (Idol, West, & Lloyd, 1988; Kimbrough & Hill, 1981). Johnston, Allington, and Afflerbach (1985) assessed the congruence between the reading programs used by reading specialists and regular classroom teachers. The results indicated that only one third of the remedial reading specialists could identify the reading materials employed in the regular classroom, while only 10 per cent of the regular classroom teachers could identify the reading materials used in the remedial education setting. These incompatible and conflicting educational programs confuse students rather than facilitate their educational progress (Johnston, Allington, & Afflerbach, 1985; Vernon, 1958). For example, confusion can occur when students receive remedial reading instruction using a phonetic approach in the resource room and a sight-word approach in the regular classroom.

Allington and Shake (1986) propose two remedial instruction models for coordinating instruction so that the remedial program supports learning in the regular education setting: an *a priori model* and a *post hoc model*. In the a priori model, the supportive services personnel and special educator teach content that supports the material taught in the regular classroom. Instruction in the remedial class lays the foundation for instruction in the regular education setting. For example, the remedial educator might introduce the mainstreamed student to the spelling words on Monday that will be tested on Friday in the regular classroom.

The post hoc model ensures congruence by focusing the instruction in the remedial setting on reinforcing skills previously introduced in the regular education classroom. Thus, rather than introducing new content to the learner, the remedial teacher reviews and reteaches content previously covered in the regular education program. For example, while a student is receiving instruction in adding fractions in the mainstreamed setting, the remedial teacher would help the student understand the process and develop automaticity in responding to similar items.

Team Teaching

Congruence also can be promoted through *team teaching*, whereby regular educators and supportive service personnel work jointly to develop and teach the instructional program in the mainstreamed setting (Reynolds & Volkmar, 1984; Sargent, Swartzbaugh, & Sherman, 1981). Team teaching infuses specialized materials and teaching strategies into the regular education setting. Thus, rather than pulling a student out of the mainstream for supportive services, the supportive services are delivered in the regular classroom setting (Bean & Eichelberger, 1985). Successful team teaching arrangements require educators to meet frequently to define roles and expectations, set schedules, select and transport appropriate materials if necessary, and determine space requirements and arrangements within the regular education setting (Bean & Eichelberger, 1985). The main focus of the team is the mainstreamed students; team members also can provide support and assistance to nonhandicapped students (Sargent, Swartzbaugh & Sherman, 1981).

Several team teaching programs have been successful in meeting the needs of students with disabilities in mainstreamed settings (Reynolds & Volkmar, 1984). Sargent, Swartzbaugh, and Sherman (1981) employed a team teaching approach to mainstream students in English. The teaching team consisted of a reading specialist, a regular education English teacher, and a special educator. The team cooperatively designed an instructional program to teach reading, writing, listening, and speaking skills. For example, in the area of reading, students' needs were assessed by the teachers; then the reading specialist developed an instructional program that was implemented in the regular education setting by all three professionals. The team noted positive improvement in students' skills in all four content areas.

IEP Meetings

The IEP meeting also can serve as a framework for establishing congruence by involving regular classroom teachers and supportive services

personnel in planning and implementing the IEP (Helge, 1987). At the meeting, educators can align their instructional programs by agreeing on a common set of objectives, appropriate instructional strategies and materials, and evaluation procedures to assess student mastery of objectives. As students master existing IEP objectives, the team can hold additional meetings to revise the IEP and evaluate congruence.

Student Interviews

Students can be a source for ensuring and evaluating congruence. Both regular education teachers and remedial personnel can periodically discuss with students aspects of the instructional environment in other classes. Specifically, they can ask students, "What things are you learning in (*class*)?"; "What type of activities do you do in (*class*)?"; "What materials do you use in (*class*)?"; and "Does (*class*) help you in other classes?" (Johnston, Allington, & Afflerbach, 1985).

Notecard Systems

Congruence and communication between professionals serving mainstreamed students can be built into the network through a *notecard system* (Everston & Heshusius, 1985). Each professional working with a mainstreamed student completes a notecard, an ongoing record of the student's performance in that class for that week. The information on the card could include a rating of the student's progress, a listing of the skills mastered or not mastered, upcoming assignments and tests, successful strategies, instructional materials being used, and skills other teachers should attempt to foster. An educator can be assigned the task of categorizing the information and sharing it with others to ensure the continuity of instruction. Thus, if a resource room teacher were aware that a mainstreamed student was scheduled to have a test, time in the resource room can be devoted to preparing for that test. A sample notecard is presented in Figure 5.4.

Safran and Safran (1985) have developed the *Something's Out of Sync (SOS) form* to facilitate communication between regular and special educators. The regular classroom teacher completes the SOS form to indicate that a student is having a problem in a specific content area. The regular classroom teacher can then request that the student receive additional work in the resource room in that area, or that a meeting be held to discuss the problem.

FIGURE 5.4. Sample Notecard System.

Student's Name: _____   **Time Period:** _____

Class/Supportive Service: _____   **Educator:** _____

Skills taught:

Instructional strategies and materials used:

Upcoming assignments/tests:

Assignment/Test   *Date due*

Skills to be reinforced in other settings:

Suggested activities to reinforce skills:

Comments:

Other Strategies for Promoting Congruence

Teachers can establish congruence in educational programs in several ways:

- remedial educators aligning their assessment procedures, curriculum, and instructional strategies with those employed in the regular classroom program;
- regular educators assisting in the design of remedial programs;
- regular and special educators sharing lesson plans and materials;

- administrators scheduling time for teachers to collaborate in the planning of the student's instructional program;
- regular and special educators observing each other's classrooms;
- educators using similar behavior management techniques so that they respond in the same manner to student behavior and promote the maintenance and generalization of the behavior change process;
- special educators teaching study skills and learning strategies using the textbooks of the regular education program;
- speech and language therapists discussing with regular education teachers language concepts to be reinforced in the mainstreamed setting;
- bilingual educators sharing strategies for use with limited English-proficient students;
- social workers contacting community agencies to coordinate services;
- educators communicating instructional goals and student progress to parents;
- educators compiling and sharing folders containing student products; and
- educators participating in staff development sessions that facilitate the coordination of services.

Migrant Student Record Transfer System (MSRTS)

The nomadic lifestyle of migrant students is a stumbling block to the delivery of congruent educational services. Frequent mobility hinders access to and continuity of appropriate educational services for migrant handicapped students. The need for greater communication between educators serving these students has been recognized (California National Policy Workshop on the Special Education Needs of Migrant Handicapped Students, 1986; National Policy Workshop on the Special Education Needs of Migrant Handicapped Students, 1984).

One means of establishing communication between educators serving migrant students is the *Migrant Student Record Transfer System (MSRTS)*. The MSRTS, a nationwide computerized communication system housed in Little Rock, Arkansas, collects and maintains health and academic records for more than a half million migrant students throughout the United States.

When a migrant student enters school, his or her file should be obtained from or started in the MSRTS. School personnel can request or start a file by contacting their local migrant education center or the state education department. Starting files and updating them with current in-

formation can provide others with the data, ensuring the continuity of services to migrant students.

The MSRTS also provides information on the delivery of special education services to migrant students. The special education component of the MSRTS includes prior information related to the existence of a handicapping condition, assessment results, previous services provided, and IEPs. Because the amount of special education information is limited by the space available in the system as well as by the quality of information entered, data are also provided in the MSRTS for directly contacting a migrant student's previous educational institutions to obtain more detailed information.

Because migrants travel intrastate and interstate, educators of migrants students have developed numerous programs other than the MSRTS to promote cooperation among educators. These model programs, directed at interstate and intrastate cooperation between state and local educational agencies serving migrant students and their families, are funded by the federal government. For example, the *Portable Assisted Study Sequence (PASS)* is designed to help migrant students make up or earn credits necessary to graduate from high school by completing an approved curriculum. The material for the curriculum is portable, so it can be worked on independently as the student travels from state to state. Individualized tutoring also is available to students who need it. The students can complete the work at their own pace. School districts then award credits toward graduation based on completion of the PASS materials. Because of the success of PASS with high school students, the PASS model has been adapted to assist migrant students in completing the middle school curriculum. Educators interested in PASS and other interstate and intrastate cooperative projects should contact their local migrant center or the office of their state director of migrant education.

Students Who Move During the School Year

Educators also can facilitate the continuity and delivery of services to mainstreamed students who are moving to a new school by teaching parents to maintain current records and share relevant information with the new school's personnel. Available, up-to-date information can assist the new school district and the parents in determining an appropriate educational program quickly. Therefore, before the family moves, educators should encourage and help parents obtain and update such relevant documents as birth certificates; immunization records; lists of illnesses, accidents, special problems, and medications; papers from medical personnel; IEPs; report cards; transcripts; important correspondence between parents and school; and names, addresses, and phone numbers of medi-

cal and educational personnel who can provide information concerning the child's needs (Sarda, et al., 1988).

School Administrators

School administrators can be instrumental in communication between educators. They can set a tone of communication by planning lunch and preparation periods so that regular and ancillary support personnel who work with the same mainstreamed students can meet to discuss and coordinate their work; requesting at the beginning of the school year that regular classroom teachers list the times that are most convenient for the students in their class to receive individualized supportive services; asking special education teachers to give a presentation at a faculty meeting or in-service day; conducting a faculty meeting in a special education teacher's classroom; giving faculty a tour of the school's special education classrooms; encouraging regular and special educators to visit and observe each other's teaching activities; asking faculty members to switch roles for a day; designating an area of the teachers' lounge as a "materials table" where teachers leave certain materials that they think would be of value to others; including special education classes in all schoolwide activities; sending all school memos to special education teachers; and having special education teachers serve as coaches, school club advisors, and representatives of the school at community events (Salend, 1980).

IN-SERVICE TRAINING.   Administrators also can foster a sense of communication and congruence between school personnel through in-service training (Tymitz–Wolf, 1982). In-service programs can help educators involved in mainstreaming acquire the skills to work together and perform new roles. Effective in-service programs should address teacher-identified needs; employ competent personnel to deliver training; be coordinated by school districts, state education departments, teacher training institutions, and professional organizations; offer educators incentives to participate; deliver instruction using a variety of methods, including demonstrations and activities that require active participation; provide teachers with feedback and the chance to experiment with the training in the classroom; and be evaluated based on teacher satisfaction, teacher and student change data, and acquisition of knowledge skills (Browder, 1983; Powers, 1983; Skrtic, Knowlton & Clark, 1979).

In-service training has been effective in promoting positive attitudes toward mainstreaming and helping teachers improve their skills (Hoben, 1980; Johnson & Johnson, 1980). Hoben (1980) and Johnson and Johnson (1980) found that teacher attitudes could be positively influenced by providing in-service training that emphasized direct experiences with mainstreamed students. Similarly, results of field-based programs showed that teachers exited the training sessions with increased skills and more positive attitudes toward mainstreaming (Carlson & Potter, 1972; Yates, 1973).

In-service training should be directed at promoting the necessary positive attitudes that teachers need to create the proper psychological and educational environment for mainstreamed students (Kauffman & Hallahan, 1981; Turnbull & Schulz, 1979). Donaldson (1980) identified several different modes for promoting attitude change that can be employed by in-service trainers. Because positive teacher attitudes toward mainstreaming appear to be related to the ability of teachers to instruct mainstreamed students (Salend & Johns, 1983; Stephens & Braun, 1980), in-service training should also focus on skill acquisition, which should be directed at the competencies educators need in order to implement mainstreaming successfully. Redden and Blackhurst (1978) identified six functions and thirty-two competency statements relating to the skills necessary to teach disabled students in mainstreamed settings (see Figure 5.5).

In-service instructional activities should be designed to address teachers' needs in relation to these competencies. Training should include interaction with peers who have been involved in successful mainstreaming efforts (Stokes & Axelrod, 1980), exposure to students who have been

FIGURE 5.5.   Competencies for Teaching Mainstreamed Students.

In order to effectively teach mildly handicapped students who are integrated with regular students in a mainstream elementary classroom setting, the teacher must be able to

Function 1.0: Develop Orientation Strategies for Mainstream Entry
   1.1 Participate in schoolwide planning for mainstreaming activities.
   1.2 Set up a training plan that will provide supplementary instruction in areas necessary to teach effectively in a mainstream setting.
   1.3 Participate in parent and community orientation programs on mainstreaming.
   1.4 Seek out consultative relationships with specialists or school staff.
   1.5 When appropriate, develop a program to prepare the special student for entry into a regular class.
   1.6 Prepare members of the regular class for the entry of special students into the class.

Function 2.0: Assess Needs and Set Goals
   2.1 Gather information to determine the educational needs of each student.
   2.2 Evaluate each student's present level of functioning.
   2.3 Determine for each student in the class individual goals that are appropriate, realistic, and measurable.
   2.4 Determine group goals for the class as a whole and for subsets within the class.
   2.5 Involve parents in setting goals for their child and for the class as a whole.

FIGURE 5.5. *(continued)*

Function 3.0: Plan Teaching Strategies and Use of Resources
  3.1 Design a system of teaching procedures that provides for individual differences in students.
  3.2 Specify and prepare a variety of activities that will involve the entire class in grouping patterns that are varied and flexible.
  3.3 Develop and design a variety of alternate teaching strategies.
  3.4 Develop a plan for use of human and material resources.
  3.5 Develop a flexible time schedule that provides for the learning, physical, and social needs of each student.
  3.6 Provide an optimal classroom climate through appropriate arrangement and adaptation of the physical properties of the classroom.

Function 4.0: Implement Teaching Strategies and Use Resources
  4.1 Select and use a variety of individualized teaching methods to instruct each student within the student's level or capability of functioning.
  4.2 Develop, schedule, and maintain on a regular basis a variety of grouping patterns that provide opportunities for students to reach class goals, both social and academic.
  4.3 Use the efforts of the special education resource staff with the special students' classroom activities.
  4.4 Acquire, adapt, and develop materials necessary to achieve learning goals.
  4.5 Plan and maintain a system to use the assistance of volunteers (other students, parents, etc.) to reinforce and supplement classroom activities.
  4.6 Develop a plan to use the talents of parents in supporting the learning activities of their child and those of other students in the class.

Function 5.0: Facilitate Learning
  5.1 Identify and differentiate between a variety of behavior management techniques and develop skills in selecting appropriate techniques to manage individual and/or group behavior.
  5.2 Select and apply adequate behavior management techniques and measures to meet the learning goals set for the class and each individual student.
  5.3 Acknowledge appropriate behaviors in each student in order to stimulate continued effort.
  5.4 Conduct class activities in a way to encourage interaction between and among students.
  5.5 Provide ample instruction and practice for each child to develop and refine adequate coping strategies.
  5.6 Plan with class for systematic appraisal and improvement of the psychological climate of the class.

Function 6.0: Evaluate Learning
  6.1 Organize a system to collect and record data by which to evaluate student progress toward goal attainment.
  6.2 Develop a feedback system that will furnish continuous data to student, teacher, and parents on goal attainment.
  6.3 Use evaluation data to assess goal attainment in order to measure terminal outcomes and set new goals.

Source: M. R. Redden and A. E. Blackhurst, *Exceptional Children,* Vol. 44 (Reston, Virginia: Council for Exceptional Children, 1978), p, 617. Reprinted by permission of the publisher.

successfully mainstreamed, contact with disabled students (Noar & Milgram, 1980), and followup in teachers' current work setting should be an integral part of the in-service program.

Fostering Parental Involvement

An essential component of a congruent mainstreaming network is the student's parents. Research indicates that when educators share information with parents, they can be instrumental in promoting their children's academic and social progress (Allen, 1978; Imber, Imber, & Rothstein, 1979). McLoughlin, Edge, & Strenecky (1978) identified several ways to involve parents in the educational program. These include

1. *Identification.* Often parents are the first ones to notice that their child is experiencing difficulty in a certain area.
2. *Assessment.* Because of their extensive experience with their children, parents are a valuable resource for assessing the student's educational and health-related needs.
3. *Programming.* Parents can give input into the selection of educational goals, instructional procedures and modifications, testing adaptations, and related services.
4. *Teaching.* Parents can supplement the educational program by tutoring their child, assisting with homework assignments, and participating in behavior change projects.

The National Institute of Education (1985) also suggests that teachers involve parents as partners in their child's educational program in several ways, such as

- Ask the parents to read aloud to the child or listen to him or her read.
- Ask the parents to sign the child's homework.
- Encourage parents to drill students on math and spelling.
- Suggest the parents help the child with workbook and homework lessons.
- Encourage parents to ask the child to discuss his or her school day activities.
- Suggest things at home that parents can use to teach their children.

- Send home suggestions for game or group activities related to the child's schoolwork that can be played by parents and child.

- Invite parents to the classroom to watch how the child is taught.

- Encourage parents to take their child to the library regularly and frequently (National Institute of Education, 1985, p. 2).

5. *Evaluation.* Feedback from the parents' perspective on the effectiveness of the student's educational program can offer educators data to validate aspects of the program and identify program characteristics that need to be revised (McLoughlin, Edge, & Strenecky, 1978).

Parents also can be involved in schools by meeting with teachers, providing transportation, observing in the classroom, conducting educational activities in the home, attending parent education groups, volunteering to work in the classroom, providing support to other parents, serving as an advocate, working with administrators, raising funds, and sharing information with others (Cone, Delawyer, & Wolfe, 1985).

PL94-142 and Parents

In addition to being an educationally sound practice, involving parents in the educational program of students with disabilities is mandated by PL94-142.

DUE PROCESS.   PL94-142 requires that parents be informed when a referral for consideration of a handicapping condition has been made; placement teams determine the need for testing to assess eligibility for special education services; results of an assessment are available and being discussed; IEPs are being formulated; a recommendation for special education services is made by the placement team; IEPs are reviewed; and changes in the student's educational program are planned (McLoughlin & Lewis, 1986). To ensure parent awareness of and participation in the process, school districts must attempt to inform parents by telephone, written communication, or home visit in the parents' primary language or mode of communication. Each attempt at communication with parents should be documented and communicated.

Throughout each of these steps, parents should be aware of their right to *due process,* which offers parents the right to appeal and contest each decision made by the placement team. If parents and the placement team cannot agree on an aspect of the student's educational program, either party may initiate a due process hearing—a quasi-judicial proceeding by which local and educational agencies and parents of special education students seek to resolve educational disputes (Kammerlohr, Henderson, & Rock, 1983). The hearing is conducted by an impartial hearing officer who makes a decision regarding the issues in question. The hearing officer is selected by the local educational agency from a list of qualified individuals. As part of their due process rights, parents have the right to have their case presented by an attorney or another knowledgeable representative, present evidence, subpoena witnesses, cross-examine witnesses, obtain a written or electronic transcript of the proceedings, and receive a copy of the hearing officer's decision. Either party can appeal the hearing officer's decision to the state educational agency. The decision of the state educational agency can be challenged through a civil action.

If a due process hearing is held, it is likely that professionals who work closely with the student will be called on to give testimony. Before the hearing, professionals should ask questions so that they understand the relationship between their testimony and the issues of contention (Scandary, 1981). Because they may be called upon to testify to support the parent's case against the district, teachers should seek information and advice from their local teachers' organization concerning potential conflicts and retaliation. Scandary (1981) has developed several guidelines to help educators prepare to serve as witnesses in a due process hearing. She suggests that educators be prepared to

- Establish their credibility by reviewing their professional credentials, such as certification(s), years of experience, training, career experiences, professional awards, and recognition received.
- Outline the services they provide to the student and the student's response to these services.
- Describe in clear and observable terms the student's educational and behavioral strengths and weaknesses.
- Support statements by citing the formal and informal assessment methods used.
- Discuss the technical adequacy (reliability, validity, standardization, and so on) of the standardized assessment instruments used.
- Explain professional jargon so that all parties can understand it.

CONFIDENTIALITY.   PL94–142 also provides parents with the right to *confidentiality*. In other words, those educators directly involved in delivering services to a student may have access to his or her records, but, before a school district can allow individuals not involved in a student's program to review a student's records, it must obtain parental consent. Confidentiality also guarantees parents the opportunity to obtain, review, and challenge their child's educational records. Parents can obtain their child's records by requesting a copy, which the school district must furnish upon request. However, parents may be responsible for the expenses incurred in duplicating their child's records. If parents disagree with the contents of their child's records, they can challenge them by asking school officials to correct or delete the information, or by writing their own response to be included in the child's record.

Parent Conferences

Research indicates that many parents of students with disabilities are willing to and do attend meetings with educators (Turnbull, Strickland, & Brantley, 1982). However, although parents are interested in attending conferences with educators, they often are not satisfied with these interactions (Hoff, Fenton, Yoshida, & Kaufman, 1978) and characterize them as confusing (Kotin & Eager, 1977; McKinney & Hocutt, 1982), disorganized, and poorly attended by professionals (Scanlon, Arick & Phelps, 1981). While parental input is mandated by PL94–142, parents tend to assume a passive role in conferences and appear to be intimidated by technical jargon and test scores (Gilliam & Coleman, 1981; Knoff, 1983).

Educators can take several steps to improve the quality of parent/teacher conferences. Educators should

1. *Plan the meeting.* Before the meeting, educators should carefully plan for it (Swick, Flake–Hobson, & Raymond, 1980). During the planning step, teachers should identify the objectives of the meeting and develop an agenda that corresponds to those objectives. McNamara (1986) suggests that teachers send a letter to parents soliciting their input concerning the meeting's agenda. The agenda should allow enough time to discuss and resolve issues and address concerns of parents and educators. Therefore, it is helpful to share the agenda with parents and other educators before the meeting, and provide them with the necessary background information to participate in the meeting (Goldstein & Turnbull, 1982). Materials such as work samples, test results, and other teachers' comments that relate to agenda items should be organized and available before the meeting.

   The planning phase also should ensure that the meeting time is appropriate for parents and professionals. They should be contacted early in the planning process to determine what times and dates are most appropriate for them. Once a meeting has been scheduled, teachers should contact parents and professionals in advance to inform them of the time, place, purpose, and duration of the meeting, and to confirm their participation (McNamara, 1986; Price & Marsh, 1985). Follow-up reminders to parents via mail or telephone can increase the likelihood that parents will attend the conference (Wolf & Troup, 1980).

2. *Structure the environment to promote communication.* The room in which the conference will take place should be organized to make it easy and comfortable to share information (Kroth & Simpson, 1977). Comfortable, same-size furniture should be used by all participants and arranged to promote communication. Barriers, such as desks and chairs, should not be placed between parents and educators. Chairs should be seated around a table or positioned so that all participants can make eye contact with each other (de Bettencourt, 1987). Lockavitch (1983) suggests that teachers arrange chairs so that they are no closer together than four feet and no farther apart than six to eight feet.

To make sure the meeting is not interrupted, teachers should post a note indicating that a conference is in session on the room's door. Additionally, distractions caused by the telephone can be minimized by taking the phone off the hook, asking the switchboard to hold all calls, or using a room that doesn't have a phone (Kroth & Simpson, 1977).

3. *Conduct the conference.* Educators should conduct the conference in a manner that encourages parent understanding and participation. Initially, review the agenda and the stated purpose of the meeting. To encourage parental participation, teachers can offer parents pads and pencils with which to take notes (Humphrey, Hoffman, & Crosby, 1984).

The meeting should start on a positive note, with educators discussing positive aspects of the student's performance. Next, educators can review any concerns they have about the student. They should present data in a format that is understandable to parents, and share with parents materials such as work samples, test results, and anecdotal records to support their comments (McLoughlin & Lewis, 1986).

They can then solicit information from parents by asking them to discuss the issues or situations from their perspective (Swick, Flake-Hobson, & Raymond, 1980). Educators can increase parental sharing at meetings by using language that parents can understand (de Bettencourt, 1987); listening attentively (Swick, Flake-Hobson, & Raymond, 1980); maintaining eye contact; acknowledging and reinforcing parent participation (*That's a good point,* or *I'll try to incorporate that.*) (Goldstein & Turnbull, 1982); avoiding asking parents questions that have yes/no or implied answers; referring to parents and students by their names (Swick, Flake-Hobson, & Raymond, 1980); refraining from criticizing parents (Swick, Flake-Hobson, & Raymond, 1980); speaking to parents using language that is understandable but not condescending (Lockavitch, 1983); checking periodically for understanding; paraphrasing parents' comments; and showing respect.

Conclude the conference with a summary of the issues discussed, points of agreement and disagreement, strategies to be taken to resolve problems, and roles to be assumed by parents and educators (Goldstein & Turnbull, 1982). At the end of the meeting, parents and educators should establish ongoing communications systems and determine appropriate dates for the next meeting (Schulz, 1987). A sample schedule of activities for a parent/professionals conference is presented in Figure 5.6.

4. *Evaluate the conference.* Parents and teachers should evaluate the conference. Feedback can be solicited by asking them to respond to a series of questions regarding the conference. Educators can be asked to respond to the following questions:

- Were the content and timeliness of the agenda appropriate?
- Was the meeting organized appropriately?
- Did parents have enough information prior to the meeting to participate in and understand the conference?
- Did the room create the right atmosphere for sharing information?
- Were points communicated to parents in a clear, nonthreatening manner using jargon-free language?

FIGURE 5.6. Sample Schedule for Parent/Professionals Conference.

1. Welcome participants.
2. Introduce parents and professionals, including explaining the roles of each professional and the services they provide to the student.
3. Discuss the purpose of this meeting and review the agenda.
4. Review relevant information from prior meetings.
5. Discuss student's needs and performance from the professionals' perspective. Educators support their statements with work samples, test results, and anecdotal records.
6. Provide parents with the opportunity to discuss their view of their child's progress and needs.
7. Discuss comments of parents and professionals attempting to meet a consensus.
8. Determine a plan of action.
9. Summarize and review results of meeting.
10. Determine appropriate dates for the next meeting.
11. Adjourn the meeting.

- Was parental participation encouraged and supported?
- Were parents' and their child's rights violated?

Similarly, the parents' view of the conference can be obtained by asking them

- Were you prepared for the meeting?
- Did the meeting address the issues you wanted to discuss?
- Did the room make you feel comfortable?
- Did you have sufficient time to present your opinion?
- Were you satisfied with the way the meeting was conducted?
- What aspects of the meeting did you like the best? the least?
- Were you satisfied with the outcome(s) of the meeting?

Hudson and Graham (1978) provide additional guidelines for obtaining feedback from parents after IEP meetings.

Written Communication

Teachers often employ written communication to inform parents of their child's performance and needs. While this method can be effective, it is not suited for information that requires two-way communication. Because it is a time-consuming procedure, it is difficult for teachers to communicate in writing detailed information tailored to the unique needs of students and parents.

Furthermore, correspondence from teachers may not reach parents if students fail to deliver it. Teachers can improve the likelihood that parents receive messages by communicating positive comments to parents, sharing notes with students, and checking periodically to ensure that correspondence has been received. One positive written communication device that some teachers employ is the *happygram,* a brief note that alerts parents to the positive accomplishments and improvements of their children (de Bettencourt, 1987). The value of positive notes and happygrams can be increased by pairing them with parental praise. Therefore, when parents receive positive notes from educators, they should be encouraged to read the note promptly, deliver praise to their child in the presence of family members and friends, put the note in a prominent location (such as the refrigerator door) where their child and others are likely to see it, and share their desire to receive additional notes of praise (Imber, Imber, and Rothstein, 1979).

Another form of written communication to parents is the newsletter, which can inform parents of school and classroom events, extracurricular activities, parent meetings, school policies, and lunch menus. Parent education also can be accomplished through a newsletter.

DAILY REPORT CARDS.   The *daily report card,* a written record of student performance in school, has been effective in establishing communication with parents (Fairchild, 1987). This system also can be employed with teachers to share information and promote continuity. The content and format of the daily report card, which will vary depending upon the needs of students and teachers, could include information on academic performance, effort, behavior, peer relationships, and homework completion. The format should be easy for teachers to complete and simple for parents to interpret. As students demonstrate success over a period of time, the report card can be shared with parents on a weekly, bimonthly, and then a monthly basis. Two sample daily report cards are presented in Figures 5.7 and 5.8.

Teachers also can communicate with parents by sending completed assignments home. Everston, Emmer, Clements, Sanford, & Worsham (1989) suggest that teachers send home work in a large envelope or folder that is taped closed. The envelope or folder should have the student's name on it as well as a place for parents' signatures, the date, and the number of assignments included.

Home-School Contracts

The daily report card system also has been used as part of a *home-school contract* (Fairchild, 1987), which allows parents to reinforce their children's improved academic performance or behavior in school. Here's how it works: Teachers observe students in school and report their observations to parents. Parents then deliver reinforcers to their children. For example, Baily, Wolf and Phillips (1970) used a home-school contract in which students earned home privileges to decrease inappropri-

SAMPLE DAILY REPORT CARD (PRIMARY GRADE) Name: *Joshua*	Reading	Language	Math	Resource Room
Remains seated	★			★
Watches teacher when giving instructions	★	★	★	★
Follows directions	★		★	★
Avoids disrupting				★
Attends to lessons	★	★		
Finishes assignments	★	★		★
Sits up in seat	★	★	★	★
Lines up quickly and quietly				★

FIGURE 5.7.   Elementary-Level Daily Report Card.   Source: T. N. Fairchild. *Teaching Exceptional Children,* Vol. 19 (Reston, VA: Council for Exceptional Children, 1987), p. 72. Reprinted by permission of the publisher.

SAMPLE DAILY REPORT CARD (INTERMEDIATE GRADE)

Date: 2/22/89   Name: Wendy

Class	Behavior	Effort	Homework	Teacher
English	2	2	none	LS
History	1	1	—	MK
Crafts	3	3	project due	BL
Science	2	3	read chapter 5	RM
Art	3	2	—	CB
Math	1	2	quiz tomorrow	AR

Rating Scale: 1 = Poor   2 = Satisfactory   3 = Good

FIGURE 5.8.   Secondary-Level Daily Report Card.   Source: T. N. Fairchild. *Teaching Exceptional Children,* Vol. 19 (Reston, VA: Council for Exceptional Children, 1987), p. 73. Reprinted by permission of the publisher.

ate behavior in school and increase study behavior. Involving parents through home-school contracts has several advantages, including promoting home-school communication, alleviating the demands on teachers in terms of time and finances, and lessening the likelihood that the student's peers will be affected by the provision of reinforcers to mainstreamed students.

Parents can provide a variety of reinforcers to their children. Edible and tangible reinforcers that parents can dispense include special foods, clothes, records, software programs, money toward the purchase of a desired item, or a new pet. Parents can dispense activity reinforcers, such as fewer chores, a family activity, trips, a party at the house, a rented video, or a special privilege (Reynolds, Salend, & Beahan, 1988).

Before implementing a home-school contract, parents and teachers should meet to discuss the specifics of the program. This discussion should provide both parties with an understanding of the behavior to be changed, details of the communication system between home and school, potential reinforcers, and when and how to deliver the reinforcers. Once the system is implemented, follow-up communication is critical. It should address these questions:

• Are parents being promptly informed of their child's behavior?
• Are the reinforcers effective or do they need to be changed?
• Are parents delivering the reinforcement as planned?
• How is the system affecting the interaction between family members?

Telephones and Telephone Answering Machines

An alternative to conferences and written correspondence that educators can employ to communicate with parents is the telephone. Although the telephone provides parents and teachers with direct access to each other, frequent telephone calls from and to parents can place an excessive demand on teacher time. However, a telephone answering machine (TAM) can be an inexpensive, easy-to-use, effective communication strategy that minimizes the demands on teacher time. Chapman and Heward (1982) and Bittle (1975) found that recorded messages led to a significant increase in the number of parent-initiated contacts with teachers and improved spelling scores of students. Additionally, teachers liked TAMs because they allowed for greater communication with parents and required less time than traditional ways of sharing information with parents (Chapman & Heward, 1982). Parents liked the system because it was readily available and kept them informed about their child's assignments.

In such a system, teachers record a daily message on a TAM. Parents then call and receive the message. The message could communicate to parents academic assignments (*Today in class we studied weather. The homework assignment for today is to keep a calendar of the day's weather for a week. The assignment is due on _____.*), special events (*Next Tuesday, the class will be going on a trip to the Children's Museum. Please make sure your child brings _____.*), and reminders (*Tomorrow, please have your child bring a magic marker to school.*) (Chapman & Heward, 1982). Minner, Beane, and Porter (1986) propose that educators also use TAMs to provide parents with suggestions for teaching specific skills to their children; report on student performance in school; provide information to parents concerning their rights and special education programs; offer information on local events of interest for students and their families; encourage parents to attend parent meetings; and recommend movies, television shows, books, and other learning activities to parents.

Questions or comments parents have also can be recorded and played back by teachers. Teachers can respond to parents' concerns via follow-up phone calls, notes, or meetings. Individualized messages also can be communicated to parents by a coded system that protects confidentiality (Minner, Beane, & Prater, 1986). Teachers can assign parents and their children a code name or number, and then they can record a message tailored to the parents. For example, a message for a parent of a mainstreamed student can be stated as *Student 5 is showing an improved effort. However, we need to continue to check that all homework assignments have been recorded and completed.*

Parental Observations

Communication between home and school can be enhanced by allowing parents to observe in the classroom. Observations allow parents to see and understand different aspects of the school environment and student behavior. This experience can help provide parents with the necessary background information for discussing school-related concerns with educators (McLoughlin & Lewis, 1986).

Teachers should carefully structure the observation to ensure that it provides parents with meaningful information. Initially, permission for parents to observe in the schools should be obtained from the appropriate school authorities and staff (McLoughlin & Lewis, 1986). Once permission is granted, parents should be prepared for the observation by reviewing ways to enter the room is an unobtrusive manner; locations in the room to sit; suitable times to observe; appropriate reactions to their child and other students; and the need to maintain confidentiality (McLoughlin & Lewis, 1986). Before the observation, parents and teachers should discuss the purpose of the observation and the unique aspects of the educational setting, such as token economy systems, reading programs, and the like. When the observation is completed, teachers should meet with parents to discuss what they saw.

Parent and Sibling Training

Parents may need training to perform varied roles in the educational process (McKinney & Hocutt, 1982). Many schools and community agencies offer parent training as part of their comprehensive delivery of services to students and their families. Calvert (1969) has identified several guidelines for setting up and evaluating parent training programs. These guidelines include

- *Who* should be involved?
- *What* is the content of the training program?
- *When* will training take place?
- *Where* will training occur?
- *How* do you train parents?

WHO.   Although most programs train mothers, training should be available to both parents. Training should also be offered to siblings to help them understand the nature of their brother's or sister's disability and deal with the impact of having a brother or sister with special needs. Banta (1979) noted that the impact of a child with disabilities on the family may affect siblings more than parents. Seligman (1983) reported that siblings' reactions to their disabled sibling depended on

1. the extent to which the sibling is held responsible for a handicapped brother or sister;

2. the extent to which a handicapped sibling takes advantage of a normal brother or sister;

3. the extent to which a handicapped sibling restricts one's social life or is considered a source of embarrassment;

4. the extent to which a handicapped sibling requires time and attention from the parents;

5. the extent to which the family's financial resources are drained by services for the handicapped child;

6. the number of siblings; and

7. the overall accommodation parents have made to their special circumstances. (p. 164)

Training for siblings can focus on providing information on the etiology and needs of the various disabilities; dispelling myths and misconceptions about disabilities; discussing ways of interacting with and assisting

Having a child with a disability may affect the whole family—siblings as well as parents. (Photo: Ray Solomon/Monkmeyer Press Photo Service)

their disabled sibling; (d) responding to the reactions of their friends and other individuals; understanding human services; and understanding the long-term needs and future of their disabled sibling (Meyer, Vadasy, & Fewell, 1985). Training also should address the concerns siblings may have about their own children being born with a disability.

Several formats for providing information to siblings have been developed. Meyer, Vadasy, and Fewell (1985) have written a book for parents and educators to help siblings adjust to life with a brother or sister with special needs. The book introduces siblings to disabilities, causes of disabilities, services for disabled individuals and their families, and future considerations. Support groups for siblings of the disabled have been established. Additional information on working with siblings can be obtained by contacting support groups for siblings (see Figure 5.9).

WHAT.   The content of the training program should focus on parents' needs. Generally, training should provide parents with the skills to teach their child in the home; the ability to interact with professionals serving their child; information relative to the delivery of special education services; counseling to provide emotional support and develop a positive self-image; and information to assist them in obtaining services for their child.

FIGURE 5.9.   Sibling Support Groups.

Sibling Information Network
Connecticut's University Affiliated Program
991 Main Street
East Hartford, CT 06108

Siblings Understanding Needs
Department of Pediatrics
University of Texas Medical Branch
Galveston, TX 77550

Siblings for Significant Change
823 United Nations Plaza
New York, NY 10017

Siblings Helping Persons with Autism through Resources and Energy
National Society for Children and Adults with Autism
Washington, D. C. 20005

Siblings of Disabled Children
535 Race Street, Suite 220
San Jose, CA 95126

WHEN. The frequency of training will depend on the parents' needs and teachers' time. However, parent training should be ongoing, as should evaluation of the training.

WHERE. Training can occur in the home or in the school. Home-based training, which occurs in the parents' and child's natural environment, can promote the maintenance and generalization of skills learned. Home-based training programs are especially appropriate for parents who have difficulty attending school meetings because of transportation problems or work schedules. School-based training allows parents to be trained as a group, which can make sharing information and experiences with parents easier. Additionally, school-based programs provide parents with the opportunity to meet and interact with a wide variety of professionals (Heward & Orlansky, 1984).

HOW. Educators can use a variety of strategies to train parents, including lecture, group discussion, role-plays, simulations, presentations by service providers and other parents, and demonstrations. Additionally, print materials and training programs for parents are available from state education departments, local organizations serving families, and professional organizations (McDonald, 1984; New York State Education Department, 1984). Excellent parent training programs and materials can be previewed by contacting some of the parental organizations listed in Appendix A.

Other programs that teach parents how to interact with their children are available, including Parents as Teachers (Becker, 1971), Games People Play (Berne, 1964), Systematic Training for Effective Parenting (Dinkmeyer & McKay, 1976), Between Parent and Child (Ginott, 1965), and Parent Effectiveness Training (Gordon, 1970).

Because some parents may have difficulty with the readability of print materials, videocassettes are an excellent format for presenting content to parents. Video presentations have the advantages of providing a visual image and model for parents; allowing parents and teachers to stop the video at any time to discuss, review, or replay the content; and being available to parents to view in school or at home. Sarda, et al. (1987) have developed seven nontechnical videocassettes for training parents. Three of the videos focus on infants and introduce parents to infant development, early intervention, and working with professionals to obtain and deliver services. The other four videos deal with developmental stages of school aged children; services, agencies, and educational alternatives for individuals with disabilities; participation of parents in the multidisciplinary team process; and the impact of a disability on the individual and the family.

Experienced and skilled parents of mainstreamed students can be a valuable resource for training other parents (Ball, Coyne, Jarvis, & Pease, 1984; Kroth, 1980). These parents can share their knowledge and experience with other parents, and provide emotional support and information concerning disabilities and the availability of services in the local community (Berger, 1981). In selecting parents to serve as trainers, educators should ask:

- Do parents respect and trust this individual?
- Does the individual have the time and skills to communicate and work with other parents?
- Does the individual possess the necessary skills to facilitate group interactions?
- Does the individual have a good understanding of special education, school policies, school curriculum, teaching strategies, and services within the local community?
- Has the individual completed any training to serve as a trainer of other parents?
- Will the individual seek assistance when he or she confronts a problem that he or she cannot solve? (Heward, Dardig, & Rossett, 1979).

Parents from Multicultural Backgrounds

It is important that parents from multicultural backgrounds be involved in the educational programs of their children. These parents are interested in their children's education, but long working hours, child care needs, and language and cultural differences may be barriers to establishing traditional parent-school communication (Lynch & Stein, 1987). For example, Hispanic parents of mainstreamed children may be less likely to participate in their children's IEP development because they "trust" the decisions made by school personnel (Stein, 1983), or they may feel that they are "intruding" on the teacher's role or the principal's domain (Herrera–Escobedo, 1983). Teachers can establish greater communication with parents from multicultural backgrounds by

- conducting parent conferences in the primary language of the parents (a bilingual educator can serve as an interpreter);
- considering the parents' transportation needs and work schedule when planning meetings;
- understanding and interpreting parental behaviors within the social and cultural context;

- preparing materials that parents can use in their homes;
- exchanging information with parents through local community organizations;
- enlisting the support of leaders of local community groups and other significant individuals in the family's life;
- using other minority parents as liaisons with parents; and
- offering opportunities during the school year for parental participation in special school events (Coballes–Vega & Salend, in press; Lynch & Stein, 1987).

Educators can facilitate communication with parents whose dominant language is not English by printing any written communication to parents in the language they understand best. In addition, it also is desirable to communicate with parents verbally (Taylor & Pitts, 1986). If parents do not have a telephone, messages to parents can be conveyed through a bilingual educator, an educator making a home visit, or the child.

Enlisting Community Resources

For some students, the mainstreaming network should include community agencies that assist in everyday school and community activities. Through these agencies and activities, needs identified by educators and parents can be remedied. For example, if a student with a visual impairment must have an adaptive device to function in the mainstreamed setting, parents and teachers can contact the local Lions Club to help buy the equipment. Therefore, educators should be aware of the supportive organizations, agencies, institutions, and resources available in their communities (Coballes–Vega & Salend, in press). Some community agencies that may be involved in a network for mainstreamed students include

- community and governmental agencies that specifically address the needs of individuals with disabilities and their families;
- organizations providing crisis intervention and counseling services;
- job training and career counseling centers;
- organizations working with culturally and linguistically different and/or minority groups;
- child-care agencies;
- local hospitals, clinics, mental health, and rehabilitation centers;
- service-oriented agencies;

- local volunteer groups;
- national service and fraternal organizations; and
- college or university centers, which may offer assessment and remediation clinics and other services (Coballes–Vega & Salend, in press).

In enlisting the support of community organizations, educators should consider the unique medical, behavioral, and social needs of students as well as the financial resources of the student's family (Taylor & Salend, 1983). Since many students may require similar services from agencies, it may prove helpful for educators to maintain a file of community agencies and the services that they provide. A sample file card is presented in Figure 5.10.

Paraprofessionals and Volunteers

A community resource that may benefit many mainstreamed students is the services of paraprofessionals and volunteers (Boomer, 1981; Platt & Platt, 1980). Paraprofessionals and volunteers can assist teachers and mainstreamed students by

- preparing individualized learning materials and modifying written materials;
- providing remedial instruction and reinforcing concepts taught previously;
- assessing learning needs;
- administering teacher-made tests;
- monitoring seatwork activities;

FIGURE 5.10.   Sample Community Organization File Card.

Name and Address of Community Organization:

Services Provided:

Contact Person: Phone:

- delivering small-group instruction;
- assisting students with motor and mobility problems;
- reading to students;
- playing educational games;
- listening to problems and offering guidance;
- correcting and grading papers;
- completing paperwork and performing clerical duties;
- working with media;
- supervising students during activities outside the classroom;
- assisting with behavior management; and
- observing and recording behavior (Boomer, 1980; Buffer, 1980; Cuninggim, 1980; McKenzie & Houk, 1986; Platt & Platt, 1980).

Hedges (1972) noted that the use of volunteers allowed elementary school teachers to increase their performance of higher-level functions by approximately 20 per cent, and increase three-fold the amount of attention provided to students.

Cuninggim (1980) and Buffer (1980) offer several steps educators can employ when working with paraprofessionals and volunteers. To make effective use of paraprofessionals and volunteers, educators should

1. *Determine the roles of the paraprofessionals and volunteers.* The roles paraprofessionals and volunteers perform in the classroom should be directly related to the needs of teachers and mainstreamed students.

2. *Recruit them.* Potential volunteers can be recruited by contacting principals, parent-teacher associations, service organizations, and senior citizen groups. When contacting potential paraprofessionals or volunteers, educators should carefully interview them to determine their suitability for the job (Boomer, 1980) and provide them with a job description, including roles to be performed, time commitments, and schedules.

3. *Train them.* Paraprofessionals and volunteers need to be prepared for the roles they will perform. Therefore, they need an orientation program. The orientation should include a tour of the school; introduction of key school personnel; explanation of the need for and rules relating to confidentiality; delineation of the roles and responsibilities inside and outside the classroom; review of the dress code and other standards of decorum; identification of the specialized medical, social, and academic needs of mainstreamed students; a review of the communication system; demonstration of how to operate media and office equipment; and discussion of scheduling, major school events, school

Volunteers can assist teachers and mainstreamed students. (Photo: Alan Carey/The Image Works)

calendars, absences, approaches to emergencies, and other school procedures (Boomer, 1980, 1981; Buffer, 1980; Cuninggim, 1980).

4. *Acknowledge their accomplishments.* Educators can acknowledge the contributions of paraprofessionals and volunteers by showing appreciation via notes from students and teachers, graphs or examples that depict student progress, certificates of appreciation, and verbal comments.

5. *Evaluate their performance.* Periodically, educators should observe paraprofessionals and volunteers in action, and provide them with feedback on their performance. Evaluation should focus on performance of duties as well as rapport with students and other school personnel. Information on how to improve job performance also should be provided. The perceptions of the paraprofessionals and volunteers concerning their roles in the school should also be solicited.

Professional and Parent Organizations

Many professional and parent organizations offer a variety of services to professionals and parents for meeting the needs of mainstreamed students. Local chapters of national organizations can provide teachers with information on techniques and materials for working with exceptional students, and help parents function as advocates for their children. For example, national organizations such as the March of Dimes, Federation of the Blind, Epilepsy Foundation, Council for Exceptional Children, and the Association for Children with Learning Disabilities offer instruction on new developments in the field, showcase new materials, organize parent groups, provide small grants to stimulate the development of innovative programs, and assist individuals in acquiring specialized aids and prosthetic devices. Some national organizations are listed in Appendix A.

Summary

Successful mainstreaming requires ongoing communication and cooperation, and establishing an interdisciplinary communication network of educators, parents, and community agencies to expand and coordinate the range of services provided to mainstreamed students. Important aspects of the communication network are communication between regular and special educators, consultation to assist regular educators, congruence in the student's educational program, in-service training, parental involvement, use of paraprofessionals and volunteers, services provided by community agencies, and parent and professional organizations.

References

Allen, K. E. (1978). The teacher therapist: Teaching parents to help their children through systematic contingency management. *Journal of Special Education Technology, 2,* 47–55.

Allington, R. L., & Broikou, K. A. (1988). Development of shared knowledge: A new role for classroom and specialist teachers. *The Reading Teacher, 41,* 806–811.

Allington, R. L., & Shake, M. C. (1986). Remedial reading: Achieving curricular congruence in classroom and clinic. *The Reading Teacher, 39,* 648–654.

Baily, J. S., Wolf, M. M., & Phillips, E. L. (1970). Home-based reinforcement and the modification of predelinquents' classroom behavior. *Journal of Applied Behavior Analysis, 3,* 223–233.

Ball, T. S., Coyne, A., Jarvis, R. M., & Pease, S. F. (1984). Parents of retarded children as teaching assistants for other parents. *Education and Training of the Mentally Retarded, 19,* 64–69.

Banta, E. M. (1979). Siblings of deaf-blind children. *Volta Review, 81,* 363–369.

Bean, R. M., & Eichelberger, R. T. (1985). Changing the role of the reading specialists: From pull-out to in-class programs. *The Reading Teacher, 38,* 648–653.

Becker, W. C. (1971). *Parents as teachers,* Champaign, Ill.: Research Press.

Bergan, J. R. (1977). *Behavioral consultation.* Columbus: Charles E. Merrill.

Berger, E. H. (1981). *Parents as partners in education.* St. Louis: C. V. Mosby.

Berne, E. (1964). *Games people play.* New York: Grove Press.

Bittle, R. G. (1975). Improving parent-teacher communication through recorded telephone messages. *Journal of Educational Research, 69,* 87–95.

Boomer, L. W. (1980). Special education paraprofessionals: A guide for teachers. *Teaching Exceptional Children, 12,* 146–149.

Boomer, L. W. (1981). Meeting common goals through effective teacher-paraprofessional communication. *Teaching Exceptional Children, 13,* 51–54.

Breyer, N. S., & Allen, G. J. (1975). Effects of implementing a token economy system on teacher attending behavior. *Journal of Applied Behavior Analysis, 8,* 373–380.

Browder, D. (1983). Guidelines for inservice planning. *Exceptional Children, 49,* 300–306.

Buffer, L. C. (1980). Recruited retired adults as volunteers in special education. *Teaching Exceptional Children, 12,* 113–115.

California Policy Workshop on the Special Education Needs of Migrant Handicapped Students (1986). *Proceedings Report.* Sacramento: California State Department of Education.

Calvert, D. R. (1969). *Dimensions of family involvement in early childhood education.* Reston, Va.: Council for Exceptional Children (ERIC Document Reproduction Service No. ED 013 371).

Carlson, L. B., & Potter, R. E. (1972). Training classroom teachers to provide in-class educational services for exceptional children in rural areas. *Journal of School Psychology, 10,* 147–150.

Chadwick, B. A., & Day, R. C. (1971). Systematic reinforcement: Academic performance of underachieving students. *Journal of Applied Behavior Analysis, 4,* 311–319.

Chapman, J. E., & Heward, W. L. (1982). Improving parent-teacher communication through recorded phone messages. *Exceptional Children, 49,* 79–81.

Coballes-Vega, C., & Salend, S. (in press). *Guidelines for assessing migrant handicapped students. Diagnostique.*

Cobb, S. (1978, February). *Social support and health through the life cycle.* Paper presented at the meeting of the American Association for the Advancement of Sciences, Washington, D.C.

Cone, J. D., Delawyer, D. D., & Wolfe, V. V. (1985). Assessing parent participation: The parent/family involvement index. *Exceptional Children, 51,* 417–424.

Conway, R. N. F., & Gow, L. (1988). Mainstreaming special students with mild handicaps through group instruction. *Remedial and Special Education, 9*(5), 34–41.

Cuninggim, W. (1980). Recruited volunteers: A growing resource for teachers and students. *Teaching Exceptional Children, 12,* 108–112.

Curtis, M. J., & Watson, K. (1980). Changes in consultee problem clarification skills following consultation. *Journal of School Psychology, 18,* 210–221.

de Bettencourt, L. U. (1987). How to develop parent relationships. *Teaching Exceptional Children, 19,* 26–27.

Dinkmeyer, D., & McKay, G. (1976). *Systematic training for effective parenting.* Circle Pines, Minn.: American Guidance Services.

Donaldson, J. (1980). Changing attitudes toward handicapped persons: A review and analysis of research. *Exceptional Children, 46,* 504–512.

Dorr, D. (1977). Some practical suggestions on behavioral consultation with teachers. *Professional Psychology, 8,* 95–102.

Everston, C. M., Emmer, E. T., Clements, B. S., Sanford, J. P., & Worsham, M. E. (1989). *Classroom management for elementary teachers (2nd ed.).* Englewood Cliffs, N.J.: Prentice-Hall.

Everston, J., & Heshusius, L. (1985). Feedback in secondary mainstreaming. *Teaching Exceptional Children, 17,* 223–224.

Fairchild, T. N. (1987). The daily report card. *Teaching Exceptional Children, 19,* 72–73.

Friend, M., & Bauwens, J. (1988). Managing resistance: An essential consulting skill for learning disabilities teachers. *Journal of Learning Disabilities, 21,* 556–561.

Gearheart, B. R., Weishahn, M. W., & Gearheart, C. J. (1988). *The exceptional student in the classroom (4th ed.).* Columbus: Charles E. Merrill.

Gilliam, J. E., & Coleman, M. C. (1981). Who influences IEP committee decisions. *Exceptional Children, 47,* 642–644.

Ginott, H. (1965). *Between parent and child.* New York: Macmillan.

Gordon, T. (1970). *Parent effectiveness training.* New York: Peter Hayden.

Goldstein, S., & Turnbull, A. P. (1982). Strategies to increase parent participation in IEP conferences. *Exceptional Children, 48,* 360–361.

Goodman, G. (1979). From residential treatment to community-based education: A model for reintegration. *Education and Training of the Mentally Retarded, 14,* 95–100.

Gutkin, T. B. (1980). Teacher perceptions of consultation services provided by school psychologists. *Professional Psychology: Research and Practice, 11,* 637–642.

Gutkin, T. B., Singer, J. H., & Brown, R. (1980). Teacher reactions to school-based consultation: A multivariate analysis. *Journal of School Psychology, 18,* 126–134.

Hedges, H. G. (1972). *Volunteer parental assistance in elementary schools.* Unpublished doctoral dissertation. University of Toronto.

Helge, D. (1987). Effective partnership in rural America. *OSERS News in Print, 1,* 2-3.

Herrera-Escobedo, T. (1983). Parent and community involvement. A blueprint for a successful program. In O.N. Saracho & B. Spodek (Eds.) *Understanding the multicultural experience in early childhood education* (pp. 107-122). Washington, D.C.: National Association for the Education of Young Children.

Heward, W. L., Dardig, J. C., & Rossett, A. (1979). *Working with parents of handicapped children.* Columbus: Charles E. Merrill.

Heward, W. L., & Orlansky, M. D. (1984). *Exceptional children (2nd. Ed.).* Columbus: Charles E. Merrill.

Hoben, M. (1980). Toward integration in the mainstream. *Exceptional Children, 47,* 100-105.

Hoff, M. K., Fenton, K. S., Yoshida, R. K., & Kaufman, M. J. (1978). Notice and consent: The school's responsibility to inform parents. *Journal of School Psychology, 16,* 265-273.

Humphrey, M. J., Hoffman, E., & Crosby, B. M. (1984). Mainstreaming LD students. *Academic Therapy, 19,* 321-327.

Hudson, F. G., & Graham, S. (1978). An approach to operationalizing the IEP. *Learning Disability Quarterly, 1,* 13-32.

Hughes, J., & Falk, R. (1981). Resistance, reluctance, and consultation. *Journal of School Psychology, 19,* 130-142.

Hundert, J. (1982). Some considerations of planning the integration of handicapped children into the mainstream. *Journal of Learning Disabilities, 15,* 73-80.

Idol, L., Paolucci-Whitcomb, P., & Nevin, A. (1986). *Collaborative consultation.* Rockville, Md.: Aspen Systems.

Idol, L., West, J. F., & Lloyd, S. R. (1988). Organizing and implementing specialized reading programs: A collaborative approach involving classroom, remedial, and special education teachers. *Remedial and Special Education, 9*(2), 54-61.

Idol-Maestas, L. A. (1981). A teacher training model: The resource/consulting model. *Behavioral Disorders, 6,* 108-121.

Imber, S. C., Imber, R. B., & Rothstein, C. (1979). Modifying independent work habits: An effective teacher-parent communication program. *Exceptional Children, 46,* 218-221.

Jackson, R. M., Cleveland, J. C., & Merenda, P. F. (1975). The longitudinal effects of early identification and counseling of underachievers. *Journal of School Psychology, 13,* 119-128.

Jason, L. A., & Ferone, L. (1978). Behavioral v. process consultation interventions in school settings. *American Journal of Community Psychology, 6,* 531-543.

Johnson, D. W., & Johnson, R. T. (1980). Integrating handicapped students into the mainstream. *Exceptional Children, 47,* 90-98.

Johnston, P., Allington, R., & Afflerbach, P. (1985). The congruence of classroom and remedial reading instruction. *Elementary School Journal, 83,* 465-477.

Kammerlohr, B., Henderson, R. A., & Rock, S. (1983). Special education due process hearings in Illinois. *Exceptional Children, 49,* 417–422.

Kasl, S. (1975). Issues in patient adherence to health care regimens. *Journal of Human Stress, 1,* 5–17.

Kauffman, J. M., & Hallahan, D. P. (1981). *Handbook of special education.* Englewood Cliffs, N.J.: Prentice-Hall.

Kimbrough, J., & Hill, P. (1981). *The aggregate effects of federal education programs.* Santa Monica, Calif.: Rand Corporation.

Knoff, H. M. (1983). Investigating disproportionate influence and status in multidisciplinary child study teams. *Exceptional Children, 49,* 367–369.

Kotin, L., & Eager, N. (1977). *Due process in special education: A legal analysis.* Cambridge: Research Institute for Educational Problems.

Kroth, R. L. (1980). The mirror model of parental involvement. *The Pointer, 25,* 18–22.

Kroth, R. L., & Simpson, R. (1977). *Parent conferences as a teaching strategy.* Denver: Love.

Lockavitch, J. F. (1983). The teaching connection. *Academic Therapy, 19,* 199–203.

Lynch, E. W., & Stein, R. C. (1987). Parent participation by ethnicity: A comparison of hispanic, black, and anglo families. *Exceptional Children, 54,* 105–111.

Martin, R. (1978). Expert and reference power: A framework for understanding and maximizing consultation effectiveness. *Journal of School Psychology, 16,* 49–55.

McClelland, D. C. (1977). Power, motivation and impossible dreams. *Wharton Magazine, 1,* 33–39.

McDonald, A. (1984). *Planning together: A handbook for parental involvement.* Frankfort: Kentucky Department of Education.

McKenzie, R. G., & Houk, C. S. (1986). Use of paraprofessionals in the resource room. *Exceptional Children, 53,* 41–45.

McKinney, J. D., & Hocutt, A. M. (1982). Public school involvement of parents of learning disabled and average achievers. *Exceptional Education Quarterly, 3,* 64–73.

McLoughlin, J. A., Edge, D., & Strenecky, B. (1978). Perspective on parental involvement in the diagnosis and treatment of learning disabled children. *Journal of Learning Disabilities, 13,* 295–300.

McLoughlin, J. A., & Lewis, R. B. (1986). *Assessing special students.* (2nd ed.). Columbus: Charles E. Merrill.

McNamara, B. E. (1986). Parents as partners in the IEP process. *Academic Therapy, 21,* 309–315.

Meyer, D. J., Vadasy, P. F., & Fewell, R. (1985). *Living with a brother or sister with special needs: A book for sibs.* Seattle: University of Washington Press.

Miller, T. L., & Sabatino, D. (1978). An evaluation of the teacher consultant model as an approach to mainstreaming. *Exceptional Children, 45,* 86–91.

Minner, S., Beane, A., & Prater, G. (1986). Try telephone answering machines. *Teaching Exceptional Children, 19,* 62–63.

National Institute of Education (1985, February). *Research in Brief.* Washington, D.C.: Author.

National Policy Workshop on the Special Education Needs of Migrant Hand-icapped Students. (1984). *Proceedings Report.* San Antonio: Interstate Migrant Education Council.

New York State Education Department, Office for Education of Children with Handicapping Conditions. (1984). *A parent's guide to special education: Your child's right to an education in New York State.* Albany, N.Y.: Author.

Noar, M., & Milgram, R. M. (1980). Two preservice strategies for preparing regular class teachers for mainstreaming. *Exceptional Children, 47,* 126-127.

Pinkerton, R. S., Miller, F. T., & Martin, P. L. (1974). Consultation—or how we while away the hours. *Professional Psychology, 5,* 13-27.

Platt, J. M., & Platt, J. S. (1980). Volunteers for special education: A main-streaming support system. *Teaching Exceptional Children, 13,* 31-36.

Ponti, C. R., Zins, J. E., & Graden, J. L. (1988). Implementing a consultation-based service delivery system to decrease referrals for special education: A case study of organizational considerations. *School Psychology Review, 17,* 89-100.

Powers, D. A. (1983). Mainstreaming and the inservice education of teachers. *Exceptional Children, 49,* 432-439.

Price, B. J., & Marsh, G. E. (1985). Practical guidelines for planning and conducting parent conferences. *Teaching Exceptional Children, 17,* 274-278.

Redden, M. R., & Blackhurst, A. E. (1978). Mainstreaming competency specifications for elementary teachers. *Exceptional Children, 44,* 615-617.

Reynolds, C. J., Salend, S. J., & Beahan, C. (1988). *Motivating secondary students: Bringing in the reinforcements.* Manuscript submitted for publication.

Reynolds, C. J., & Volkmar, J. N. (1984). Mainstreaming the special educator. *Academic Therapy, 19,* 585-591.

Rodin, J., & Janis, I. (1979). The social power of health-care practitioners as agents of change. *Journal of Social Issues, 35,* 60-81.

Safran, J., & Safran, S. P. (1985). Organizing communication for the LD teacher. *Academic Therapy, 20,* 427-435.

Salend, S. J. (1980). How to mainstream teachers. *Education Unlimited, 2,* 31-33.

Salend, S. J. (1984). Factors contributing to the development of successful mainstreaming programs. *Exceptional Children, 50,* 409-419.

Salend, S. J. (in press). A migrant education guide for special educators. *Teaching Exceptional Children.*

Salend, S. J., & Hankee, C. (1981). Successful mainstreaming: A form of communication. *Education Unlimited, 3,* 47-48.

Salend, S. J., & Johns, J. (1983). Changing teacher commitment to main-streaming. *Teaching Exceptional Children, 15,* 82-85.

Salend, S. J., & Salend, S. M. (1984). Consulting with the regular teacher: Guidelines for special educators. *The Pointer, 28,* 25-28.

Salend, S. J., Tintle, L., & Balber, H. (1988). Effects of a student-managed response-cost system on the behavior of two mainstreamed students. *Elementary School Journal. 89,* 89-97.

Sarda, L., Crockett, L., Lazzaro, V., Mastrocola, C., Richmann, S., Neugebauer, J., & Warren-Blum, M. (1988). *Training manual for training video
for outreach workers and migrant parents of children with special needs.*
New Paltz, N.Y.: Mid-Hudson Migrant Education Center.

Scandary, J. (1981). What every teacher should know about due process hearings. *Teaching Exceptional Children, 13,* 92–96.

Scanlon, C., Arick, J., & Phelps, N. (1981). Participation in the development of
the IEP: Parents' perspective. *Exceptional Children, 47,* 373–376.

Schulz, J. B. (1987). *Parents and professionals in special education.* Boston:
Allyn & Bacon.

Seligman, M. (1983). *The family with a handicapped child: Understanding and
treatment.* New York: Grune & Stratton.

Skrtic, T., Knowlton, H. E., & Clark, F. L. (1979). Action versus reaction.
A curriculum development approach to inservice education. *Focus on
Exceptional Children, 11,* 1–16.

Stein, R. C. (1983). Hispanic parents' perspectives and participation in their
children's special education program: Comparisons by program and race.
Learning Disability Quarterly, 6, 432–439.

Stephens, T. M., & Braun, B. L. (1980). Measures of regular classroom teachers'
attitudes toward handicapped children. *Exceptional Children, 46,* 292–
294.

Stokes, S., & Axelrod, P. (1980). Staff support teams: Critical variables. In L.
Burello (Ed.), *What works in inservice* (pp. 15–23). Bloomington, Ind.:
National Inservice Network.

Sargent, L. R., Swartzbaugh, T., & Sherman, P. (1981). Teaming up to mainstream in English: A successful secondary program. *Teaching Exceptional Children, 13,* 100–104.

Swick, K. J., Flake-Hobson, C., & Raymond, G. (1980). The first step-
Establishing parent-teacher communication in the IEP conference.
Teaching Exceptional Children, 12, 144–145.

Taylor, L., & Salend, S. J. (1983). Reducing stress-related burnout through a
network support system. *The Pointer, 27,* 5–9.

Taylor, M., & Pitts, I. M. (1986). Career education for migrant handicapped
youth. *The Forum, 12,* 13–14.

Turnbull, A. P., & Schulz, J. B. (1979). *Mainstreaming handicapped students.*
Boston: Allyn & Bacon.

Turnbull, A. P., Strickland, B. B., & Brantley, J. C. (1982). *Developing and
implementing individualized education programs (2nd ed.).* Columbus:
Charles E. Merrill.

Tymitz-Wolf, B. L. (1982). Extending the scope of inservice training for mainstreaming effectiveness. *Teacher Education and Special Education, 5,*
17–23.

Vernon, M. D. (1958). *Backwardness in reading.* New York: Cambridge University Press.

West, J. F., & Cannon, G. S., (1988). Essential collaborative consultation competencies for regular and special educators. *Journal of Learning Disabilities, 21,* 56–63.

West, J. F., & Idol, L. (1987). School consultation (Part 1): An interdisciplinary perspective on theory, models, and research. *Journal of Learning Disabilities, 20,* 388–408.

Wolf, J. S., & Troup, J. (1980). Strategy for parent involvement: Improving the IEP process. *The Exceptional Parent, 10,* 31–32.

Yates, J. R. (1973). A model for preparing regular classroom teachers for mainstreaming. *Exceptional Children, 39,* 471–472.

Zins, J. E., Curtis, M. J., Graden, J. L., & Ponti, C. R. (1988). *Helping students succeed in the regular classroom.* San Francisco: Josssey-Bass.

CHAPTER 6

Modifying Instruction for Mainstreamed Students

(Photo: Barbara Hadley)

Teachers teach in many different ways. They use large and small group instruction, print materials, instructional programs, peers, and media to convey new information to their students. Although most students learn from these teaching strategies, mainstreamed students may have unique learning needs that will require teachers to make modifications in their instructional programs.

Research indicates that when teachers make adaptations in their instructional practices, mainstreamed students are often successful learners and can meet the academic and social rigors of the regular classroom setting (Madden & Slavin, 1983; Wang & Birch, 1984). Most of the instructional accommodations for mainstreamed students can even aid the performance of other students in the regular classroom (Stainback, Stainback, Courtnage, & Jaben, 1985). Chapter 3 discussed a variety of strategies that *students* can use to benefit from instruction in the regular education setting; this chapter offers strategies that *teachers* can employ to facilitate students' mastery of classroom content. Specifically, this chapter offers guidelines for determining instructional modifications. This chapter also presents ways to modify large and small group instruction, instruction via textbooks and other print materials, instruction for specific learners, classroom behavior, and the classroom design.

Determining Instructional Modifications

The types of instructional modifications mainstreamed students need can be determined by the placement team and should be specified in the students' IEPs. Since teachers are more likely to implement instructional modifications that they helped design, regular classroom teachers should be included in planning instructional modifications for their mainstreamed students (Margolis & McGettigan, 1988). Whenever possible, mainstreamed students should participate in planning adaptations; they can be a reliable source of information concerning modifications they have found most useful and effective.

While a variety of techniques exist for adapting the learning environment to promote the optimal performance of mainstreamed students, the selection of an appropriate modification will depend on several factors, including students' learning needs and teachers' instructional styles. For example, if content is presented in lectures but students have difficulty taking notes, teachers will need to use strategies such as writing main points on the board, providing lecture outlines, and summarizing main points at the end of the class.

Treatment Acceptability

Another important factor that teachers and placement teams should consider in adapting instructional techniques for mainstreamed students is *treatment acceptability* (Martens, Peterson, Witt, & Cirone, 1986), the extent to which teachers view a specific instructional strategy as easy to use, effective, and appropriate for their settings (Kazdin, 1980) as well as its reasonableness. Brown (1988) noted that reasonableness can be assessed by examining the instructional modification in terms of how much extra time it will take to implement, whether it will require significant changes in the teachers' styles, and how much it will cost. In general, teachers are more likely to implement an instructional strategy that is practical, easy to use, immediately effective, and nondisruptive to their classroom routine and teaching style (Margolis & McGettigan, 1988).

A second aspect of treatment acceptability examines the impact of the proposed intervention on the mainstreamed students and their classroom peers. For example, placing a mainstreamed student in a cubicle who has difficulty attending to seatwork, or assigning a mainstreamed student a math assignment while the other students are working on social studies, can have the negative effect of isolating a student within the mainstreamed setting. Care must be taken to ensure that proposed modifications do not adversely affect either the mainstreamed student or his or her classmates. Therefore, in selecting, designing, and implementing modifications of the students' and teachers' needs, placement teams should consider the following:

- What are the student's strengths, weaknesses, and unique needs?
- How do the teacher's presentation method and the course content affect the student's performance?
- How do the teacher's response mode and the course content affect the student's performance?
- Does the student require specialized material or adaptive devices?
- Are there any architectural barriers that affect the student's performance?
- Does the modification adequately address the problems?
- Does the modification protect the integrity of the course and the grading system?
- What are the implications of the modification on the teacher, the mainstreamed student, other students, and staff?

Modifying Large and Small Group Instruction

Oral Presentations

Data indicate that the instructional strategy most frequently used by teachers is lecturing (Wood, 1988). In preparing and delivering lectures, teachers can help students follow along by

- initially stating the objectives, purpose, and relevance of the lecture;
- reviewing prerequisite information and defining key terminology needed to understand the main points;
- organizing the lecture so that the sequence of the presentation of information is appropriate;
- using ordinal numbers and temporal cues (*first, second, finally*) to organize information for students;
- emphasizing important concepts and critical points by using cue words, varying voice quality, writing them on the blackboard, and repeating them;
- employing examples, illustrations, charts, diagrams, and maps to make the material more concrete;
- using visual aids to supplement oral material;
- referring to individuals, places, or things using nouns rather than pronouns;
- employing specific numerical quantification terms instead of ambiguous ones (for example, using the term *two* instead of *a couple*);
- decreasing the use of vague terms (*these kinds of things, somewhere*) and avoidance phrases (*to make a long story short, as you all know*);
- reducing extraneous information and stimuli;
- asking students questions that require them to think about information presented and assess comprehension and recall;
- discussing and summarizing all main points;
- assigning readings and other assignments that prepare students for class;
- providing the opportunities for questions during and after the class; and
- offering students time at the end of class to review, summarize, and organize their notes (Bos & Vaughn, 1988; Carman & Adams, 1972; Chilcoat, 1987; Wallace, Cohen, & Polloway, 1987).

Teachers also can help students retain lecture content by pausing for two minutes after every five to seven consecutive minutes of lecturing (Guerin & Male, 1988; Ruhl, Hughes, & Schloss, 1987). Hawkins (1988) and Hughes, Hendrickson, and Hudson (1986) found that pausing periodically during lectures facilitated the retention of information. During the two-minute pause, students should be directed to discuss and review their notes, jot down questions, rehearse important points, associate the lecture information with their experiences and interests, and engage in visual imagery. To ensure that students are active during the instructional pause, teachers can structure the pause by using a cue card that focuses students on activities related to specific content presented in the lecture (Hawkins, 1988).

GUIDED LECTURE PROCEDURE. One technique that teachers can use to help the mainstreamed student benefit from lectures is the *Guided Lecture Procedure* (Kelly & Holmes, 1979). In this procedure, teachers review objectives of the lecture and allow students to record them in their notes before beginning the lecture; focus students' attention on the lecture by periodically reminding them to listen carefully and not allowing them to take notes; pause midway through the lecture to offer students the opportunity to take notes on the content presented; place students in small groups at the end of the lecture to review content and share and develop notes; offer assistance to the small groups; and provide time for students to study and verbally summarize their notes. Because this technique requires students to be able to retain information for a period of time, it may not be effective with students who have memory deficits unless more frequent pauses are made during the lecture to allow for note taking.

OVERHEAD PROJECTOR. Teachers can supplement their lectures with transparencies projected on an overhead projector (Wood, 1988). Transparencies can help students by providing visual support (charts, graphs, and lists) during an oral presentation. For example, teachers might begin a lecture with a transparency—an advance organizer to orient students to the main and supporting points to be presented. The overhead projector allows teachers to present content and highlight main points and key vocabulary simultaneously on the overhead while maintaining eye contact with students. When presenting information using prepared transparencies, it may be best to focus the students' attention by covering the transparency with a piece of paper and presenting one piece of information at a time.

ENCOURAGING QUESTIONS. In order to benefit from oral instruction and understand assignments and directions, students should ask questions to clarify teacher comments and instructions. However, many mainstreamed students may be reluctant to ask questions (Alley & Deshler, 1979). To help these students overcome their fear, teachers can reinforce student questioning with praise (*I'm glad you asked that question, That's a good question. It shows you're really thinking*); listen attentively and make eye contact; offer students time to write down and ask questions during class; provide students with the correct response and ask them to state the corresponding question; and teach students when and how to ask questions (Alley & Deshler, 1979; Fraenkel, 1973).

Note-Taking Skills

The amount of information gleaned from lectures also will depend on the students' ability to take notes. Teachers can engage in several behaviors that can help students take quality notes (see Chapter 3 for a review of student behaviors that make note taking easier).

OUTLINES.   Giving students a teacher-prepared outline of the class session can provide them with a foundation for notes. Initially, the outline should include headings with main points, as well as subheadings with secondary supporting information. It should be read and discussed with the class. As students develop note-taking skills, teachers should introduce a skeletal outline of main points with enough space after each main point to record supporting information.

If providing students with outlines is not feasible, then teachers can facilitate note taking by listing the major points of each lecture on the blackboard or an overhead (Devine, 1981). Teachers also can structure students' notes at the beginning of class by listing questions on the blackboard relating to the day's class, then discussing answers at the end of class (Hoover, 1986).

Teachers can provide students with a framework for note taking by using a listening guide or a slot/frame outline. Shields & Heron (1989) note that a *listening guide,* a list of important terms and concepts that parallels the order they will be presented in class, can facilitate the identification and retention of key terms and major concepts. Students add to the guide by writing supplemental information and supportive details. A sample listening guide is presented in Figure 6.1. Some students may need a *slot/frame outline* (Lovitt, Rudsit, Jenkins, Pious, & Benedetti, 1986; Wood & Rosbe, 1985), a sequential overview of the key terms and main points of the class or textbook chapter presented as an outline of sentences that are incomplete statements. Students listen to the lecture or read the textbook chapter and fill in the blanks to complete the outline. The completed outline then serves as the students' notes.

FIGURE 6.1. Sample Listening Guide.

Civil War

A. The sides

  1. The Union:

  2. The Confederacy:

  3. The Border States:

    a.   c.

    b.   d.

B. Advantages of each side

  1. The Union:

    a.   d.

    b.   e.

    c.   f.

  2. The Confederacy:

    a.

    b.

C. The strategy of each side:

  1. The Union:

    a.

    b.

    c.

    d.

  2. The Confederacy:

    a.

    b.

    c.

D. Key individuals to know

  1. Abraham Lincoln:

  2. Jefferson Davis:

  3. Stonewall Jackson:

  4. Robert E. Lee:

  5. Ulysses S. Grant:

  6. Clara Barton:

Developed by Peter Goss, Social Studies Teacher, New Paltz Central Schools, New Paltz, New York.

HIGHLIGHTING MAIN POINTS. To help students determine important points to be recorded in their notes, teachers can emphasize these points by pausing for attention, using introductory phrases (*I want you to remember this, This is critical to you*), and changing inflection (Spargo, 1977). Another method that can aid students in identifying important classroom content is *oral quizzing,* in which the teacher allots time at the end of the class session to respond to student questions and to ask students questions based on the material presented in class (Spargo, 1977). Similarly, end-of-class time can be devoted to summarizing and reviewing main points from class content and discussing what points should be in the students' notes (Lock, 1981). Pairing students to check each others' notes after class also can ensure that mainstreamed students' notes are in the desired format and include relevant content (Mercer &

Mercer, 1985). Teachers can check student notes' accuracy, completeness, usability, and style by periodically collecting and reviewing them.

✗PEER NOTE TAKERS AND AUDIOCASSETTE RECORDERS.   The notes of students who have difficulties recording verbal information can be supplemented by the aid of peers or audiocassette recorders. Teachers or mainstreamed students can ask classmates who are proficient at note taking to share their notes with mainstreamed students. In selecting note takers, teachers should consider the peer note takers' mastery of the class content, sensitivity to mainstreamed students, and ability to work independently (Wilson, 1981). Notes can be photocopied or duplicated with carbon paper.

Students can record class sessions on an audiocassette, which can be replayed after class to allow students to take notes at their own pace (Devine, 1981). As with other notes, teachers periodically should review notes from tape-recorded classes. Because replaying audiocassettes can be time-consuming, students can use a *harmonic compressor,* which allows them to play back the recording at a faster speed without distorting the speech. Whether mainstreamed students are using peer note takers or audiocassettes, they should be encouraged to take notes during class sessions. This will allow them to practice their note-taking skills and keep alert in class. It also can help prevent resentment from other students who may feel that the mainstreamed students must do less work.

Listening Skills

A skill critical to taking notes is the ability to listen. Since communication is a two-way process, the speaker can assist students in developing their listening skills (see Chapter 3 for a review of student behaviors that can facilitate listening skills).

One strategy is to offer students some incentives for listening. For example, students can be given extra credit, free time, or no homework when they identify a carefully placed contradiction or a mistake in a teacher presentation. Motivation to listen also can be fostered by teachers' using gestures, eye contact, facial expressions, pauses, and voice changes. Keeping students actively involved in learning motivates them to listen. Teaching students to ask questions of their peers; expanding and using students' responses; employing activities that require students to use objects or work in small groups; relating lesson content to the students' lives and interests; using high interest materials; and varying the schedule so that students are not passive for long periods of time are all good strategies for actively involving students (Jones & Jones, 1986).

Teachers also can engage in several behaviors during class presentations that can promote listening skills. They can ask students to repeat or paraphrase instructions, assignments, and important statements. They can periodically intersperse questions relating to critical content into class presentations, and have students try to predict what will be discussed next (Wallace & Kauffman, 1986). Listening also can be facilitated by supplementing oral statements with visual aids, varying the pace of the oral presentation to emphasize critical content, moving around the room, placing the student near the speaker, and minimizing nonessential and distracting noises and activities (Robinson & Smith, 1981).

GAINING ATTENTION.   Students spend much of their classroom time listening. An important aspect of listening to and following directions is paying attention. However, because many mainstreamed students may have difficulty focusing their attention (Lerner, 1985), teachers may have to use several attention-getting strategies, such as directing them to listen carefully (*Listen carefully to what I say*); giving clear, emphatic instructions (*Put your finger on the top of the page*); pausing before speaking to make sure all students are paying attention; limiting distractions by having students remove unnecessary materials from their desks; and eliminating noise and visual distractions (Jones & Jones, 1986; Wallace & Kauffman, 1986). Jones and Jones (1986) suggest that teachers use a cue such as a verbal statement or physical gesture (raising a hand, blinking the lights, or ringing a bell) to alert students of the need to pay attention. To motivate students to respond to the cue, teachers can involve students in determining the cue and changing it on a monthly basis.

MAINTAINING ATTENTION.   In addition to gaining attention, teachers can maintain that attention by

- delivering material at a fast pace;
- having students respond frequently;
- using repetition—asking students to answer the same questions several times;
- reinforcing with descriptive statements correct responses and appropriate behavior;
- cuing correct responses;
- supplementing statements with visual aids;
- decreasing distractions from extraneous stimuli;
- placing students closer to the speaker;
- assigning one activity at a time;
- grouping students with peers who can maintain attention;
- maintaining eye contact with all students;
- creating suspense;

- selecting students randomly to respond;
- reminding students that they may be called on next;
- asking students to add additional information or explain an answer given by a peer;
- supplementing the presentation or discussion with a visual display; and
- decreasing the complexity and syntax of statements (Everston, Emmer, Clements, Sanford, & Worsham, 1989; Gearheart, Weishahn, & Gearheart, 1988; George, 1986; Robinson & Smith, 1981).

Teachers also can maintain attention by changing activities frequently and varying the presentation and response modes of instructional activities.

They can also maintain attention by using color. Zentall and Kruczek (1988) found that color could enhance the performance of students with attention problems. However, they caution that color should focus attention to the salient features of the task, rather than just increasing the attractiveness of the task.

FOLLOWING DIRECTIONS.   Research indicates that teachers give more than 200 instructional statements each day (Lovitt & Smith, 1972). Attention and listening skills are therefore important if students are to understand and follow directions to complete their assignments. Teachers can modify the ways they give instructions to help the class attend to and follow directions for assignments.

In general, instructions should inform students about the content of the assignment; the rationale for the assignment; the type of assistance allowed from adults, peers, reference materials, and aids; the amount of time allowed to complete the assignment, the assignment's format; and the way they will evaluate the assignment. Teachers can help students remember the materials they will need to complete the assignment by listing them on the assignment sheet (Cohen & de Bettencourt, 1988). Students should be told where and when to hand in a completed assignment and given guidance on activities that they can work on if they complete a task early.

Teachers should use specific techniques for giving directions to students. When explaining assignments, make certain all students are attentive, pausing when they are not. Present directions to students visually via the blackboard, overhead, or a flip chart, and review them orally using terminology that the students understand. When giving directions orally, teachers should simplify the vocabulary, decrease the use of extraneous words and irrelevant information, and use consistent terminology from assignment to assignment (Gillet, 1986). Students should copy the directions in their notebooks. If some students have difficulty copying from the blackboard or writing, the assignment can be given via a teacher-prepared handout using the writing style (manuscript or cursive) to which the students are accustomed. Directions for completing assignments can also be recorded on audiocassette. Students who have difficulty can copy at their seat using the teacher's or a peer's notes, or a peer can copy the assignment for the student. In presenting directions that have several steps, teachers should number and list the steps in sequential order. For example, an assignment using dictionary skills can be presented to students by listing the steps as

1. Use the dictionary guide words;
2. check the pronunciation of each word; then
3. write the definition.

Teachers also can facilitate the students' understanding of the directions by providing students with a model of the assignment, encouraging students to ask questions concerning the assignment, and having students paraphrase and explain the directions to the rest of the class. Similarly, students can be verbally questioned to assess their understanding of the instructions (*What steps are you required to follow in doing this assignment? Can you anticipate any problems in doing this assignment? If you have a problem, who should you ask for help? What can you do if you finish before time?*). Finally, to ensure understanding, students can complete several problems from the assignment under teaching supervision before beginning to work independently.

For students who continue to experience problems following directions, teachers should break directions into shorter, more meaningful statements (Wallace, Cohen, & Polloway, 1987). When possible, teachers should give no more than two instructions at a time. These students should work on one part of the assignment at a time, and check with the teacher before advancing to the next phase of the activity (Jones & Jones, 1986). For example, long assignments can be divided into several shorter ones, with students completing one assignment at a time before working on the next part of the assignment (Glazzard, 1980).

Teachers can help students with reading problems understand written directions via a *rebus system,* whereby important words in the directions are depicted pictorially (Cohen & de Bettencourt, 1988). Recurring direction words and their corresponding rebus can be placed in a convenient location in the room so that all students have visual access to it. A sample rebus direction list developed by Cohen and de Bettencourt (1988) is presented in Figure 6.2.

Teachers also can help students follow directions on assignments by periodically providing time for students to receive teacher assistance.

	Direction Word	Picture Stimulus
1.	circle	
2.	cross out	
3.	book	
4.	read	
5.	page	
6.	cut	
7.	color	
8.	look (at, over)	
9.	listen	
10.	underline	
11.	do	
12.	write	
13.	think	
14.	tape (record)	
15.	remember	

FIGURE 6.2.   Sample Rebus Directions List. Source: S. Cohen and L. de Bettencourt, *Effective Instructional Strategies for Exceptional Children* in E. L. Meyen, G.A. Vergason, and R. J. Whelan (Denver, CO: Love, 1988) p. 332. Reprinted by permission of the publisher.

A sign-up sheet posted in the classroom can encourage scheduling of teacher-student meetings (Cohen & de Bettencourt, 1988). The times teachers are available to provide assistance can be listed, and students can request assistance by signing their names next to the allotted time interval.

Since teachers in the regular classroom may not be available to check students' work, independent work skills also can be fostered through use of self-correcting materials (Cohen & de Bettencourt, 1988). Potential self-correcting materials in the classroom include flash cards, puzzles, matching cards, tape-recorded answers, and transparency overlays (Cohen & de Bettencourt, 1988).

Motivating Students

An important aspect of learning, listening, and following directions is motivation. Because of their past history of negative experiences, mainstreamed students may lack the motivation they need to be successful learners. Teachers can help motivate these students by

- having students identify what they would like to learn during the upcoming school year or semester;
- developing a unit or several lessons based on students' interests;
- surveying students at the beginning of a unit to determine their existing knowledge base and what questions they have concerning the content of the unit;
- devoting class time periodically to student-selected content areas;
- allowing students to select learning and practicing activities from a variety of options;

 offering activities that require students to be active rather than passive;
- varying the instructional format;
- relating content to students' interests and their lives;
- using high-interest materials;
- teaching content that is appropriate to the students' skill levels;
- personalizing instruction by using the students' names, interests, and experiences in the lesson;
- providing them with choices and a range of options in terms of content and process; and
- allowing students to demonstrate mastery of content in a variety of ways (Adelman & Taylor, 1983; D'Zamko & Hedges, 1985; Jones & Jones, 1986).

Organizing Notebooks and Work Areas

In addition to helping students take notes, pay attention, and listen, teachers may need to help students organize and maintain their notebooks. Teachers can help students who have difficulties with this task by monitoring notebooks and desks periodically; offering class time to review notebooks, folders, and desks to reorganize them and throw out unnecessary materials; providing students with the space to store materials; teaching students to use folders and how to organize their notebooks and desks; using incentives to motivate students to keep organized; and training peers to provide feedback to mainstreamed students on organizing their materials and desks (Archer, 1988). Marking a reminder to purchase a new notebook on a notebook page about twenty pages from the last sheet can be helpful (Glazzard, 1980). To help prevent students losing notebooks when they travel back and forth to school, teachers can encourage the use of folders to transport assignments and other relevant necessary materials, and remind students to put their names in and on the cover of all textbooks.

Some students also may need assistance in keeping their work areas neat and orderly. A weekly work area cleanup can help students eliminate unnecessary papers and materials and make sure they bring papers home to their parents. They can keep a basket in their desks for storage of important materials, such as pencils, pens, scissors, and scotch tape (Terranova, 1984).

Elements of Direct Instruction

There has been a growing emphasis on identifying effective teaching behaviors that promote student mastery of content (Englert, 1984). A major focus of the teacher effectiveness research has been an examination of the components of effective lesson presentation (Hunter, 1981; Rosenshine, 1983; Stevens & Rosenshine, 1981). The elements of effective lessons for teaching concepts and skills that appear to be successful are

- start the lesson with a brief explanation of goals and objectives;
- briefly review previously learned, relevant prerequisite information;
- perform task analysis and present new content in discrete steps, followed by practice;
- provide unambiguous, straightforward, descriptive directions and explanations;
- program for opportunities that offer active and guided practice to all students;

- check for comprehension by having all students respond to questions;
- give prompt and specific feedback;
- offer independent seatwork practice activities; and
- summarize main points and evaluate mastery (Rosenshine, 1986).

Elements of effective lessons that teachers can use to guide large and small group instruction are presented below.

ELEMENT 1   ESTABLISH THE PURPOSE BY EXPLAINING GOALS AND OBJECTIVES.   Teachers should begin the lesson by identifying its purpose so that students can focus their attention on the new content (Rosenshine, 1986). Research indicates that students' achievement increases when they understand their teachers' goals, the importance of the content, and its relationship to information they previously learned (Kennedy, 1968).

Teachers should start the lesson with an *anticipatory set,* a statement or an activity that introduces the students to the content and offers some motivation to learn (Hunter, 1981). Usually, teachers then establish the purpose of the lesson by either telling students the objectives and goals of the lesson, or writing them on the blackboard and establishing a relationship between the new content and previously learned material (Anderson, 1984). It also is helpful for students if teachers offer a review of the schedule of activities in the daily lesson and discuss the value of learning the material to students (Englert, 1984).

ELEMENT 2   REVIEW PREREQUISITE SKILLS.   After the lesson's purpose has been communicated to students, it is important for teachers to start the lesson with a review of previously learned, relevant skills. The review should be a five- to ten-minute synopsis of prerequisite skills that they will need to learn the new material (Rosenshine, 1986). For example, in learning to tell time, it might help students if the teacher reviews such skills as discriminating the big and small hands of the clock, and identifying the numerals 1 through 12. Effective teachers typically review prerequisite skills by correcting and discussing the previous night's homework, asking students to define key terms, requiring students to apply concepts, or assigning an activity that requires students to demonstrate mastery of prior relevant material (Englert, 1984; Rosenshine, 1986).

ELEMENT 3   PERFORM TASK ANALYSIS AND INTRODUCE CONTENT IN DISCRETE STEPS.   Once the teacher has reviewed prerequisite skills, specific points should be presented to students in small, in-

FIGURE 6.3.   Task Analysis of Telling Time.

Each skill completes the statement *The student will*

1. verbally identify the clock and its function.
2. verbally identify the numbers on the clock.
3. discriminate the big hand as the hour hand and the little hand as the minute hand.
4. state the number of minutes in a hour and number of seconds in a minute.
5. state the time when the time is set
    a. on the hour.
    b. on the half-hour.
    c. on the quarter-hour.
    d. in 10-minute intervals.
    e. in 5-minute intervals.
    f. in 1-minute intervals.
6. position the hands of the clock when given a specific time
    a. on the hour.
    b. on the half-hour.
    c. on the quarter-hour.
    d. in 10-minute intervals.
    e. in 5-minute intervals.
    f. in 1-minute intervals.
7. write the time when the time is set
    a. on the hour.
    b. on the half-hour.
    c. on the quarter-hour.
    d. in 10-minute intervals.
    e. in 5-minute intervals.
    f. in 1-minute intervals.

---

cremental, and sequential steps (Hunter, 1981; Rosenshine, 1986). *Task analysis* can aid teachers in identifying the sequential, discrete steps that make up mastery of a skill. Task analysis is a systematic process of stating and sequencing the salient components of a specific task to determine the subtasks students should perform to master the task. A task analysis can help teachers identify skills that need to be taught, as well as superfluous skills that are not essential to learning a task; establish a sequence of instruction; define the prerequisite skills needed to master the task; record data and pinpoint errors; understand the inherent difficulties associated with tasks; individualize the lesson to meet the multiple skill levels of students; and fill in the gaps in the curriculum. A sample task analysis is presented in Figure 6.3.

Teachers can follow several steps in performing the task analysis.

1. *Determine the Terminal Goal and Present Level of Functioning.* Initially, teachers should identify the behavior that they want the students to learn (ask yourself, "What do I want the students to be able to do at the end of the lesson?") and determine the students' present level of functioning on the skill ("What skills related to the task can students perform?") to decide the last and first steps of the task analysis, respectively.

2. *Identify Prerequisite Skills.* Teachers can begin to analyze the task by examining the prerequisite skills needed to perform it. For example, a prerequisite skill related to the task of telling time is the ability to distinguish the numerals 1 through 12. Prerequisite skills mastered by students should be introduced in the daily review section of the lesson, while those skills not mastered should be incorporated into the task.

3. *Determine the Behavior's Components and Their Sequence.* Next, teachers should determine the subskills that constitute the behavior and list them in sequential order from easiest to hardest. Depending on the behavior, teachers can determine the components and the appropriate sequence by performing the task, consulting print materials, and examining the presentation and response modes.

    Perform the Task. Some linear tasks, such as motor tasks, can be broken down into their component parts by performing the task, verbalizing the steps, and writing them down. For example, the steps in tying a shoe can be identified by performing the task and recording each step. Similarly, observing others who perform the task well or interviewing them can help identify the sequence of steps necessary to be proficient in the task.

    Consult Print Materials. Teachers can consult professional publications to supplement information on the order of skills to be presented in learning a new task. Technical manuals, commercially developed instructional materials, criterion-referenced tests, developmental scales, and behavioral checklists frequently contain skill sequences for a variety of content areas. For example, the Brigance Inventories (Brigance, 1980, 1983) and the Keymath Diagnostic Diagnostic Inventory of Essential Mathematics (Connolly, 1988) provide skill sequences that can guide educators.

    Examine the Presentation Modes. Teachers can determine and vary the task's level of difficulty by examining the different ways that it can be presented. Therefore, in performing a task analysis, teachers should consider complexities related to the content's presentation. For example, in a bingo game that requires students to match colored shapes, the task's level of difficulty can be varied from showing students the colored shape and simultaneously verbalizing it (*Who has the yellow circle?*) to verbalizing the colored shape only (*Who has the red square?*).

Cues and prompts also can affect the level of difficulty in which teachers present material. For example, when initially introducing addition of fractions, the visual cue of a shaded portion of a shape can be paired with corresponding numerical representation of a fraction (such as ◖½ + ◖½ = ●1). Similarly, the types of devices that students are allowed to use to assist them in performing a task (ruler, calculator, dictionary, compass, number line) also should be considered in the task analysis. For example, the level of difficulty of a simple addition task will be affected by the use of a number line. However, since the goal of instruction often is for students to master skills without cues or aids, gradually phasing out their use should be part of the task analysis.

Teachers' behavior during content presentation also can be varied to promote student performance. Teachers can structure the task's presentation so that they initially model and guide students in their performance of the task. As students demonstrate proficiency, the teacher's role should fade. Figure 6.4 presents an example of the task analysis based on varying the teacher's role.

Examine the Response Mode. Another teaching variable that teachers should consider in performing a task analysis is the type or level of the response mode associated with the task. In other words, analyze the memory, language, and motor requirements of the response. In addition to the complexity of the response, teachers also should examine the time limits associated with the task. This is especially true when automaticity is important in such skills as number facts and phonetic rules.

ELEMENT 4   GIVE CLEAR DIRECTIONS, EXPLANATIONS, AND RELEVANT EXAMPLES.   Research indicates that teachers who give longer and more detailed explanations and examples of content are more successful in promoting learning in their students (Everston, Emmer, & Brophy, 1980). Thus, when explaining points to students and giving directions on tasks, teachers should present content and activities with clear and explicit statements. Instructions and directions should be directly related to the objectives of the lesson and should vary in length and language used at the beginning of the statement (Lovitt & Smith, 1972). Teachers should avoid using confusing phrases (*you know, a lot, these things*) and try to use terminology that students can understand (Smith & Land, 1981). The rate of presentation of the materials will depend upon the students' skills and the complexity of the content; it is suggested that teachers try to maintain a swift pace for instruction (Englert, 1984). However, to ensure understanding, teachers should repeat

FIGURE 6.4.   Task Analysis Based on Varying the Teacher's Role.

Skill to be taught: When given one to five objects and asked, *How many do you have?*, the student will state correctly the number of objects given.

Step 1. Teacher Guidance
  Teacher takes one object and says, "I have one." Teacher gives student one object and says, "You have one."

Step 2. Teacher Modeling without Student Failure
  Teacher takes one object and says, "I have one." With only one object available so that the student can't fail, teacher says to student, "You take one."

Step 3. Teacher Modeling with Possible Student Failure
  Teacher repeats Step 2 with more than one object available.

Step 4. Fade Out Teacher Modeling
  Teacher repeats Step 3 without the teacher serving as a model.

Step 5. Student Responds Receptively to Teacher Requests
  Teacher asks student to find or make a specific number of objects on command. For example, teacher asks student to show a chair, show two fingers, draw three circles, erase four letters, and so on.

Step 6. Student Responds Expressively to Teacher Requests
  Teacher gives student the similar objects from one to five, and asks student, "How many do you have?"

Note: Each step should be repeated using different types of objects and numbers so that students don't associate the object name as a number.

---

key points, terminology, and concepts (Mastropieri & Scruggs, 1987), and adjust the pace of the lesson to allow for reteaching and repetition if students appear confused or bored (Jones & Jones, 1986).

ELEMENT 5   PROVIDE TIME FOR ACTIVE AND GUIDED PRACTICE. Students need opportunities to practice what they have learned. Therefore, it is often best for teachers to structure time for practice after they introduce small amounts of difficult or new material (Rosenshine, 1986). Since high rates of success during practice are associated with student learning, teachers should strive for a practice success rate of at least 75 per cent to 80 per cent, and should prepare practice activities that require students to respond to items of various levels of difficulty (Rosenshine, 1986). Some good practice activities include responding to teacher-directed questions, summarizing major points, and engaging in peer tutoring (Rosenshine, 1986). Practice activities should be directed to provide all students with the chance to respond overtly so that the teacher can ensure that they have mastered the skill. Rosenshine (1986) lists a variety of student response strategies for teachers to encourage all students to become actively involved in practice.

Model-Lead-Test. When introducing new concepts, teachers can model the new concept or strategy, carefully identifying and emphasizing the salient features of each point (Englert, 1984). One effective modeling procedure for teaching new skills is the *model-lead-test strategy,* which requires teachers to model and orally present the technique or concept, guide students in understanding the process through prompts and practice, and test student mastery (Carnine & Silbert, 1979). When modeling new content, teachers should make the demonstration very clear and exaggerate the salient features of the task. It also is desirable to offer specific examples and nonexamples (Rosenshine, 1986). Examples should be relevant to student experiences to help make abstract information more concrete.

Physical Guidance. When introducing skills that require a motor response, the teacher sometimes needs to physically guide the student through the steps of the skill (Deutsch–Smith, 1981). Teachers also should simultaneously verbalize the steps being executed during the physical guidance. For example, in teaching the cursive letter *a,* the teacher could place his or her hand over the student's hand holding the writing utensil and physically guide the student in the formation of the letter while verbalizing the stroke by saying *Start at the top . . . go around . . . and down . . . back up to the start . . . down again.* Physical guidance is highly intrusive and should be used only during the initial stages of learning a skill, then faded quickly (Deutsch–Smith, 1981).

Time Delay. Another strategy that has been successful in promoting mastery of spelling words, reading sight words, computing math facts, and defining vocabulary words is *time delay* (Stevens & Schuster, 1988). The steps in time delay are

- the teacher presents the task to the student(s) and requests the student(s) to respond—for example, the teacher shows a card with addition problem 11 + 5 and says, *How much is 11 +5?;*
- the teacher prompts the student(s) immediately (zero-second delay) by providing the correct answer during several trials—for instance, after presenting the problem in step one, the teacher shows a card with the answer *11 + 5 = 16* and says, *Eleven plus five equals sixteen;*
- students respond and receive feedback based on their response;
- repeat prior steps while increasing in increments the amount of time between the presentation of the content and the teacher's providing the correct response; and

- fade out assistance so that the students can respond quickly and independently.

Stevens and Schuster (1988) provide additional guidelines for using time delay.

ELEMENT 6 CHECK FOR COMPREHENSION. Rather than asking students if they have questions, teachers should check for understanding after presenting each new point (Rosenshine, 1986). When checking for understanding, teachers should sample behaviors from all students in the class by having them identify main points or state agreement or disagreement with peers' comments and responses (Rosenshine, 1986).

Questioning. Teachers can check for comprehension by asking students questions, which should be stated so that they direct all students to respond in an overt manner (Mastropieri & Scruggs, 1987). Thus, rather than targeting a question for a specific student by linking the question with a student's name (*Jack, who was president during the Civil War?*), teachers should start a question using such terms as *Everyone listen and then tell me* or *I want you all to think before you answer.* Also, teachers should randomly select students to respond to questions, giving them at least five to ten seconds to formulate their answers (Rowe, 1974), and ask students to respond to answers given by their peers (Jones & Jones, 1986). To encourage full participation, teachers can use *choral questioning,* in which students answer simultaneously on a cue from the teacher, such as, *Everyone whisper the answer when I say three* (Mastropieri & Scruggs, 1987), or have students write down their answer and then check each student's response.

Similarly, group physical responses that allow each group member to indicate a response through an overt physical gesture also are desirable (Englert, 1984). For example, students can respond to a question that elicits a *yes* or *no* by placing their thumbs up or down, respectively. More complex questions, such as identifying whether a word is a verb or an adjective, can be responded to by having students arrange their fingers in the shape of a V (verb) or an A (adjective) to indicate their choice, or display a card with the answer. It can be motivating for students to plan with teachers different ways to indicate their responses using physical gestures. When questioning students, teachers should not promote student inattention by repeating questions, vitiate the need for students' responses by answering questions for students, or supplement students' incomplete answers (Hoover, 1976).

Teachers should adjust their questions to meet the content level and the skill levels of the students. To check student understanding of simple facts or basic rules, teachers can use questions that ask students to restate information and procedures, such as, *What is the "i" before "e" rule?* (Mastropieri & Scruggs, 1987). To survey students' ability to apply complex skills, teachers should use questions that require students to apply basic rules or generalizations (Rosenshine, 1986). For example, asking students to spell *receive* is a more complex skill than merely asking students to repeat the rule. Sanders (1966) has developed a hierarchy of questions that teachers can use to tailor their questions to the ability levels of students. The hierarchy, sequenced from easiest to hardest, includes seven levels of questioning: memory, translation, interpretation, application, analysis, synthesis, and evaluation.

Encouraging LEP Students to Respond. Teachers may need to encourage limited English-proficient students and students with speech and language difficulties to respond verbally. Wood (1976) noted that teachers can aid these students in responding by creating an atmosphere that facilitates speaking, offering frequent chances for students to engage in oral discussions, allowing students to use gestures initially until they develop language competence, and acknowledging the student's contribution and seeking additional information when necessary.

Teachers also can stimulate students' use of language by providing experiences that encourage verbalizations, such as introducing new objects into the classroom, making periodic changes in the classroom environment, allowing students to work and play cooperatively, conducting interviews, sending students on errands, creating situations in which students need to request assistance, and employing visuals that display pictorial absurdities (Spekman & Roth, 1984).

ELEMENT 7   OFFER PROMPT AND SPECIFIC FEEDBACK.   Students' responses during comprehension checks, practice activities, and other lesson phases should be followed by feedback from the teacher. The type of feedback should relate to the nature of the students' responses. Therefore, in determining what type of feedback to employ, teachers should categorize the students' responses as *correct and confident, correct but unsure, partly correct,* or *incorrect.* If the answer is correct and presented with a degree of certainty, teachers should confirm the response with praise and ask additional questions at the same or a more difficult level (Mastropieri & Scruggs, 1987; Rosenshine, 1986). If the answer is not correct and confident, teachers should deliver another type of feedback.

Process Feedback. While teachers can reinforce a correct student response with praise, mainstreamed and other students who are unsure of their correct responses may need to receive *process feedback* (Good & Grouws, 1979), a technique that allows teachers to praise students verbally, and reinforce their response by restating why the answer was correct. For example, if a student correctly answers a question applying a rule of possessives, the teacher would confirm the answer by stating it was correct and repeating the possessive rule that the student applied successfully.

In addition to responding to correct answers, it is also important for teachers to provide feedback to students whose responses are partly correct. Teachers should confirm the aspect of the response that is correct, then restate or simplify the question to address the incorrect part of the answer.

Teachers also can respond to the students' errors in a variety of ways, including corrective feedback, prompting, and cuing. If these strategies are not effective, teachers can call on other students to provide the answer, and recheck understanding of the question later in the session (Mastropieri & Scruggs, 1987).

Corrective Feedback. Corrective feedback guides students on how to perform the task more effectively (Wallace & Kauffman, 1986). When using corrective feedback, teachers identify errors and offer instructional support to assist students in modifying these errors (Cohen, Perkins, & Newmark, 1985). Research suggests that corrective feedback is more effective in promoting learning than *general feedback,* in which responses are identified for students simply as correct or incorrect; *right-only feedback,* where only correct responses are identified for students; and *wrong-only feedback,* where only incorrect responses are identified for students (Kulhavy, 1977; Mims & Gholson, 1977).

If the students' responses are obviously incorrect, and extensive teacher assistance will not help the students determine the correct answer, teachers can respond by clarifying the directions, rechecking mastery of prerequisite skills, teaching a lower-level skill from the task analysis, providing additional practice, and modifying the presentation style (Mastropieri & Scruggs, 1987). When the students' incorrect answers appear to be caused by a lack of effort, attention, or preparation, the teacher should emphasize the need to improve in these areas.

Prompting. Teachers can help students correct errors by using a variety of *prompting procedures.* Schloss (1986) defines prompting as "visual, auditory, or tactile cues that assist the learner in performing a subskill of the terminal behavior." (p. 181) Prompts can be categorized from most to least intrusive, including *manual prompts,* during which the student is physically guided through the task; *modeling prompts,* in which the student watches another individual perform the task; *oral prompts* that provide students with a description of how to perform the task; and *visual prompts,* whereby the student is shown the correct process or answer via a graphic presentation (Schloss, 1986). Teachers should use prompts in a sequential fashion, depending on the skill level of the students and the degree of complexity of the task. Highly intrusive prompts should be coupled with more natural prompts.

Cuing. One type of prompt is a *cue,* which can increase students' abilities to deal with a difficult task because it relates the task or the components of the task to the students' existing skill repertoire (Salend, 1980). Deutsch–Smith (1981) suggests the use of movement, position, and redundancy cues when students need assistance on worksheet assignments. *Movement cues* require the teacher to physically indicate the response. For example, when working on a reading comprehension worksheet with multiple choice responses, the teacher might indicate the correct response by pointing, touching, or circling it. When using *position cues,* teachers ensure that the correct response is located nearest to the student. *Redundancy cues* allow teachers to highlight the correct response through such variables as color, shape, size, and position. Other cuing strategies include highlighting salient features of a task, modeling correct answers, and presenting verbal statements—words, phrases, and sounds (George, 1986).

Praising. Research indicates that while teachers are very likely to acknowledge a correct and appropriate response, they are less likely to use praise frequently in their classrooms (Sadker & Sadker, 1985). Effective use of praise can promote self-esteem in students, establish a greater bond between teachers and students, reinforce appropriate behavior, and create a positive environment in the classroom. Because many students tend to rate their performance in negative terms (Meunier & Rule, 1967), praise coupled with comments concerning strengths and weaknesses can provide valuable feedback to students and increase their proficiency (Page, 1958).

Despite the fact that praise is more effective with lower-achieving students and students from lower socioeconomic backgrounds, they are less likely than their more proficient peers to receive teacher praise (Brophy & Everston, 1976). Teachers can increase their use of praise with these students by recording the number of praise statements they direct to them. Additionally, displaying a cue in a location of the room that teachers frequently see (for example, a smiling face on the back wall of the classroom) and finding a student to praise each time eye contact is made with the cue can promote an increase in the teacher's use of praise.

Brophy (1981) analyzed the components of effective praise. He suggests that teachers follow several guidelines when using praise in their classrooms, such as

* delivering praise after the appropriate response has occurred;
* describing the specifics of the behavior being praised (rather than saying *This is a good paper,* the teacher should say, *You really did a good job of using topic sentences to begin your paragraphs in this paper;*

- increasing the credibility of the praise by using diverse, spontaneous statements;
- considering the age and skill level of the students when phrasing praise statements;
- acknowledging effort as well as specific outcomes;
- focusing students on the behaviors that helped them to be successful; and
- individualizing praise 'so that the students' achievements are evaluated in comparison to their own performance, rather than the performance of their peers.

In addition to verbal statements, praise also can be delivered through nonverbal gestures, such as a smile, a hug, a pat on the back, the O.K. sign, or the thumbs-up sign. Since some researchers have shown that frequent praise can minimize students' independence, self-confidence, and creativity (Brophy, 1981), teachers should distribute praise evenly and examine its effect on students. Thus, rather than just praising on-task behavior and task correctness, praise also can be delivered to encourage independence, determination, and creativity.

Student-Directed Feedback. Students also can be a valuable source of feedback. Students can be encouraged and taught to use self-monitoring techniques to record and analyze their progress. They can chart their mastery of a specific skill by graphing their percentage or number correct every day. In addition to graphing performance, it may be desirable for students to identify the variables that led to their success (Jones & Jones, 1986). Identifying these factors can help students learn to attribute their success to competence and effort rather than believing that they had little control over the outcome. Additionally, students can be taught to exchange papers and offer feedback to peers on each other's performance.

ELEMENT 8   OFFER TIME FOR SEATWORK ACTIVITIES.   Teachers often conclude successful lessons by giving students seatwork activities that allow them to demonstrate mastery of the material presented (Rosenshine, 1986). Seatwork activities should be directly related to the content provided in the lesson so that students are developing automaticity of the skill. Teachers should direct (*Now I want to see you do these math problems*) rather than ask students to perform a task (*Would you like to do these math problems?*) when presenting assignments (Wallace & Kauffman, 1986). Because students frequently exhibit off-task behaviors during seatwork (Berliner & Rosenshine, 1977), teachers can do several things to keep their students actively engaged in the task, including informing students of the purpose of the assignment and its objectives (Wong, Wong, & Lemare, 1982); explaining the relationship between the seatwork assignment and the material covered in the lesson (Anderson, 1984); giving clear directions concerning expectations (Mastropieri & Scruggs, 1987); perusing the room to monitor student behavior (Englert, 1984); walking around the classroom to help students who need assistance (Englert & Thomas, 1982); providing prompt feedback (Rosenshine, 1980); and reviewing seatwork after it is completed (Englert, 1984).

Teachers also can improve student completion levels of seatwork by establishing, communicating, and enforcing their expectations in terms of accuracy, time, format, and appearance (Englert, 1984). If students fail to complete an assignment according to the teacher's expectations, they should be required to rework it until it complies with the teacher's standards (Everston & Emmer, 1982). Levels of accuracy demonstrated by students are especially important for promoting learning; so, it is recommended that teachers strive for seatwork accuracy levels of 90 per cent or more (Rosenshine, 1983).

For mainstreamed students, it may be appropriate to adapt seatwork by decreasing the number of items they are required to answer; interspersing items relating to content they have mastered previously with items addressing the new material; providing cues to highlight key parts of directions, details of items, and changes in item types; using a similar worksheet format repeatedly; using color cues to note starting and ending points; dividing worksheets into sections by folding, drawing lines, cutting off parts of the page, boxing, and blocking out with an index card or with a heavy crayon; limiting the amount of distracting visual stimuli; modifying the content of the assignment to meet the skill levels of the students; giving several shorter assignments rather than a single lengthy one; and providing students with additional time to complete the assignment (Gillet, 1986; Humphrey, Hoffman, & Crosby, 1984).

Teachers also can modify seatwork by providing students with assistance. Students can indicate that they need help by placing a help sign or card on their desks, raising their hands, or signing a list for students needing teacher assistance. Although it is appropriate to modify the seatwork tasks, it is inappropriate to have mainstreamed students work on a content area that is different from the rest of the class; this differentiation might isolate them within the class.

ELEMENT 9   SUMMARIZE MAIN POINTS AND EVALUATE MASTERY.   At the end of the lesson, teachers should summarize main points and evaluate students' mastery of the content. The summary can be a brief review of the main points and procedures presented in the lesson. Following the summary, teachers should assess students' mastery of content via a one- to five-minute probe. Maintenance of skills is critical for establishing a foundation for learning additional skills; maintenance probes on a weekly and monthly basis also are desirable (Mastropieri & Scruggs, 1987). (Additional guidelines for evaluating student mastery and progress are presented in Chapter 9.)

Student-Directed Small Group Activities

Several techniques for modifying instruction are particularly valid for use with student-directed small group activities. These strategies include cooperative learning arrangements and academic games.

Cooperative Learning

Teachers usually structure learning so that students work individually or competitively (Johnson & Johnson, 1986). However, teachers can adapt their instructional programs by employing *cooperative learning,* a technique found to be highly effective in simultaneously promoting academic and affective skills of all students and facilitating the mainstreaming of students with disabilities (Johnson & Johnson, 1986; Slavin, Madden, & Leavey, 1984). Cooperative learning is especially worthwhile for heterogeneous student populations because it encourages mutual respect and learning among students of various academic abilities, handicapping conditions, and racial and ethnic backgrounds (Sharan, 1980; Slavin, et al., 1985).

Cooperative learning refers to a method for organizing learning, in which students are working with their peers toward a shared academic goal rather than competing against or working separately from their peers. Teachers structure the learning environment so that each class member contributes to the group's goal. When learning is structured cooperatively, students are accountable not only for their own achievement, but also for the performance of other group members; the group's evaluation is based on the group's product. Schniedewind and Salend (1987) have reviewed several guidelines for implementing cooperative learning. These guidelines are discussed below.

SELECTING A COOPERATIVE LEARNING FORMAT. Teachers can begin to implement cooperative learning in their classrooms by selecting a format for structuring the cooperative learning experience. The format teachers choose for their classes will depend on the unique needs and characteristics of their students and classrooms, as well as their experiences in working cooperatively. For example, a teacher might choose to introduce peer teaching first because it is easy to manage. Groups with varying levels of ability who need structure might do best with the jig-saw technique (discussed below), which ensures that all students actively participate. Finally, when working with students who have had prac-tice with cooperative learning, teachers should consider using the group project, which optimizes student responsibility.

The type of cooperative learning format selected also will depend on the content of the assignment. According to Kagan (1985), peer teaching and STAD are best for teaching basic skills; the jigsaw is most appropriate for text mastery; TAI adapts well for math; and the group project gives the desired format for teaching higher-level cognitive material.

PEER TUTORING.   One widely used cooperative format that has been effective in increasing the amount of time students are engaged in learn-ing, promoting educational progress, and fostering positive attitudes to-ward school and learning is *peer tutoring* (Allen, 1976; Jenkins & Jenk-ins, 1981). In addition to benefitting tutees, peer tutoring can promote a greater sense of responsibility and improved self-concept, as well as increased academic skills in tutors (Gerber & Kauffman, 1981).

In peer tutoring, one student tutors and assists another in learning a new skill. Teachers should

- establish specific goals for the sessions;
- plan particular learning activities to meet the identified goals;
- select tutors who have demonstrated proficiency in the content to be taught;
- train students to function as successful tutors;
- match tutors and tutees;
- schedule sessions for no longer than thirty minutes and no more than three times per week;
- periodically monitor the tutoring process and provide feedback to both members of the dyad; and
- allay potential parental concerns by explaining to parents the role and the value of peer tutoring.

Teachers should carefully plan tutoring sessions so that nonhandicapped students are not constantly teaching mainstreamed students. For exam-ple, if a mainstreamed student performs well in math, the teacher could structure the peer tutoring format so that this student would teach math to a student who provides tutoring to him or her in learning capitaliza-tion rules. Students who are not capable of teaching academic skills can teach nonacademic skills related to their hobbies or interests.

Jones and Jones (1986) propose two ways that peer tutoring systems can be incorporated into classrooms on a continuing basis. Students can be given symbols that they display on their desks to indicate whether they need or can provide help. For example, they suggest using a red card to indicate the need for assistance and a green card to announce that the student is willing to aid others. Similarly, recording on the blackboard the names of students who are available to provide assistance for a specific assignment can guide students in selecting peer tutors.

STUDENT TEAMS-ACHIEVEMENT DIVISIONS (STAD).   Another cooperative learning structure for teachers is Student Teams-Achievement Divisions (STAD) (Slavin, 1980). Kagan (1985) outlines the steps in implementing STAD as

1. Content is presented to students by the teacher;
2. teams are formed, work on study sheets, and prepare for quizzes related to the content presented;
3. students take quizzes individually; their improvement above an individually assigned "base score" earns points for their respective teams (base scores are averages of the students' two latest quizzes); and
4. teachers recognize team and individual improvement by distributing a newsletter concerning the teams' performance or providing special activities to teams.

JIGSAW.   The *jigsaw format* divides students into groups, with each student assigned a task essential to the accomplishment of the group's goal (Aronson, et al., 1978). Every group member contributes an individualized part that is integrated with the work of others to produce the group's product. When teams are working on the same task, expert groups can be formed by having a member of each group meet with peers from other groups who have been assigned the same subtask. The expert group members work together to complete their assignment, then share their results with their original jigsaw groups.

Teachers should structure the students' assignment so that each group member can succeed. For example, a regular classroom teacher taught a lesson about Dr. Martin Luther King by giving each student one segment of Dr. King's life to learn about and teach to others in their group. Students who had the same aspect of Dr. King's life met in expert groups to complete their part; then the original group answered a worksheet on all segments of Dr. King's life.

Variations of the jigsaw have been developed. Slavin (1980) has developed the Jigsaw 2, which incorporates elements of STAD into the jigsaw format. Kagan (1985) suggests several modifications on expert groups; Gonzalez and Guerro (cited in Kagan, 1985) have adapted the jigsaw for use with bilingual students.

GROUP PROJECT.   A cooperative format that places more responsibility on the group members is the *group project,* which is based on Johnson and Johnson's (1975) *Learning Together Approach.* In this format, students are assigned to teams; each team is given an assignment. Teams decide whether to divide the task into its component parts or approach the task as a whole group. All group members are involved in the team's decisions by offering their knowledge and skills and seeking assistance and clarification from others. Every group produces one product, which represents a composite of the contributions of every group member. The teacher grades this product, with each student in the group receiving the group grade. For example, a teacher used a group project to teach students about mammals. The teacher divided the class into groups and assigned each group the task of developing part of a bulletin board display containing descriptive information and artwork about a particular mammal. Individual students within each group then contributed to the group's display by reporting information, doing artwork, or dictating material about mammals.

TEAM-ASSISTED INSTRUCTION (TAI).   *Team-Assisted Instruction (TAI)* is a cooperative learning system in which heterogeneous groups of students work to master individualized assignments (Slavin, Madden, & Leavey, 1984). While other cooperative learning formats are group-paced, TAI is unique in that it combines cooperatively structured learning with individualized instruction. In TAI, individual group members work on their own assignments and assist other group members with their assignments. Group members are then rewarded if their team's performance meets or exceeds preestablished criteria.

To implement TAI in their classrooms, teachers initially develop individualized units of instruction for each student. These units contain a list of instructions, skill sheets, quizzes, and answer sheets. Team members exchange answer sheets and work on the skill sheets in their individualized units, seeking assistance from their teammates when necessary. When a student completes a skill sheet, a teammate checks the answers using the unit answer sheet. If the answers are correct, the student proceeds to the other skill sheets in the unit. If the problems are answered incorrectly, the student reworks them.

After completing the unit and obtaining the consent of all teammates, students take a practice test, and then a final test on content that parallels the content of the student's unit skill sheets. If teammates do not give the student approval to take a test, the teacher gives the student additional skill sheets and assistance if necessary. When each member of the team has taken at least one final test, the team's average is computed. If the team's average meets or exceeds set criteria established by the teacher, reinforcement to the whole group is delivered (Salend & Washin, 1988).

ESTABLISHING GUIDELINES FOR WORKING COOPERATIVELY. Teachers and students should establish guidelines for working cooperatively. Johnson (1988) outlines several classroom guidelines that can help students work cooperatively:

- Each group will produce one product.
- Each group member will assist other group members to understand the material.
- Each group member will seek assistance from his or her peers.
- Each group member will stay in his or her group.
- No group member will change his or her ideas unless logically persuaded to do so.
- Each group member will indicate acceptance of the group's product by signing his or her name.

Teachers also should remind students that the standard classroom behavior expectations must be followed during cooperative learning lessons.

FORMING COOPERATIVE GROUPS.   Teachers should assign students to heterogeneous groups, considering such variables as sex, race, handicapping condition, and academic skill level. Another factor to consider in forming groups is the students' ability to work together. Information on how well students can work together can be obtained through observation and/or administration of a sociogram (see Chapter 4). While it is possible to change groups for each cooperative lesson, keeping the students in the same group for several weeks can provide the continuity that is helpful in developing cooperative skills. Initially, teachers should form small groups of two or three students, increasing the size to no more than five when students become accustomed to cooperative learning (Johnson & Johnson, 1986).

ARRANGING THE CLASSROOM FOR COOPERATIVE LEARNING. Teachers can structure their classrooms for cooperative work by arranging the students' desks or tables in clusters, placing individual desks in pairs for peer tutoring, or blocking off a carpeted corner of the room. For larger groups, desks should be placed in circles rather than rectangles, which can prevent eye contact and communication (Johnson & Johnson, 1986). Bookshelves, screens, movable chalkboards, and easels can divide the classroom into discrete areas. Since the time required to complete co-operative projects may vary, teachers should provide the groups with a safe area to store in-progress projects and other necessary materials.

DEVELOPING COOPERATIVE SKILLS.   Many students have only lim-ited experience in working cooperatively, so teachers may have to de-vote some time to helping students learn to work together. Cooperative learning skills should be taught gradually, building on the students' ex-periences. Teachers can vary the complexity of the cooperative learning activity by modifying the task to meet students' needs. For classes with little experience with cooperative learning, it is best to start with small groups of two on a short-term, discrete, cooperative learning task with well-defined roles. For example, pairs of students can study for the first quiz together and receive their average grade score.

Teachers can also help students learn to work cooperatively by pro-viding opportunities for them to practice specific skills. For example, put-downs of group members can hinder cooperation. Because main-streamed students may be the targets of negative statements from peers, teachers could help the class practice how to respond appropriately to put-downs. First, teachers should have their students brainstorm all con-structive ways to respond to put-downs directed at themselves or other group members. Students should be given time to practice responding to put-downs. As a followup, teachers can lead their students in a discus-sion of the most effective responses to put-downs, possibly listing them on a chart.

Another method of helping students gain the skills necessary for pro-ductive group functioning is *role delineation,* whereby each member of the group is assigned a specific role to enable the group to work cooper-atively. For example, for tasks involving written products, a team might need a reader, a discussion leader to promote brainstorming and deci-sion making, a secretary to record all contributions, and a writer to edit the product. Other students might be assigned the roles of keeping the group on task, explaining word meanings, and providing positive com-ments. Specific roles for group members have been identified by Kagan (1985).

Monitoring groups and providing feedback can build cooperative skills in classes. Therefore, it is important for teachers to observe groups, model appropriate cooperative skills, intervene as a consultant, and pro-vide feedback regarding group processing skills (Reynolds & Salend, in press). After students complete a cooperative lesson, they can be encour-aged to reflect on their experience by responding to such processing questions as

• What did group members do to help your group accomplish its goal?

- What did group members do that hindered your group in achieving its goal?
- What will your group do differently next time to work together?

Gillespie (1976) has identified several processing questions that can help students assume greater responsibility and improve their cooperative skills.

EVALUATING COOPERATIVE LEARNING. Teachers should evaluate groups based on their mastery of subject matter as well as their ability to work together. To promote peer support and group accountability, evaluate students as a group; each student's individual learning contributes to the group's evaluation. Teachers can build in individual accountability by having each group member complete a quiz, or by randomly selecting a teammate to respond for the group (Johnson, 1988).

A popular method for evaluating cooperative learning is the *group project/group grade format*. The group submits for evaluation one final product (a worksheet, report, or oral presentation) that is a composite of the individual group members' contributions. Teachers then evaluate the product and assign each group member the same grade.

In another evaluation format, *contract grading*, groups contract for a grade based on the amount of work they agree to accomplish according to a set of criteria. Thus, group members who have differing skill levels can perform different parts of the task according to their ability. For example, a cooperative lesson might contain five activities of varying degrees of difficulty, with each activity worth ten points. The contract between the teacher and the groups might then specify the criteria the groups must meet to achieve an A (fifty points), B (forty points), and C (thirty points). Once a contract for a grade is made, group members can divide the tasks, choosing tasks commensurate with their abilities. Additional guidelines for using contract grading are discussed in Chapter 8.

One evaluation system that provides students with particular incentives to assist others in learning the material is the *group average*. Individual grades on a quiz or part of a project are averaged into a group grade. Each group member receives the average grade. For example, each group member could be given an individualized test tailored to his or her unique abilities in math. Thus, one student might be tested on addition, while other students might be tested on subtraction and multiplication. During the week, group members help each other master their assignments and prepare for their tests. Some students initially may be resistant to the concept of group grades. Teachers can minimize their resistance by assuring students that group members will only be assigned work that is possible for them to complete. Inform students that if all group members do their best and assist others, high grades will be received by all of them.

In addition to evaluating the group in terms of mastery of content, teachers also might grade students in terms of effort and ability to work together by assigning each team member a percentage grade that represents a measure of their efforts and ability to work together. Since team members will have a greater idea of the relative contributions of each group member, the group can determine the effort and teamwork grade for each of its members. However, since students may feel uncomfortable rating their peers, teachers should exercise caution in requiring an effort grade. Kagan (1985) has developed several forms that teachers can employ to solicit evaluations from teammates.

Some other useful resources to help teachers learn more about cooperative learning are Dishon and O'Leary (1985), Johnson, Johnson, Holubec, and Roy (1984), Kagan (1985), Slavin (1980), and Schniedewind and Davidson (1987).

Academic Games

One small group instructional format that is particularly motivating for students is the learning game (Jones & Jones, 1986). Salend (1979) defines academic learning games as "a pleasure-invoking, rule-based interaction between at least two persons, with successful movement toward an agreed upon goal dependent on mastery of academic skills" (p. 4). Academic games may take several formats. When space is limited, a game board format (Regional Support and Technical Assistance Centers Coordinating Office, 1976) would be a feasible alternative; if space is available, a movement-oriented format is appropriate (Cratty, 1971; Humphrey, 1969).

An important facet of academic games that makes them particularly suitable for mainstreaming is the fact that the teacher controls the academic component, so they can vary the skill level, presentation mode, and the response to match the needs and levels of a wide variety of students. Thus, students of varying ability levels can interact within the same instructional format, yet perform skills differing in complexity. For example, the academic content for several students in the game can be addition of fractions with a common denominator; other students' movement toward the winning criteria may involve solving problems requiring the division of fractions.

Salend (1979) identified four phases in developing academic games for mainstreamed settings:

Phase 1: Foundation. The foundation phase allows teachers to develop
a framework from which the game can evolve, and determine the

game's rules. Rules should specify the criteria for completion of
the game, penalties or bonuses, criteria for movement toward
an agreed end point, order of participation, nature of player ex-
changes, use of materials, schedule of events, record keeping, and
game modifications.

Phase 2: Formulation. The formulation phase requires teachers to
match the game's characteristics to the specific abilities of their
students. Questions and activities related to students' academic
skills and needs are formulated to constitute the academic component of the game.

Phase 3: Experimentation. In the experimentation phase, teachers
initially focus on the construction of the game and its materials.
During this phase, teachers should train students in the rules and
prerequisite skills needed to play the game.

Phase 4: Evaluation. The evaluation phase is a feedback mechanism.
Evaluation data regarding rules, prerequisites, learner response
variables, academic content, and other game variables are gathered,
analyzed, and interpreted.

Games should stress cooperation rather than competition (Salend,
1981). One cooperative goal strategy requires players to strive for a
common goal. In this technique, winning is not confined to one player
who arrives at the terminal goal first; rather, winning occurs when the
whole group arrives at the goal. Devising game movers as puzzle pieces
also can foster the cooperative effect of an academic game. For example,
each player's mover can be part of a puzzle that is completed when each
player reaches a specified terminal goal. Competition with self can be
built into common goal games by setting individualized time limits or
increasing the level of difficulty of the content. The time limits and
content levels should be based on a previously established standard or a
prior level of performance.

Teachers can increase the cooperation among players by phrasing
questions so that they require the input of more than one player to
be completed correctly. For example, the academic question *Add the
number of players on a baseball team to the number of eggs in a dozen,
then multiply that number by the number of ships on Columbus' voyage
to America, and then divide that number by the number of students in
this class* can be answered by having players collaborate.

Rules can be designed to optimize cooperation among players. A rule
that requires players to periodically change teams or movers during the
game can promote cooperation. Similarly, a rule that periodically requires one player to move toward the goal dependent on the academic
performance of another player tends to foster a coalition of game par-

ticipants. Another cooperative rule allows a player who has reached the terminal goal to aid the other players.

Homework

Homework can be an effective and valuable instructional tool that supplements large and small group instruction (Coulter, 1980; Keith, 1982). Teachers can use homework with mainstreamed students to individualize instruction, facilitate learning through practice and application, complete work not finished in school, teach independent study skills and work habits, and communicate to parents the skills and materials that are being covered in school (Turner, 1984).

Teachers should pay attention to the amount of homework they assign to students. It should depend on the students' ages and educational placement. As students proceed beyond third grade, the amount of homework should be increased to two to four nights each week, for thirty to sixty minutes per night. Because mainstreamed students may be taught in several settings, teachers should attempt to coordinate homework assignments—particularly for secondary-level students who may have different teachers in each content area.

A critical factor in making homework meaningful is the content of the assignment. Not only *what* but *how* teachers taught the material should be incorporated into the assignment. Many mainstreamed students may have difficulty with generalization, so applying skills to other conditions should not be assigned as homework unless it has been taught in class. For example, students instructed in how to solve addition problems presented in the vertical format should not be given homework in horizontal form until specifically taught the procedure.

The type of homework teachers give depends on the instructional purpose in giving the assignment. Lee and Pruitt's (1979) homework taxonomy delineated four possible instructional purposes of homework: practice, preparation, extension, and creativity. If the goal of homework is to practice material learned in class, teachers can assign some type of drill-oriented assignment (*Rewrite these sentences using commas*). When the instructional purpose of homework is to prepare students for upcoming lessons, assignments should be structured to provide students with the prerequisite information necessary to perform successfully in class (*Read pages forty-five to fifty-three and define the terms "weathering" and "erosion"*). Assignments requiring abstract thinking and transfer of prior knowledge to different conditions (*Based on what you learned, read the following paragraph and write down all the reasons this location is a good site for a city*) should be employed when the teacher's intention is to extend and apply skills mastered to more complex and varied situations. Finally, when teachers seek to foster creativity in their students, they should use long-term assignments that require the integration of many skills and processes (science projects, book reports, historical time lines, oral reports, or term papers).

The type of homework assignments given also should be related to the way students acquired the content. Material taught via analysis, synthesis, or problem-solving techniques would best be reviewed by creative, open-ended homework assignments (such as responding to essays), whereas homework on factual and memorized material should use a drill format.

Some mainstreamed students may need to be motivated to complete their homework (Salend & Schliff, in press). Teachers can motivate these students by making homework creative and enjoyable. For example, an assignment on computing averages may be made more interesting by using the scoring records of the members of the school's basketball teams. Teachers also can increase motivation to complete homework by grading it and displaying exemplary homework assignments on a bulletin board. Similarly, motivation to complete homework can be fostered by praising students and granting free time or extra computer time, and giving tangible reinforcers such as stickers or erasers to students who successfully complete their homework.

Frequent evaluation by teachers also can motivate students to complete their homework. Therefore, teachers should provide immediate feedback to students' homework assignments. Feedback should encompass recognition of correct responses as well as identification of responses that need further refinement. Teachers can deliver feedback through daily reviews of homework during class time or by writing comments on the students' products. Homework evaluation also could include homework grades, which should then become part of a report card grade.

Parents can be instrumental in monitoring and assisting with their children's homework. Make them a part of the homework process by periodically communicating with them about the purpose of homework and the amount and type of homework given. Teachers could offer parents suggestions on how to help their children complete their homework, including how to give feedback, employ positive reinforcement, schedule time to do homework, establish a proper distraction-free environment, deal with frustration, and avoid completing homework for the child (Salend & Schliff, 1988). Clary (1986) developed a check list that can help parents monitor the homework and study behaviors of their children.

Modifying Instruction via Textbooks and Other Print Materials

Teachers also present content to students using print materials, such as textbooks. However, since many mainstreamed students may have difficulty reading and gaining information from print materials, teachers may need to modify reading selections to assist students in developing reading comprehension skills (Burnette, 1987). (See Chapter 3 for a review of strategies for students to improve their text comprehension skills.)

Text Comprehension

Before assigning a selection for reading, teachers should review new vocabulary and word pronunciation. Scanning the selection and discussing the meaning of boldfaced terms within the context of the chapter also can aid students. New vocabulary words can be placed in an index card file by chapter, with each new term placed on a separate card that includes the definition and the page number on which the word appears (Wood & Wooley, 1986).

Previews, structured overviews, and prereading organizers can direct the students' attention to the relevant information in the selection. For example, teachers can give an outline of the selection's main points to students and discuss it before they read the material; or, they can give students an outline to complete as they read the selection (Bos & Vaughn, 1988). As students read the assignment, teachers emphasize key points by underlining, repeating, and discussing them, and questioning students about graphs, pictures, and diagrams. Similarly, teachers can improve students' text comprehension skills by asking them to perform a writing activity related to the reading assignment before they actually read the passage (Marino, Gould, & Haas, 1985). Students' memory of key terms can be improved by limiting the amount of new material presented, summarizing main points, and assigning study questions.

Questioning

A frequently used strategy for guiding text comprehension, having students respond to questions about the text (Beck & McKeown, 1981), can focus the students' attention on the reading assignment's purpose. Teachers can help students answer chapter questions correctly by modifying the type and timing of the questions. In varying the type of question, teachers should initially present questions that deal with factual information and move to those which require inference and more complex skills. Rather than using questions that are open ended, teachers can rephrase questions by using simpler language or by employing a multiple choice format. Students gain information from textbooks more readily if teachers use *prequestions*—those posed before the selection is read—and *postquestions*—those posed after the materials have been read

(Beck, 1984). Postquestions are particularly effective in promoting recall by establishing the need for review (Harris & Sipay, 1985). However, teachers should exercise some caution in using prequestions; their use can result in students focusing too much on information related to the answers and ignoring other content in the text (Tierney & Cunningham, 1984).

Reciprocal Teaching

Text comprehension skills also can be strengthened by *reciprocal teaching*, which involves the teacher assigning students to read a selection silently, summarizing the content, discussing and clarifying problem areas, using questions to check student comprehension, and providing students with the opportunity to predict future content (Palinscar & Brown, 1983). After students observe the teacher modeling these strategies, students assume the role of teacher.

Guided Reading Procedure

Teachers can use a *guided reading procedure* to help students comprehend material presented in a reading passage (Manzo, 1975). The steps in implementing the guided reading procedure are

1. Students read the selection and attempt to remember as much as possible.
2. Students share the information they remember with the class, and the teacher records their responses on the chalkboard.
3. Students review the selection and correct inconsistencies or errors in information presented on the chalkboard, then add new information.
4. Students organize the information on the chalkboard into an outline or pattern.
5. Teachers promote understanding of the material by questioning students about the information.
6. Teachers assess the students' short-term memory of the information.
7. Repeat steps 1 through 6 as needed (Manzo, 1975).

Modifying Materials

Teachers also can facilitate students' comprehension of reading matter by modifying the materials. To help students identify main points, framing the page and highlighting critical information via underlining can help students locate essential content and foster reading anticipation (Burnette, 1987). Cues linking a chapter question with the location of the answer in the selection can help students learn how to find correct answers to reading assignments. For example, teachers can color-code study question 1 and its corresponding answer in the text using a yellow magic marker, then color-code question 2 and its answer using a blue magic marker. Similarly, pairing chapter questions with the page numbers that contain the answers, or recording questions on cassettes, including the corresponding pages of the correct response, can help students (Wood & Wooley, 1986).

When reviewing texts with students, the readability of the text can be enhanced by teachers decreasing the number of words in a sentence; breaking long sentences into two or three sentences; converting complex language into language the students can understand; eliminating extraneous sections that may distract students; using words that show relationships, such as *because, after, since*; rephrasing paragraphs so that they begin with a topic sentence followed by supporting details; presenting a series of events or actions in chronological order; clustering information that is related; using words that are known to students; embedding the definition of new words in paragraphs and selections; refraining from using different words that have identical meanings; and inserting text and examples to clarify main points (Beech, 1983; Wood & Wooley, 1986).

Audiotapes

In addition to using reading selections with lower readability indices, teachers can supply students with audiotapes of the text that are commercially produced or volunteer-made (volunteers can be peers, parents, teacher aides, community group members, drama club members, or honor society members) (Smith & Smith, 1985). For example, groups of students can be assigned the creative cooperative task of preparing an audiocassette of a textbook chapter. So that tapes can be used repeatedly by many students, they can be stored in the library for circulation (Smith & Smith, 1985).

When preparing tapes of written materials, the quality of the tape can be improved by the speaker reading in a clear, coherent voice, presenting 120 to 175 words per minute with pauses long enough for punctuation (Deshler & Graham, 1980). The clarity of the tape can be enhanced by recording in a quiet location, keeping the microphone in a fixed position approximately six inches from the speaker's mouth, and adjusting the volume so that clicks are minimized (Mercer & Mercer, 1985).

Each tape should begin with a statement of the title of the textbook, the authors' names, and the chapters or sections recorded. The beginning of the tape can include study questions or an advance organizer to orient the listener to the important points of the selection (Bos & Vaughn, 1988; Mercer & Mercer, 1985). In preparing audiotapes for students, it is often helpful for the teacher to limit the amount of information presented. Teachers can encourage students to rehearse or apply the content presented by including study questions on the tape. For example, an inserted reminder to the listener to *Stop here, and list three changes in America that were a result of the Industrial Revolution* can guide students. At strategic points throughout the tape, teachers also should summarize the information.

Deshler and Graham (1980) suggest the use of a marking system to help students follow along in the text while they are listening to the tape. They propose that teachers place symbols in the text that relate to a specific section of the tape. For example, a # in the text may indicate a section that has been paraphrased. To enhance the motivational aspect or the dramatic effects of the audiocassettes, some teachers and commercial producers add music, sound effects, and other strategies (Burnette, 1987). Audiocassettes adapting several history books and including supplemental print materials are available commercially from

DLM Teaching Resources
DLM Park, P.O. Box 4000
Allen, TX 75002

Audiocassette readings of textbooks also are available to students with learning and physical disabilities, and visually and print-impaired individuals. Educators can obtain these materials by contacting

The National Library Service for the Blind and Physically Handi-
    capped
Library of Congress
1291 Taylor Street, N.W.
Washington, D.C. 20542
(202) 287-5100

American Printing House for the Blind
1839 Frankfort Avenue
Louisville, KY 40206
(502) 895-2405

Recording for the Blind, Inc.
20 Roszel Road
Princeton, NJ 08540

Franklin County Special Education Cooperative
Box 44
Union, MO 63084
(314) 583-8936

Some of these organizations charge a registration fee, which the school district can pay if the student's IEP states that the student needs recorded textbooks. Time delays are common before students receive the cassettes, so it is important that teachers inform the individuals responsible for obtaining the cassettes (such as students, parents, guidance counselors, special educators) early, so they are available at the appropriate time in the school year (Vogel, 1988). Commercially recorded books are quite popular; in fact, many novels are available on cassette in local stores.

Previewing

An alternative to audiotapes, *previewing*, has been defined as "any method that provides an opportunity for a learner to read or listen to a selection or passage prior to instruction and/or testing" (Rose, 1984b, p. 544). The most popular previewing strategies employed by teachers include *oral previewing*, where students read the passage aloud prior to the reading session; *silent previewing*, where students read the passage silently before reading the selection; and *listening previewing*, in which students listen and follow along as an adult reads the passage aloud (Hansen & Eaton, 1978). Research indicates that oral previewing is superior to silent previewing in promoting the reading skills of students with disabilities (Rose, 1984a; Rose, 1984b; Rose & Sherry, 1984).

One type of listening previewing that has been effective with students with mild handicaps is *peer previewing* (Salend & Nowak, 1988). In this system, mainstreamed students listen and follow along while peer previewers read the selection. Before using peer previewing, teachers should train the previewers by modeling effective previewing and emphasizing that previewers should read clearly and at a rate that the listener can follow.

Computer Software

Some students with poor reading comprehension skills may benefit from using computer-presented texts, which allow teachers to incorporate effective strategies for reading comprehension into the reading passage via strategy prompts (Keene & Davey, 1987). Strategy prompts can be placed throughout the selection to remind students to engage in effective reading comprehension practices. Strategy prompts can remind students to review material, look ahead to preview material, ask questions about the material, repeat words silently to themselves, pay attention to underlined or highlighted information, and construct mental pictures (Keene & Davey, 1987).

Print materials, including textbooks, have been adapted into computer software (Burnette, 1987). These software programs introduce students to the textbook material by defining terms and reviewing prerequisite skills, demonstrating concepts, individualizing the lesson through help menus, self-pacing, sound effects, and pauses, involving them actively in the lesson through games and simulations using computer-generated graphics, providing corrective feedback, and assessing mastery of the content. In addition to providing printouts of student progress, these programs also include supplementary materials for teachers and strategies that teachers can use to modify each student's disk to meet his or her specific needs. Information on software programs modifying textbooks is available by contacting

D. C. Heath and Company
2700 N. Richardt Ave.
Indianapolis, IN 46219

Modifying Instruction for Specific Learners

Teachers also may find it necessary to adapt their instructional techniques and programs to address the unique needs of their mainstreamed students. For example, students with sensory impairments may need specific adaptations and help from computer technology to understand classroom content.

Adapting Instruction for Students with Sensory Impairments

Students with sensory impairments have unique needs that teachers must address. For students with visual impairments, teachers must emphasize presenting information orally; for students with hearing impairments, teachers must focus on visual stimuli to provide meaningful instruction. Suggestions for adapting instruction for students with visual and hearing impairments are presented in Figures 6.5 and 6.6, respectively.

FIGURE 6.5.   Suggestions for Adapting Instruction for Students with Visual Impairments.

1. Provide experiences that allow students with visual impairments to learn by doing and by using manipulatives.

2. Give test directions, assignments, notes, and important directions verbally.

3. Use *o'clock* directions to describe the location of an object on a flat surface, such as "Your book is at three o'clock and your pencil is at nine o'clock." Guide the student's hand to an object if it is near and in danger of being knocked over. Hand students objects by gently touching their hands with the object.

4. Avoid use of purple dittos and multicolored chalk; they are often difficult for students with visual impairments to see. Tracing over the letters, numerals, and pictorials with a felt-tip marker can facilitate the viewing of dittos. Placing a piece of yellow acetate over a page of print enhances the contrast and darkens the print.

5. Provide students with writing paper that has a dull, cream-colored finish, a rough texture, and wide-spaced green lines. Felt or nylon-tipped markers, black ball point pens, and thick pencils with soft lead are helpful for writing.

6. Make letters and numerals on the blackboard, flash cards, handouts, and assignments larger. The distance between lines of print should be equivalent to the height of the tallest letter in the line.

7. Use tactile illustrations and graphics that avoid clutter and emphasize contrast. Students with visual impairments will find it difficult to read print surrounded by small pictures and print superimposed over pictures.

8. Provide additional time to complete assignments and tests. Be aware that students may suffer from visual fatigue during activities that require continuous use of visual skills. Minimized visual fatigue by reducing the number and length of activities that require visual concentration.

9. Use and allow students to use typewriters with large, clear type when preparing written assignments.

10. Record assignments or present information on an audiocassette.

11. Teach manuscript writing first; it helps some partially sighted students to differentiate between letters and words that look similar. Students also may benefit from having a larger space in which to write.

12. Allow the student to look directly into the overhead projector from behind it while the transparency is projected on the wall or screen.

13. Phrase questions and comments directed to visually impaired students by using their names.

14. Identify yourself by name or voice when walking up to a visually impaired student. Don't leave a room without telling the student that you are leaving.

15. Give directions to specific destinations within the classroom or school by using statements that are nonvisual. Directions for going left and right should be in relation to the student's body rather than yours.

FIGURE 6.5. *(continued)*

16. Initially assign the student a buddy to facilitate the student's movement through the school. When the student becomes proficient in traveling around the school, ask the student to perform errands and class jobs. A peer also can read directions and materials, describe events in the classroom, take notes, and assist the student during fire drills and other emergencies.

17. Be aware that with some individuals with visual impairments, particularly those born blind, their facial expressions may not accurately indicate their feelings. The way they hold their hands and fingers may give a better indication of their feelings.

18. Provide audible warning signals accompanied by simultaneous visual signals to alert the visually impaired students to dangerous situations, such as fire drills.

19. Use cues to help students develop proper posture.

20. Obtain specialized materials by contacting

The American Printing House for the Blind
1839 Frankfort Avenue
Louisville, KY 40206

American Foundation for the Blind
15 West 16th Street
New York, NY 10011

Division for the Blind and Physically Handicapped
Library of Congress
1291 Taylor Street
Washington, D.C. 20542

Association for the Education of the Visually Handicapped
919 Walnut Street
Philadelphia, PA 19107

National Association for the Visually Handicapped
3201 Balboa Street
San Francisco, CA 94121

Adapting Instruction for Students with Written Language Problems

Many teachers require students to respond and demonstrate mastery of specific content by producing a written product. However, while many mainstreamed students may master the content of the assignment, their writing difficulties can interfere with their performance. In addition to allowing students to respond in other means (orally, via audiocassette,

FIGURE 6.6.   Suggestions for Adapting Instruction for Students with Hearing Impairments.

1. Use an overhead projector to present material; it simultaneously allows the student to view a visual presentation of the material and the teacher's lips.
2. Assign a peer to take notes using carbon paper for the hearing-impaired student and to point to speakers during a group discussion. A peer also can ensure that the student is following along in the correct place when the class is working on an assignment.
3. Speak clearly in a normal tone of voice and at a moderate pace.
4. Use visual signals to gain the student's attention.
5. Ask questions to check understanding of orally presented directions and content.
6. Rephrase content or questions to make it more understandable to hearing-impaired students.
7. Supplement information presented orally with visual aids.
8. Give test directions, assignments, and lecture outlines in writing.
9. Cue the student visually to indicate that someone is talking over the intercom. Make sure that someone explains the intercom message to students with hearing impairments.
10. Provide the student with outlines, assignments, vocabulary lists, and the like before introducing new material. Encourage the student's parents to review these materials with their child.
11. Remember to present all spelling and vocabulary words in sentences; many words presented in isolation look alike to lip-readers.
12. Establish a visual signal to alert students to dangerous situations.
13. Shine a light on the speaker's face when the room is darkened for films or slides. Providing the student with the script of a record or a filmstrip can help the student follow along.
14. Try to limit the movement and unnecessary gestures when speaking to students with hearing impairments.
15. Repeat and summarize main points of orally presented information.
16. Provide written models to aid hearing-impaired students in checking the accuracy of their assignments.
17. Teach the student to look up difficult-to-pronounce words in the dictionary.
18. Use an interpreter to help deaf students coordinate the visual and auditory messages associated with the class presentation. Waldron, Diebold, & Rose (1985) suggest that the interpreter sit slightly in front of the student without blocking the view of the chalkboard or the teacher, focus the student's attention by pointing with one hand to the visuals as the teacher refers to them, and use the other hand to communicate the dialogue of the teacher or the other students.

or artistically), teachers can help students improve their written products by

- scheduling and audiotaping writing conferences with students to clarify and develop ideas, outline responses, and provide feedback;
- encouraging students to use the dictionary and the thesaurus;
- providing checkpoints during the process to monitor students' work;
- allowing students to redo assignments for an improved grade by responding to teacher comments;
- giving separate grades for content, grammar, and spelling (Vogel, 1988).

Teachers can provide mainstreamed students with writing samples that depict the correct format, writing style, and organization of content as a model for their written product. The value of the model can be enhanced by reviewing it with students and marking it with comments that direct students to the qualities that contribute to making it an excellent product. For example, the use of a topic sentence can be emphasized by the teacher circling it and writing the comment, *This is a good topic sentence. It introduces the reader to the content in the paragraph.* Similarly, the inclusion of specific sections that make up the report (an hypothesis, procedures, results, or discussion) can be noted to ensure that the student's paper includes all the necessary sections.

In addition to providing students with a model, teachers also can facilitate writing by providing a checklist of items by which the paper will be evaluated. The checklist can then guide students in evaluating their papers before handing them to the teacher. A checklist also can be given to students to help them proofread their written products (Wood, 1988). A sample proofreading checklist is presented in Figure 6.7.

Peers also can assist with assignments that require written language proficiency. A peer proofreader can check a mainstreamed student's grammar, punctuation, and spelling. When only the content of an assignment is important, mainstreamed students can dictate their response to a peer scribe, who writes it with correct grammar, spelling, and punctuation (Perreira, Franke, and Woych, 1988).

Technology

With today's technology, teachers can modify instruction for mainstreamed students. They can implement computer applications to individualize instruction, modify the ways they present material, facilitate writing, and create adaptive devices for physically and sensory-impaired students.

FIGURE 6.7. Sample Proofreading Checklist.

Form

_____ 1. I have a title page with centered title, subject, class, name, and date.

_____ 2. I have a thesis statement telling the main idea of my paper.

_____ 3. I have an outline that structures the major topics and minor subheadings.

_____ 4. I have footnoted direct quotes and paraphrased material.

_____ 5. I have made a footnote page using correct form.

_____ 6. I have made a bibliography, using correct form, of all reference materials.

Grammar

_____ 1. I have begun all sentences with capital letters.

_____ 2. I have put a period at the end of each sentence and a question mark at the end of questions.

_____ 3. I have used other punctuation marks correctly.

_____ 4. I have checked words for misspelling.

_____ 5. I have reread sentences for correct noun-verb agreement and awkward phrasing.

_____ 6. I have checked all sentences to be sure each is complete.

Content

_____ 1. I have followed my outline.

_____ 2. I have covered each topic from my outline thoroughly and in order.

_____ 3. Each paragraph has a topic sentence.

_____ 4. The paper has an introduction.

_____ 5. The paper has a conclusion.

_____ 6. I have proven my thesis statement.

Source: J. W. Wood and K. W. Rush. _Academic Therapy,_ Vol. 23 (Austin, Texas: Pro-Ed), p. 244. Reprinted by permission of the publisher.

MICROCOMPUTERS.   Teachers can supplement and individualize instruction for mainstreamed students with microcomputers and computer-assisted instruction (Lerner, 1985). Microcomputers can

- individualize instruction by branching students to items that relate to their skill levels;
- allow students to work at their own pace;
- provide opportunities for automaticity through constant drill, repetition, and practice;
- offer multisensory presentations of content;
- deliver direct instruction to teach new concepts and multistep processes;
- facilitate problem-solving skills;
- provide immediate feedback and deliver reinforcement; and
- offer instruction in a nonthreatening manner (Ellis & Sabornie, 1988; Lerner, 1985; Taber, 1984).

McCormick and Haring (1986) identified five types of computer-assisted instruction:

1. Drill and practice programs, which seek to promote mastery of content through repetition and feedback;
2. Tutorials, which are designed to introduce new material, concepts, and skills;
3. Simulations, which teach problem solving within a realistic context;
4. Problem-solving programs, which provide students with a systematic approach to solving problems; and
5. Word processing programs, which help students write.

However, the effectiveness of using computer-assisted instruction is dependent on the software program used (Ellis & Sabornie, 1988). Many commercial software programs are open to criticism (LeBlanc, Hoko, Aangeenbrug, and Etzel, 1985; Carlson & Silverman, 1986); teachers should carefully evaluate the software programs they use with students. A form for evaluating software programs is presented in Figure 6.8.

WORD PROCESSING.   The computer's word processing capabilities can be especially helpful in assisting with students' writing. While the superiority of word processing over handwriting as a vehicle for improving the quality of student writing has not been clearly established (Vacc,

FIGURE 6.8.   Computer Software Evaluation Form.

Learner/Teacher Needs	YES	NO		YES	NO
1. Does the program reach the target population for which it was designed?	☐	☐	5. Is the content presented clearly?	☐	☐
2. Will the program motivate the students to learn?	☐	☐	6. Does the program use a multisensory approach?	☐	☐
3. Is the content relevant to the instructional needs of the students?	☐	☐	7. Are the use of graphics, sound, and color appropriate?	☐	☐
4. Will the material be effective with individual learning styles?	☐	☐	8. Does the program provide meaningful interaction for the students?	☐	☐
5. Does the format appeal to the students?	☐	☐	9. Does the program provide for user self-pacing?	☐	☐
6. Is the material relevant to daily living experiences?	☐	☐	10. Does the material require the purchase of accompanying printed material, or is it self-sufficient?	☐	☐
Instructional Integrity	YES	NO	11. Does the material prescribe to a number of sources or just the publisher's own materials?	☐	☐
1. Does the program state behavioral/instructional objectives?	☐	☐	12. Does the material provide direct instruction?	☐	☐
2. Is the teaching/learning mode identified (drill and practice, diagnosis, tutorial, simulation, inquiry, game, problem solving)?	☐	☐	13. Does the material provide immediate feedback?	☐	☐
3. Is the program organized and presented in a sequential manner and in appropriate developmental steps?	☐	☐	14. Does the material provide a variety of built-in reinforcements?	☐	☐
			15. Does the program offer supplementary materials or suggested activities for reinforcement?	☐	☐
4. Is the material presented at a concrete level and in a variety of ways?	☐	☐	16. Does the content use past learning or experiential background?	☐	☐

FIGURE 6.8. (*continued*)

	YES	NO
17. Is the material presented on a meaningful and appropriate language level?	☐	☐
18. Is the required reading presented at the students' level of functioning?	☐	☐
19. Does the program provide "flexible" branching so the content and reading levels meet the needs of individual student levels?	☐	☐
20. Does the program allow the student adequate time to complete learning segments?	☐	☐
21. Is the program designed to alert the teacher to a student who is experiencing difficulty with the content?	☐	☐
22. Does the material meet race, sex, and cultural distributions of the student population?	☐	☐

Technical Adequacy and Utility

	YES	NO
1. Are the teacher's instructions well organized, useful, and easy to understand?	☐	☐

	YES	NO
2. Does the material require extensive preparation or training on the teacher's part?	☐	☐
3. Is the material of high quality?	☐	☐
4. Is the material reusable?	☐	☐
5. Is the material durable for repeated and prolonged use?	☐	☐
6. Is the size of the print clear and well spaced?	☐	☐
7. Does the speed of presentation match individual learning styles?	☐	☐
8. Does the student need typing skills to use the program?	☐	☐
9. Is it "kid-proof?"	☐	☐
10. Can a student use the program without supervision?	☐	☐
11. Is a printout of student performance available, if desired?	☐	☐
12. Is the initial cost of this nonconsumable material reasonable?	☐	☐
13. Is the program packaged so that it can be easily and safely stored?	☐	☐
14. Can the program be used in a regular classroom, resource room, media center, agency, or institution?	☐	☐

FIGURE 6.8.   (*continued*)

	YES	NO		YES	NO
15. Does the publisher provide a policy for replacement of parts?	☐	☐	17. Has the publisher produced the program so that it is available for use on at least two different models of microcomputer hardware?	☐	☐
16. Does the publisher provide for preview and/or demonstration of the program?	☐	☐			

Source: A. Hannaford and E. Sloane. *Teaching Exceptional Children*, Vol. 14 (Reston, Virginia: Council for Exceptional Children, 1981), p. 56. Reprinted by permission of the publisher.

1987), word processing has several advantages for mainstreamed students, such as minimizing spelling errors; overcoming handwriting problems so that all students produce a neat, clean copy; providing students with a novel experience that motivates them to write; making text revision easy by allowing students to move text around and insert words; improving the variety of words used in writing via a thesaurus program; eliminating the tedious process of copying; and searching for word repetitions (Smith, 1988; Vogel, 1988). Although in their infancy, grammar-check programs are on the market and can be helpful (Kaufman, 1988).

Mainstreamed students may experience some difficulties using word processing. Degnan (1985) noted that students with memory problems may have difficulty remembering functions that require multiple keys or syntax codes. MacArthur and Shneiderman (1986) found that the keyboarding skills of students with learning disabilities were characterized by inefficient cursor movements and inappropriate use of deletion procedures. Students also experienced problems saving and loading files and using the return key to organize text on the monitor.

Therefore, to benefit from word processing, students may need to receive some instruction in keyboarding skills and the word processing program. Morocco and Neuman (1986) suggest that students strengthen keyboarding skills by exploring the computer every day for brief periods of time. Schloss and Sedlak (1986) note that word processing instruction should teach students to enter and save text, return to the menu, print copies, load disks, clear memory, center, justify, add, delete and move text, skip lines, and move the cursor. Teachers should monitor student progress, initially emphasizing accuracy and correct hand placement rather than speed.

It's a good idea to teach students typing skills via such typing programs as Typing Tutor and Typing Keys for Computer Ease (Kaufman, 1988). Ellis and Sabornie (1988) recommend that teachers select a typing program that accepts only correct responses, provides numerous practice activities, introduces skills gradually, and offers frequent reinforcement. Prompt cards that display the keys and their functions help students remember single and multiple key functions. Most word processing programs include tutorials to teach students to use the program. The program to train students to use word processing also should teach students how to load, save, and exit the program.

Talking word processors, which have synthesized speech output capabilities, may benefit mainstreamed students (MacArthur, 1988). Talking word processors allow students to detect syntax errors, receive feedback on spelling as they enter words, and hear their text read. Rosegrant (1986) found that students who use a talking word processor spend more time writing, revise more, and write longer pieces of a higher quality than when they use a nontalking word processor.

VIDEOCASSETTES/VIDEODISCS. Videocassette recorders can help teachers present information. The taping, stopping, and starting capabilities of videocassettes allow demonstrations, experiments, and other classroom activities to be taped, then played back for students to highlight or repeat key parts or information. Videocassettes also can facilitate modeling, and establish an environment that promotes simulation activities or group discussions. For example, a videocassette of a student giving an oral presentation is a model that mainstreamed students can take home to help them master the task; a video of excerpts from a television show on the homeless can stimulate a class discussion on the plight of the homeless.

Videos also can serve as an advance organizer (Walla, 1988). For example, the video *West Side Story* can introduce and orient students to the characters and plot of *Romeo and Juliet*. In addition, this use of videocassettes can motivate students.

Teachers can present content via videodiscs connected to a computer (Thorkildsen & Friedman, 1986). Kelly, Carnine, Gersten, & Grossen (1987) used videodisc-guided instruction to teach basic fractions concepts to a group of remedial and mildly handicapped students. Each disc can present up to 54,000 realistic graphic displays or motion pictures, which can be accessed in a random or continuous fashion. Thus, videodisc instruction allows students to interact with colorful and expressive visual displays and demonstrations, computer graphics, and sound effects that accurately depict concepts and material in a gradual and systematic way (Gersten, Carnine, & Woodward, 1987). Although videodisc programs have been developed, availability is limited by their high cost (Cartwright, Cartwright, & Ward, 1985).

Adaptive Devices

Computer technology has been used to develop many adaptive devices. These adaptive devices can promote the independence of students with physical, visual, and hearing impairment.

STUDENTS WITH PHYSICAL DISABILITIES.   Students who have difficulty making the motor responses necessary to produce intelligible

A closed circuit television system can be used to magnify print materials.
(Photo: Alan Carey/The Image Works)

speech may find microcomputers with speech synthesis capabilities invaluable. Computer programs and output devices are available that can transform word input into speech. For example, the student can input a phrase or press a key that activates the computer's speech capabilities. Because these students also may have problems inputting information into the computer in traditional ways, alternative methods have been developed (See Figure 6.9).

Computer technology has also helped increase the range of movements and thus the independence of individuals with physical disabilities. For example, Schneider, Schmeisser and Seamone (1981) developed a computer-controlled robotic arm which attaches to a worktable. The arm allows individuals with physical disabilities to perform a variety of motor activities, such as feeding themselves and using a typewriter. Personal robots can also perform manual functions for individuals with physical disabilities. Computerized systems in the home can be programmed to

FIGURE 6.9.   Alternative Methods of Inputting Information into Computers.

1. *Voice recognition.* The computer recognizes speech of user and converts speech into action.

2. *Key guard.* A device that modifies the traditional keyboard to change the size and spacing of the keys.

3. *Graphics tablet.* A small slate that may be covered by templates of words, pictures, numerals, and letters that are input when touched by a special stylus.

4. *Adapted switches.* The student activates the system by using an adapted switch, which is controlled by pressure or body movements. Switches can be activated by foot, head, cheek, chin, and eye movements.

5. *Scanning systems.* An array of letters, phrases, and numerals are displayed on the screen at a rate that is adjusted to the student's need. The student selects the message from the scanner by use of the keyboard or a switch.

6. *Touch screens/light pens.* Devices that allow the student to activate the computer by touching the screen.

7. *Joysticks.* The student controls the movement of the cursor by moving a stick in different directions.

8. *Mouthsticks.* A tool that is placed in the mouth and used to press buttons and activate switches.

9. *Headbands.* The student wears a headband that allows control of the computer through head or eye movements.

10. *Sip and puff systems.* The student sucks on a long command tube attached to a computer or wheelchair.

11. *Skateboard.* A block of wood on rollers attached to the student's arm is moved in different directions to control cursor movements.

perform such activities as turning on the oven, shutting lights, locking doors, and adjusting the sound of the television so that these individuals can live on their own.

STUDENTS WITH VISUAL IMPAIRMENTS.   Although expensive, several adaptive devices have been developed to help visually and print-impaired students acquire information from print materials. The Kurzweil Reading Machine is programmed to recognize letters, group letters into words, pronounce words, and provide the correct pronunciation to words in a sentence in several different languages. Here's how it works: printed materials are placed on the glass top of a machine that resembles a photocopy machine. Students then punch buttons on a panel. The functions allow them to pause the machine, rewind to hear one or more lines read again, move ahead to a particular section, find a specific word and spell it out, and control volume, pitch, and speech rate.

Another device that can help students read print materials is the Optacon. The student moves a camera-like device along a printed page, and the Optacon translates the image to a tactile Braille-type representation, or converts it to synthesized speech. The Talking Terminal also provides individuals with visual impairments with access to large bodies of information by reading aloud computerized material.

A variety of optical aids, including hand-held magnifiers, magnifiers mounted on a base, and magnifiers that are attached to eyeglass frames or are part of the lenses, magnify printed materials for individuals with visual impairments. One technology-oriented optical aid, the Apollo Laser Electronic Aid, employs a closed-circuit television system that enlarges visual stimuli aimed through its lens. It helps students obtain information presented on the blackboard by enlarging white lettering on a black background, or gain information from a book by enlarging black lettering on a white background. The visual acuity of students varies, so the Apollo Laser allows them to adjust the size of print on the screen.

Technology also has been developed to establish communication systems for individuals with visual impairments. The Tele-Braille facilitates communication for deaf and blind individuals by converting a message typed on a Braille keyboard into print on a video monitor, which is read by a sighted person. The sighted person then types a response, which is converted into a Braille display.

Electronic travel aids can increase the independent mobility skills of individuals with visual impairments. The Mowat Sensor is a hand-held electronic device that uses vibrations to alert students to barriers in their paths and indicate the distance to obstacles. Similarly, the Laser Cane emits three laser beams that provide auditory feedback to sensitize the user to objects, drop-offs, or low-hanging obstacles in the individual's path.

STUDENTS WITH HEARING IMPAIRMENTS.   Technology is having a profound impact on improving adaptive devices for individuals with hearing impairments. For some individuals whose hearing loss is related to cochlea damage, a small microprocessor can be implanted into the ear to improve hearing. The microprocessor translates auditory stimuli into electrical signals, which are transmitted to the nerve fibers that lead to the brain. Following the implant, individuals must be taught to convert the sounds into meaningful messages.

Systems that convert verbal statements to print can promote communication between hearing-impaired and hearing individuals. The teletypewriter can translate speech into a visual display on a screen for reading by hearing-impaired individuals. The dialogue that accompanies closed-caption television shows and films can be presented visually on the screen via a device connected to the television. The device receives closed-caption signals. Telecommunication Devices for the Deaf (TDD) allow individuals with hearing impairments to communicate using the telephone.

Modifying Classroom Behavior

Mainstreamed students may exhibit behaviors that interfere with their learning and socialization, and disrupt the learning environment (Alberto & Troutman, 1986). Therefore, teachers may need to employ a variety of behavior management strategies to increase appropriate behavior and decrease inappropriate behavior.

Antecedents-Behavior-Consequences (ABC) Analysis

The behavior management strategy a teacher selects often depends on the antecedents and consequences associated with the behavior. The *antecedents* refer to the events, stimuli, objects, actions, and activities that precede and trigger the behavior, while the *consequences* relate to the events, stimuli, objects, actions, and activities that follow and maintain the behavior. Teachers can identify the relevant antecedents and consequences related to the behavior by performing an *Antecedents-Behavior-Consequences (ABC) analysis*. Questions to guide teachers in performing an ABC analysis and a sample ABC analysis for out-of-seat behavior are presented in Figures 6.10 and 6.11, respectively.

The results of the ABC analysis can help the teacher plan an appropriate intervention. For example, based on the ABC analysis in Figure 6.11, the teacher could plan to modify the student's out-of-seat behav-

FIGURE 6.10.   ABC Analysis Questions.

In analyzing the antecedents, consider the following:
1. Is it related to the content area or the task?
2. Is it related to the way the material is presented?
3. Is it related to the way the student responds?
4. Is it related to the physical design of the classroom (e.g., location of the students' seats, proximity of the teacher, seating arrangements, furniture, and so on)?
5. Is it related to the behavior of the teacher? the teacher's aide?
6. Is it related to the behavior of peers?
7. Is it related to the time of day?
8. Is it related to events outside the classroom (e.g., seeing other students in the halls)?
9. What other events happen before the behavior?

In analyzing the consequences, consider the following:
1. How do the teacher and the teacher aide respond to the behavior?
2. How do the other students respond to the behavior?
3. What is the effect of the behavior on the classroom atmosphere?
4. What progress or lack of progress is made on the activity or the assigned task?
5. What has encouraged the behavior?
6. What has stopped the behavior?

FIGURE 6.11.   Sample ABC Analysis for Out-of-Seat Behavior.

Antecedents	Behavior	Consequences
What happens before?	*Out-of-seat*	*What happens after?*
1. Location of the student's work area		1. Attention from peers and/or adults
2. Placement of peers' work areas		2. Makes friends, antagonizes enemies
3. Type and difficulty level of in-seat activity		3. Avoids unpleasant in-seat activity
4. Proximity of adults		4. Performs pleasant out-of-seat activity
5. Duration of in-seat activity		5. Releases physical energy after sitting for a period of time
6. Prior activity required sitting		
7. Auditory stimuli in the room		
8. Peer out-of-seat behavior		
9. Availability of other activities		

ior by placing the student's work area near the teacher or the teacher's aide; adjusting the in-seat activity to the level of the student; allowing the student to work with a peer tutor or to serve as a peer tutor; limiting the distractions in the classroom; varying the activity so that the student is not required to sit for long periods of time; reprimanding peers out-of-seat and praising peers in-seat; praising the student for in-seat behavior; circulating around the room to monitor students; and allowing the student to perform a desired activity when the in-seat activity is completed.

Rules

An important aspect of behavior management is establishing, teaching, and enforcing classroom rules, which set the expectations for behavior in the classroom and provide a structure to guide interactions in the classroom (Herr, 1988). Since most important classroom behaviors can be addressed using five to seven rules, teachers should limit the number of rules to those that relate to classroom needs and help create an environment of academic and social growth. In devising rules, teachers should be aware of the schoolwide rules and procedures students are expected to follow. To determine if a rule is necessary, teachers can examine the rules in terms of the following questions:

- Is the rule necessary to prevent harm to others or their property?
- Does the rule promote the personal comfort of others?
- Does the rule facilitate learning?
- Does the rule encourage the development of friendships in the classroom?
- Does the rule prevent disrespectful behavior directed at peers, the teacher, the teacher's aide, or others in school?
- Is the rule logical and reasonable?
- How will the rule affect the class?

Once they have identified the areas that require rules, teachers can follow several guidelines to make their rules meaningful to students (Heward, Dardig, & Rossett, 1979). Rules should be phrased so that they are concise, simple, and easily understood. Each rule should include a behavioral expectation defined in observable terms; the consequences of following the rules should be explained. When exceptions to rules exist, discuss the exceptions in advance. Whenever possible, state rules in positive terms. For example, a rule for in-seat behavior can be stated as *Work at your desk* rather than *Don't get out of your seat*.

After rules are selected and phrased, they should be taught to students. Teachers can help students learn the rules by verbally describing and physically modeling the observable behaviors that make up the rules, and discussing the positive aspects of each (Everston, Emmer, Clements, Sanford, & Worsham, 1989). Teachers should initially review the rules frequently with the class. Students can be asked periodically to recite the rules or to practice a rule. Displaying the rules on a neat, colorful sign in a prominent location in the room can help students remember them. Some mainstreamed students and younger students may have difficulty reading, so pictorial representations of the rules can be beneficial. Foster an understanding of the rules and a commitment to following them by enforcing the rules immediately and consistently, and reminding students of the rules when a class member has complied with them.

Cues

Cues can be employed as part of a teacher's behavior management system. For example, color cues can indicate acceptable noise levels in the classroom. Red can alert students that the noise level is excessive, yellow can suggest that a moderate noise level is appropriate, and green can indicate that there are no restrictions on the noise level (D'Zamko & Hedges, 1985).

Positive Reinforcement

A widely used, highly effective method of maintaining and increasing compliance with rules is *positive reinforcement,* the contingent presentation of a stimulus after a behavior occurs that increases the rate of the behavior or the likelihood that the behavior will occur again. Stimuli and consequences that increase the probability of a behavior's occurrence are called *positive reinforcers.*

When using positive reinforcement, teachers should

- make sure that reinforcers are delivered after the desired behavior occurs;
- be consistent in the delivery of reinforcement;
- deliver reinforcement immediately after the behavior occurs, especially when the behavior is being learned;
- gradually decrease the frequency and immediacy of reinforcement;

- gradually increase the behavior that students must demonstrate to receive reinforcement; and
- use reinforcers desired by the students.

One form of positive reinforcement used by many classroom teachers is the *Premack Principle* (Premack, 1959). Teachers can apply the Premack Principle by making a desired activity available to students contingent on the completion of an undesired activity. For example, a student who works on an in-seat assignment for a period of time can earn an opportunity to work on the computer.

Classroom Lottery

A positive reinforcement system that can motivate students to demonstrate appropriate behavior is the *classroom lottery,* where teachers acknowledge appropriate behavior by writing a student's name on a lottery ticket and placing it in a jar located in full view of the class (George, 1975). At the end of the class or at various times during the day, a drawing is held to award prizes or free time to students whose names are picked out of the jar. Students can earn several tickets in the lottery to increase their probability of winning. The lottery system can be modified by having the class earn a group reward when the number of tickets accumulated exceeds a pre-established number specified by the teacher.

Selecting Reinforcers

A key component in the success of positive reinforcement and other behavior management systems is the reinforcer that students receive. Teachers can use a variety of edible, tangible, activity, social, and group reinforcers.

EDIBLE REINFORCERS. *Edible reinforcers* are the least sophisticated type because of their highly intrusive nature. Exercise caution in choosing this form of reinforcement; student satiation can easily result. However, edibles have the advantages of being highly desirable, available, and dispensable in varying quantities.

A variety of edible reinforcers can be used, including a pizza party, a fast food coupon, pretzels, potato chips, candy, and cookies. These reinforcers have limited nutritional value and can have negative effects (Shevin, 1982), so educators, parents, and health professionals should carefully evaluate them with respect to student health needs and allergic reactions. Consider more nutritious alternatives, such as raisins, peanuts, popcorn, fruit, sugar-free gum, or cereal.

TANGIBLE REINFORCERS.   *Tangible reinforcers,* such as pins, stickers, posters, magazines, bumper stickers, stencils, bookcovers, t-shirt transfers, records, comic books, and books that reflect the current fads or heroes and heroines, can be powerful reinforcers. Tangible reinforcers that are not directly related to current fads are also a good idea. These potential reinforcers include frisbees, mechanical pencils, magic markers, and bracelets. Identify additional tangible items by visiting a toy store, novelty shop, or the school store.

ACTIVITY REINFORCERS.   *Activity reinforcers,* which give students the privilege to perform a desired task or activity, are highly motivating alternatives to tangible and edible reinforcers. One flexible activity reinforcer is free time, which can be varied according to individual preference to provide students with the opportunity to work alone, with a peer, or with the teacher. Students can also take free time to go to the library, play a favorite game, sit in a location of their choice in the room, make an arts project, or perform a supervised activity in the gymnasium.

Class jobs also can motivate students. Initially, class jobs—handing out and collecting papers, cleaning the classroom, making class announcements, taking attendance, and running errands—can be assigned. As students demonstrate the skill to perform these jobs, they can be given jobs that require more responsibility, such as working in the main office, assisting the janitorial staff, running media, tutoring peers and younger students, and helping teachers grade papers.

Another activity that can be a reinforcing event is access to media and technology (Salend & Santora, 1985). The opportunity to listen to music on headphones, play an electronic keyboard, have extra time at the computer, watch a video on the VCR, and view a filmstrip can motivate behavior.

REINFORCEMENT SURVEYS.   Many behavior management systems fail because teachers do not identify appropriate, effective reinforcers. One way to help ensure that reinforcers are motivating is by soliciting student preferences through a *reinforcement survey* (Raschke, 1981; Swanson & Reinert, 1979). While a variety of these tools exist (Fox & Wise, 1981; Phillips, Fischer, & Singh, 1977), teachers can develop their own surveys to encompass the special characteristics of their students and classrooms.

Raschke (1981) identified three formats for reinforcement surveys: open-ended, multiple choice, and rank order. The *open-ended format* asks students to identify reinforcers by completing statements concerning their preferences (*If I could choose the game we will play the next time we go to recess, it would be_____*). The *multiple choice format* allows students to select one or more choices from a list of potential reinforcers (*If I had 15 minutes of free time in class, I'd like to (a) work on the computer; (b) play a game with a friend; (c) listen to music on the headphones*). For the *rank order format,* students are asked to grade their preferences from strong to weak through a numbering system. Excellent examples of all these formats are available (Raschke, 1981).

Teachers should consider several factors when developing reinforcement surveys. Phrase items using student language rather than professional jargon (*reward* rather than *reinforcer*) and reflect a range of reinforcement. In addition, examine the availability (*Will I be able to provide the reinforcer at the appropriate times?*), practicality (*Is the reinforcer consistent with the class and school rules?*) and cost (*Will the reinforcer prove too costly to maintain?*) of survey reinforcers. Finally, since mainstreamed students may have reading and/or writing difficulties, teachers may need to read items for students as well as record their responses.

Contingency Contracts

An agreement between students and teachers concerning the exchange of reinforcers is formalized by a *contingency contract,* a written agreement between two parties, usually teachers and students, that outlines the behaviors and consequences of a specific behavior management system. Homme (1970) suggests that contracts provide immediate and frequent reinforcement, be structured for success by initially calling for small changes in behavior, should be perceived as fair by both parties, and be stated in language the student can understand.

A contract should include

- a statement of the behavior(s) the student(s) are to increase or decrease in observable terms;
- a statement of the environmental conditions during which the strategy will be implemented;
- a listing of the type and amount of reinforcers that will be provided and who will provide them;
- a schedule of when the delivery of reinforcers will take place;
- a listing of the roles teachers and students can perform to increase the success of the system;
- a time frame for the length of the contract, including a date for renegotiation; and
- signatures of the students and teacher.

An outline of a sample contingency contract is presented in Figure 6.12.

FIGURE 6.12.   Sample Contingency Contract Outline.

This is a contract between _____ and

Student's or class's name

_____ . The contract starts on _____ and ends

Teacher's name

on _____. We will renegotiate it on _____.

During _____,

Environmental conditions (times, classes, activities)

I (we) agree to _____.

Behavior student(s) will demonstrate

If I (we) do, I (we) will _____.

Reinforcer to be delivered

The teacher will help by _____.

The class will help by _____.

_____

Teacher's Signature

_____

Student or Class Representative's Signature

_____

Date

Self-Management

A variety of student-management techniques have been successful in modifying a wide range of student behaviors (Alberto & Troutman, 1986). Student-managed interventions teach students strategies for monitoring and modifying their own behaviors. These strategies are described in Chapter 3.

Group-Oriented Behavior Management Strategies

One behavior management strategy that employs the group's influence to promote appropriate behavior and decrease disruptive behavior is the *group-oriented management system* (Salend, 1987), which has been used successfully in a variety of educational settings to modify a wide range of behaviors, including hyperactivity, calling out, obscene gestures and verbalizations, on-task behavior, and academic performance (Gresham & Gresham, 1982; Nelson, 1981).

Group systems have several advantages over traditional methods for managing classroom behavior: they foster group cohesiveness and cooperation among members; teach responsibility to the group and enlist the support of the class in solving classroom problems; allow the teacher to manage behavior effectively and efficiently; are adaptable to a variety of behaviors and classrooms; and offer peers a positive, practical, and acceptable method of dealing effectively with peer-related problems.

INTERDEPENDENT GROUP SYSTEMS.   When a behavior problem is common to several students in a class, an appropriate intervention strategy is an *interdependent group system* (Hayes, 1976; Litow & Pumroy, 1975), where the contingency is applied to the entire group and is dependent on the behavior of the group. Some potential reinforcers that can be highly motivating to groups of students are free time; a class trip; a party for the class; time to play a group game in class, the gymnasium, or the schoolyard; or a special privilege, such as renting a video. Because the success of an interdependent system depends on the behavior of the class, a single classmate can prevent the class from receiving reinforcement by repeatedly engaging in disruptive behavior. If one student continually prevents the group from achieving its goal, the offender can be removed from the group system and dealt with individually.

GROUP RESPONSE-COST SYSTEM.   One interdependent group system that has been effective is a *group response-cost system* mediated by free tokens (Salend & Allen, 1985; Salend & Kovalich, 1981). In this system, the group is given a predetermined number of tokens, which are placed in full view of the students and within easy access of the teacher (such as paper strips on an easel, checks or marks on the chalkboard). The teacher removes a token each time a class member displays an inappropriate behavior. If any tokens remain at the end of the time period, the agreed-upon reinforcement (for example, ten minutes of free time) is delivered to the whole group.

Initially, the number of tokens should guarantee success for the group. As the group is successful, the number of tokens given should gradually be decreased. Adaptations to this system include allowing students within the class to be responsible for removing the tokens (Salend & Lamb, 1986) and making each token worth a set amount. An illustration of the group-response cost system is presented in Figure 6.13.

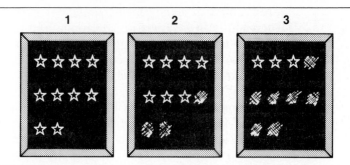

FIGURE 6.13.   Illustration of a Group-Response Cost System.
The class is given free tokens (Blackboard 1), which are removed when a disruptive behavior occurs (Blackboard 2). If any tokens remain at the end of the class, the group receives reinforcement (Blackboard 3).   Source: S. J. Salend, *Teaching Exceptional Children* (1987), Vol. 20, 54.

THE GOOD BEHAVIOR GAME.   The *Good Behavior Game* is an interdependent group system where class members are divided into two or more groups. Each inappropriate behavior is recorded by a slash on the blackboard. If a group's total slashes are fewer than the limit specified by the teacher, the group earns special privileges (Barrish, Saunders, & Wolf, 1969). Salend, Reynolds, and Coyle (1989) individualized the Good Behavior Game to account for the differences in the types and frequencies of inappropriate behaviors engaged in by class members.

An example of the Good Behavior Game is illustrated in Figure 6.14. The slashes indicate the number of inappropriate behaviors exhibited by each group. In this example, if the number of inappropriate behaviors allowed by the teacher was six, only Groups A and C would receive reinforcement. Group B's slashes exceed the criteria specified by the teacher, so they lost the opportunity to receive reinforcement.

THE GROUP TIME-OUT RIBBON.   The *group time-out ribbon* employs a ribbon, leather string, piece of rope, or piece of colored paper, which is placed where all students can see it and within easy access of the teacher. While the class is behaving appropriately, the ribbon remains in its location and the class earns tokens that can be exchanged for reinforcers (Salend & Gordon, 1987). As the class is successful, the time interval for receiving a token is increased.

If a group member exhibits an inappropriate behavior, the ribbon is removed for one to five minutes, during which time the group loses the

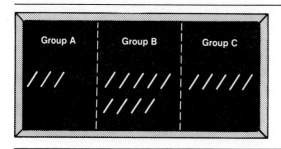

FIGURE 6.14.   Illustration of the Good Behavior Game.   Source: S.J. Salend, *Teaching Exceptional Children* (1987), Vol. 20, 54.

opportunity to earn tokens. After the group has behaved appropriately for a specified brief period of time, the ribbon is returned and the group can earn tokens again. However, if a group member engages in inappropriate behavior while the ribbon is removed, the time-out period is extended. As the class becomes acquainted with the system, students can assume responsibility for removing the ribbon and dispensing tokens. An example of a group time-out ribbon system is shown in Figure 6.15.

DEPENDENT GROUP SYSTEMS.   A *dependent group system* is used when an individual student's behavior problem is reinforced by his or her peers. In the dependent group system, the contingency is applied to the whole class, dependent on the behavior of one of the class' members (Litow & Pumroy, 1975; Nelson, 1981).

THE HERO METHOD.   The *hero-method* is a dependent group system where one student earns special privileges for the whole class by improv-

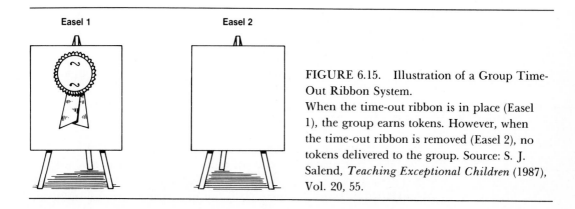

FIGURE 6.15.   Illustration of a Group Time-Out Ribbon System.
When the time-out ribbon is in place (Easel 1), the group earns tokens. However, when the time-out ribbon is removed (Easel 2), no tokens delivered to the group. Source: S. J. Salend, *Teaching Exceptional Children* (1987), Vol. 20, 55.

ing his or her behavior (Patterson, 1965). For example, a student can earn extra recess time for the class by reducing the number of call outs during teacher-directed instruction. However, because failure to earn the reward for the class can have a negative impact on the social status of the "hero," this system must be carefully structured to ensure success.

PEER-MEDIATED EXTINCTION.   A group-oriented system that has elements of interdependent and dependent systems is the *peer-mediated extinction system* (Salend & Meddaugh, 1985), in which the group is rewarded for not exhibiting behaviors that reinforce the inappropriate behavior of one of their peers. Salend and Meddaugh (1985) reduced a student's use of obscenities by providing his peers with free time if they did not laugh or respond to the student's obscenities. The teacher initiates the system by asking students to help the disruptive student improve his or her school behavior, and leading a discussion about the negative consequences of the student's behavior.

If the students consent to participate in the peer-mediated extinction, the teacher should inform them that the inappropriate behavior initially may get worse. Peer attention during the implementation of the extinction system can serve as intermittent reinforcement and interfere with the success of the system, so the teacher should monitor the group's adherence to the procedure.

PEER CONFRONTATION.   Another group-oriented management procedure that possesses characteristics of both interdependent and dependent systems is the *peer confrontation system* (Bellafiore & Salend, 1983). Whenever a behavior is deemed inappropriate, it and its consequences on others are verbally acknowledged by the group. The procedure can be initiated by the teacher or a class member by asking the class to respond to the following questions:

- "(Helena) seems to be having a problem. Who can tell (Helena) what the problem is?"
- "Can you tell (Helena) why that is a problem?"
- "Who can tell (Helena) what (she) needs to do to solve the problem?"

Making Transitions

Transitions from one period to the next and activities within a class period make up approximately 15 per cent of the school day (Rosenshine, 1980). These times can lead to disruptive behaviors that interfere with student learning (Jones & Jones, 1986). Teachers can minimize problems with transitions by incorporating several adaptations into the classsroom routine. At the beginning of the school day or class period, post and discuss a schedule of class events for that day. Pay particular attention to schedule modifications that deviate from the typical school day. Many mainstreamed students will be receiving the services of ancillary support personnel (speech and language therapists, guidance counselors) on different days of the week; these students should be alerted to the unique aspects of their schedules.

A particularly difficult part of transitions for mainstreamed students may be ending one activity and beginning another. Teachers can facilitate the students' ability to make this change by using a cue to signal students that they have five minutes left to complete their work, reviewing before the end of an activity several motivating aspects of the next activity, rewarding groups or individual students for making an orderly and smooth transition, and having materials necessary for the subsequent lesson prepared in advance (Jones & Jones, 1986).

Giving students specific directions about how to move to the next activity can be helpful in making transitions. For example, rather than telling students to *get ready for physical education class,* the teacher can provide them with specific directions, such as *finish working on your assignment, put all your materials neatly in your desk or bookbag, check to see that you have your sneakers and gym uniform, and line up quietly.*

Transitional activities also can make transitions smoother (Jones & Jones, 1986). When students come from a less structured, social activity like recess to a setting that requires quiet and attention, a transitional activity is important. For example, having students write in a journal one thing that was discussed in social studies class the day before can help prepare students for the day's lesson and facilitate transition from lunch time.

Modifying the Classroom Design

An important variable for teachers to consider in adapting instruction for mainstreamed students is classroom design, which should complement the teachers' teaching style and accommodate the students' unique learning needs. In planning their classroom's design, teachers should consider several variables: objects and areas in the room that cannot be altered easily (doors, windows, lights, outlets, cabinets, shelves, chalkboards, and bulletin boards), unique classroom and student needs and problems, and teaching style and educational philosophy (Hayes, 1986).

Teachers can tailor their classrooms to their teaching style by drawing a map of the classroom, including seating arrangements, centers, and furniture. Have a colleague observe a class session, noting the teacher's movement patterns on the map. Analyze the map to determine what parts of the existing classroom design are congruent with the teacher's style, and those aspects that need to be changed (Jones & Jones, 1986). The observer also should note student movement patterns and places where students work in groups. Adequate space to create aisles that facilitate movement throughout the classroom as well as sections of the room for group activities can be planned based on these identified teacher and student needs. Everston, Emmer, Clements, Sanford, and Worsham (1989) suggest that teachers can assess the effectiveness of their room arrangements by simulating the various movements they make during a typical day. Similarly, they note that the effect of the room on students can be determined by the teacher pretending to be a student and examining the visibility, movement patterns, and accessibility of materials from the student perspective.

Seating Arrangements

The seating arrangement of the classroom will depend on the type of instruction the teacher employs. Generally, students should be seated in areas that allow clear sight lines to instructional presentations and displays (Everston, Emmer, Clements, Sanford, & Worsham, 1989). When using small group, teacher-directed instruction, it is suggested that students be seated in a semi-circle arrangement facing the teacher (Carnine & Silbert, 1979). In a larger group, teacher-directed activity, such as lecturing, it is most conducive for learning if all students face the teacher, with their seats in rows, circular, or horseshoe arrangements. When the instructional format requires students to work in groups (role plays, simulations, or cooperative learning), teachers should have students arrange their desks in groups so that they face each other and can share information efficiently and quietly (Jones & Jones, 1986).

Because some students may perform better in different settings, it is recommended that for appropriate assignments, teachers allow students the chance to select the location in the room in which they can best complete their work (Hoover, 1986). For example, a mainstreamed student may feel more comfortable working on a seatwork assignment on a rug-covered floor than at a desk. To encourage academic performance and neatness, mainstreamed students who work in areas other than their desks should be given a clipboard or another hard surface on which to mount and secure their work (Jones & Jones, 1986). Teachers use a variety of instructional formats, so the design of their classrooms should allow flexibility in seating arrangements. Students should be taught how to move their desks into the appropriate layout.

Each student's desk should be of the correct size and be placed so that it ensures that the student can participate in all classroom activities

(Kerr & Nelson, 1983). Teachers should pay special attention to the seating location of their mainstreamed students. Teachers should seat their mainstreamed students nearby to facilitate those students' participation in discussions, on-task behavior, listening, and attending skills, as well as academic performance (Delefes & Jackson, 1972; Schwebel & Cherlin, 1972). It is easier for teachers to monitor student performance, deliver cues and nonverbal feedback, and assess understanding when students are sitting near them. Sitting students near the teacher also allows for proximity control and can make implementation of a behavior management system easier.

The space around students' desks should be large enough for teachers to have easy access to students in order to monitor performance and distribute papers. Space also should be provided so that students have a place to store their materials. When students' desks do not provide adequate storage, tote trays can supplement storage (Everston, Emmer, Clements, Sanford, & Worsham, 1989).

Teacher's Desk

An important factor in managing the classroom is the location of the teacher's desk, which should allow teachers to monitor behavior and progress and to move quickly if a situation warrants intervention. So teachers can monitor students, the teacher's desk should be placed in an area that gives a barrier-free view of the whole classroom. Remove any obstacles that prevent teachers from periodically scanning different parts of the room. Similarly, when working with students in other parts of the room, teachers should sit facing the other students in the class.

Instructional Materials

An important element of classroom design is the organization of the teacher's instructional materials. Paine, Radicchi, Rossellini, Deutchman, and Darch (1983) suggest that a materials area should be located in the front or center of the room and include room for storing extra pencils, papers, and other supplies students will need to complete classroom activities.

Employing a system for storing, organizing, and categorizing materials can make the classroom a more orderly and efficient place, and help teachers individualize instruction. Teachers can help organize their instructional materials in the classroom by keeping frequently used materials together in a location that is accessible to all adults and students, and labeling storage areas and materials so students can find them easily (Lund & Bos, 1981). Cohen and de Bettencourt (1988) offer teachers a five-step system for categorizing their instructional materials:

1. Create a file box of all classroom materials, with each card including the material's name, objectives, level of difficulty, and potential modifications.
2. Develop a code. Label each material by the type of activity. For example, * could indicate a software program; # can indicate a role play.
3. Assign each material a level of difficulty.
4. Color-code and place materials in separate locations by content areas.
5. Individualize assignments for students using the system.

Bulletin Boards and Walls

The inclusion of bulletin boards in the classroom design can help teachers create a pleasant, visually appealing environment that promotes learning and class pride. Hayes (1985) delineated four types of bulletin boards: decorative, motivational, instructional, and manipulative. *Decorative bulletin boards* make the room attractive and interesting, and often relate to a theme. *Motivational bulletin boards* encourage students by providing a place where teachers acknowledge student progress and publicly display students' work. *Instructional bulletin boards* or *teaching walls* (Cummins & Lombardi, 1989) often include an acquisition wall, which introduces new concepts and material, and a maintenance wall, which emphasizes review of previously learned concepts (Creekmore, 1987). *Manipulative bulletin boards* also promote skill mastery by using materials that students can manipulate to learn new skills.

Since it is the students' room as well as the teacher's, displays should be planned so that they are at the students' eye level. Whenever possible, students should be involved in decorating areas of the room. Mobiles, posters, pictures, and student artwork can make the walls and ceiling of the classroom colorful and attractive. For example, place a class collage that includes a contribution from each class member on a bulletin board.

When planning how to use wall space around the room, teachers also should include a space for displaying students' work. Such a space can help motivate students to produce exemplary products because seeing their work posted is a visible reminder of their success. Posting the daily assignment schedule and examples of products on a part of the bulletin board or wall can help students remember to perform all assigned tasks. Wall displays can include a clock and calendar large enough to be seen from all parts of the classroom, and a listing of class rules (Everston, Emmer, Clements, Sanford, & Worsham, 1989).

Specialized Areas

Teachers also may want to establish specialized areas of the room for specific functions. For example, an old couch or rocking chair can be placed in a quiet part of the room to offer students a place they can go to relax when the classroom pace is hectic, to process what they have just learned, to be alone, or to gain control of their behavior (Hayes, 1985). Similarly, a location of the room that is available to groups of students to read together or share time with a peer can be valuable in promoting socialization (Jones & Jones, 1986). High-traffic areas, such as learning centers, small group instruction areas, the teacher's desk, and the pencil sharpener area, should be free from congestion, separated from each other, easily accessible, and spacious (Everston, Emmer, Clements, Sanford, & Worsham, 1989).

Learning Centers

Learning centers can provide variety in the classroom and help teachers individualize instruction. They also can help students develop independent skills and learn to work in small groups.

Gearheart, et al. (1988) delineate four types of learning centers: skill centers, discovery/enrichment centers, listening centers, and creativity centers. *Skill centers* allow students to practice skills such as math facts, spelling words, alphabetizing, and defining vocabulary. *Discovery/enrichment centers* employ a variety of learning activities (science experiments, math applications) that require students to add to their knowledge base. A *listening center* is designed to offer students instruction or recreation through listening. Arts and crafts, music, creative writing, and poetry are often the focus of activities in a *creativity center*.

Teachers can establish centers by

- identifying students' academic levels, abilities, interests and needs;
- determining relevant objectives;
- offering students a variety of activities that allow them to explore new skills and practice previously learned skills;
- developing appropriate materials that students can use independently or in small groups;
- training students to work at learning centers;
- providing students with directions that are easily understood and guidelines on the use of the materials and accompanying media;

- explaining to the students appropriate times for using the center and the number of students that the center can accommodate at one time; and

- monitoring student progress and changing materials and activities as students master new skills.

Study Carrels

Some students may have difficulty screening out noise and visual distractions in the classroom. When these students are working on individualized assignments that require concentration, teachers might allow them to move to a quiet area of the room, away from the teacher's desk and other high-traffic, visually loaded areas. When it is necessary for students to work in a self-contained area, they should be continuously monitored. Consequently, the barriers around the area should be low enough to allow an unobstructed view of the students, and high enough to eliminate distractions. Although some educators advocate use of study carrels for students with attention problems (Hewett, 1967), teachers should be careful to avoid frequent use of study carrels because they may isolate or stigmatize the students that use them. Teachers can lessen the potential problems associated with study carrels by discussing how individuals learn and function best in different ways, allowing all students to use the study carrel, and using the study carrel for several purposes (such as relaxation areas or computer or media centers).

Classroom Design Modifications

Many mainstreamed students will require specific classroom design modifications in order to perform at their optimal levels. Guidelines for adapting regular classroom physical environments to address the needs of students with a variety of handicapping conditions are outlined below.

STUDENTS WITH HEARING IMPAIRMENTS.   Because students with hearing impairments have difficulty receiving auditory stimuli, classroom design adaptations for this group should promote their ability to gain information from teachers and interact with peers. The placement of hearing-impaired students' desks can affect their performance in the mainstreamed setting (Salend, 1983). To facilitate lip reading and the use of residual hearing, hearing-impaired students' desks should be in a central location, about two rows from the front, where these students can have visual access to the teacher's and other students' lips. Hearing and lip reading also can be fostered by having the student sit on a swivel chair on casters, giving easy movement and the ability to follow the flow of conversation. If students with hearing impairments have an obstructed view of the speaker's lips, they should be allowed to leave their seat to assume a position that will maximize their lip-reading skills. During lectures or other teacher-directed activities, the student should be seated near the teacher and to one side of the room, where he or she has a direct line of sight to the lips of peers and teachers. A semicircular seating arrangement can facilitate lip reading during small group instruction (Gearheart, Weishahn, and Gearheart, 1988).

Teachers also should consider lighting and noise levels in determining the location of their hearing-impaired students' work area (Salend, 1983). Light glaring into the hearing-impaired student's eyes can hinder lip reading; therefore, avoid locating the teacher or source of information in a poorly lighted area or where the light is behind the speaker. Noise can also interfere with the residual hearing abilities of students with hearing impairments. Internal noises, such as heating units, footsteps, furniture movements, and external noises, such as cars or construction outside the school, can be lessened by carpets on the floor and draperies on windows (Niemoeller, 1968) as well as putting hearing-impaired students in classrooms that are situated in quiet locations and away from noise centers (gymnasiums, cafeterias, and busy hallways and corridors) (D'Alonzo, D'Alonzo, & Mauser, 1979).

Students with hearing impairments can benefit from sitting next to an alert and competent peer. During verbal conversations, peers can help hearing-impaired students follow along by indicating changes in the speaker. A peer also can be assigned the role of alerting students when and what information is being conveyed on the intercom system. Peers also can be responsible for assisting students in reacting to fire drills. However, as students with hearing impairments make the adjustment to the regular classroom, the assistance they receive from peers should be faded out, if possible.

Teachers should exercise caution in using media with hearing-impaired students. The overhead projector allows teachers to present content visually and orally while standing in one place facing students, so it is a valuable instructional apparatus for students with hearing impairments. However, other media, such as audiocassette recorders, films, and filmstrips, can cause frustration (Salend, 1983). When using these types of media, teachers can reduce the potential frustration of hearing-impaired students by providing students with a script of the audio segments of the media, stopping periodically and explaining the content of the material, and illuminating the speaker's lips with a flashlight when the lights are dimmed.

STUDENTS WITH VISUAL IMPAIRMENTS.   Several classroom design adaptations can help students with visual impairments function successfully in mainstreamed settings. Because students with visual impairments should be encouraged to use their residual vision (Barraga, 1964), their work area should be glare free and well-lighted (Salend, 1983). Teachers can reduce problems associated with glare by using a gray-green chalkboard, placing translucent shades on windows (Wolf, 1967), installing furniture and equipment with matte finishes (Abend, 1974), and positioning desks so that the light comes over the shoulder of the student's nondominant hand (Salend, 1983). During teacher-directed activities, the teacher should be positioned so that the student is not looking directly into the light. To reduce the fatigue associated with bending over, desks should have adjustable tops.

The work area for students with visual impairments should offer the students an unobstructed and direct trail to the major parts of the room, including the teacher's desk, learning centers, storage areas, media, chalkboards, bookshelves, and waste baskets. When students with visual impairments are initially placed in the regular classroom setting, they should be shown how to move around the room and from their desks to the major classroom locations. Students can be taught to move around the classroom by using *trace trailing*, directing them to the routes between their desks and major classroom landmarks by having them touch the surfaces of objects on the path. Visual descriptions of the room and routes also can supplement trace trailing and help students develop a mental picture of the room. When the room is rearranged, teachers should again give these students time to adjust to the new arrangement.

Because of the unique needs of students with visual impairments, teachers should locate their work areas in a quiet area, away from potentially harmful objects. To enhance students' abilities to compensate for their visual impairment by increased attention to verbal information, students should be seated in an area conducive to listening. To prevent injuries, visually impaired students' desks should be located away from such potentially dangerous objects as hot radiators, half-open doors, and paper cutters. Masking tape markers on the floor can assist students with visual impairments in keeping their desks in the proper alignment.

Students with visual impairments may require cumbersome prosthetic devices and optical aids, such as large-print books, Braillers, and magnifiers, to benefit from instruction in the mainstream setting. Therefore, teachers should consider the placement and storage of these aids when designing their classrooms to accommodate these students. A music stand or drafting table can be placed adjacent to the students' work areas to lessen the problems related to the use of large-print books. When the devices students use are electrically powered, visually impaired students' desks should be positioned near electrical outlets. Teachers also should provide these students with a sufficient, convenient, safe space to store aids when they are not being used.

STUDENTS WITH PHYSICAL DISABILITIES. Students with physical disabilities who use wheelchairs or prostheses need several classroom design modifications (Salend, 1983). Wheelchair-bound students should be provided the space to maneuver in the classroom. Therefore, consider placing desks and classroom furniture in a configuration that allows aisles to accommodate crutches, canes, and adequate turning for wheelchair-bound students. Additionally, some wheelchair-bound students may need space in which to recline during the school day. Students with electrically charged wheelchairs should be seated near an electrical outlet.

The ability of wheelchair-bound students also will be affected by the types of floor coverings in the classroom (Salend, 1983). Floors should have a nonslip surface. Deep pile, shag, or sculptured rugs limit mobility, so floors should be covered with tightly looped, commercial-grade carpet, which is smooth enough to allow wheelchairs to move easily and strong enough to withstand frequent use. To keep the rug from fraying or rippling, tape it down from wall to wall without padding underneath it.

The type and size of furniture in the classroom can be a critical factor in meeting the needs of students with physical disabilities in the regular education setting. The height of the student's work area should be adjusted to accommodate wheelchairs or to allow a prosthesis to function properly (Gearheart, Weishahn, & Gearheart, 1988). Some students with cerebral palsy may require stand-up desks; students in wheelchairs may use desk tops or lap boards placed on the wheelchair (Gearheart, Weishahn, & Gearheart, 1988). Furniture that is rounded with padding on the edges and no protrusions is appropriate for students with physical disabilities (Abend, 1974). Work areas should be at least twenty-eight inches wide to allow students in wheelchairs to get close to them. Because the reach of wheelchair-bound students is restricted, work tables should not be wider than forty-two inches. For comfortable seating, chairs should be curvilinear, have seat heights at least sixteen inches above the ground, and be strong enough so that students can pull themselves up on and out of the chairs (Salend, 1983). Work areas of students with physical disabilities should include space for computers or other adaptive devices that they may need.

In addition to working at their desks, students with physical disabilities also will be required to work at the blackboard. Therefore, at least one blackboard in the classroom should be lowered to twenty-four inches from the floor. To assist students in working at the chalkboard, attach a sturdy vertical bar as a handrail (Wolf, 1967).

Glazzard (1980) identified several classroom adaptations that can assist students whose movements are limited. Assign buddies the role of bringing assignments and materials to the students' desks. Teachers should consider allowing these students to leave class early to get to their next class and avoid the rush in the hallway. Securing papers by taping them to the students' desks can help with writing. Similarly, connecting writing utensils to strings taped to students' desks can help students retrieve them when dropped. Desks with textured surfaces or with a barrier around the periphery of the student's desks also can help prevent papers, books, and writing utensils from falling (D'Zamko & Hedges, 1985; Gearheart, Weishahn, & Gearheart, 1988). Gearheart, et al. (1988) suggest that students with restricted arm movement can benefit by using paper holders, such as a clipboard attached to the work area or an unbleached muslin cloth sprayed with a nonskid liquid glued to the desk.

STUDENTS WITH SEIZURES.   Students who experience seizures will require few modifications in the mainstream setting, but the potential deleterious effects of a seizure can be minimized by carefully structuring the classroom physical environment (Salend, 1983). Teachers can help prevent students from hurting themselves during a seizure by staying composed and keeping the other students calm (it often helps to remind the class that the seizure is painless); avoiding attempting to restrain the student, placing fingers or objects in the student's mouth, or giving the student anything to eat or drink; helping the student be as comfortable as possible by helping him or her to lie down and loosening tight clothing; protecting the student by placing a soft cushioned object under his or her head; ensuring that the spaces around the student's work areas are large enough to thrash around in; and keeping the area surrounding the student's desk free of objects that could cause harm to students during seizures (Gearheart, Weishahn, & Gearheart, 1988; Salend, 1983). After the seizure, position the student's head to one side to allow discharge of saliva that may have built up in the mouth, contact the student's parents and other necessary school and medical personnel, and briefly discuss the seizure with the class, encouraging acceptance rather than fear or pity. Since seizures often result in students being fatigued, a rest area with a cot may be necessary. Materials that provide guidelines for helping teachers and peers learn about epilepsy and seizures are available from

Epilepsy Foundation of America
1828 L. St. N.W.
Washington, D.C. 20036

STUDENTS WITH BEHAVIOR DISORDERS.   An important factor to consider when designing the classroom for students who exhibit inappropriate behaviors is the location of their desks. In addition to seating students with behavior disorders near teachers, placing these students near positive peer models can help them learn appropriate classroom behaviors. To enhance their effectiveness, models should be praised periodically in the presence of students with behavior disorders. The praise can function as vicarious reinforcement and promote positive behaviors in behaviorally disordered students (Kazdin, 1979; Strain & Timm, 1974).

Teachers also should examine the movement patterns within the classroom when determining the work areas for students with behavior disorders (Salend, 1983). Avoid putting behaviorally disordered students' desks in parts of the room that have a lot of activity, such as learning centers, media, and pencil sharpeners. Since many students with behavior disorders may experience problems with staying on task, avoid sitting them near open doors and windows. Reith and Everston (1988) and Paine, et al. (1983) identified several classroom organization strategies that can be used to reduce off-task behavior:

- locating the teacher's desk near the front of the room and positioning it so that it faces the class;
- using borders and partitions to minimize distractions in the room;
- placing teaching stations and centers in corners of the room so that they can be more easily monitored;
- establishing activity centers for special projects;
- using bulletin boards to post scores and to showcase materials;
- establishing systematic routines for performing nonacademic tasks (attendance, lunch money); and
- organizing and arranging teacher and student materials before class begins.

Summary

When teachers make adaptations in their instructional programs, mainstreamed students can perform successfully in the regular classroom setting. Teachers can modify instruction for mainstreamed students by structuring oral presentations, textbooks, and homework assignments to help students gain information; giving clear directions; teaching concepts and skills using the elements of direct instruction, academic games, and cooperative learning arrangements; employing technology and adaptive devices; changing behavior via behavior management strategies; and designing classrooms to address the needs of mainstreamed students. In selecting appropriate modifications, consider the effectiveness of the strategy and its reasonableness from the perspective of the teacher.

References

Abend, A. C. (1974). Criteria for selecting school furniture and equipment for the disabled. *CEEP Journal, 12,* 4–7.

Adelman, H. S., & Taylor, L. (1983). Enhancing motivation for overcoming learning and behavior problems. *Journal of Learning Disabilities, 16,* 384–392.

Allen, V. L. (1976). *Children as teachers.* New York: Academic Press.

Alley, G., & Deshler, D. (1979). *Teaching the learning disabled adolescent: Strategies and methods.* Denver: Love.

Alberto, P. A., & Troutman, A. C. (1986). *Applied behavior analysis for teachers. 2nd ed.* Columbus, Ohio: Charles E. Merrill.

Anderson, L. M. (1984). The environment of instruction: The function of seatwork in a commercially developed curriculum. In G.G. Duffy, I. R. Roehler, & J. Mason (Eds.). *Comprehension instruction: Perspectives and suggestions* (pp. 93–103). New York: Longman.

Archer, A. L. (1988). Strategies for responding to information. *Teaching Exceptional Children, 20,* 55–57.

Aronson, E. (1978). *The jigsaw classroom.* Beverly Hills: Sage Publications.

Aronson, E., Blaney, N., Stephan, C., Sikes, J., & Snapp, M. (1978). *The jigsaw classroom.* Beverly Hills: Sage Publications.

Barraga, N. C. (1964). *Increased visual behavior in low vision children.* New York: American Foundation for the Blind.

Barrish, H. H., Saunders, M., & Wolf, M. M. (1969). Good behavior game: Effects on individual contingencies for group consequences on disruptive behavior in the classroom. *Journal of Applied Behavior Analysis, 2,* 119–124.

Beck, I. L. (1984). Developing comprehension: The impact of the directed reading lesson. In R. Anderson, J. Osburn, and R. Tierney (Eds.), *Learning to read in American schools: Basal readers and context texts.* (pp. 3–20). Hillsdale, N.J.: Lawrence Erlbaum Associates.

Beck, I. L., & McKeown, M. C. (1981). Developing questions that promote comprehension: The story map. *Language Arts, 58,* 913–918.

Beech, M. C. (1983). Simplifying text for mainstreamed students. *Journal of Learning Disabilities, 16,* 400–402.

Bellafiore, L., & Salend, S. J. (1983). Modifying inappropriate behaviors through a peer confrontation system. *Behavioral Disorders, 8,* 274–279.

Berliner, D. C., & Rosenshine, B. V. (1977). The acquisition of knowledge in the classroom. In R. C. Anderson, F. J. Spiro, & W. E. Montague (Eds.). *Schooling and the acquisition of knowledge* (pp. 375–396). Hillsdale, N.J.: Erlbaum.

Bos, C. S., & Vaughn, S. (1988). *Strategies for teaching students with learning and behavior problems.* Boston: Allyn & Bacon.

Brigance, A. H. (1980). *Brigance diagnostic inventory of essential skills.* N. Billerica, Mass.: Curriculum Associates.

Brigance, A. H. (1983). *Brigance diagnostic comprehensive inventory of basic skills.* N. Billerica, Mass.: Curriculum Associates.

Brophy, J. E. (1981). Teacher praise: A functional analysis. *Review of Educational Research, 5,* 301–318.

Brophy, J. E. (1982). Classroom organization and management. *Elementary School Journal, 83,* 254–285.

Brophy, J. E., & Everston, C. (1976). *Learning from teaching: A developmental perspective.* Boston: Allyn & Bacon.

Brown, J. (1988, March). *Preventing classroom failure: Small modifications make a big difference.* Paper presented at the meeting of the Council for Exceptional Children, Washington, D.C.

Burnette, J. M. (1987). *Adapting instructional materials for mainstreamed students.* Reston, Va.: Council for Exceptional Children.

Carlson, S. A., & Silverman, R. (1986). Microcomputers and computer-assisted instruction in special classrooms: Do we need the teacher? *Learning Disabilities Quarterly, 9,* 105–110.

Carman, R. A., & Adams, W. R. (1972). *Study skills: A student's guide for survival.* New York: John Wiley & Sons.

Carnine, D. W., & Silbert, J. (1979). *Direct instruction reading.* Columbus: Charles E. Merrill.

Cartwright, G. P., Cartwright, C. A., & Ward, M. E. (1985). *Educating special learners. (2nd Ed.).* Belmont, Calif.: Wadsworth.

Chilcoat, G. W. (1987). Teacher talk: Keep it clear. *Academic Therapy, 22,* 263–271.

Clary, L. M. (1986). Help for the homework hassle. *Academic Therapy, 22,* 57–60.

Cohen, S. B., & de Bettencourt, L. (1988). Teaching children to be independent learners: A step by step strategy. In E. L. Meyen, G. A. Vergason, & R. J. Whelan (Eds.), *Effective instructional strategies for exceptional children.* (pp. 319–334). Denver: Love.

Cohen, S. B., Perkins, V. L., & Newmark, S. (1985). Written feedback strategies used by special education teachers. *Teacher Education and Special Education, 8,* 183–187.

Connolly, A. J. (1988). *Keymath revised: A diagnostic inventory of essential mathematics.* Circle Pines, Minn.: American Guidance Services.

Coulter, F. (1980). *Secondary school network. Cooperative research report No. 7.* Perth, Australia: University of Western Australia Education Department and Perth Department of Education (ERIC Document Reproduction Service No. ED 209 200).

Cratty, B. J. (1971). *Active learning.* Englewood Cliffs, N.J.: Prentice Hall.

Creekmore, W. N. (1987). Effective use of classroom walls. *Academic Therapy, 22,* 341–348.

Cummins, G. J., & Lombardi, T. P. (1989). Bulletin board learning center makes spelling fun. *Teaching Exceptional Children, 21,* 33–35.

Dahl, P. R. (1979). An experimental program for teaching high speed word recognition and comprehension skills. In J. E. Button, T. C. Lovitt, & T. D. Rowland (Eds.), *Communications research in learning disabilities and mental retardation.* (pp. 633–655). Baltimore: University Park Press.

D'Alonzo, B. J., D'Alonzo, R. L., & Mauser, A. J. (1979). Developing resource rooms for the handicapped. *Teaching Exceptional Children, 11,* 91–96.

Degnan, S. C. (1985). Word processing for special education students: Worth the effort. *Technological Horizons in Education Journal. 12,* 80–82.

Delefes, P., & Jackson, B. (1972). Teacher-pupil interaction as a function of location in the classroom. *Psychology of the Schools, 9,* 119–123.

Deshler, D. D., & Graham, S. (1980). Tape recording educational materials for secondary handicapped students. *Teaching Exceptional Children, 12,* 52–54.

Deutsch-Smith, D. (1981). *Teaching the learning disabled.* Englewood Cliffs, N.J.: Prentice-Hall.

Devine, T. G. (1981). *Teaching study skills.* Boston: Allyn & Bacon.

Dishon, D., & O'Leary, P. W. (1985). *A guidebook for cooperative learning.* Holmes Beach, Fla.: Learning Publications.

D'Zamko, M. E., & Hedges, W. D. (1985). *Helping exceptional students succeed in the regular classroom.* West Nyack, N.Y.: Parker.

Ellis, E. S., & Sabornie, E. J. (1988). Effective instruction with microcomputers: Promises, practices, and preliminary findings. In E. L. Meyen, G. A. Vergason, & R. J. Whelan (Eds.), *Effective instructional strategies for exceptional children* (pp. 355–379). Denver: Love.

Englert, C. S. (1984). Measuring teacher effectiveness from the teacher's point of view. *Focus on Exceptional Children, 17* (2), 1–14.

Englert, C. S., & Thomas, C. C. (1982). Management of task involvement in special education classrooms. *Teacher Education and Special Education.* 5, 3–10.

Everston, C. M., & Emmer, E. T. (1982). Effective management in the beginning of the school year in junior high classes. *Journal of Educational Psychology, 74,* 485–498.

Everston, C. M., Emmer, E. T., & Brophy, J. E. (1980). Predictors of effective teaching in junior high mathematics classrooms. *Journal of Research in Mathematics Education, 11,* 167–178.

Everston, C. M., Emmer, E. T., Clements, B. S., Sanford, J. P., & Worsham, M. E. (1989). *Classroom management for elementary teachers (2nd ed.).* Englewood Cliffs, N.J.: Prentice-Hall.

Fox, R., & Wise, P. S. (1981). Infant and preschool reinforcement survey. *Psychology in the Schools, 18,* 92.

Fraenkel, J. R. (1973). *Helping students think and value: Strategies for teaching social studies.* Englewood Cliffs, N.J.: Prentice-Hall.

Gearheart, B. R., Weishahn, M. W., & Gearheart, C. J. (1988). *The exceptional student in the regular classroom (4th ed.).* Columbus: Charles E. Merrill.

George, P. (1975). *Better discipline: Theory and practice.* Gainesville: Florida Educational Research and Development Council.

George, P. (1986). Teaching handicapped children with attention problems: Teacher verbal strategies make the difference. *Teaching Exceptional Children, 18,* 172–175.

Gerber, M. A., & Kauffman, J. M. (1981). Peer tutoring in academic settings. In P.S. Strain (Ed.), *The utilization of classroom peers as behavior change agents* (pp. 155–187). New York: Plenum.

Gersten, R., Carnine, D., & Woodward, J. (1987). Direct instruction research: The third decade. *Remedial and Special Education, 8*(6), 48–56.

Gillespie, D. (1976). Processing questions: What they are and how to ask good ones. In M.L. Silberman, J.S. Allender, & J.M. Yanoff (Eds.), *Real Learning: A sourcebook for teachers* (pp. 235–238). Boston: Little, Brown and Company.

Gillet, P. (1986). Mainstreaming techniques for LD students. *Academic Therapy, 21,* 389–399.

Glazzard, P. (1980). Adaptations for mainstreaming. *Teaching Exceptional Children, 13,* 26–29.

Good, T. L., & Grouws, D. A. (1979). The Missouri mathematics effectiveness project. *Journal of Educational Psychology, 71,* 143–155.

Gresham, F. M., & Gresham, G. N. (1982). Interdependent, dependent and independent group contingencies for controlling disruptive behavior. *Journal of Special Education, 16,* 101–110.

Guerin, G., & Male, M. (March 1988). *Models of best teaching practices.* Paper presented at the meeting of the Council for Exceptional Children, Washington, D.C.

Hansen, C. L., & Eaton, M. D. (1978). Reading. In N. G. Haring, T. C. Lovitt, M. D. Eaton, & C. L. Hansen (Eds.), *The fourth R: Reading in the classroom* (pp. 41–92). Columbus: Charles E. Merrill.

Harris, A. J., & Sipay, E. R. (1985). *How to increase reading ability: A guide to developmental and remedial methods (8th ed.).* New York: Longman.

Hawkins, J. (1988). Antecedent pausing as a direct instruction tactic for adolescents with severe behavioral disorders. *Behavioral Disorders, 13,* 263–272.

Hayes, M. L. (1985). Materials for the resource room. *Academic Therapy, 20,* 289–297.

Hayes, M. L. (1986). Resource room: Space and concepts. *Academic Therapy, 21,* 453–464.

Hayes, L. A. (1976). The use of group contingencies for behavioral control: A review. *Psychological Bulletin, 83,* 628–648.

Herr, C. M. (1988). Strategies for gaining information. *Teaching Exceptional Children. 20,* 53–55.

Herr, D. E. (1988, March). Behavior management techniques effective for both the regular and special educator. Paper presented at the meeting of the Council for Exceptional Children, Washington, D.C.

Heward, W. L., Dardig, J. C., & Rossett, A. (1979). *Working with parents of exceptional children.* Columbus: Charles E. Merrill.

Hewett, F. M. (1967). Educational engineering with emotionally disturbed children. *Exceptional Children, 33,* 459–467.

Homme, L. (1970). *How to use contingency contracting in the classroom.* Champaign, Ill.: Research.

Hoover, J. J. (1986). *Teaching handicapped students study skills.* Lindale, Tex.: Lindale.

Hoover, K. H. (1976). *The professional teacher's handbook: A guide for improving instruction in today's middle and secondary schools.* Boston: Allyn & Bacon.

Hughes, C. A., Hendrickson, J. M., & Hudson, P. J. (1986). The pause procedure: Improving factual recall from lectures by low- and high-achieving middle school students. *International Journal of Instructional Media, 13,* 217–226.

Humphrey, J. H. (1969). Active games as a learning medium. *Academic Therapy, 5,* 15–24.

Humphrey, M. J., Hoffman, E., & Crosby, B. M. (1984). Mainstreaming LD students. *Academic Therapy, 19,* 321–327.

Hunter, M. (1981). Increasing your teaching effectiveness. Palo Alto: Learning Institute.

Jenkins, J. R., & Jenkins, L. M. (1981). *Cross-age and peer tutoring: Help for children with learning problems.* Reston, Va.: Council for Exceptional Children.

Johnson, D. W. (1988). *The power of positive interdependence.* Paper presented at conference on Designing the Future Together: Cooperative Learning, Team Building and Collaboration at Work, New Paltz, New York.

Johnson, D. W., & Johnson, R. T. (1986). Mainstreaming and cooperative learning strategies. *Exceptional Children, 52,* 553–561.

Johnson, D. W., & Johnson, R. (1975). *Learning together and alone.* Englewood Cliffs, N.J.: Prentice-Hall.

Johnson, D. W., Johnson, R., Holubec, E., & Roy, P. (1984). *Circles of learning.* Alexandria, Va.: The Association for Supervision and Curriculum Development.

Jones, V. F., & Jones, L. S. (1986). *Comprehensive classroom management: Creating positive learning environments.* Boston: Allyn & Bacon.

Kagan, S. (1985). *Cooperative learning: Resources for teachers.* Riverside: University of California Press.

Kaufman, T. (1988, April). *Computers, composition and the LD writer.* Paper presented at the conference on Writing Models and Programs for the Learning Disabled College Student, New Paltz, New York.

Kazdin, A. E. (1979). Vicarious reinforcement and punishment in operant programs for children. *Child Behavior Therapy, 1,* 13–26.

Kazdin, A. E. (1980). Acceptability of alternative treatments for deviant child behavior. *Journal of Applied Behavior Analysis, 13,* 259–297.

Keene, S., & Davey, B. (1987). Effects of computer-presented text on LD adolescents reading behaviors. *Learning Disability Quarterly, 10,* 283–290.

Keith, T. (1982). Time spent on homework and high school grades: A large-sample path analysis. *Journal of Educational Psychology, 74,* 248–253.

Kelly, B. W., Carnine, D., Gersten, R., & Grossen, B. (1987). The effectiveness of videodisc instruction in teaching fractions to learning handicapped and remedial high school students. *Journal of Special Education Technology, 8*(2), 5–17.

Kelly, B. W., & Holmes, J. (1979). The guided lecture procedure. *Journal of Reading, 22,* 602–604.

Kennedy, B. (1968). *Motivational effect of individual conferences and goal setting on performances and attitudes in arithmetic.* Madison: University of Wisconsin (ERIC Document Reproduction Service No. ED 032 113).

Kerr, M. M., & Nelson, C. M. (1983). *Strategies for managing behavior problems in the classroom.* Columbus: Charles E. Merrill.

Kulhavy, R. W. (1977). *Feedback in written instruction. Review of Educational Research, 47,* 211–232.

LeBlanc, J. M., Hoko, J. A., Aangeenbrug, M. H., & Etzel, B. C. (1985). Microcomputers and stimulus control: From the laboratory to the classroom. *Journal of Educational Technology, 7,* 23–30.

Lee, J. F., & Pruitt, K. W. (1979). Homework assignments: Classroom games or teaching tools? *The Clearing House, 53,* 31–37.

Lerner, J. (1985). *Children with learning disabilities: Theories, diagnosis, and teaching strategies (4th ed.).* Boston: Houghton Mifflin.

Lenz, B. K. (1983). Using advance organizers. *The Pointer, 27,* 11-13.

Litow, L., & Pumroy, D. K. (1975). A brief review of classroom group-oriented contingencies. *Journal of Applied Behavior Analysis, 8,* 341-347.

Lock, C. (1981). *Study skills.* West Lafayette, Ind.: Kappa Delta Pi.

Lovitt, T. C., Rudsit, J., Jenkins, J., Pious, C., & Benedetti, D. (1986). Adapting science materials for regular and learning disabled seventh graders. *Remedial and Special Education, 7*(1), 31-39.

Lovitt, T. C., & Smith, J. O. (1972). Effects of instructions on an individual's verbal behavior. *Exceptional Children, 38,* 685-693.

Lund, K. A., & Bos, C. S. (1981). Orchestrating the preschool classroom: The daily schedule. *Teaching Exceptional Children, 14,* 120-125.

MacArthur, C. A. (1988). The impact of computers on the writing process. *Exceptional Children, 54,* 536-542.

MacArthur, C. A., & Shneiderman, B. (1986). Learning disabled students' difficulties in learning to use a word processor: Implications for instruction and software evaluation. *Journal of Learning Disabilities, 19,* 248-253.

Madden, N., & Slavin, R. (1983). Mainstreaming students with mild handicaps: Academic and social outcomes. *Review of Educational Research, 53,* 519-659.

Manzo, A. (1975). Guided reading procedure. *Journal of Reading, 18,* 287-291.

Margolis, H., & McGettigan, J. (1988). Managing resistance to instructional modifications in mainstreamed environments. *Remedial and Special Education, 9*(4), 15-21.

Marino, J., Gould, S., & Haas, L. (1985). The effects of writing as a prereading activity on delayed recall of narrative text. *Elementary School Journal, 86,* 199-205.

Martens, B. K., Peterson, R. L., Witt, J. C., & Cirone, S. (1986). Teacher perceptions of school-based interventions. *Exceptional Children, 53,* 213-223.

Mastropieri, M. A., & Scruggs, T. E. (1987). *Effective instruction for special education.* San Diego: College-Hill.

Mercer, C. D., & Mercer, A. R., (1985). *Teaching students with learning problems.* Columbus: Charles E. Merrill.

Meunier, C., & Rule, B. (1967). Anxiety, confidence and conformity. *Journal of Personality, 35,* 498-504.

McCormick, L., & Haring, N. G. (1986). Technological applications for children with special needs. In L. McCormick and N. G. (Eds.), *Exceptional children and youth (4th ed.).* (pp. 42-69). Columbus: Charles E. Merrill.

Mims, R. M., & Gholson, B. (1977). Effects and type and amount of feedback upon hypothesis sampling systems among 7- and 8-year-old children. *Journal of Experimental Psychology, 24,* 358-371.

Morocco, C. C., & Neuman, S. B. (1986). Word processors and the acquisition of writing strategies. *Journal of Learning Disabilities, 19,* 243-247.

Nelson, C. M. (1981). Classroom management. In J. M. Kaufman & D. P. Hallahan (Eds.), *Handbook of special education* (pp. 663-687). Englewood Cliffs, N.J.: Prentice-Hall.

Niemoeller, A. F. (1968). Acoustical design of classrooms for the deaf. *American Annals of the Deaf, 113,* 1040-1045.

Page, E. (1958). Teacher comments and student performance. *Journal of Educational Psychology, 49,* 172-181.

Paine, S. C., Radicchi, J., Rossellini, L. C., Deutchman, L., & Darch, C. B. (1983). *Structuring your classrooms for academic success.* Champaign, Ill.: Research Press.

Palinscar, A., & Brown, A. L. (1983). *Reciprocal teaching of comprehension-monitoring activities. Technical Report No. 269.* Champaign, Ill.: Center for the Study of Reading, University of Illinois.

Patterson, G. R. (1965). An application of conditioning techniques to the control of a hyperactive child. In L. P. Ullman & L. Krasner (Eds.), *Case studies in behavior modification* (pp. 370-375). New York: Holt, Rinehart & Winston.

Pauk, W. (1984). *How to study in college.* Boston: Houghton Mifflin.

Perreira, D., Franke, S., & Woych, J. (1988). *Aiding the writing skills of learning disabled college students.* Paper presented at the conference on Writing Models and Programs for the Learning Disabled College Student, New Paltz, New York.

Phillips, D., Fischer, S. C., & Singh, R. (1977). A children's reinforcement survey schedule. *Journal of Behavior Therapy and Experimental Psychiatry, 8,* 131-134.

Premack, D. (1959). Toward empirical behavior laws. *Psychological Review, 66* (4), 219-233.

Raschke, D. (1981). Designing reinforcement surveys—Let the student choose the reward. *Teaching Exceptional Children, 14,* 92-96.

Regional Support and Technical Assistance Centers Coordination Office. (1976). *The game bag.* Raleigh, N.C.: Author.

Reith, H., & Everston, C. (1988). Variables related to the effective instruction of difficult-to-teach children. *Focus on Exceptional Children, 20* (5), 1-8.

Reynolds, C.J., & Salend, S. J. (in press). Using cooperative learning in special education teacher training programs. *Teacher Education and Special Education.*

Robinson, S. M., & Smith, D. D. (1981). Listening skills: Teaching learning disabled students to be better listeners. *Focus on Exceptional Children, 13,* 1-15.

Rose, T. L. (1984a). Effects of previewing on the oral reading of mainstreamed behaviorally disordered students. *Behavioral Disorders, 10,* 33-39.

Rose, T. L. (1984b). The effects of two prepractice procedures on oral reading. *Journal of Learning Disabilities, 17,* 544-548.

Rose, T. L., & Sherry, L. (1984). Relative effects of two previewing procedures on LD adolescents' oral reading performance. *Learning Disability Quarterly, 7,* 39-44.

Rosegrant, T. J. (1986, April). *It doesn't sound right: The role of speech output as a primary form of feedback for beginning text revision.* Paper presented at the annual meeting of the American Research Association, San Francisco.

Rosenshine, B. V. (1980). How time is spent in elementary classrooms. In C.

Denham & A. Lieberman (Eds.), *Time to learn* (pp. 107–126). Washington, D.C.: National Institute of Education.

Rosenshine, B. V. (1983). Teaching functions in instructional programs. *Elementary School Journal, 83,* 335–352.

Rosenshine, B. V. (1986). Synthesis of research on explicit teaching. *Educational Leadership, 43*(7), 60–69.

Robinson, S., & Smith, D. D. (1981). Listening skills: Teaching learning disabled students to be better listeners. *Focus on Exceptional Children, 13,* 1–15.

Rowe, M. (1974). Wait-time and rewards as instructional variables, their influence on language, logic, and fate control: Part one, wait-time. *Journal of Research in Science Teaching, 11,* 81–94.

Ruhl, K. L., Hughes, C. A., & Schloss, P. J. (1987). Using the pause procedure to enhance lecture recall. *Teacher Education and Special Education, 10*(1), 14–18.

Sadker, D., & Sadker, M. (1985). Is the o.k. classroom o.k.? *Phi Delta Kappan, 66,* 358–361.

Salend, S. J. (1979). Active academic games: The aim of the game is mainstreaming. *Teaching Exceptional Children, 12,* 3–6.

Salend, S. J. (1981). Cooperative games promote positive student interactions. *Teaching Exceptional Children, 13,* 76–80.

Salend, S. J. (1983). Classroom design adaptations for mainstreamed settings: Making the least restrictive environment less restrictive. *Journal for Special Educators, 20,* 51–57.

Salend, S. J. (1987). Group-oriented behavior management strategies. *Teaching Exceptional Children, 20,* 53–55.

Salend, S. J., & Allen, E. M. (1985). A comparison of self-managed response-cost systems on learning disabled children. *Journal of School Psychology, 23,* 59–67.

Salend, S. J., & Gordon, B. (1987). A group-oriented timeout ribbon procedure. *Behavioral Disorders, 12,* 131–137.

Salend, S. J., & Kovalich, B. (1981). A group response-cost system mediated by free tokens: An alternative to token reinforcement in the classroom. *American Journal of Mental Deficiency, 86,* 184–187.

Salend, S. J., & Lamb, E. M. (1986). The effectiveness of a group-managed interdependent contingency system. *Learning Disability Quarterly, 9,* 268–274.

Salend, S. J., & Meddaugh, D. (1985). Using a peer-mediated extinction procedure to decrease obscene language. *The Pointer, 30,* 8–11.

Salend, S. J., & Nowak, M. R. (1988). Effects of peer-previewing on LD students oral reading skills. *Learning Disability Quarterly, 11,* 47–54.

Salend, S. J., Reynolds, C. J., & Coyle, E. M. (1989). Individualizing the good behavior game across type and frequency of behavior with emotionally disturbed adolescents. *Behavior Modification, 13,* 108–126.

Salend, S. J., & Santora, D. (1985). Employing access to the computer as a reinforcer for secondary students. *Behavioral Disorders, 11,* 30–34.

Salend, S. J., & Schliff, J. (in press). An examination of the homework practices of teachers of students with learning disabilities. *Journal of Learning Disabilities.*

Salend, S. J., & Schliff, J. (1988). The many dimensions of homework. *Academic Therapy, 23,* (4), 397–403.

Salend, S. J., & Washin, B. (1988). The effects of team-assisted individualization on the academic, behavioral, and social skills of handicapped adjudicated youth. *Exceptional Children, 55,* 174–180.

Sanders, N. M. (1966). *Classroom questions: What kinds?* New York: Harper & Row.

Schloss, P. J. (1986). Sequential prompt instruction for mildly handicapped learners. *Teaching Exceptional Children, 18,* 181–184.

Schloss, P. J., & Sedlak, R. A. (1986). *Instructional methods for students with learning and behavior problems.* Boston: Allyn & Bacon.

Schneider, W., Schmeisser, G., & Seamone, W. (1981). A computer-aided robotic arm/worktable system for high-level quadriplegics. *Computer, 14,* 41–47.

Schniedewind, N., & Davidson, E. (1987). *Cooperative learning: Cooperative lives.* Dubuque: Wm. C. Brown.

Schniedewind, N., & Salend, S. J. (1987). Cooperative learning works. *Teaching Exceptional Children, 19,* 22–25.

Schwebel, A., & Cherlin, D. (1972). Physical and social distancing in teacher-pupil relationships. *Journal of Educational Psychology, 63,* 543–550.

Sharan, S. (1980). Cooperative learning in teams: Recent methods and effects on achievement, attitudes, and ethnic relations. *Review of Educational Research, 50,* 241–272.

Shields, J. M., & Heron, T. E. (1989). Teaching organizational skills to students with learning disabilities. *Teaching Exceptional Children, 21,* 8–13.

Slavin, R. E. (1980). *Using student team learning.* Baltimore: Johns Hopkins University.

Slavin, R. E., Madden, N. A., & Leavey, M. (1984). Effects of cooperative learning and individualized instruction on mainstreamed students. *Exceptional Children, 50,* 434–443.

Slavin, R. E., Sharan, S., Kagan, S., Hertz-Lazarowitz, R., Webb, C. W., & Schmuck, R. (1985). *Learning to cooperate, cooperating to learn.* New York: Plenum.

Smith, G., & Smith, D. (1985). A mainstreaming program that really works. *Journal of Learning Disabilities, 18,* 369–372.

Smith, J. B. (1988). Connecting WP and LD: Students write! *The Forum, 14* (3), 12–15.

Smith, L., & Land, M. (1981). Low-inference verbal behaviors related to teacher clarity. *Journal of Classroom Interaction, 17,* 37–42.

Spargo, E. (1977). *The now student: Reading and study skills.* Jamestown, R.I.: Jamestown.

Spekman, N. J., & Roth, F. P. (1984). Intervention strategies for learning disabled children with oral communication disorders. *Learning Disability Quarterly, 7,* 7–18.

Stainback, W., Stainback, S., Courtnage, L., & Jaben, T. (1985). Facilitating mainstreaming by modifying the mainstream. *Exceptional Children, 52,* 144–152.

Stevens, K. B., & Schuster, J. W. (1988). Time delay: Systematic instruction for academic tasks. *Remedial and Special Education, 9*(5), 16–21.

Stevens, R., & Rosenshine, B. V. (1981). Advances in research on teaching. *Exceptional Education Quarterly, 2,* 1–9.

Strain, P. S., & Timm, M. A. (1974). An experimental analysis of social interaction between a behaviorally disordered preschool child and her classroom peers. *Journal of Applied Behavior Analysis, 7,* 583–590.

Swanson, H. L., & Reinert, H. R. (1979). *Teaching strategies for children in conflict.* St. Louis: C.V. Mosby.

Taber, F. M. (1984). The microcomputer—Its applicability to special education. In E. L. Meyen, G. A. Vergason, & R. J. Whelan (Eds.). *Promising practices for exceptional children: Curriculum implications.* Denver: Love Publishing.

Terranova, L. (1984). Instructor's terrific timesaver tips. In S. Fenner (Ed.) *Readings in student teaching and special education.* (p. 21). Guilford, Conn.: Special Learning Corp.

Thorkildsen, R. J., & Friedman, S. G. (1986). Interactive videodisc: Instructional design of a beginning reading program. *Learning Disability Quarterly, 9,* 111–117.

Tierney, R. J., & Cunningham, J. W. (1984). Research on teaching reading comprehension. In P. D. Pearson (Ed.), *Handbook of reading research* (pp. 609–655). New York: Longman.

Turner, T. (1984). The joy of homework. *Tennessee Education, 14,* 25–33.

Vacc, N. N. (1987). Word processor versus handwriting: A comparative study of writing samples produced by mildly mentally handicapped students. *Exceptional Children, 54,* 156–165.

Vogel, S. (1988). *Characteristics of LD college writers.* Paper presented at the conference on Writing Models and Programs for the Learning Disabled College Student, New Paltz, New York.

Waldron, M. B., Diebold, T. J., & Rose, S. (1985). Hearing-impaired students in regular classrooms: A cognitive model for educational services. *Exceptional Children, 52,* 39–43.

Walla, D. (1988, April). *A secondary modified program in English/Language Arts.* A paper presented at the conference on Writing Models and Programs for the Learning Disabled College Student, New Paltz, New York.

Wallace, G., Cohen, S. B., & Polloway, E. A. (1987). *Language arts: Teaching exceptional students.* Austin, Tex.: Pro-Ed.

Wallace, G., & Kauffman, J. M. (1986). *Teaching students with learning and behavior problems.* Columbus: Charles E. Merrill.

Wang, M., & Birch, J. (1984). Effective special education in regular class. *Exceptional Children, 50,* 391–399.

Wilson, J. J. (1981). Notetaking: A necessary support for hearing-impaired students. *Teaching Exceptional Children, 14,* 38–40.

Wolf, J. M. (1967). Physical facilities guidelines for handicapped children: Fitting facilities to the child, Part III. *School Management, 11,* 40–54.

Wong, B. Y. I., Wong, R., & LeMare, I. (1982). The effects of knowledge of criterion task on comprehension and recall in normally achieving and learning disabled children. *Journal of Educational Research, 76,* 119-126.

Wood, B. J. (1976). *Children and communication.* Englewood Cliffs, N.J.: Prentice-Hall.

Wood, J. W. (1988, March). *Adapting instruction for the mildly handicapped student: A national perspective.* Paper presented at the meeting of the Council for Exceptional Children, Washington, D.C.

Wood, J. W., & Rosbe, M. (1985). Adapting the classroom lecture for the main-streamed student in the secondary schools. *The Clearing House, 58,* 354-358.

Wood, J. W., & Wooley, J. A. (1986). Adapting textbooks. *The Clearing House, 59,* 332-335.

Zentall, S. S., & Kruczek, T. (1988). The attraction of color for active attention-problem children. *Exceptional Children, 54,* 357-362.

CHAPTER 7

Content-Area

Thurs. 6:00
Fri. ✓
Sat. ✓
Sun. ✓
Mon. —

$60
×5
$300.

(Alan Carey/The Image Works)

A variety of strategies for adapting classroom instruction to enhance learning, motivation, and social development span academic disciplines (see Chapter 6). However, teachers may find they must make other adaptations unique to a specific content area to promote learning in mainstreamed students. This chapter offers guidelines for teaching reading, math, science, social studies, writing, spelling, and handwriting, and presents strategies for adapting instruction to meet the needs of mainstreamed students in specific content areas.

Reading

In addition to adapting textbooks (see Chapter 6) and teaching text comprehension strategies (Chapter 3), teachers may need to help mainstreamed students develop word recognition skills. *Word recognition,* the ability to establish the relationship between the printed word and its correct pronunciation, is an important component of reading comprehension (Harris & Sipay, 1985).

Selecting an Appropriate Reading Approach

Teachers can choose from among a variety of approaches to teach students word recognition skills. Most reading programs are based on a particular philosophy for teaching reading; therefore, they differ in their instructional approach. Teachers should select a reading approach appropriate to the student's learning needs and characteristics. There are few guidelines for matching a student with a specific reading approach (Zigmond, Vallecorsa, & Leinhardt, 1980); Harris and Sipay (1985) suggest that the student's rate of learning and emotional responsiveness be the guide for determining appropriate instructional procedures. Cohen and Plakson (1978) provide guidelines for examining the advantages and disadvantages of the different reading approaches with mainstreamed students.

PHONETIC APPROACHES. *Phonetic approaches* provide students with a strategy for decoding new, unknown words. Phonics instruction is geared toward teaching students the relationship between letters and sounds. It also teaches students to focus on the letter sequences and the sounds within words. The curriculum of most phonics programs includes auditory discrimination of sounds in words; letters and their corresponding sounds; initial and final consonant sounds; consonant blends and digraph sounds; vowel sounds; vowel digraphs, double vowels, and diphthong sounds; sounds of vowels followed by the letter *r;* sounds related to the final *e;* and the final *y* sound (Heilman, Blair, & Rupley, 1981).

Phonetics approaches are categorized as synthetic or analytic. The *synthetic approach* develops phonetic skills by teaching students the specific symbol to sound (grapheme to phoneme) correspondence rules. Once students learn the sound and symbol rules, they are taught to synthesize the sounds into words through blending. When using this approach, teachers

1. Introduce letters and their names to students.
2. Instruct students in the corresponding sounds associated with each letter.
3. Provide students with opportunities to develop automaticity in grapheme-phoneme relationships.
4. Teach students how to blend sounds into words.
5. Offer activities that allow students to apply their skills to unknown words. (Vaca, Vaca, & Gove, 1987).

In an *analytic approach* to phonics instruction, grapheme-phoneme correspondence is taught by showing students how to analyze words. These word analysis skills help students develop an understanding that letters within words sound alike and are written in the same way (Vaca, Vaca, & Gove, 1987). When using the analytic approach, teachers

1. Present students with a list of words that share a common phonic element.
2. Question students concerning the similarities and differences in the look and sound of the words.
3. Help students determine the common phonetic patterns in the words.
4. Have students state the rule concerning the phonetic pattern. (Vaca, Vaca, & Gove, 1987).

An alternative analytic method uses a *linguistic approach* to teach reading. Based on the work of Fries (1963) and Bloomfield and Barnhart (1961), students learn to read and spell word families that share the same phonetic patterns. Through repeated presentations of these word families, students learn the rules of sound and symbol correspondence. For example, introduce the *-at* family as a group, using such words as *bat, cat, fat, hat, rat,* and *sat.* In a linguistic approach, blending is not taught; little emphasis is placed on meaning and comprehension during the early stages of reading.

Phonetic approaches may present some problems for mainstreamed students (Cohen & Plakson, 1978). Students taught using these phonetic approaches tend: not to guess words that do not follow phonetic rules, to read more regular words than irregular words; and to pronounce words based on graphic and phonetic cues rather than semantic and syntactical cues (Barr, 1975; Dank, 1977). Students may have difficulty differentiating words that do not follow phonetic patterns and have difficulty isolating and blending sounds, so teachers may need to supplement phonics instruction with other approaches. For example, Lewandowski (1979) found that only 41 per cent of high-utility words followed phonetically regular patterns.

WHOLE WORD APPROACHES.   *Whole word approaches* help students make the link between whole words and their oral counterparts. In the whole word approach, meaning also is emphasized. New words are taught within sentences and passages, or in isolation. Teachers can modify whole word approaches for mainstreamed students by decreasing the number of words to be learned, offering spaced practice sessions, and providing opportunities for overlearning and delivering more frequent reinforcement (Harris & Sipay, 1985). Students taught through whole word methods tend to attempt to read unfamiliar words, use context cues rather than graphic cues, and substitute familiar words for new words (Biemiller, 1970).

Basal Readers. Perhaps the most widely used whole word approach is the *basal reader* (Britton, Lumpkin, & Britton, 1984). Students learn to recognize, read, and define the common words that constitute the basal reader. More complex words are introduced gradually as students progress through the series.

Basal readers cover a wide range of reading levels, usually from readiness kindergarten materials to eighth grade, allowing students to work at different levels within the regular classroom (Vaca, Vaca & Gove, 1987). Students progress throughout the series to develop reading proficiency (Heilman, Blair, & Rupley, 1981). Each level may have several books that correspond to specific skills within the skill sequence on which the series is based. The skill sequence usually follows a continuum of reading readiness, word identification, vocabulary, comprehension, and study skills. As students develop their skills, phonics and word analysis skills are taught to increase word recognition skills.

The content of the series is controlled so that vocabulary and new skills are introduced in a gradual, logical sequence. Teachers guide groups of students through a story, using a *directed reading activity,* which comprises three components (Harris & Sipay, 1985). During the preparation stage, the teacher stimulates the students' interest and presents new words and concepts from the selection. Next, the students read the selection silently after participating in a discussion about the story title and the accompanying pictures. When the silent reading is completed, the group discusses the story; then each member takes a turn reading the story aloud. Students then practice skills and words introduced in the story through some type of follow-up activity.

In addition to the readers, basal reader programs also include criterion-referenced tests to assess mastery; alternative follow-up activities such as comprehension questions, workbooks, ditto masters, and games; media, such as films, videocassettes, filmstrips, and audiocassettes; a teacher's manual to guide and train educators in the use of the program; and record-keeping forms to chart student progress.

WHOLE LANGUAGE APPROACH.   One methodology for promoting literacy that may be particularly appropriate for students from multi-cultural backgrounds is a *whole language approach*, which employs students' language and experiences in and outside of school to increase their reading and writing abilities (Goodman, 1986). The emphasis is on reading for meaning rather than learning decoding skills. Students are motivated to read and improve their reading by reading real, relevant, and functional materials. Rather than using basal readers or skill development programs, the reading materials in a whole language approach are fiction and nonfiction books and resources the students need to or want to read (Goodman, 1986). Thus, the whole language approach classroom is stocked with books of varying degrees of difficulty and content, such as novels, short stories, dictionaries, and encyclopedias.

The whole language curriculum is organized around themes and units that increase language and reading skills. Teachers and students develop and structure curricula to offer instructional experiences relating to real problems and ideas. Initially, students start to read meaningful, predictable whole words. Next, they use these familiar words to begin to learn new words and phrases. While learning to read, students also are learning to write. Students are encouraged to write about their experiences through composing letters, maintaining journals, making lists, labeling objects in the classroom, and keeping records.

In the whole language approach, the teacher's role is varied. They motivate students, structure the environment, evaluate progress, supply and expose students to relevant and meaningful materials and experiences, and involve students in the learning process. Teachers can begin to implement a whole language approach in the classroom by

- establishing a center for reading and writing;
- making students aware of the meaning of written language by sharing the meaning of written messages with them;

- taking and discussing school trips to expand their range of experiences;
- labeling objects and areas of the classroom;
- reading to students and encouraging them to follow along, and providing them with the opportunity to predict events within the story;
- role playing and discussing situations;
- having students make and read recipes;
- creating a bulletin board that includes work written and read by students;
- asking students to dictate stories to an adult and then reading them;
- having students read big book editions of popular books in unison; and
- encouraging students to follow along while listening to audiocassettes of books (Goodman, 1986).

LANGUAGE EXPERIENCE APPROACH.   Another strategy to promote reading skill that employs a program incorporating reading, listening, speaking, and writing is the *language experience approach,* a program based on the belief that what students think about, they can talk about; what students can say, they can write or have someone write for them; and what students can write, they can read (Vaca, Vaca, & Gove, 1987). Language experience approaches are highly individualized; they use the students' interests, hobbies, and experiences to compose their reading materials (Hall, 1981). The incorporation of students' experiences can maintain a high level of motivation and foster creativity.

Teachers provide students with guided and varied experiences and encourage students to share their thoughts, ideas, and feelings through artwork, speaking, and writing. Initially, students share their reactions and experiences by dictating stories to the teacher; these stories form the core of the reading program. Teachers guide the formation of the story, helping students make revisions and instructing them about grammar, punctuation, spelling, syntax, and vocabulary. As students develop a sufficient number of words they can recognize, easy books are introduced (Harris & Sipay, 1985). They also are encouraged to write and then read aloud their own stories, poems, and plays.

Remedial Reading Strategies

Because many mainstreamed students have difficulty reading, regular education teachers may have to supplement their reading programs with remedial reading strategies.

MULTISENSORY STRATEGIES. *Multisensory strategies* teach letters and words using combinations of visual, auditory, kinesthetic, and tactile modalities. Several multisensory strategies are available, including students writing the words in chalk, spelling the word after saying it, tracing three-dimensional letters with students' eyes shut, and teachers tracing letters on the students' backs (Blau & Blau, 1968; Witman & Riley, 1978).

FERNALD METHOD. A multisensory, whole word, language experience strategy that was developed for students with learning problems is the *Fernald method,* which involves four steps (Fernald, 1943). The step at which students begin depends upon their reading level.

Step 1   Tracing. The teacher presents a model of the word. Students simultaneously touch trace the model with a finger while stating aloud each syllable of the word. Students also are encouraged to visualize the word while tracing it, and write a story using the new word. Step 1 is continued until students can write the word from memory. At that time, the word is filed alphabetically in a word list.

Step 2   Writing without tracing. Rather than tracing new words, students attempt to write the word after viewing the model and visualizing it with eyes closed. The students' written products are compared with the model; mastered words are placed in the word list.

Step 3   Recognition in print. Students attempt to read and write the word after looking at it in print, hearing the teacher read it, and repeating it several times. Teachers provide books and encourage students to read them.

Step 4   Word analysis. Students attempt to read new words by comparing them to familiar words they previously mastered.

THE GILLINGHAM–STILLMAN STRATEGY. *The Gillingham–Stillman strategy* employs a multisensory synthetic phonics approach to teaching reading (Gillingham & Stillman, 1973). Initially, students are taught letter and sound symbol correspondence using a visual-auditory-kinesthetic methodology, whereby students view the letters, hear the sounds they make, link the letters to their sounds, and write the letters. Once ten letters (*a, b, f, h, i, j, k, m, p, t*) are mastered, blending of the sounds is taught. Blending is followed by story writing, syllabication, dictionary skills, and instruction in spelling rules. Slingerland (1976) and Traub (1982) have developed additional classroom activities based on this strategy.

PROGRAMMED READING MATERIALS. A highly structured approach to the teaching of reading involves *programmed materials,* which are designed to present information in small, discrete steps that follow a planned skill sequence. Each skill within the skill sequence is presented so that students have an opportunity to review, practice, overlearn, and apply the skill while receiving feedback. Errors are corrected before students can proceed to the next skill. Teachers follow the sequence of the presentation by adhering to the directions outlined in the manual.

NEUROLOGICAL IMPRESS METHOD. A listening remedial strategy that has been effective in promoting the word recognition and comprehension skills of poor readers is the *Neurological Impress Method* (Bos, 1982; Heckelman, 1969). In this method, the student and the teacher read aloud in unison for fifteen minutes each day. The student is positioned in front of the teacher so that the teacher's voice is directed into the student's ear. Initially, the teacher reads louder and faster than the student, with the student ignoring errors and focusing on keeping up with the teacher. Both the teacher and the student slide their fingers along as each word is read. As the student becomes more proficient in oral reading, he or she is encouraged to read louder and faster.

Teacher and Student Cuing Strategies

Cuing can help mainstreamed students read difficult or unfamiliar words. Cues can be divided into two types: teacher cues and student cues. *Teacher cues* are strategies initiated by the teacher to help a student make the correct response; *student cues* are strategies used by students to determine the correct response.

Salend (1980) identified three types of cues that are readily available to teachers for remediating reading errors: language cues, visual cues, and physical cues. Students can improve their reading by employing configuration and context cues.

LANGUAGE CUES. *Language cues* use the students' language skills as the base for triggering the correct response. For example, if a student had difficulty decoding the word *store,* a vocabulary cue such as *You go to buy things at a—* might elicit the correct response. Other language-oriented cues include rhyming (*it rhymes with door*), word associations (*Choo! Choo!* to cue the word *train*), analogies (*Light is to day, as dark is to—*) and antonyms (*It's the opposite of hot*).

VISUAL CUES. *Visual cues* can help students focus their attention on important stimuli within words. For example, attention to medial vowels can be fostered visually by color cues (for example, make the medial vowel a different color than the other letters), size cues (make the medial vowel enlarged while keeping the other letters are kept constant, such as *cAt*), or graphic cues (accentuate the medial vowel by underlining or circling it, as in c<u>a</u>t).

Visual cues can be valuable in remediating reversals. For example, difficulty discriminating *b* and *d* can be lessened by graphically cuing one of the letters. Similarly, a picture cue technique, where pictures depicting words appear above words that are difficult to read, is especially helpful in reading nouns and prepositions. For example, if a student typically read the word *saw* as *was,* a drawing of a saw above the word would help the student make this discrimination. Finally, visual cues, such as pointing to an object in the classroom or showing a numeral, can be used to prompt the reading of words that correspond, respectively, to objects in the classroom and number words.

PHYSICAL CUES.   *Physical cues* are most effective in communicating words or concepts that possess perceptually salient features. Cue these words by miming the distinct qualities or actions associated with them. For example, cue the word *safe* by assuming the position of a baseball umpire who has just declared a runner safe on a close play at home. In addition to pantomiming, teachers can use finger spelling instead of oral presentation as a cue to elicit a correct response.

CONFIGURATION CUES.   *Configuration cues* relate to the outline of the word, and can be useful when there are noticeable differences between words in terms of shape and length. While research on the effectiveness of configuration cues is inconclusive (Haber, Haber, & Furlin, 1983), it appears that they are most effective when used with context and other cuing strategies (Haber & Haber, 1981).

CONTEXT CUES.   The context in which the word is presented in a sentence or selection can provide useful cues to students in determining the pronunciation of unknown words. Potential *context cues* include syntactical, semantic, and pictorial features of the text. When using context cues, teachers should ensure that the syntactical and semantical structures of the sentence or passage are consistent with the students' skill level and background of experience (Duffelmeyer, 1982). To provide students with the necessary syntactical and semantical information, context cues are best suited for words that are embedded near the end or the middle of the sentence (Duffelmeyer, 1982).

SYNTACTICAL CUES.   *Syntactical cues* deal with the grammatical structures of the sentence in which the word is embedded. They are dependent on the students' knowledge of word order and the nature of words (Harris & Sipay, 1985). The syntactical structure of English dictates that only certain words can fit into a particular part of a sentence or statement. Thus, students can be taught to use parts of sentences to figure out difficult words.

꒱ SEMANTICAL CUES. *Semantical cues,* available by examining the meanings of sentences, can help students improve their word recognition skills. Students can be taught to use semantic cues by having them closely examine the sentence containing the unknown word, as well as the chapter or story plot in which the word appears. These cues are particularly appropriate when students are learning to read abstract words (Durkin, 1978).

↙PICTORIAL CUES.   Many reading passages contain illustrations or pictures that are designed to promote comprehension and facilitate student motivation. These *pictorial cues* also can help students recognize new words by establishing the context of the story (Arlin, Scott, & Webster, 1979; Denburg, 1976). To maximize the effects of illustrations on word recognition, the students' attention should be directed to the word and the illustration (Ceprano, 1981).

Error-Correction Techniques

When students make word recognition errors, teachers can use a variety of error correction techniques, including phonic analysis correction, word supply, and drill (Jenkins, Larson, & Fleisher, 1983). *Phonic analysis correction* involves encouraging the student to sound out the word that was read incorrectly (Rose, McEntyre, & Dowdy, 1982). In *word supply,* the teacher provides the student with the correct pronunciation of the word after the word has been misread (Jenkins, Larson, & Fleisher, 1983). The *drill correction* procedure involves simultaneously applying the word supply technique and writing each misread word on an index card; having the student attempt to read each of the words on the index cards after the selection has been read; separating the correct and incorrect readings of the words on the index cards into two piles; reviewing the incorrect word pile by providing the student with the correct word and having him or her repeat it two times; concluding the procedure when the student can read correctly all words recorded on the index cards for two consecutive trials (Jenkins, Larson, & Fleisher, 1983).

Mathematics

Math is another content area with which many mainstreamed students may experience problems (Bley & Thornton, 1981; Garnett, 1987). Mc-

Kinney and Feagans (1980) found that as many students with learning disabilities had deficits in mathematics as in reading. McLeod and Armstrong (1982) found that teachers or intermediate and secondary students with learning disabilities reported that 66 per cent of their students had problems with math, indicating that math difficulties may intensify as students age. In particular, mainstreamed students may need assistance in mastering basic math facts and solving word problems (Bley & Thornton, 1981).

Teaching Basic Math Facts

A major portion of the K–8 math curriculum is devoted to mastery of basic math facts—the areas of numbers and numeration, addition, subtraction, multiplication and division of whole numbers, time, measurement, money, percents, decimals, and fractions. Teachers can help mainstreamed students master this material by carefully planning and organizing instruction according to several principles:

Introduce new concepts through everyday situations to which students can relate. Many math skills are important for functioning in daily life (Johnson & Blalock, 1986). Relating new concepts to everyday situations can help motivate students to learn (Bley & Thornton, 1981). For example, introduce percentages and graphing through statistics from the school's sports teams; relate time concepts to a schedule of favorite television shows; and teach measurement skills by having students follow a recipe for baking a cake.

Teach key math terms. As with other content areas, math has its own terminology. Teachers can help mainstreamed students learn math by teaching them essential math terminology. Key math terminology can be listed in a math dictionary developed and maintained by the class (Bley & Thornton, 1981). The dictionary could contain definitions and examples of math terms, such as *sum, difference, quotients, proper fractions, mixed numbers,* and *reciprocals.* For example, a student having difficulty with the term *denominator* can locate its definition and view examples (*the denominator is the bottom part of a fraction that indicates the number of parts. In the fraction 5/6, the 6 is the denominator*). Lists of key math terminology that are important for math proficiency have been developed by O'Mara (1981), Cox and Wiebe (1984), and Swett (1978).

Use drawings and diagrams to illustrate new concepts and interrelationships. Supplement oral presentations of math instruction with illustrations. Drawings and diagrams of new concepts and interrelationships can help students master many skills; they gain a visual and concrete framework for understanding the foundations of the process as well as the steps necessary to perform the operation. Because material used to present mathematics is typically difficult to read (Schell, 1982), misunderstandings related to reading mathematical language can be minimized by using drawings and diagrams that depict difficult-to-understand content (Dunlap & McKnight, 1978).

When offering depictions of math concepts, use colored chalk or marking pens to highlight and delineate important points (Bley & Thornton, 1981). For example, when initially teaching carrying, illustrate the process by highlighting the number to be carried at the top of the next column:

$$
\begin{array}{r}
① \\
48 \\
+33 \\
\hline
81
\end{array}
$$

Cluster math facts to facilitate memory of them. Rather than teaching math facts in isolation, teach related math facts together (Thornton, Tucker, Dossey, & Bazik, 1983). For example, students should learn the cluster of multiplying by two together.

Use manipulatives and concrete teaching aids. The importance of using manipulatives and concrete teaching aids in teaching concepts of varying degrees of difficulty has been recognized (Herbert, 1985; Marzola, 1987). Manipulatives are particularly valuable in helping students with language difficulties acquire math concepts (Garnett, 1989). Parkham (1983) found that students who used manipulatives scored significantly higher on math achievement tests than their counterparts who did not use them. While manipulatives are most frequently used to teach readiness and first-grade math concepts (Suydam, 1986), they have been successful in teaching place value (Beattie & Scheer, 1982), fractions and decimals (Suydam, 1984), money and percentages (Sullivan, 1981), word problem-solving skills (Canny, 1984), probability (Bruni & Silverman, 1986), statistics (Alford, 1985; Bruni & Silverman, 1986), geometry (Clements & Battista, 1986), and algebra (Williams, 1986).

When using manipulatives to teach math concepts, teachers should follow several guidelines (Marzola, 1987). Initially, introduce the manipulatives by modeling their use (Trueblood, 1986) and verbally explaining the concepts illustrated (Garnett & Fleischner, 1987; Thornton & Wilmot, 1986). Next, students should have the opportunity to experiment with the manipulatives and verbalize their actions. Teachers can structure their students' use of the materials by asking questions that guide their experimentation (Thornton & Wilmot, 1986).

Marzola (1987) offered a list of commercially produced manipulatives for teaching a variety of concepts, including place value, computations, money, time, measurement, fractions, decimals, percent, and geometry. For example, the Stern Structural Arithmetic Program (Stern, 1965) employs blocks to teach K–3 arithmetic concepts, while colored Cuisennaire rods of varying lengths have been developed to provide an understanding of many underlying principles of mathematics (Davidson, 1969).

Non-commercially produced manipulatives include number lines, money, and fingers. Number lines can be used to teach a variety of math concepts (Mercer & Mercer, 1985). However, many students have difficulty using number lines; their use should follow experiences with other manipulatives, such as cubes, popsicle sticks, and chips (Thornton et al., 1983). Carefully introduce the number line and train students to use it by drawing a large number line on which students can walk.

Manipulatives are especially important in teaching money skills. When doing so, it is best to use real money (Bley & Thornton, 1981). However, if it is not feasible, make money substitutes as authentic as possible.

Another manipulative aid that students can employ is their fingers. While fingers are often used as an aid in counting, simple addition, and subtraction, fingers also can help teach basic multiplication facts of nine. Assign each of the student's fingers a consecutive number from one to ten. To multiply four times nine, bend the student's fourth finger. The number of fingers preceding the bent finger represents the number of tens (in this case, three; the number of fingers following the bent finger represents the ones (in this case, six). Thus, the answer is 36. Try it with other multiplications of nine.

— *Use a variety of activities to promote automaticity.* One goal of instruction in basic math facts is for students to respond quickly and accurately. Teachers should offer students a variety of activities that promote automaticity (Mastropieri & Scruggs, 1987; Thornton et al., 1983). Automaticity can be developed through use of student- or peer-directed flash cards (Mastropieri & Scruggs, 1987) and having students listen to math facts on a Language Master or an audiocassette (Lambie & Hutchens, 1986). Worksheets and homework also can help students develop automaticity.

In adapting these assignments for mainstreamed students, teachers should consider reducing the number of problems on the worksheet, increasing the time limit, providing adequate space to write out solutions, and following a standard format for worksheets (Bley & Thornton, 1981). Worksheets also can be adapted by folding them so that students work on one line at a time, cutting them into halves or fourths so that students complete a portion of the sheet before working on the next part of the assignment, allowing students to skip certain items, or assigning students to work only even- or odd-numbered problems (Lambie & Hutchens, 1986). As students develop proficiency in a specific skill, increase the number of problems and decrease the time limit. When worksheets have problems requiring different operations, teachers can heighten student awareness of the operation by cuing or highlighting each operation, or grouping problems according to the operational process (Fagan, Graves, & Tessier–Switlick, 1984).

Speed and accuracy in basic math facts also can be fostered by games (Mercer & Mercer, 1985) and computer software programs (Hedley, 1987). Descriptions of math games for teaching a variety of math concepts and skills are available (Bley & Thornton, 1981; Mercer & Mercer, 1985; Thornton et al., 1983). Hedley (1987) has compiled a list of computer software games, drill and practice sessions, simulations, and tutorials that are helpful in teaching basic skills, algebra, geometry, and solving word problems.

Offer prompt feedback. The teacher should confirm the correctness of students' responses. Teachers also should acknowledge and reinforce correct responses and alert students to incorrect responses. When incorrect responses are noted, offer corrective feedback based on an analysis of the students' errors. Ashlock (1986) and Enright (1983, 1986) identify common student error patterns and offer strategies that teachers can employ to correct these patterns.

Students also should be taught to estimate and check answers. When errors are noted, they should learn to locate and correct their errors. Teach students to evaluate their mastery of concepts by graphing their performance on computer programs, worksheets, and follow-up probes. A checking center equipped with answer keys, teacher's guides, supplementary materials, peer tutors, and recordings of correct responses can facilitate self-checking and minimize the demands on teacher time (Lambie & Hutchens, 1986).

Assess mastery over time. The maintenance of skills is important for mainstreamed students, so teachers should periodically conduct cumulative reviews and timed probes to assess mastery of previously learned skills (Thornton et al., 1983).

CUING STRATEGIES.   Cues can help mainstreamed students overcome errors in computation problems that are not related to mastery of basic facts. Accentuate attention to computational signs (+, −, ×, ÷) by color coding, bolding, and underlining. Foster attention to signs by listing the sign and its operation at the top of each worksheet (+ = add, 6 + 3 = 9), and teaching students to trace the sign prior to beginning the computation (Enright, 1987a).

Cues also can be used with students who have difficulty remembering the order in which to solve computation items. Arrows can be drawn to indicate the direction in which students should proceed when working on a computation item:

$$
\begin{array}{r}
\leftarrow \\
35 \\
-28 \\
\hline
\end{array}
$$

Cues such as green and red dots, go and stop signs, and answer boxes can alert students when to proceed or stop when working on a specific computation item.

Another type of cue—*boxing*, or placing boxes around items—can focus students' attention on specific problems within a group (Bley & Thornton, 1981). When boxing items, teachers should leave enough space within the box to do the necessary calculations to solve the item. As students increase their skills, they should be encouraged to assume the responsibility for boxing items.

Boxing also can aid students who have problems aligning their answers in the correct columns. A color-coded, smaller box or broken line can be drawn to delineate columns so that students record their answers in the appropriate column (Gloeckler & Simpson, 1988; Thornton et al., 1983). Problems with aligning answers also can be minimized by having students use centimeter graph paper, which structures the task so that only one digit can be written in each box (Bley & Thornton, 1981), or by turning lined paper horizontally (Gillet, 1986). Alleviate aligning problems by teaching students to estimate and check the reasonableness of their answers. Answers that deviate significantly from their estimate may indicate an alignment problem; students should check their work accordingly.

PROVIDING A MODEL.   Some algorithms, such as long division and multidigit multiplication, require students to perform a series of different operations in a set sequence in order to arrive at the correct answer. Although many mainstreamed students may understand the process and possess the ability to perform these operations, they may need a model to guide them initially through the sequence (Bley & Thornton, 1981). Worksheets can be coded so that they provide a correct model for computing the answer. The model should vary depending upon the skill level and needs of the students. Sample models are presented in Figure 7.1.

Charts can also be placed in the room to help students. Charts can depict basic computation facts, math terminology and symbols (*subtract = take away = −*) as well as the steps to follow in doing a specific type of computation problem, such as the steps in dividing fractions (Bley & Thornton, 1981). For example, a fraction strip chart presenting strips divided into halves, thirds, fourths, and so on can be posted to assist students in learning concepts associated with fractions. In addition to class charts, some students may benefit from keeping pocket-size charts of basic math computation facts at their work areas (Garnett, 1989) (see Figure 7.2). A cutout in the shape of a backward *L* can help mainstreamed students find answers, located where the vertical and horizontal rows meet (Garnett, 1989). As these students develop their skills, encourage them to cross out number facts on the chart that they have mastered (Garnett, 1989; Thornton et al., 1983).

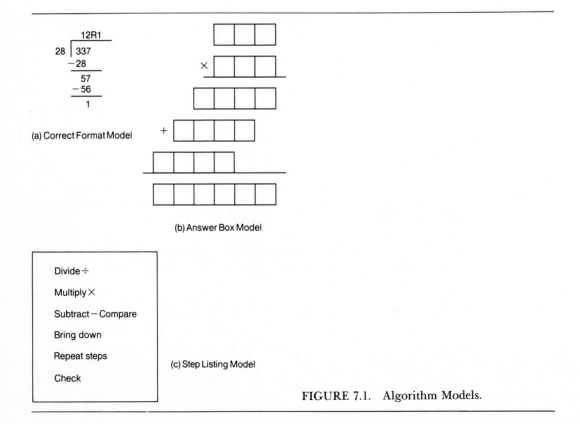

(a) Correct Format Model

(b) Answer Box Model

(c) Step Listing Model

FIGURE 7.1.   Algorithm Models.

FIGURE 7.2.   Chart of Basic Multiplication Facts.

X	0	1	2	3	4	5	6	7	8	9	10
0	0	0	0	0	0	0	0	0	0	0	0
1	0	1	2	3	4	5	6	7	8	9	10
2	0	2	4	6	8	10	12	14	16	18	20
3	0	3	6	9	12	15	18	21	24	27	30
4	0	4	8	12	16	20	24	28	32	36	40
5	0	5	10	15	20	25	30	35	40	45	50
6	0	6	12	18	24	30	36	42	48	54	60
7	0	7	14	21	28	35	42	49	56	63	70
8	0	8	16	24	32	40	48	56	64	72	80
9	0	9	18	27	36	45	54	63	72	81	90
10	0	10	20	30	40	50	60	70	80	90	100

Flip charts can offer students a model of the correct format and order in which they should approach a task (Bley & Thornton, 1981). The flip chart is sequenced so that each page represents a step the students need to perform to complete the task. A sample flip chart relating to the division of fractions appears in Figure 7.3.

A *demonstration plus model strategy* has been successful in helping students with learning problems develop computational skills (Rivera & Deutsch-Smith, 1988). The strategy involves these steps:

1. The teacher demonstrates the procedures for solving a type of computation problem while verbalizing the key words associated with each step.
2. The student views the teacher's example, and performs the steps in the computation while verbalizing the key words for each step.
3. The student completes additional problems, referring to the teacher's example, if necessary.

FIGURE 7.3.   Flip Chart for Dividing Fractions.

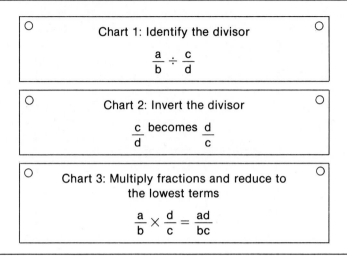

SELF-INSTRUCTION.   Because many mathematical operations follow a step-by-step approach, self-instruction can be a highly effective procedure for teaching math skills (Leon & Pepe, 1983). Verbalizing the steps and the signs while performing the computation has resulted in improved mathematical performance (Grimm, Bijou, & Parsons, 1973). The steps for self-instruction of math computation skills are

1. The teacher models the calculation by demonstrating and overtly stating the steps in the process.
2. The teacher and the student compute the answer and overtly state the steps in the process in unison.
3. The student computes the problem and overtly states the steps in the process while the teacher observes.
4. The student repeats step three, substituting internal self-instruction for overt verbalizations. If necessary, the teacher gives a cue sheet listing key steps to the student.
5. The student implements the self-instruction procedure internally with no cues and delivers self-reinforcement.

Teaching Word Problems

While many students have difficulty solving mathematics word problems (National Council of Teachers of Mathematics, 1980), mainstreamed students may experience particular difficulties in learning to solve them (Nuzum & Fleischner, 1983). Therefore, in addition to computation skills, mainstreamed students need to receive specialized instruction in approaching and solving word problems.

Such factors as syntactical complexity, amount of extraneous information, sequence, and number of ideas presented can affect students' ability to solve word problems (Bos & Vaughn, 1988; Harris & Sipay, 1985). Therefore, teachers should initially provide students with assistance in solving word problems. Teachers can foster their students' ability to understand word problems by simplifying the syntax used in the word problem (O'Mara, 1981), deleting extraneous information (Cohen & Stover, 1981), and reordering the presentation of information so that it is consistent with the order students should follow in solving the problem (O'Mara, 1981). Number cues written above parts of the word problem can also alert students to the steps they should follow in solving the problem. The National Council of Teachers of Mathematics (1980) suggests that teachers can facilitate the development of problem solving skills by

- using field trips, films, and presentations by others to provide students with experiences in a variety of situations;
- employing manipulatives and drawings to explain problems;
- de-emphasizing computations and emphasizing problem solving by having students write or state mathematical sentences without computing answers to them, substituting easier, smaller numbers to minimize the complexity of the calculations;
- having students identify needed and extraneous information by presenting them with problems that have too little or too much information, respectively;
- asking students to compose problems to be solved by their classmates;
- supplementing textbook problems with teacher-made problems;
- presenting problems orally; and
- offering numerous opportunities for practice.

In addition to teacher assistance, students should receive training in identifying the critical elements of word problems, eliminating irrelevant details and sequencing information in the order it will be needed. These skills can be developed by teaching students to underline the question and circle the given parts of the problem, providing practice items where students restate the specifics of the problem in their own words, and having students act out the problem (Enright, 1987a).

LEARNING STRATEGIES.   Several learning strategies have been developed to provide students with a step-by-step approach to solving word problems (Fleischner, Nuzum, & Marzola, 1987; Montague & Bos, 1986; Smith & Alley, 1981). In general, the steps in these strategies include

1. *Read the problem*. Initially, read the problem to determine the question and to find unknown words and clue words. Clue words are those words that indicate the correct operation to be used. For example, the words *altogether, both, together, in all, and, plus,* and *sum* suggest that the problem involves addition; words like *left, lost, spent,* and *remain* indicate that the correct operation is subtraction (Mastropieri & Scruggs, 1987; Mercer & Mercer, 1985). When students encounter unknown words, they should ask the teacher to pronounce and define them.

2. *Reread the problem*. Read the problem a second time so that the students can identify and paraphrase relevant information, which they should highlight by underlining, while deleting extraneous information and irrelevant facts. Focus their attention on determining what mathematical process and unit they should use to express the answer.

3. *Visualize the problem*. Students visualize the problem and draw a representation of the information given.

4. *Write the problem*. Students hypothesize and write the steps in solving the problem. If there is more than one step, each step is written in order with the appropriate sign.

5. *Estimate the answer*. Before solving the problem, students estimate the answer. The estimate provides a framework for determining the reasonableness of their response.

6. *Solve the problem*. The problem written in step four is solved by calculating each step in the process. Attention is given to the correctness of the calculations and the unit used to express the answer.

7. *Check the answer*. Students check their work and compare their answer to their estimate. Examine each step in terms of necessity, order, operation selected, and correctness of calculations.

CALCULATORS.   Calculators can help mainstreamed students develop their math skills (Garnett & Fleischner, 1987) by giving them the ability to learn, retrieve, and check computation facts as well as promote independence and speed in solving word problems (National Council of Teachers of Mathematics, 1976). Calculators can improve students' scores on tests and their attitudes toward math (Hembree, 1986).

Calculators are most useful when students have an understanding of the basic operations, so teachers should ensure that students have this understanding before introducing students to calculators. Before using the calculator as an alternative to memorizing basic math facts, provide students with the oppportunity to learn these facts over a period of time (Mastropieri & Scruggs, 1987). Once students are ready to use calculators, they should receive training in how to do so (Garnett & Fleischner, 1987). Some students who have difficulty computing with calculators, such as students who reverse numbers, may benefit from use of a "talking calculator," which states the names of the numerals entered and computed (Garnett & Fleischner, 1987). The Speech Plus Calculator developed by Telesensory Systems has a twenty-four-word vocabulary that can help students perform addition, subtraction, multiplication, division, square roots, and percentages by stating the function or name of each key that has been pressed.

Mathematics Remedial Programs

Several remedial math programs that can help mainstreamed students are on the market. These remedial programs can supplement the mathematics series that the school district is using. Examples of remedial math programs include Project Math (Cawley, Fitzmaurice, Sedlak, & Althaus, 1976), Computational Arithmetic Program (Smith & Lovitt,

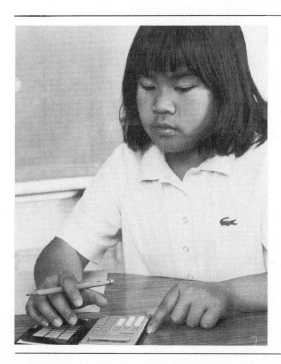

Calculators can assist students in learning, retrieving, and checking computation facts. (Photo: Stephen McBrady/PhotoEdit)

1982), Milliken Wordmath (Coffland & Baldwin, 1985), Corrective Mathematics Program (Engelmann & Carnine, 1982), Distar Arithmetic (Engelmann & Carnine, 1975, 1976), Enright S.O.L.V.E.: Action Problem Solving (Enright, 1987b), Developing Key Concepts for Solving Word Problems (Panchyshyn & Monroe, 1986) and Problem Solving Experiences in Mathematics (Charles, 1984).

Science and Social Studies

While the specific content in each area is different, science and social studies teaching methods share several commonalities. Both areas use an inquiry approach to teaching. Teachers of both science and social studies rely on lectures and textbooks to present material to students. Because mainstreamed students may experience some difficulty acquiring information through lectures and textbooks, teachers can adapt these learning formats for mainstreamed students via some key strategies.

The Key Word Method

An effective strategy for teaching science and social studies vocabulary is the *key word method* (Mastropieri, 1988; Viet, Scruggs, & Mastropieri, 1986) in areas such as single facts (Mastropieri, Scruggs, & Levin, 1985), multiple science facts (Scruggs, Mastropieri, Levin, & Gaffney, 1985), science word parts (Viet, Scruggs, & Mastropieri, 1986), and classification systems (Mastropieri, Scruggs, McLoone, & Levin, 1985). The key word method is a mnemonic device that promotes memory of the meanings of new vocabulary words by associating the new word with a word that sounds similar and an illustration that is easy to remember. Mastropieri (1988) outlined the steps in using the key word method:

1. *Recoding.* The new vocabulary word is recoded into a key word that sounds similar and is familiar to the student. The key word should be one that students can easily picture. For example, the key word for the word part *Sauro* might be *saw*.

2. *Relating.* An *interactive illustration*—a mental picture or drawing of the key word interacting with the definition of the vocabulary word— is created. A sentence describing the interaction also is formulated. For example, the definition of *Sauro* and the key word *saw* can be depicted using the sentence *A lizard is sawing*.

3. *Retrieving.* The definition is retrieved by students upon hearing the new vocabulary word by (a) thinking of the keyword; (b) creating

the interactive illustration and/or its corresponding sentence; and (c) stating the definition.

Definitions of key science and social studies terminology also can be taught by providing students with a list of definitions and asking them to write the correct word, giving students the word and having them write the definition, or matching the word with its definition from lists of words and definitions (Lovitt, Rudsit, Jenkins, Pious, & Benedetti, 1985).

Advance and Post-Organizers

Teachers can enhance students' ability to gain information from lectures and textbooks by using *advance and post-organizers* (Darch & Gersten, 1986), written or oral statements and illustrations that offer students a framework for determining and understanding the essential information in a learning activity (Lenz, 1983). To facilitate the effectiveness of advance organizers, teachers should encourage students to use them (Lenz, Alley, & Schumaker, 1987). For example, when assigning a reading selection in a science textbook, the teacher could focus students' reading via an advance organizer such as, *Read pages sixty-five to sixty-eight on mirrors, and find out how a mirror works. Pay careful attention to such terms as plane mirror, virtual image, parabolic mirror, principal axis, principal focus, and focal length.* Similarly, a class-developed outline that summarizes the main points of a presentation on the geography of California could be a post-organizer. Several types of advance and post-organizers are described below.

STRUCTURED OVERVIEWS.   An advance organizer teachers can use to present science and social studies content is a *structured overview,* also called *graphic organizers,* which identify and present key terms in science and social studies before presenting them in class lectures and textbooks (Vaca, Vaca, & Gove, 1987). A structured overview is a visual illustration of the key terms that comprise concepts and their interrelationships. Barron, cited in Vaca, Vaca, and Gove (1987), has developed a model for constructing structured overviews for students:

1. Analyze the curriculum area or textbook to identify key concepts and terms.
2. Arrange the concepts and terms based on their interrelationships.
3. Include additional terms that are important for students to know.
4. Assess the overview for completeness and organization.

5. Introduce the overview to the students.

6. Include additional information relevant to the overview.

CONCEPT TEACHING ROUTINES.   Many science and social studies concepts can be taught to students using a concept teaching routine, which Bulgren, Schumaker, and Deshler (1988) found improved performance on teacher-made tests, *Tests of Concept Acquisition,* and in note taking when used to teach new concepts. In the concept teaching routine, teachers present new concepts to students via a concept diagram that presents the relevant characteristics of the concept. A sample concept diagram is presented in Figure 7.4. Teachers use the concept teaching routine to introduce students to the concept diagram by offering an advance organizer; soliciting from students a list of key words related to the concept, which are recorded on the board; explaining the symbols in the diagram; stating the name of the concept; giving the definition of the concept; discussing the "always," "sometimes," and "never" characteristics of the concept, respectively; reviewing an example and then a nonexample of the concept; relating the examples and nonexamples to each of the characteristics; examining examples and nonexamples to determine if they are members of the concept subset; and presenting a post-organizer. Each step in the process is recorded by completing a blank concept diagram that has been presented on the blackboard or an overhead transparency. Students and teachers can also use the concept diagram to review for tests.

✳ ANTICIPATION GUIDES.   Teachers also can orient students to new science and social studies content by using *anticipation guides* by having them respond to several oral or written statements or questions concerning the new material (Vaca, Vaca, & Gove, 1987). For example, an anticipation guide might include a series of true/false statements that the students answer and discuss before reading a chapter in the textbook (see Figure 7.5). Vaca, Vaca, and Gove (1987) outline the steps in constructing anticipation guides:

1. Analyze the reading selection and determine the main points.

2. Convert main points into short, declarative, concrete statements that students can understand.

3. Present statements to students in a way that elicits anticipation and predication.

4. Have students discuss their predictions and responses to the statements.

5. Discuss the students' reading of the text selection; compare and evaluate their responses with the information presented in the text.

FIGURE 7.4.   Sample Concept Diagram.

Concept Name:	democracy

Definitions: A democracy is a form of government in which the people hold the ruling power, citizens are equal, the individual is valued, and compromise is necessary.

Characteristics Present in the Concept:

Always	Sometimes	Never
form of government	direct representation	king rules
people hold power	indirect representation	dictator rules
individual is valued		
citizens equal		
compromise necessary		

Example:

United States

Mexico

West Germany today

Athens
(about 500 B.C.)

Nonexample:

Russia

Cuba

Germany under Hitler

Macedonia
(under Alexander)

Source: J. Bulgren, J. B. Schumaker, and D. Deshler. *Learning Disability Quarterly, Vol. 11,* Overland Park, KS: Council for Learning Disabilities. Reprinted by permission.

❋SEMANTIC WEBS.   Whereas a structured overview presents critical concepts and terminology before a class lecture or reading a textbook selection, teachers can use *semantic webs* to foster understanding and retention of information after it has been read or presented (Vaca, Vaca, and Gove, 1987). Semantic webs, like structured overviews, provide a visual

FIGURE 7.5.   Anticipation Guide on Energy Resources.

Working as a group, read the statements and place a *T* next to those that are true and an *F* next to those that are false. Be prepared to explain the reasons for your rating a statement as true or false.

_____ Ninety-five percent of the energy needs of the United States are provided by fossil fuels.

_____ Spacecraft and many homes use solar energy.

_____ Hydroelectric power has no negative effects on the environment.

_____ Fossil fuels produce more energy per gram than fossil fuels.

_____ Before the radiation decays, radioactive wastes must be stored for a thousand years.

---

depiction of important points as well as the relationships between these points, and can be developed by the class (see Figure 7.6). A semantic web includes a key word or phrase that relates to the main point of the content, which serves as the focal point of the web; web strands, which are subordinate ideas that relate to the key word; strand supports, which include details and information relating each web strand; and strand ties, which establish the interrelationships between different strands (Freedman & Reynolds, 1980).

Textbooks

Much of the content in science and social studies is presented through textbooks; therefore, teachers should exercise caution when selecting textbooks. Teachers should avoid using textbooks that employ vague and indirect referents, use concepts that are unknown to the reader, fail to establish relationships between content and within chapters, and include irrelevant information (Harris & Sipay, 1985). Armbruster and Anderson (1988) suggest guidelines for choosing science and social studies textbooks for mainstreamed students in terms of structure, coherence, and audience appropriateness. These guidelines include:

1. Does the textbook offer informative headings and subheadings?
2. Does the textbook provide signals to highlight main points and key vocabulary (use of marginal notations, graphic aids, and pointer words and phrases)?

FIGURE 7.6.   Web on the Three Branches of the Federal Government.

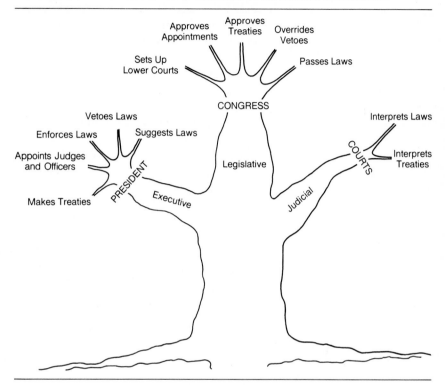

3. Does the textbook present information in an organized fashion (use of preview or introductory statements, topic sentences, summary statements, lists, enumeration words)?

4. Does the textbook offer transitions that help the reader adjust to changes in topics?

5. Are the accompanying graphic aids easy to read and interpret?

6. Are chronological sequences or events presented from first to last?

It is desirable for science and social studies textbooks to have illustrations. Illustrations that depict content can provide a visual framework for understanding the content and supplement written presentations. Illustrations are most appropriate for presenting spatial information. Therefore, science and social studies teachers can facilitate the performance of mainstreamed students by selecting textbooks that have numerous illustrations and pictures (Levin, 1981). However, it is also important that illustrations be alluded to and explained in writing in the textbook.

STUDY GUIDES.   Teachers can prepare *study guides* to help students determine critical points in science and social studies textbooks and provide activities to help master them (Lovitt et al., 1985). Horton and Lovitt (cited in Bergerud, Lovitt, & Horton, 1988) and Bergerud and Lovitt (cited in Bergerud, Lovitt, & Horton, 1988) reported that use of study guides led to a significant improvement in the social studies and science performance of mainstreamed students.

Although the components of study guides vary, they often include objectives, text references, a chapter summary, an outline, study questions and activities, definitions of key terms, and student evaluation probes (Pauk, 1984). Study guides also can take the form of a framed outline, which is an ordered list of the chapter's main points with key words blanked out. The students fill in the blanks while reading the selection or listening to a lecture in class (Lovitt, et al., 1985). In devising study guides, review and note the main points of the reading selection, state main points as questions, ensure that the order of the questions is consistent with the order of the information in the textbook, provide enough space between questions for students to write their answers, distribute study guides to students and provide enough time for them to complete them, and review answers and offer feedback to students on their performance.

ADAPTED TEXTBOOKS.   Many mainstreamed students may have difficulty reading on-grade science and social studies textbooks (Harris & Sipay, 1985; Johnson & Vardian, 1973). For these students, it may be appropriate to use *adapted textbooks,* which present content that matches the on-grade textbook, but at a lower readability level. For example, Globe's *Pathway to Science* provides junior and senior high chemistry, physics, and biology content to students reading at the fifth- to sixth-grade level. Similarly, Macmillan has adapted its elementary-level social studies textbooks for lower-level readers, and created a text called *The Reading Range Plus*. Other science and social studies adapted textbooks include *Science For You* (Steck–Vaughn), *Wonders of Science* (Steck–Vaughn), *American Adventures World History* (Scholastic), *America's Story* (Steck–Vaughn), and *American History* (Follet). Teachers can find appropriate adaptive textbooks that correspond to their on-grade textbooks by contacting a representative of their book company.

PARALLEL ALTERNATIVE CURRICULUM (PAC).   In addition to adapted textbooks, *Parallel Alternative Curriculum (PAC)* materials have been developed for mainstreamed students (Mercer & Mercer, 1985). PAC materials are designed to supplement the textbook by providing lower-achieving students with alternative ways to master critical information from content areas. For example, the Livonia (Michigan) Public Schools District has developed a PAC called Project PASS (Packets Assuring Student Success) (Mercer & Mercer, 1985) to offer assistance to mainstreamed students taking courses in U.S. history and American government. Adapted materials, such as vocabulary lists, glossaries, learning activities, content outlines, and pre- and post-tests at a third- to fifth-grade reading level were developed. Similarly, Project IMPRESS of the Tallahassee (Florida) School District has developed PAC materials for American history (grades eleven and twelve), social studies (grades eight and nine), science (grades seven and eight), basic English, economics, and human biology (Mercer & Mercer, 1985).

Specially designed science programs and science equipment also are available. Malone, Petrucchi, and Thier (1981) developed an activity-based science program for students with visual impairments called Science Activities for the Visually Impaired (SAVI). SAVI takes a laboratory approach to teaching science that stresses observations, manipulation of materials, and the development of science language concept. Similarly, Project MAVIS (Materials Adaptations for Visually Impaired Students) has adapted social studies materials to assist in mainstreaming students with visual impairments. These programs are designed for students with visual impairments, but they also can be used with nonvisually impaired mainstreamed students. Other adapted science curriculum materials include McGraw–Hill's Elementary Science Study Program, Opportunities for Learning's IDEAL Science Curriculum, and Biological Sciences Curriculum Study's Me in the Future and Hubbard's Me and My Environment, and Me Now (Mercer & Mercer, 1985). Additional information on teaching science to mainstreamed students can be obtained by contacting the Educational Resource Information Center/Science, Math, and Environmental Educational Information Clearing House (ERIC/SMEE).

Graphic Aids

Science and social studies teachers can help mainstreamed students master content by supplementing lectures and textbooks with graphic representations (Darch & Carnine, 1986). Lovitt, Stein, and Rudsit (1985) reported an increase in mastery of science facts when these facts were taught using a combination of visual displays (charts and diagrams) and direct instruction. For example, comprehension of content presented in a lecture on the brain can be enhanced by displaying a pictorial representation of the brain. Similarly, mastery of information concerning comparisons between groups, periods, individuals, countries, and geographical regions in social studies can be fostered through use of charts, tables, graphs, and maps.

Media

Films, videos, and film strips can enhance science and social studies instruction. In addition to providing students with an opportunity to observe unique aspects of the content, media can motivate students and stimulate their curiosity. To enhance the value of media as a teaching tool, teachers should orient students to the mediated presentation by focusing their attention on the main points to be presented. After viewing the film, review and discuss the main points.

Field Trips

Class field trips can make learning more meaningful and real for students. In particular, visits to historical and science museums as well as ecological and historical sites can allow students to experience what they hear and read about. Many museums offer special tours for school groups; contact local museums to arrange and preview the tour.

Written Language Instruction

One content area that cuts across all aspects of the school curriculum is written language. However, rather than assume that students are improving their writing skills by writing on content-area assignments, teachers must make instruction in written expression an ongoing part of the students' program (Graham & Harris, 1988). Instruction in writing should allow students the opportunities to write for social, creative, recreational, and occupational purposes, as well as sharing opinions and expressing factual information (Graham & Harris, 1988). Calkins (1986) believes that at least forty-five minutes of each school day should be devoted to writing; Graham and Harris (1988) propose that students receive writing instruction a minimum of four times a week. Calkins (1986) also suggests that students work on the same writing product over a period of time (writing sessions). Bos (1988) advocates the use of individual folders to facilitate the writing process and promote independence in students. Individual folders could include works in progress, completed products, ideas for future products, student- and teacher-selected goals, graphs of progress, and writing aids (a list of spelling demons, or word processing programs).

Although there is considerable overlap of stages in writing (Englert & Raphael, 1988), many researchers advocate teaching writing by using a *process-oriented approach* (Calkins, 1986; Flower & Hayes, 1981; Graves,

1983). In most process-oriented approaches, writing is divided into four subprocesses: planning, drafting, editing, and publishing (Bos, 1988; Englert & Raphael, 1988).

Planning

During the planning phase, students determine the purpose of the writing task, generate and group ideas, and plan how to present the content to the reader (Englert & Raphael, 1988). Thomas, Englert, and Gregg (1987) observed that students with disabilities use a knowledge-telling strategy, an inefficient technique for generating writing ideas. In applying the knowledge-telling strategy, students with disabilities typically list all the information they possess on a topic without screening for irrelevant details or ordering the sequence of the content. This strategy often results in a written product that is disorganized and difficult for the reader to follow (Scardamalia & Bereiter, 1986).

Teachers can help students plan their writing in several ways. They can model and verbalize the steps involved in planning writing, share written products, and solicit feedback from students (Graham & Harris, 1988). Teachers can discuss with students the different rationales for writing, and present examples of the different writing formats (Whitt, Paul, & Reynolds, 1988).

IDEA GENERATION.   Allowing students to work on self-selected topics can foster idea generation because students will probably choose topics with which they feel familiar (Graves, 1985). Similarly, a journal, in which students write about their personal reactions to events and their experiences, can be a good way to facilitate writing. For students who have difficulty generating journal entries, a *dialogue journal* may be appropriate (Graham & Harris, 1988). The dialogue journal, in which students and teachers write responses to each other, can motivate students to write, while promoting a positive relationship between teachers and students.

Simulations, trips, interviews, pictorial representations, music, sensory explorations, speakers, demonstrations, brainstorming, and researching can inspire the selection of writing topics (Tompkins & Friend, 1986; Whitt, Paul, & Reynolds, 1988). Reading and discussing passages before writing can help students select topics and add details to their writing (Graham, 1982). Englert, et al. (1988) suggest that teachers use oral questions to promote topic generation and supporting ideas to be covered in the written product.

OUTLINES AND SEMANTIC MAPS.   Ideas generated can then be organized by assisting students in developing an outline, which should include the main topics and supporting ideas grouped together, as well as the sequence in which they will be presented. Students also can be taught to organize their writing by developing a *semantic map* a diagram or a map of the key ideas and words that make up the topic (Tompkins & Friend, 1986; Whitt, Paul, & Reynolds, 1988). Mapping allows students to identify the main points and to plan the interrelationship between these parts. A sample semantic map is presented in Figure 7.7. Tompkins and Friend (1986) provide excellent, practical activities for generating ideas and organizing them before writing.

NARRATIVE STORIES.   Graham and Harris (cited in Graham, Harris, & Sawyer, 1987) have developed a self-instructional strategy for teaching students to write a narrative story. The quality of the stories written by students with learning disabilities who applied the strategy was similar to that of their age-appropriate, nonhandicapped peers who were skilled writers. The self-instructional strategy involved five steps:

1. Look at the picture (stimulus item).
2. Let your mind be free.
3. Write down the story part reminder (W–W–W; What = 2; How = 2).
4. Write down story parts for each part reminder.
5. Write your story; use good parts and make sense (Graham, Harris, & Sawyer, 1987).

The mnemonic *W–W–W; What = 2; How = 2* refers to

1. Who is the main character?; Who else is in the story?
2. When does the story take place?

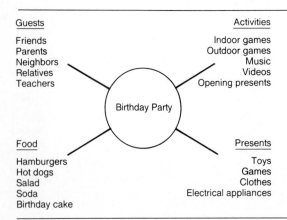

Guests	Activities
Friends	Indoor games
Parents	Outdoor games
Neighbors	Music
Relatives	Videos
Teachers	Opening presents

Birthday Party

Food	Presents
Hamburgers	Toys
Hot dogs	Games
Salad	Clothes
Soda	Electrical appliances
Birthday cake	

FIGURE 7.7.   A Sample Writing Map.

3. Where does the story take place?

4. What does the main character want to do?

5. What happens when he or she tries to do it?

6. How does the story end?

7. How does the main character feel? (Graham, Harris, & Sawyer, 1987, p. 7).

A similar strategy has been successful in helping students plan to write short stories on material they have just read (Harris & Graham, 1988).

OPINION ESSAYS.   Harris and Graham (cited in Graham & Harris, 1988) developed and tested a three-phase strategy to assist students in planning and composing opinion essays. In this strategy students are taught to

• think, "Who will read this and why am I doing this?";

• plan what to say using TREE (note Topic sentence; note Reasons, Examine reasons; note Endings); and

• write and say more (Graham & Harris, 1988, p. 510).

DIRECTED READING AND WRITING (DRAW).   A collaborative writing model that incorporates written language instruction into the content areas is *Directed Reading and Writing (DRAW)* (Cox & Woods, 1988). In DRAW, students work in groups of up to five to develop paragraphs based on common experiences, such as a taking a field trip, viewing a film, reading a passage, or discussing an issue. Cox and Woods (1988) list the steps of DRAW as

1. Students listen to the teacher read the text aloud.

2. Students read the text to themselves.

3. Students discuss the selection with the teacher and develop an understanding of the subject matter.

4. Students compose questions about the selection they just read.

5. Students and teachers discuss and expand upon the student-developed questions. Detailed answers are recorded using a question expansion grid, a sample of which is presented in Figure 7.8.

6. Students select topic sentences from information available in the question expansion grids.

7. Students plan a paragraph outline that the teacher reviews for order and relevance to the topic sentence.

8. Students work independently or in groups to write a paragraph based on the paragraph outline.

FIGURE 7.8. Sample Question Expansion Grid.

Question Expansion Grid

Question: "Why did Queequeg throw the passenger to the deck?"

Who	What	Where (How, When)	Why
Queequeg	gently tossed passenger	—to the deck —to the floor	—because he made fun of Queequeg —because he was angry

Source: J. P. Cox and E. Woods. *Teaching Exceptional Children,* Vol. 20 (Reston, Virginia: Council for Exceptional Children, 1988), p. 34. Reprinted by permission of the publisher.

Drafting

In the drafting phase, writers transform their plans into printed sentences and paragraphs. They make attempts to establish a relationship and order between these sentences and paragraphs, and make appropriate word choices. While it should not be emphasized in the drafting stage, some attention to the rules of grammar, punctuation, and spelling may be appropriate (Bos, 1988). During this step, encourage students to plan, and provide time to revise their draft.

Teachers can facilitate the drafting process in several ways. They can ask questions to help students explore alternatives, offer suggestions, encourage students, and focus attention on the writing task (Whitt, Paul, & Reynolds, 1988). Research indicates that use of self-evaluation questions during writing is more valuable to students than applying criteria after completion of the written product (Benton & Blohm, 1986), so teachers can help students monitor their drafts by providing them with self-evaluation questions (Moran, 1988). Additionally, teachers should encourage students to use the self-evaluation guidelines throughout the writing process. Since the criteria for judging the effectiveness of a written product will vary depending on the type and purpose of the writing task, tailor the self-evaluation questions to the specific writing task students will be asked to perform. For example, the self-evaluation questions used for an opinion essay will be very different from those questions applied to a business letter or a creative writing task. Sample self-evaluation questions for writing stories adapted from the work of Graham & Harris (1986) and Isaacson (1988) are presented in Figure 7.9.

Harris and Graham (1985) improved the writing skills of learning-disabled students by teaching them to apply a *self-control strategy,* designed to teach students to look at the picture and write down good action words; think of a good story idea to use the words in; write the story, making sense and using good action words; read the story and ask, "Did I write a good story? Did I use action words?"; fix the story; "Can I use more action words?" (p. 29).

Revising and Editing

In this phase, students edit their drafts by making revisions, additions, and deletions to ensure that their products adequately address their writing goals (Englert & Raphael, 1988). Teachers can introduce students to the revision process by reviewing a sample paper as a group (Tompkins & Friend, 1988). The class can identify the positive aspects of the product as well as the problems a reader would have in reading the paper. The discussion should focus on the content, organization, and word choices rather than on mechanical errors. The class can complete the revision process by correcting the problems identified in the paper as a group. For example, students and teacher can help the writer generate a list of synonyms that can replace nondescriptive words (such as *nice, great, fine, good*) that have been used repeatedly (Fagan, Graves, & Tessier–Switlick, 1984). The *Find* (*Search*) and *Replace* functions of many word processing programs can then be used to locate the nondescriptive word and replace it with the new word.

Research suggests that many mainstreamed students may have poor revision skills (MacArthur, Graham, & Skarvoed, 1986), which can be improved by auditory feedback. Espin and Sindelar (1988) found that students who listened to a written passage read to them were able to identify more errors in the passage than students who read the passage.

FIGURE 7.9. Sample Writing Evaluation Questions.

- Does each paragraph start with a topic sentence?
- Does each paragraph include relevant supporting information?
- Are the paragraphs organized appropriately?
- Are the main characters introduced and described?
- Is the location of the story presented and described?
- Is the time of the story introduced?
- Does the story include a starting event?
- Does the story include the main characters' reactions to the starting event?
- Does the story present actions to resolve conflicts?
- Does the story have an ending?
- Does the ending include the outcome's effects on the main characters?

COLLABORATIVE GROUPS.   Collaborative writing groups can be an excellent resource for students who are revising their work because it promotes a positive environment for writing (Weiner, 1988). One collaborative writing strategy is the *author's chair* (Graves & Hansen, 1983). In this technique, upon completing their product, students read it aloud to their peers, who discuss the positive features of the text and ask questions concerning the author, strategy, meaning, and writing style. Mohr (1984), Russell (1983), and Tompkins and Friend (1986) provide some specific guidelines and questions teachers can use to guide students in giving feedback to their peers. Students also can work in collaboration by reading their products to the group or individual group members; editing the products of group members; brainstorming ideas for writing; developing outlines as a group; and producing a group product, such as a class newsletter (Graham & Harris, 1988).

Students can work together in groups to offer feedback on content, sequence, and vocabulary, and to edit drafts (Isaacson, 1988). Perl (1983) suggests that peers be encouraged to provide feedback to writers concerning the clarity of their message by paraphrasing their view of the author's message. Moore, Moore, Cunningham, and Cunningham (1986) established guidelines for peer writing groups, including focusing on initial feedback that emphasizes the positive aspects of the product, phrasing negative reactions as questions, giving reactions orally or in written form, and providing writers with time to respond to the reactions of their peers.

THE COMPUTER.   The computer can aid the revision process. Word processing allows students to delete, add, and move text easily. Graham and MacArthur (cited in Graham & Harris, 1988) found that they could improve students' revising skills and the quality of their writing by teaching them to revise their essays composed on a word processor. Specifically, students were taught to

- Read your essay;
- Find the sentence that tells what you believe. Is it clear?
- Add two reasons why you believe it.
- Scan each sentence, (Does it make sense? Is it connected to my belief? Can I add more? Note errors);
- Make changes on the computer.
- Reread the essay and make final changes (Graham & Harris, 1988, p. 509).

Some word processing programs have interactive prompting capabilities that help students use effective writing strategies. These programs provide students with prompts that appear on the screen to guide them. For example, the Quill writing system (Rubin & Bruce, 1985) has a planner program that presents prompts, such as Who? What? Where? When? questions, to assist students in writing a newspaper article. Teachers can tailor these prompts to adapt to the different types of writing assignments. Prompting programs have been developed to help students generate ideas (Burns & Culp, 1980), write opinion essays (Woodruff, Bereiter, & Scardamalia, 1981), compose, and revise (Daiute, 1986).

Publishing

The computer also can be a valuable resource in the fourth stage of the writing process, publishing. Publishing students' written language products presents an excellent opportunity for sharing their work with others and receiving feedback (Graves & Hansen, 1983).

FEEDBACK.   Feedback should facilitate, not frustrate the writing process. A teacher conference can be an excellent vehicle for providing feedback. By meeting individually with students, teachers can help students learn to correct content, process, and mechanical errors (Whitt, Paul, & Reynolds, 1988). The type and amount of feedback will depend on the students' writing abilities.

Initially, teachers should focus feedback on the positive aspects of the students' written products, and acknowledge and encourage students' writing by praising them, sharing their products with others by reading their stories in class, and posting their writing in the room or the school (Graham & Harris, 1988). As students become more proficient and confident in their writing, introduce corrective feedback. Because identifying all errors can frustrate students, teachers' corrective feedback should focus on a limited number of writing problems (no more than two) at a time. Pinpoint errors that interfere with the writers' abilities to make their products understandable to the reader rather than grammatical, punctuation, spelling, and usage errors (Graham & Harris, 1988). Pinpointed errors also should relate to skills that are within the students' repertoire (Tompkins & Friend, 1988).

Students also should be involved in evaluating their own written products (Harris & Graham, 1985; Hillocks, 1984). Mainstreamed students may have difficulty judging their performance on written tasks (Englert & Raphael, 1988), so the criteria for evaluating written products should be taught explicitly. Hillocks (1984) concluded that allowing students to assess their writing products based on a clearly defined criteria can improve written expression skills. Similarly, goal setting, in which students establish goals for their writing and graph their performance, has led to positive effects on writing and motivating students to write (Graham & Harris, 1988).

COGNITIVE STRATEGY INSTRUCTION IN WRITING (CSIW).   A teaching approach that introduces students to all subprocesses of writing through use of models and think-alouds is the *Cognitive Strategy Instruction in Writing (CSIW)* program (Englert & Raphael, 1988). In the initial phase of CSIW, students are introduced to a variety of written products and strategies for improving writing through teacher modeling. Teachers use the overhead projector to show well-written and poorly written text, model, and rehearse for the class text comprehension strategies and ways to expand on text.

When the modeling phase is completed, students are given "think sheets," which offer a list of the steps and questions to guide them in each stage of the writing process. For example, the planning think sheet structures this phase of the process for students by prompting them to ask themselves:

- Who am I writing for?
- Why am I writing this?
- What do I know about the topic?
- How can I group my ideas? (Englert & Raphael, 1988, p. 518).

Feedback on drafts is provided via self-evaluation and peer editing, both of which also are structured by think sheets. Peer conferencing is used to discuss peer feedback and brainstorm ideas to assist in the revision process.

Spelling

A skill area that can impact on both writing and reading is spelling (Graham & Miller, 1979). While reading is a decoding process, spelling is an encoding process (Mercer & Mercer, 1985). Consequently, many students who experience difficulties reading also are likely to have problems with spelling (Carpenter & Miller, 1982).

Several different approaches have been offered to remediate spelling difficulties (Bos & Vaughn, 1988; Mercer & Mercer, 1985; Miller, 1987). These approaches are described below.

Rule-Governed Approaches

Rule-governed models are designed to promote spelling skills by teaching students the basic spelling rules. These approaches assume that once students master the basic rules, they can apply them to spell unfamiliar words. Mercer and Mercer (1985) suggest that *rule-governed approaches* are appropriate for spelling rules that apply at least 75 per cent of the time. In rule-governed approaches, teachers help students learn the spelling rules and patterns by asking them to analyze words that follow the same grapheme-phoneme correspondence, discuss similarities and differences in words, identify the rules that apply, practice the rule with unfamiliar words, and learn exceptions to the rule.

One rule-governed model for teaching spelling is the *linguistic approach* (Mercer & Mercer, 1985), in which spelling instruction focuses on the rules of spelling and patterns that relate to whole words. Once the student learns a series of words that follow similar spelling patterns, opportunities to generalize the rule with other words in the family arise. For example, students would be taught the *oat* family using the words *boat* and *coat*. Later, students would apply the pattern to other words from that family, such as *goat, moat,* and *float*.

A linguistic approach is based on learning spelling patterns within whole words; a *phonetic approach* is based on learning to apply phoneme-grapheme correspondence within parts of words (Mercer & Mercer, 1985). Thus, teachers using a phonetic approach to spelling teach students the sound-symbol correspondence for individual letters and combinations of letters (for instance, digraphs and diphthongs). Students then apply these rules by breaking words into syllables, pronouncing each syllable, and writing the letter(s) that correspond to each sound (Mercer & Mercer, 1985). While phonetic approaches to teaching spelling have been successful, several factors limit their use (Graham & Miller, 1979). Hanna, Hanna, Hodges, and Rudorf (1966) reviewed 17,000 words and concluded that only 49 per cent could be spelled correctly using a phonetic rule-governed approach. Horn (1960) noted the irregularities in the English language, including multiple letter sounds and word pronunciations and unstressed syllables, as deterrents to using a phonetic approach to spelling.

Cognitive Approaches

Wong (1986) proposes a *cognitive approach* to teaching spelling that employs a spelling grid and a seven-step questioning procedure. The five-column spelling grid is designed to teach structural analysis of words. Its use begins with the teacher writing a spelling word, pronouncing it, and discussing its meaning. Next, students complete the spelling grid by reading the word in column one; recording the number of syllables in the word in column two; dividing the word into syllables in column three; breaking the word into its root and suffix, and writing the suffix in column four; and writing the modification of the spelling of the root word in column five. The self-questioning strategy entails students asking themselves

1. Do I know the word?
2. How many syllables do I hear in this word? (Write down the number.)
3. I'll spell the word.
4. Do I have the right number of syllables down?
5. If yes, is there any part of the word I'm not sure of the spelling? I'll underline that part and try spelling the word again.
6. Now, does it look right to me? If it does, I'll leave it alone. If it still doesn't look right, I'll underline the part of the spelling I'm not sure of and try again. (If the word I spelled does not have the right number of syllables, let me hear the word in my head again, and find the missing syllable. Then I'll go back to steps 5 and 6. and
7. When I finish spelling, I tell myself I'm a good worker. I've tried hard at spelling. (Wong, 1986, p. 172)

Whole Word Approaches

In light of the concerns about the usability of the rule-governed approaches to spelling, several educators have advocated use of a *whole word approach* to increasing spelling vocabulary (Graham & Miller, 1979). These approaches help students focus on the whole word through a variety of multisensory activities (Miller, 1987). Whole word approaches include test-study-test procedures, corrected test methods, and word study techniques.

TEST-STUDY-TEST PROCEDURES. Perhaps the most popular method of spelling instruction is the *test-study-test method*. In this method, students receive a pretest on a fixed list of words, study those words they misspell, and take a posttest to assess mastery. Some teachers use a study-test procedure, where students study all the week's spelling words and then take a test. Research indicates that test-study-test procedures are superior to study-test procedures (Stephens, Hartman, & Lucas, 1982). When posttesting students with these procedures, it is recommended that teachers intersperse known and unknown words into the test (Neef, Iwata, & Page, 1977).

Teachers can adapt this procedure for mainstreamed students in several ways. Bryant, Drabin, and Gettinger (1981) found that decreasing the number of spelling words given to students with learning disabilities from five to three increases their spelling performance. Thus, rather than having students try to master a large list of words each week, teachers can break down the spelling list so that students study and are tested on three words each day.

Teachers also can modify this method of spelling instruction by using a flow word list rather than a fixed list (McGuigan, 1975; Mercer & Mercer, 1985). Flow lists can help teachers individualize spelling by allowing students who master spelling words to delete those words from the list and replace them with new words. Whether using a fixed or flow list of spelling words, teachers should allow students the time to work at their own rate, and require them to demonstrate mastery over a period of time.

CORRECTED TEST METHODS. Feedback on spelling in-class activities and tests can have a significant positive impact on spelling performance (Graves, 1977). In addition to receiving feedback from teachers, students should be actively involved in correcting their spelling errors (Graham & Miller, 1979). One method of allowing students to correct their own errors is the *corrected-test method* (Graham & Miller, 1979). Teachers can guide students in correcting their spelling errors by spelling words orally while the student corrects them; spelling words and accentuating each letter as the student simultaneously points to each letter in the word (Allred, 1977); spelling words while the student writes the correct letter above the crossed-out, incorrect letter (Hall, 1964); writing the correct spelling on the student's paper near the incorrectly spelled word, which the student then corrects (Kauffman, Hallahan, Haas, Brame, & Boren, 1978); and copying the student's error, spelling the word correctly, and observing as the student writes the word correctly (Kauffman et al., 1978).

Nulman and Gerber (1984) found that contingent imitation and modeling was a highly effective procedure for improving spelling performance. Teachers implement the contingent imitation and modeling procedure by acknowledging the accuracy of all words spelled correctly, verbalizing and then writing each word the student misspelled, verbalizing and writing the correct spelling for each word misspelled, and asking the student to copy the correct spelling of each misspelled word.

WORD STUDY TECHNIQUES. An integral part of spelling programs, *word study techniques,* include a wide range of activities designed to help students remember spelling words. Graham and Freeman (1985) and Harris, Graham and Freeman (1988) found that a student-controlled, five-step word study procedure was effective in helping students learn new spelling words. The five-step strategy included verbalizing the word; writing and saying the word; comparing the written word to a model; tracing and saying the word; writing the word from memory and checking it; and repeating prior steps as necessary. Fitzsimmons and Loomer (1978) advocate use of a word study method that encourages students to close their eyes and visualize the spelling word, while others employ strategies that teach students to verbalize the word while writing it. A summary of several proposed word study techniques is presented in Figure 7.10.

Radabaugh and Yukish (1982) suggest that teachers match the word study strategies to the learning styles of their students. For visual learners, they recommend that

1. Students view the word while the teacher reads the word to them.
2. Students study the word, read it, spell it, and read it again.
3. Students attempt to spell the word orally without the model three times.
4. Students write the word and check its spelling.

For auditory learners, they recommend that

1. Students observe the teacher reading, spelling, and reading the word.
2. Students read the word and then attempt to spell it.
3. Students listen to the teacher spell the word, then repeat after the teacher.
4. Students spell the word without assistance.

Adapting Spelling Instruction

Many mainstreamed students may exhibit problems in spelling (Graham & Miller, 1979), so teachers must adapt their spelling instruction by

1. *Teaching dictionary skills.* Spelling problems can be minimized by consulting the dictionary (Graham & Miller, 1979). Gloeckler & Simpson (1988) note that the dictionary can help students confirm the spelling of irregular words, spelling demons, confusing rules, and difficult word combinations. Therefore, students need to learn how to use the dictionary, including alphabetizing skills, locating words, using guide words, and understanding syllabication and pro-

FIGURE 7.10. Word Study Techniques.

Fitzgerald Method (Fitzgerald, 1951a)

1. Look at the word carefully.
2. Say the word.
3. With eyes closed, visualize the word.
4. Cover the word and then write it.
5. Check the spelling.
6. If the word is misspelled, repeat steps 1–5.

Horn Method 1 (E. Horn, 1919)

1. Look at the word and say it to yourself.
2. Close your eyes and visualize the word.
3. Check to see if you were right. (If not, begin at step 1.)
4. Cover the word and write it.
5. Check to see if you were right. (If not, begin at step 1.)
6. Repeat steps 4 and 5 two more times.

Horn Method 2 (E. Horn, 1954c)

1. Pronounce each word carefully.
2. Look carefully at each part of the word as you pronounce it.
3. Say the letters in sequence.
4. Attempt to recall how the word looks, then spell the word.
5. Check this attempt to recall.
6. Write the word.
7. Check this spelling attempt.
8. Repeat the above steps if necessary.

Visual-Vocal Method (Westerman, 1971)

1. Say word.
2. Spell word orally.
3. Say word again.
4. Spell word from memory four times correctly.

Gilstrap Method (Gilstrap, 1962)

1. Look at the word and say it softly. If it has more than one part, say it again, part by part, looking at each part as you say it.
2. Look at the letters and say each one. If the word has more than one part, say the letters part by part.
3. Write the word without looking at the book.

Fernald Method Modified

1. Make a model of the word with a crayon, grease pencil, or magic marker, saying the word as you write it.
2. Check the accuracy of the model.
3. Trace over the model with your index finger, saying the word at the same time.
4. Repeat step 3 five times.
5. Copy the word three times correctly.
6. Copy the word three times from memory correctly.

Cover-and-Write Method

1. Look at word. Say it.
2. Write word two times.
3. Cover and write one time.
4. Check work.
5. Write word two times.
6. Cover and write one time.
7. Check work.
8. Write word three times.
9. Cover and write one time.
10. Check work.

References to Other Techniques

Aho, 1967
Bartholome, 1977
Clanton, 1977
Glusker, 1967
Hill & Martinis, 1973
Phillips, 1975
Stowitschek & Jobes, 1977

Source: S. Graham and L. Miller. *Focus on Exceptional Children*, Vol. 12 (Denver, Colorado: Love, 1979), p. 11. Reprinted by permission of the publisher.

nunciation. Students in primary grades can use a picture dictionary until they acquire the word skills to use a regular dictionary (Mercer & Mercer, 1985).

2. *Teaching students to proofread for spelling errors.* Spelling errors can be reduced by students proofreading their work. Train students to proofread for spelling errors by giving students a list of words and having them identify and correct the misspellings (Hardin, Bernstein, & Shands, 1978), assigning them to find the spelling errors in the assignments of their peers (Rudman, 1973), listing the number of errors in a student's assignment and having students locate and correct the errors (Valmont, 1972), and marking words that may be incorrectly spelled and having students check them (Personkee & Yee, 1971). Posting an alphabetical list of words frequently misspelled in a central location in the room, encouraging students to maintain a list of words they frequently misspell in their notebooks, and assigning peers to serve as a "human dictionary" or "super speller" to assist their classmates can help students learn to identify and vanquish spelling demons (Fagan, Graves, & Tessier–Switlick, 1984).

3. *Using spelling games.* Games can motivate students and provide them with the opportunity to practice spelling skills in a non-threatening environment. A variety of teacher-made and commercially produced spelling games are available (Gloeckler & Simpson, 1988). Teacher-made games include spelling bingo, hangman, spelling baseball, and spelling lotto; commercially produced games include Scrabble, Spello, and Boggle.

4. *Employing a combination of approaches.* Graham and Miller (1979) advocate use of a spelling program that combines several approaches. They propose that spelling instruction encompass a list of common reading and vocabulary words used by students. Similarly, spelling words should be selected that are consistent with the students' reading and vocabulary levels (Bos & Vaughn, 1988; Shinn, 1982). These words can then be taught using a variety of spelling vocabulary instructional methods. Supplement spelling vocabulary by use of rule-governed approaches to teach essential spelling rules and phonetic skills such as prefixes, suffixes, blends, and digraphs. To assist mainstreamed students in learning spelling rules, it is suggested that only one rule be taught at a time.

5. *Teaching students to use cues.* Students can employ both mnemonic devices and configuration clues to cue them to the correct spelling of words (Gloeckler & Simpson, 1988). For example, some students may benefit from placing blocks around the outline of the word to remember the configuration of the word.

6. *Having students self-record their progress.* Self-recording motivates students by providing them with a visual representation of their progress. For example, students can keep a cumulative chart or graph of words they spelled correctly, or maintain weekly graphs that measure their performance on pretests and posttests.

7. *Providing time to review words previously learned.* Since mainstreamed students may experience difficulty remembering words previously mastered, teachers should provide time to review and study previously learned words. Graham and Miller (1979) suggest that previously mastered spelling words should be periodically tested during the school year. When assessing mastery of spelling words, students should check their work under the teacher's supervision (Vallecorsa, Zigmond, & Henderson, 1985).

8. *Modeling appropriate spelling techniques.* Teachers can facilitate the spelling skills of their students by providing them with oral and written models that they can imitate (Kauffman, et al., 1978; Stowitschek & Jobes, 1977). When writing on the blackboard, periodically emphasize the spelling of words, and occasionally spell words or have peers spell them for the class.

9. *Using a computerized spell checker.* Many word processing programs come with a *spell checker* that reviews written text and identifies spelling errors. Students can then correct the spelling errors by typing in the correct spelling or choosing from a list of spelling alternatives presented by the spell checker. Students can add words to the spell checker's dictionary to tailor it to their unique spelling needs. However, spell checkers cannot differentiate between words that are spelled correctly but used in the wrong context, such as homonyms.

10. *Choosing relevant spelling words.* Teachers can motivate students and improve their spelling by focusing initially on a core of frequently used spelling words as well as those words that are part of the student's listening and spelling vocabulary (Vallecorsa, Zigmond, & Henderson, 1985).

Handwriting

Students need to develop the legibility and fluency of their handwriting so that they can express themselves in writing (Mercer & Mercer, 1985). *Legibility*—the clarity and correctness of letter formations—includes such variables as size, slant, proportion, alignment, and spacing of letters, as well as the thickness and evenness of the lines that constitute the letters. *Fluency* refers to the speed with which students write, and is measured in terms of letters produced per minute. Poor handwriting skills can hinder the appearance of written products and result in mainstreamed students receiving lower grades on their assignments (Hagin, 1983; Markham, 1976).

Initial Handwriting Instruction

Handwriting instruction should be an integral part of the school curriculum. Schedule at least fifteen minutes for handwriting instruction each day (Milone & Wasylyk, 1981; Wiederholt, Hammill, & Brown, 1978). Initial instruction in handwriting should focus on helping students develop the prerequisite fine motor, visual motor, and visual discrimination skills (Mercer & Mercer, 1985). Therefore, early handwriting instruction can include activities such as cutting, tracing, coloring, finger painting, discriminating, and copying shapes.

Before receiving formal handwriting instruction, students should be able to draw vertical, horizontal, curved, and slanted lines; make backward and forward circles; discriminate and verbally identify letters and shapes; and reproduce simple shapes when provided with a model. Because instruction is predicated on teachers using directionality concepts to verbalize the formation of letters, students should develop an understanding of the meaning of such directionality terms as *up, down, top, center, bottom, around, left, right, across, middle,* and *diagonal* (Miller, 1987). Initial writing instruction also should focus on teaching students proper posture, writing utensil grip, and paper positioning.

SITTING CORRECTLY.   Proper posture is necessary for good handwriting (Milone & Wasylyk, 1981). Poor posture such as resting the head on the desk can distort motor movements and the visual feedback necessary for good handwriting. Therefore, teachers should teach students good posture including: (a) sitting upright with the lower back positioned against the back of the seat and both feet on the floor; (b) leaning the shoulders and upper back forward in a straight line; (c) placing the elbows extended slightly at the edge of the writing surface; and (d) using the forearms as a pivot for movements (Graham & Miller, 1980; Milone & Wasylyk, 1981).

HOLDING THE WRITING UTENSIL.   In addition to posture, students also need to learn the proper way to hold the writing utensil (Graham & Miller, 1980; Milone & Wasylyk, 1981). Students should position the writing utensil in their hands so that the utensil is held lightly between the index finger and the middle finger, with the thumb to the side and index finger on top; the thumb is bent to hold the pencil high in the hand and the pencil rests near the knuckle of the index finger; and the pinky and ring finger touch the paper (Milone & Wasylyk, 1981). Right-handers hold the writing utensil about an inch from the point, with the eraser pointing toward the right shoulder. Left-handers should hold their writing utensil one-and-a-half inches from the point, with the eraser facing toward the left elbow. The nonwriting hand rests on the desk surface and helps by keeping the paper in place. This hand also moves the page as lines are completed (Hagin, 1983).

Teachers can help students learn the correct way to hold their writing utensil by modeling and demonstrating the correct grip, physically guiding students, and placing the student's fingers in the correct position (Graham & Miller, 1980; Radabaugh & Yukish, 1982). Teachers can cue students on how to hold the writing utensil by using tape, rubber bands, or a rubber device that can be slipped over the writing utensil (Foerster, 1975; Mendoza, Holt, & Jackson, 1978). Some mainstreamed students may require specialized writing utensils, such as large-diameter pencils, crayons, holders, and writing frames (Milone & Wasylyk, 1981).

POSITIONING THE PAPER.   Since the position of the paper is important in facilitating good handwriting (Bos & Vaughn, 1988; Mercer & Mercer, 1985), instruction should include training in how to position the paper (Milone & Wasylyk, 1981). For manuscript writing, the paper should be located perpendicular to the front of the student, with the left side placed so that it is aligned with the center of the student's body. For cursive writing, right-handers should be taught to slant the paper counterclockwise, while left-handers should slant it clockwise (Bos & Vaughn, 1988). Harrison (1981) suggests that left-handers hold their papers more to the right than do right-handers and turn their bodies to the right.

For some students, special writing paper may help overcome writing difficulties. Fagan, Graves, and Tessier–Switlick (1984) recommend that teachers adapt writing paper by emphasizing the base lines and marking the starting and end points with green and red dots, respectively. Problems with keeping letters on the writing lines of standard writing paper can be alleviated through use of right-line paper, a specialized writing sheet that allows students to see and feel the base lines that provide the boundaries for forming letters (Mercer & Mercer, 1985). Paper with colored, solid, and dashed lines can help students learn correct letter heights; paper with perpendicular lines can teach proper spacing (Gloeckler & Simpson, 1988).

Manuscript vs. Cursive Writing

Once students possess the readiness skills necessary to begin formal handwriting instruction, they are typically taught manuscript writing, which is traditionally followed by instruction in cursive writing. Advocates of teaching manuscript first argue that it is easy to learn because it consists of simple motor movements, is more legible, promotes reading and spelling skills, because it resembles book print, and is used to complete applications and documents (Hagin, 1983; Johnson & Myklebust, 1967; Graham & Miller, 1980).

However, some educators propose that students with handwriting difficulties be taught only cursive writing. These proponents note that cursive writing can help some students write faster; decreases the likelihood that students will reverse letters; is easier for many students as the strokes are continuous, rhythmic, and connected; and is the style of handwriting used by peers and required by teachers in the intermediate grades (Bos & Vaughn, 1988; Graham & Miller, 1980; Mercer & Mercer, 1985).

Whether students are learning cursive or manuscript, teachers should individualize instruction and provide feedback to students on their performance. Analyze writing errors and suggest remedial strategies. Mercer and Mercer (1985) offer an excellent framework for linking student errors with remedial strategies (see Figure 7.11).

TRANSITIONAL MODELS.   In an extensive review of handwriting research, Graham and Miller (1980) suggest that students learn manuscript writing first. Once manuscript writing is mastered, they recommend teaching cursive writing as a distinct but related skill. Several models for promoting the transition from manuscript to cursive are available (Hagin, 1983; Mann, Suiter, and McClung, 1979). Mann, Suiter, and McClung (1979) offer a transitional writing model requiring that students

1. Print words in manuscript.
2. Connect the letters within the words with a colored dotted line.
3. Trace over the letters and dotted lines so that the words are converted from manuscript to cursive writing.

Another transitional program is Hagin's Write-Right-or-Left approach, which teaches students to use the vertical downstroke rather than the diagonal slant (Hagin, 1983). Students are taught cursive writing through use of letter motifs (waves, pearls, wheels, and arrows), which are a means for learning the cursive writing strokes. Initially, introduce the letter motifs to students at the chalkboard. After students practice at the chalkboard, they move to their desks, where they trace motifs and letters on an acetate sheet placed over a model; try to write the letters on an acetate without the model; match and compare their letters with the models to determine if additional practice is needed; and produce a final product that is used to assess student progress and mastery.

FIGURE 7.11.   Diagnostic Chart for Manuscript and Cursive Writing.

Factor	Problem	Possible Cause	Remediation
		Manuscript Writing	
Shape	Letters slanted	Paper slanted	Place paper straight and pull straight line strokes toward center of body.
	Varies from standard	Improper mental image of letter	Have pupil write problem letters on chalkboard.
Size	Too large	Poor understanding of writing lines	Reteach size concept by pointing out purpose of each line on writing paper.
		Exaggerated arm movement	Reduce arm movement, especially on circle and part-circle letters.
		Improper mental image of letter	Have pupil write problem letters on chalkboard.
	Too small	Poor understanding of writing lines	Reteach size concept by pointing out purpose of each line on writing paper.
		Overemphasis on finger movement	Stress arm movement; check hand-pencil and arm-desk positions to be sure arm movement is possible.
		Improper mental image of letter	Have pupil write problem letters on chalkboard.
	Not uniform	Adjusting writing hand after each letter	Stress arm movement; move paper with nonwriting hand so writing hand can remain in proper writing position.
		Overemphasis on finger movement	Stress arm movement; check arm-desk and pencil-hand positions.
Space	Crowded letters in words	Poor understanding of space concepts	Reteach uniform spacing between letters (finger or pencil width).
	Too much space between letters	Improper lowercase letter size and shape	Review concepts of size and shape; provide appropriate corrections under size and shape.
Alignment	Letters not sitting on base line	Improper letter formation	Evaluate work for letter shape; stress bringing straight line strokes all the way down to base line.
		Poor understanding of base line concept	Review purpose of base line on writing paper.

FIGURE 7.11.   (*continued*)

Factor	Problem	Possible Cause	Remediation
		Manuscript Writing	
		Improper hand-pencil and paper-desk positions	Check positions to make sure pupil is able to reach base line with ease.
	Letters not of consistent height	Poor understanding of size concept	Review concept of letter size in relationship to lines provided on writing paper.
Line quality	Too heavy or too light	Improper writing pressure	Review hand-pencil position; place wadded paper tissue in palm of writing hand to relax writing grip; demonstrate desired line quality.
		Cursive Writing	
Shape	Letters too oval in size	Overemphasis of arm movement and poor image of letter size and shape	Check arm-desk position; review letter size and shape.
	Letters too narrow in shape	Finger writing	Check positions to allow for arm movement.
		Overemphasis of straight line stroke	Make sure straight line stroke does not come all the way down to base line in letters like *l*, *b*, and *t*.
		Poor mental image of letter shape	Use transparent overlay for pupil's personal evaluation of shape.
			In all problems of letter shape review letters in terms of the basic strokes.
Size	Letters too large	Exaggerated arm movement	Check arm-desk position for over-movement of forearm.
		Poor mental image of letter size	Review base and top line concepts in relation to ¼ space, ½ space, and ¾ space; use transparent overlay for pupil's personal evaluation of letter size.
	Letters too small or letters not uniform	Finger movement	Check arm-desk and pencil-hand positions; stress arm movement.
		Poor mental image of letter size	Review concept of letter size (¼ space, ½ space, and ¾ space) in relation to base and top lines; use transparent overlay for pupil's personal evaluation of letter size.

FIGURE 7.11. (*continued*)

Factor	Problem	Possible Cause	Remediation
		Cursive Writing	
Space	Letters in words crowded or spacing between letters uneven	Finger movement	Check arm-desk, pencil-hand positions; stress arm movement.
		Poor understanding of joining strokes	Review how letters are joined; show ending stroke of one letter to be beginning stroke of following letter; practice writing letters in groups of five.
	Too much space provided between letters in words	Exaggerated arm movement	Check arm-desk position for over-movement of forearm.
		Poor understanding of joining strokes	Review joining strokes; practice writing groups of letters by rhythmic count.
	Uneven space between words	Poor understanding of between-word spacing	Review concept of spacing between words; show beginning stroke in second word starting under ending stroke of preceding word.
Alignment	Poor letter alignment along base line	Incorrect writing position; finger movement; exaggerated arm movement	Check all writing positions; stress even, rhythmic writing movement.
		Poor understanding of base line concept	Use repetitive exercise with emphasis on relationship of base line to written word.
		Incorrect use of joining strokes	Review joining strokes.
	Uneven alignment of letters in words relative to size	Poor understanding of size concept	Show size relationships between lower- and uppercase, and ¼ space, ½ space, and ¾ space lowercase letters; use repetitive exercise with emphasis on uniform height of smaller letters.

FIGURE 7.11. *(continued)*

Factor	Problem	Possible Cause	Remediation
		Cursive Writing	
Speed and Ease	Writing becomes illegible under stress and speed (grades 4, 5, and 6)	Degree of handwriting skill is insufficient to meet speed requirements	Improve writing positions; develop more arm movement and less finger movement.
	Writing becomes illegible when writing activity is too long	Handwriting positions have not been perfected to allow handwriting ease	Improve all writing positions, especially hand-pencil position; stress arm movement.
Slant	Back slant	Left-handedness	Correct hand-pencil and paper-desk positions.
	Vertical	Poor positioning	Correct hand-pencil and paper-desk positions.
	Too far right	Overemphasis of finger movement	Make sure pupil pulls slant strokes toward center of body if right-handed and to left elbow if left-handed.
			Use slant line instruction sheets as aid to teaching slant.
			Use transparent overlay for pupil's personal evaluation.
			Review all lowercase letters that derive their shape from the slant line.
			Write lowercase alphabet on chalkboard; retrace all slant strokes in colored chalk.

Source: C. D. Mercer and A. R. Mercer. *Teaching Students with Learning Problems,* second edition. (Columbus, Ohio: Merrill, 1985), pp. 419–422. Reprinted by permission of the publisher.

An instructional writing strategy that eases the transition from manuscript to cursive writing is the D'Nealian system. In this system, the formation of most manuscript and cursive letters involves similar continuous and slanted strokes. Brown (1984) and Thurber (1981) offer suggestions for using the D'Nealian method, including slant and letter size, letter spacing, and writing rhythm.

Instructional Strategies and Models

Several letter formation strategies and models have been used to teach handwriting skills (see Figure 7.12). Writing strategies and models for students with special needs should teach handwriting directly, establish the importance of handwriting, use overlearning to promote automaticity, encourage students to visualize the task, and teach students to monitor their work and make corrections (Hagin, 1983; Milone & Wasylyk, 1981). Graham (1983) and Salend (1984) propose that educators use a combination of procedures, such as modeling, self-instruction, copying, cuing, and teaching basic strokes.

MODELING.   A variety of modeling strategies can be employed to teach students handwriting skills. Teachers can introduce students to letter formations by modeling the strokes used to form the letters. Additionally, physically guiding students through the sequence of strokes can help them learn the necessary motor movements. Teacher modeling and physical guidance should be accompanied by verbal descriptions of how to form letters (*We start at the top, swing down to the right, and then go up*) as well as statements that point out the critical and unique features of each letter. Verbal descriptions that create visual images of the letters using real objects can be especially effective in promoting letter formation skills (Bos & Vaughn, 1988). For example, when modeling the letters *j* and *m,* relate their formation to a fishhook and a camel's hump, respectively.

Such visual mnemonics also can help remediate reversals in writing (Bos & Vaughn, 1988). Graham and Miller (1980) identified several strategies for remediating reversals, including teaching students to simultaneously trace and name the letter, write the letter to the right of the paper's midline, write the letter by linking it with a letter that is not typically reversed, use directionality cues, such as heavy lines, color coding, and drawings; and employ verbal cues.

In addition to presenting models depicting appropriate letter formations, teachers should provide students with models of poorly written letters so that they can learn to compare and assess their writing to identify areas that need improvement (Mercer & Mercer, 1985). Student evaluation of writing also can be fostered by use of *self-checking transparencies,* overlays of correct letter formations that students can place over their work to examine their letter formation accuracy (Mastropieri & Scruggs, 1987).

A chart presenting the lower-case and upper-case letters, the numerals 1 through 10, and their corresponding stroke directions should be placed in the room so that all students can view it. The chart can guide students in

FIGURE 7.12. Letter Formation Strategies.

Fauke Approach (Fauke et al., 1973)

1. The teacher writes the letter, and the student and teacher discuss the formational act.
2. The student names the letter.
3. The student traces the letter with a finger, pencil, and magic marker.
4. The student's finger traces a letter form made of yarn.
5. The student copies the letter.
6. The student writes the letter from memory.
7. The teacher rewards the student for correctly writing the letter.

Progressive Approximation Approach (Hofmeister, 1973)

1. The student copies the letter using a pencil.
2. The teacher examines the letter and, if necessary, corrects by overmarking with a highlighter.
3. The student erases incorrect portions of the letter and traces over the teacher's highlighter marking.
4. The student repeats steps 1–3 until the letter is written correctly.

Furner Approach (Furner, 1969a, 1969b, 1970)

1. Student and teacher establish a purpose for the lesson.
2. The teacher provides the student with many guided exposures to the letter.
3. The student describes the process while writing the letter and tries to write or visualize the letter as another child describes it.
4. The teacher uses multisensory stimulation to teach the letter form.
5. The student compares his or her written response to a model.

VAKT Approach

1. The teacher writes the letter with crayon while the student observes the process.
2. The teacher and student both say the name of the letter.
3. The student traces the letter with the index finger, simultaneously saying the name of the letter. This is done successfully five times.
4. The student copies and names the letter successfully three times.
5. Without a visual aid, the student writes and names the letter correctly three times.

Niedermeyer Approach (Niedermeyer, 1973)

1. The student traces a dotted representation of the letter 12 times.
2. The student copies the letter 12 times.
3. The student writes the letter as the teacher pronounces it.

Handwriting with Write and See (Skinner & Krakower, 1968)

The student traces a letter within a tolerance model on specially prepared paper. If the student forms the letter correctly, the pen writes gray; if it is incorrect, the pen writes yellow.

Source: S. Graham and L. Miller, *Focus on Exceptional Children*, Vol. 13 (Denver: Love, 1980), p. 11. Reprinted by permission of the publisher.

the formation of letters and numerals and assist them in evaluating their performance. Because the stroke directions are different for left-handers, those students should be provided with chart and teacher models that are appropriate for their unique style.

Teachers can use a multisensory approach to provide students with a visual and verbal model that guides their formation of the letters (Mercer & Mercer, (1985). The steps in this approach include the teacher writes or presents the letter to the students, the teacher states the name of the letter and verbalizes the sequence of the strokes, students trace the letters with their fingers and verbalize their movements, students repeat that step using a pencil, and students write the letter while viewing the model.

Mercer and Mercer (1985) propose use of a *fading model* to teach handwriting skills. Initially, students are given a model made up of solid, dark, heavy lines, which students trace. Next, parts of the model are gradually and progressively faded, then eliminated; students trace over them with their writing utensils. Finally, the model is completely eliminated, and the student produces the letter from memory.

SELF-INSTRUCTION.   Self-instructional procedures have been found to be effective for increasing the handwriting skills of students (Graham, 1983; Kosiewicz, Hallahan, Lloyd, & Graves, 1982; Salend, 1984). Salend (1984) used a combination of cues, tracing, fading, and verbal self-instruction to teach appropriate letter formation, alignment, and proportion. Graham (1983) used a six-step, self-instructional procedure to improve learning-disabled students' handwriting performance:

Step 1. Students watch as the teacher writes the letter. Students and teacher discuss writing the letter, with both outlining the steps in the formation of the letter. Step one is concluded when the process is repeated three times.

Step 2. The teacher writes and verbalizes the process while students observe. Students delineate the process in unison with the teacher.

Step 3. Students trace the letters while verbalizing the process with the teacher. Students demonstrate mastery of this phase by verbalizing the steps without teacher assistance.

Steps 4 through 6. Students learn the self-instructional task. In step four, the teacher writes the letter, traces it, then models the self-instructional procedure, which includes defining the task (*What do I have to do?*); verbalizing the steps in forming the letter (*How do I make this letter?*); correcting errors (*How does it look? Do I need to make any changes?*); and delivering reinforcement (*That looks good. I did a good job*). Steps five and six resemble step four. However, teacher assistance is faded out in steps five and six.

Self-instructional techniques may be difficult for younger students to learn and use (Robin, Armel, & O'Leary, 1975).

CUING.   Salend (1984) used a variety of visual and verbal cues to help teach letter formation skills:

1. Place a green dot to indicate the correct starting point for each letter.
2. Darken bottom and midlines of the student's paper to assist the student in aligning the letters correctly.
3. Provide one-centimeter blocks, into which the student can write the letters.
4. Put masking tape on the student's desk to indicate the correct position of the paper.
5. Teach the students a rhyme to remind them how to perform the task.

COPYING.   Copying also can improve handwriting skills. Research indicates that copying is superior to tracing in promoting letter formation skills (Askov & Greff, 1975; Hirsch & Niedermeyer, 1973). Two types of copying activities are available to teachers: near-point and far-point copying. Teachers should begin with *near-point copying*, where students copy a model placed on their desk. As students become proficient at near-point copying, *far-point copying*—where the model is placed away from the students' desks—can be employed. However, although students may be successful with near-point copying, far-point copying requires them to transfer through space and from different planes, and thus may create problems for many students. Minimize problems in spacing by teaching students to establish the space between words and sentences by using their fingers or the size of the lower-case *o* as a guide. For example, teach students that they can determine the space between letters within a word by estimating the size of one lower-case *o*, while the space between words within a sentence would be the size of two of those letters (Miller, 1987).

TEACHING BASIC STROKES.   Most of the letters in manuscript and cursive writing are made up of a series of basic strokes. Handwriting skills can be strengthened by teaching students these basic strokes (Milone & Wasylyk, 1981). The basic strokes in manuscript writing are the top-bottom line (↓|), left to right line (⇌), backward circle (◯), forward circle (◯) and slant lines (// \\ ). In cursive writing, the basic strokes are the slant stroke (//), understroke (⟋⟍), downstroke (⟋⟍) and overstroke (⟋⟍) (Milone & Wasylyk, 1981).

The Hanover method teaches handwriting skills by grouping them in families based on the nature of the strokes that form the letters (Hanover, 1983). In this method, students are taught the similarities and differences between letters within each family.

Teaching Left-Handers Handwriting

Because writing progresses from left to right, left-handed students may have difficulties with handwriting (Harrison, 1981; Salend, 1984). Compared to right-handed students, left-handed students are more likely to write slower (Burns, 1968), feel awkward and uncomfortable while writing, experience fatigue (Clark, 1959), and reverse letters (Enstrom & Enstrom, 1970). In addition to instruction in posture, writing utensil grip, and paper positioning, teachers can facilitate handwriting for their left-handed students by grouping them together, offering them left-handed models, teaching them to write letters vertically or with a slight backslant, having them eliminate elaborate and excessive loops and curves, and having them write on the left side of the blackboard (Graham & Miller, 1980; Harrison, 1981). If the classroom does not have full-sized desks, teachers should make sure that left-handed students have left-handed desks.

Summary

Mainstreamed students may require specific adaptations for learning various aspects of reading, math, social studies, science, written expression, handwriting, and spelling. This chapter presented guidelines and strategies for adapting instruction in these specific content areas.

References

Alford, I. (1985). Manipulating mathematics. *Mathematics Teaching. 114*, 44–45.

Allred, R. (1977). *Spelling: The application of research findings.* Washington, D.C.: National Education Association.

Arlin, M., Scott, M., & Webster, J. (1979). The effects of pictures on rate of learning sight words: A critique of the focal attention hypothesis. *Reading Research Quarterly, 14*(4), 645–660.

Armbruster, B. B., & Anderson, T. H. (1988). On selecting "considerate" content-area textbooks. *Remedial and Special Education, 9*(1), 47–52.

Ashlock, R. B. (1986). *Error patterns in computation: A semi-programmed approach (4th ed.)*. Columbus: Charles E. Merrill.

Askov, E., & Greff, K. (1975). Handwriting: Copying versus tracing as the most effective type of practice. *Journal of Educational Research, 69*, 96–98.

Barr, R. (1975). Influence of reading materials on response to printed words. *Journal of Reading Behavior, 7*, 123–135.

Bartalo, D. B. (1983). Calculators and problem solving instruction: They are made for each other. *Arithmetic Teacher, 30*, 18–21.

Beattie, I. D., & Scheer, J. K. (1982). *Using the diagnostic stamp kit*. Port Roberts, Wash.: Janian Educational Materials.

Benton, S., & Blohm, P. (1986). Effect of question type and position on measures of conceptual elaboration in writing. *Research in the Teaching of English, 20*, 98–108.

Bergerud, D., Lovitt, T. C., & Horton, S. (1988). The effectiveness of textbook adaptations in life science for high school students with learning disabilities. *Journal of Learning Disabilities, 21*, 70–76.

Biemiller, A. (1970). Changes in the use of graphic and contextual information as functions of passage difficulty and reading achievement level. *Journal of Reading Behavior, 11*, 308–318.

Blau, H., & Blau, H. (1968). A theory of learning to read. *The Reading Teacher, 22*, 126–129, 144.

Bley, N. S., & Thornton, C. A. (1981). *Teaching mathematics to the learning disabled*. Rockville, Md.: Aspen.

Bloomfield, L., & Barnhart, C. L. (1961). *Let's read—A linguistic approach*. Detroit: Wayne State University Press.

Bos, C. S. (1982). Getting past decoding: Assisted and repeating readings as remedial methods for learning disabled students. *Topics in Learning Disabilities, 1*, 51–57.

Bos, C. S. (1988). Process-oriented writing: Instructional implications for mildly handicapped students. *Exceptional Children, 54*, 521–527.

Bos, C. S., & Vaughn, S. (1988). *Strategies for teaching students with learning and behavior problems*. Boston: Allyn & Bacon.

Britton, G., Lumpkin, M., & Britton, E. (1984). The battle to imprint citizens for the 21st century. *The Reading Teacher, 37*, 724–733.

Bruni, J. V., & Silverman, H. J. (1986). Developing concepts in probability and statistics—and much more. *Arithmetic Teacher, 33*, 34–37.

Brown, V. L. (1984). D'Nealian handwriting: What it is and how to teach it. *Remedial and Special Education. 5*, 48–52.

Bryant, N. D., Drabin, I. R., & Gettinger, M. (1981). Effects of varying unit size on spelling achievement in learning disabled children. *Journal of Learning Disabilities, 14*(4), 200–203.

Bulgren, J., Schumaker, J. B., & Deshler, D. (1988). Effectiveness of a concept teaching routine in enhancing the performance of LD students in secondary-level mainstream classes. *Learning Disability Quarterly, 11*, 3–17.

Burns, H., & Culp, G. H. (1980). Stimulating invention in English composition through computer-assisted instruction. *Educational Technology, 20*(8), 5–10.

Burns, P. C. (1968). *Improving handwriting instruction in elementary schools.* Minneapolis: Burgess.

Calkins, L. M. (1986). *The art of teaching.* Portsmouth, N.H.: Heinemann.

Canny, M. E. (1984). The relationship of manipulative materials in achievement in three areas of fourth-grade mathematics: Computation, concept development and problem-solving. *Dissertation Abstracts International, 45a,* 775–776.

Carpenter, D., & Miller, L. J. (1982). Spelling ability of reading disabled l.d. students and able readers. *Learning Disability Quarterly, 5,* 65–70.

Cawley, J. F., Fitzmaurice, A. M., Sedlak, R., & Althaus, V. (1976). *Project math.* Tulsa: Educational Progress.

Ceprano, M. A. (1981). A review of selected research on methods of teaching sight words. *The Reading Teacher, 35,* 314–322.

Charles, R. I. (1984). *Problem-solving experiences in mathematics.* Menlo Park, Calif: Addison-Wesley.

Clark, M. M. (1959). *Teaching left-handed children.* New York: Philosophical Library.

Clements, D. C., & Battista, M. (1986). Geometry and geometric measurement. *Arithmetic Teacher, 33,* 29–32.

Cohen, S., & Plakson, P. (1978). Selecting a reading approach for the mainstreamed child. *Language Arts, 55,* 966–970.

Cohen, S. A., & Stover, G. (1981). Effects of teaching sixth-grade students to modify format variables of math word problems. *Reading Research Quarterly, 16*(2), 175–200.

Coffland, J. A., & Baldwin, R. S. (1985). *Wordmath.* St. Louis: Milliken.

Cox, J., & Wiebe, J. H. (1984). Measuring reading vocabulary and concepts in mathematics in the primary grades. *The Reading Teacher, 37,* 402–410.

Cox, J. P., & Woods, E. (1988). Directed reading and writing. *Teaching Exceptional Children, 20,* 33–35.

Daiute, C. A. (1986). Physical and cognitive factors in revising: Insights from studies with computers. *Research in Teaching of English, 20,* 141–159.

Dank, M. (1977). What effect do reading programs have on the oral reading behavior of children? *Reading Improvement, 14,* 66–69.

Darch, C., & Carnine, D. (1986). Teaching content-area materials to learning disabled students. *Exceptional Children, 53,* 240–246.

Darch, C., & Gersten, R. (1986). Direction setting in reading comprehension: A comparison of two approaches. *Learning Disability Quarterly, 9,* 235–243.

Davidson, J. (1969). *Using the Cuisenaire rods.* New Rochelle, N.Y.: Cuisenaire.

Denburg, S. D. (1976). The interaction of picture and print in reading instruction. *Reading Research Quarterly, 12*(2), 176–189.

Duffelmeyer, F. A. (1982). Introducing words in context. *Wisconsin Reading Association Journal, 26,* 4–6.

Durkin, D. (1978). *Teaching them to read.* Boston: Allyn & Bacon.

Dunlap, W. P., & McKnight, M. B. (1978). Vocabulary translations for conceptualizing math word problems. *The Reading Teacher, 32,* 183–189.

Englemann, S., & Carnine, D. (1975). *Distar arithmetic level 1.* Chicago: Science Research Associates.

Engelmann, S., & Carnine, D. (1976). *Distar arithmetic level 2*. Chicago: Science Research Associates.

Engelmann, S., & Carnine, D. (1982). *Corrective mathematics program*. Chicago: Science Research Associates.

Englert, C. S., & Raphael, T. E. (1988). Constructing well-formed prose: Process, structure, and metacognitive knowledge. *Exceptional Children, 54,* 513–520.

Englert, C. S. Raphael, T. E., Anderson, L. M., Anthony, H. M., Fear, K. L., & Gregg, S. L. (1988). A case for writing intervention: Strategies for writing informational text. *Learning Disabilities Focus, 3,* 98–113.

Enright, B. E. (1983). *Enright diagnostic inventory of basic arithmetic skills*. North Billerica, Mass.: Curriculum Associates.

Enright, B. E. (1986). *Enright computation series*. North Billerica, Mass.: Curriculum Associates.

Enright, B. E. (1987a). Basic mathematics. In J. S. Choate, T. Z. Bennett, B. E. Enright, L. J. Miller, J. A. Poteet, & T. A. Rakes, (Eds.), *Assessing and programming basic curriculum skills* (pp. 121–145). Boston: Allyn & Bacon.

Enright, B. E. (1987b). *Enright S.O.L.V.E.: Action problem-solving series*. North Billerica, Mass.: Curriculum Associates.

Enstrom, E. A., & Enstrom, D. (1970). Right writing. *Grade Teacher, 87,* 105–106.

Espin, C. A., & Sindelar, P. T. (1988). Auditory feedback and writing: Learning disabled and nondisabled students. *Exceptional Children, 55,* 45–51.

Fagan, S. A., Graves, D. L., & Tessier-Switlick. (1984). *Promoting successful mainstreaming: Reasonable classroom accommodations for learning disabled students*. Rockville, Md.: Montgomery County Public Schools.

Fernald, G. (1943). *Remedial techniques in basic school subjects*. New York: McGraw-Hill.

Fitzsimmons, R. J., & Loomer, B. M. (1978). *Excerpts from spelling: Learning and instruction-research and practice*. Wellesley, Mass.: Curriculum Associates.

Fleischner, J. E., Nuzum, M. G., & Marzola, E. S. (1987). Devising an instructional program to teach arithmetic problem-solving skills to students with learning disabilities. *Journal of Learning Disabilities, 20,* 214–217.

Flower, L., & Hayes, J. R. (1981). A cognitive process theory of writing. *College Composition and Communication, 32,* 365–387.

Foerster, L. (1975). Sinistra power! Help for lefthanded children. *Elementary English, 52,* 213–215.

Freedman, G., & Reynolds, E. G. (1980). Enriching basal reader lessons with semantic webbing. *The Reading Teacher, 33,* 677–684.

Fries, C. C. (1963). *Linguistics and reading*. New York: Holt, Rinehart & Winston.

Garnett, K. (1987). Math learning disabilities: Teaching and learners. *Journal of Reading Writing and Learning Disabilities, 3,* 1–8.

Garnett, K. (1989). Math learning disabilities. *The Forum, 14* (4), 11–15.

Garnett, K., & Fleischner, J. E. (1987). Mathematical disabilities. *Pediatric Annals, 16,* 159–176.

Gillet, P. (1986). Mainstreaming techniques for LD students. *Academic Therapy, 21,* 389–399.

Gillingham, A., & Stillman, B. W. (1973). *Remedial training for children with specific disability in reading, spelling and penmanship.* Cambridge, Mass.: Educators Publishing Service.

Gloeckler, T., & Simpson, C. (1988). *Exceptional students in regular classrooms: Challenges, services and methods.* Mountain View, Calif.: Mayfield.

Goodman, K. (1986). *What's whole in whole language?* Portsmouth, N.H.: Heinemann.

Graham, S. (1982). Composition research and practice: A unified approach. *Focus on Exceptional Children, 14,* 1–16.

Graham, S. (1983). The effect of self-instructional procedures on LD students' handwriting performance. *Learning Disability Quarterly, 6,* 231–234.

Graham, S., & Freeman, S. (1985). Strategy training and teacher vs. student-controlled study conditions: Effects on LD students spelling performance. *Journal of Learning Disabilities, 8,* 267–274.

Graham, S., & Harris, K. R. (April, 1986). *Improving learning disabled students' compositions via story grammar training: A component analysis of self-control strategy training.* Paper presented at the Annual Meeting of the American Educational Research Association, San Francisco.

Graham, S., & Harris, K. R. (1988). Instructional recommendations for teaching writing to exceptional students. *Exceptional Children, 54,* 506–512.

Graham, S., Harris, K. R., & Sawyer, R. (1987). Composition instruction with learning disabled students: Self-instructional strategy training. *Focus on Exceptional Children, 20,* 1–11.

Graham, S., & Miller, L. (1979). Spelling research and practice: A unified approach. *Focus on Exceptional Children, 12*(2), 1–16.

Graham, S., & Miller, L. (1980). Handwriting research and practice: A unified approach. *Focus on Exceptional Children, 13*(2), 1–16.

Graves, D. H. (1977). Spelling texts and structural analysis. *Language Arts, 54,* 86–90.

Graves, D. H. (1983). *Writing: Teachers and children at work.* Exeter, N.H.: Heinemann.

Graves, D. H. (1985). All children can write. *Learning Disabilities Focus, 1,* 36–43.

Graves, D. H., & Hansen, J. (1983). The author's chair. *Language Arts, 60,* 176–183.

Grimm, J. A., Bijou, S. W., & Parsons, J. A. (1973). A problem-solving model for teaching remedial arithmetic to handicapped children. *Journal of Abnormal Child Psychology, 1,* 26–39.

Haber, R. N., & Haber, L. R. (1981). The shape of a word can specify its meaning. *Reading Research Quarterly, 16*(3), 334–345.

Haber, L. R., Haber, R. N., & Furlin, K. R. (1983). Word length and word shape as sources of information in reading. *Reading Research Quarterly, 18,* 165–189.

Hagin, R. A. (1983). Write right or left: A practical approach to handwriting. *Journal of Learning Disabilities, 16*(5), 266–271.

Hall, M. (1981). *Teaching reading as a language experience (3rd ed.).* Columbus: Charles E. Merrill.

Hall, N. (1964). The letter mark-out corrected test. *Journal of Educational Research, 58,* 148–157.

Hanna, P., Hanna, J., Hodges, R., & Rudorf, E. (1966). *Phoneme-grapheme correspondences as cues to spelling improvement.* Washington, D.C.: U.S. Government Printing Office.

Hanover, S. (1983). Handwriting comes naturally? *Academic Therapy, 18,* 407–412.

Hardin, B., Bernstein, B., & Shands, F. (1978). The "Hey what's this?" approach to teaching spelling, *Teacher, 94,* 64–67.

Harris, A. J., & Sipay, E. R. (1985). *How to increase reading ability: A guide to developmental and remedial approaches. 8th ed.* New York: Longman.

Harris, K. R., & Graham, S. (1985). Improving learning disabled students' composition skills: Self-control strategy training. *Learning Disability Quarterly, 8,* 27–36.

Harris, K. R., & Graham, S. (1988). Self-instructional strategy training. *Teaching Exceptional Children, 20,* 35–37.

Harris, K. R., Graham, S., & Freeman, S. (1988). Effects of strategy training on metamemory among learning disabled students. *Exceptional Children, 54,* 332–338.

Harrison, S. (1981). An open letter from a left-handed teacher: Some sinistral ideas on the teaching of handwriting. *Teaching Exceptional Children, 13,* 116–120.

Heckelman, R. G. (1969). A neurological-impress method of remedial-reading instruction. *Academic Quarterly, 4,* 277–282.

Hedley, C. N. (1987). Software feature: What's new in software? Computer programs in math. *Journal of Reading Writing and Learning Disabilities, 3,* 103–107.

Heilman, A. W., Blair, T. R., & Rupley, W. H. (1981). *Principles and practices of teaching reading (5th ed.).* Columbus: Charles E. Merrill.

Hembree, R. (1986). Research gives calculators a green light. *Arithmetic Teacher, 34,* 18–21.

Herbert, E. (1985). One point of view: Manipulatives are good mathematics. *Arithmetic Teacher, 32,* 4.

Hillocks, G. (1984). What works in teaching composition: A meta-analysis of experimental treatment studies. *American Journal of Education, 93,* 133–170.

Hillocks, G. (1986). *Research on written composition: New directions for teaching.* Urbana, Ill.: National Conference for Research in English.

Hirsch, E., & Niedermeyer, F. C. (1973). The effects of tracing prompts and discrimination training on kindergarten handwriting performance. *Journal of Education Research, 67* (2), 81–86.

Horn, E. (1960). *Spelling. Encyclopedia of Educational Research (4th ed).* New York: Macmillan.

Isaacson, S. (1988). Assessing the writing product: Qualitative and quantitative measures. *Exceptional Children, 54,* 528–534.

Isaacson, S. (1989). Teaching written expression to mildly handicapped students. *The Forum, 14* (3), 5–7.

Jenkins, J. R., Larson, K., & Fleisher, L. (1983). Effects of error correction on word recognition and reading comprehension. *Learning Disability Quarterly, 6,* 139–145.

Johnson, D., & Blalock, J. (1986). *Adults with learning disabilities: Clinical studies.* Orlando, Fla.: Grune & Stratton.

Johnson, D. J., & Myklebust, H. R. (1967). *Learning disabilities: Educational principles and practices.* New York: Grune & Stratton.

Johnson, R., & Vardian, E. R. (1973). Reading, readability, and the social studies. *The Reading Teacher, 26,* 483–488.

Kauffman, J., Hallahan, D., Haas, K., Brame, T., & Boren, R. (1978). Imitating children's errors to improve spelling performance. *Journal of Learning Disabilities, 11,* 33–38.

Kosiewicz, M. M., Hallahan, D., Lloyd, J., & Graves, A. (1982). Effects of self-instruction and self-correction procedures on handwriting performance. *Learning Disability Quarterly, 5,* 71–78.

Lambie, R. A., & Hutchens, P. W. (1986). Adapting elementary school mathematics instruction. *Teaching Exceptional Children, 18,* 185–189.

Lenz, B. K. (1983). Using the advance organizer. *The Pointer, 27,* 11–13.

Lenz, B. K., Alley, G. R., & Schumaker, J. B. (1987). Activating the inactive learner: Advance organizers in the secondary content classroom. *Learning Disability Quarterly, 10,* 53–67.

Lenz, B. K., Schumaker, J. B., Deshler, D. D., & Beals, V. L. (1984). *The word identification strategy.* Lawrence: University of Kansas.

Leon, J. A., & Pepe, H. J. (1983). Self-instructional training: Cognitive behavior modification for remediating arithmetic deficits. *Exceptional Children, 50,* 54–60.

Levin, J. R. (1981). On functions of pictures in prose. In F. Pirozzolo & M. Wittrock, eds. *Neuropsychological and cognitive processes in reading* (pp. 203–228). New York: Academic Press.

Lewandowski, G. (1979). A different look at some basic sight-word lists and their use. *Reading World, 18,* 333–341.

Lovitt, T. C., Rudsit, J., Jenkins, J., Pious, C., & Benedetti, D. (1985). Two methods of adapting science materials for learning disabled and regular seventh graders. *Learning Disabilities Quarterly, 8,* 275–285.

Lovitt, T. C., Stein, M., & Rudsit, J. (1985). *The use of visual spatial displays to teach science facts to learning disabled middle school students.* Unpublished manuscript. Experimental Education Unit, University of Washington, Seattle.

MacArthur, C. A., Graham, S., & Skarvoed, J. (1986). *Learning disabled students' composing with three methods: Handwriting, dictation, and word processing.* Technical Report No. 109. College Park, Md.: Institute for the Study of Exceptional Children and Youth.

Malone, L., Petrucchi, L., & Thier, H. (1981). *Science activities for the visually impaired (SAVI).* Berkeley: Center for Multisensory Learning, University of California.

Mann, P. H., Suiter, P. A., & McClung, R. M. (1979). *Handbook in diagnostic-prescriptive teaching (Abridged 2nd ed.).* Boston: Allyn & Bacon.

Markham, L. (1976). Influence of handwriting quality on teacher evaluation of written work. *Educational Research Journal, 13,* 277–283.

Marzola, E. S. (1987). Using manipulatives in math instruction. *Journal of Reading Writing and Learning Disabilities, 3,* 9–20.

Mastropieri, M. A. (1988). Using the keyword method. *Teaching Exceptional Children, 20,* 4–8.

Mastropieri, M. A., & Scruggs, T. E. (1987). *Effective instruction for special education.* Boston: College-Hill.

Mastropieri, M. A., Scruggs, T. E., & Levin, J. R. (1985). Memory strategy instruction with learning disabled adolescents. *Journal of Learning Disabilities, 18,* 94–100.

Mastropieri, M. A., Scruggs, T. E., McLoone, B., & Levin, J. R. (1985). Facilitating the acquisition of science classifications in LD students. *Learning Disabilities Quarterly, 8,* 299–309.

McGuigan, C. A. (1975). *The effects of a flowing words list vs. fixed word lists and the implementation of procedures in the add-a-word spelling program (Working paper No. 52).* Seattle: University of Washington Experimental Education Unit.

McKinney, J. D., & Feagans, L. (1980). *Learning disabilities in the classroom (Final project report).* Chapel Hill: University of North Carolina, Frank Porter Graham Child Development Center.

McLeod, T. M., & Armstrong, S. W. (1982). Learning disabilities in mathematics skill deficits and remedial approaches at the intermediate and secondary level. *Learning Disability Quarterly, 5,* 305–311.

Mendoza, M., Holt, W., & Jackson, D. (1978). Circles and tapes: An easy teacher-implemented way to teach fundamental writing skills. *Teaching Exceptional Children, 10,* 48–50.

Mercer, C. D., & Mercer, A. R. (1985). *Teaching students with learning problems (2nd ed.).* Columbus: Charles E. Merrill.

Milone, M. N., & Wasylyk, T. M. (1981). Handwriting in special education. *Teaching Exceptional Children, 14,* 58–61.

Miller, L. J. (1987). Spelling and handwriting. In J.S. Choate, T.Z. Bennett, B.E. Enright, L.J. Miller, J. A. Poteet, & T. A. Rakes (Eds.), *Assessing and programming basic curriculum skills* (pp. 177–204). Boston: Allyn & Bacon.

Mohr, M. M. (1984). *Revision: The rhythm of meaning.* Upper Montclair, N.J.: Boynton/Cook.

Montague, M., & Bos, C. S. (1986). The effect of cognitive strategy training on verbal math problem-solving performance of learning disabled adolescents. *Journal of Learning Disabilities, 19,* 26–33.

Moore, D. W., Moore, S. A., Cunningham, P. M., & Cunningham, J. W. (1986). *Developing teachers and writers in the content areas.* White Plains, N.Y.: Longman.

Moran, M. R. (1988). Rationale and procedures for increasing the productivity of inexperienced writers. *Exceptional Children, 54,* 552–558.

National Council of Teachers of Mathematics. (1976). Minicalculators in schools. *The Arithmetic Teacher, 23,* 72–74.

National Council of Teachers of Mathematics. (1980). *An agenda for action: Recommendations for school mathematics of the 1980s.* Reston, Va.: Author.

Neef, N., Iwata, B., & Page, T. (1977). The effects of known-item interspersal on acquisition and retention of spelling and sight word reading. *Journal of Applied Behavior Analysis, 10,* 738.

Nulman, J. A., & Gerber, M. M. (1984). Improving spelling performance by imitating a child's errors. *Journal of Learning Disabilities, 17,* 328–333.

Nuzum, M. (1987). Teaching the arithmetic story problem process. *Journal of Reading Writing and Learning Disabilities, 3,* 53–61.

Nuzum, M. & Fleischner, J. (1983). *Technical report. Institute for the study of learning disabilities.* New York: Teachers College, Columbia University.

O'Mara, D. H. (1981). The process of reading mathematics. *Journal of Reading, 25,* 22–30.

Panchyshyn, R., & Monroe, E. E. (1986). *Developing key concepts for solving word problems.* Baldwin, N.Y.: Barnell Loft.

Parkham, J. L. (1983). A meta-analysis of the use of manipulative materials and student achievement in elementary school machematics. *Dissertation Abstracts International, 44a,* 96.

Pauk, W. (1984). *How to study in college.* Boston: Houghton Mifflin.

Perl, S. (1983). How teachers teach the writing process: Overview of an ethnographic research project. *Elementary School Journal, 84,* 19–24.

Personkee, C., & Yee, A. (1971). *Comprehensive spelling instruction: Theory, research, and application.* Scranton: Intext Educational Publishers.

Radabaugh, M. T., & Yukish, J. F. (1982). *Curriculum and methods for the mildly handicapped.* Boston: Allyn & Bacon.

Rivera, D., & Deutsch-Smith, D. (1988). Using a demonstration strategy to teach middle school students with learning disabilities how to compute long division. *Journal of Learning Disabilities, 21,* 77–81.

Robin, A., Armel, S., & O'Leary, K. (1975). The effects of self-instruction on writing deficiencies. *Behavior Therapy, 6,* 178–187.

Rose, T. L., McEntyre, E., & Dowdy, C. (1982). Effects of two-error correction procedures on oral reading. *Learning Disability Quarterly, 5,* 100–105.

Rubin, A., & Bruce, B. (1985). *Learning with QUILL: Lessons for students, teachers and software designers.* Reading Report No. 60. Washington, D.C.: National Institute of Education.

Rudman, M. (1973). Informal spelling in the classroom: A more effective approach. *Reading Teacher, 26,* 602–604.

Russell, C. (1983). Putting research into practice: Conferencing with young writers. *Language Arts, 60,* 333–340.

Salend, S. J. (October, 1980). Using cues and clues. *Early Years,* 32–33.

Salend, S. M. (1984). A multidimensional approach to remediating sinistral handwriting deficits in a gifted student. *The Pointer, 29,* 23–28.

Scardamalia, M., & Bereiter, C. (1986). Research on written composition. In M. C. Wittrock (Ed.), *Handbook of research on teaching* (pp. 778–803). New York: Macmillan.

Schell, V. J. (1982). Learning partners: Reading and mathematics. *The Reading Teacher, 35,* 544–548.

Scruggs, T. E., Mastropieri, M. A., Levin, J. R., & Gaffney, J. S. (1985). Facilitating the acquisition of science facts in learning disabled students. *American Educational Research Journal, 22,* 575–586.

Slingerland, B. H. (1976). *A multi-sensory approach to language arts for specific language disability children: A guide for primary teachers.* Cambridge, Mass.: Educators Publishing Service.

Smith, D. D., & Lovitt, T. C. (1982). *The computational arithmetic program.* Austin, Tex.: Pro-Ed.

Smith, E. M., & Alley, G. R. (1981). *The effect of teaching sixth graders with learning difficulties a strategy for solving verbal math problems (Research Report #39).* Lawrence, Kan.: Institute for Research in Learning Disabilities.

Stephens, T. M., Hartman, A. C., & Lucas, V. H. (1982). *Teaching children basic skills: A curriculum handbook. 2nd ed.* Columbus: Charles E. Merrill.

Stern, C. (1965). *Structural arithmetic.* Boston: Houghton Mifflin.

Stowitschek, C. E., & Jobes, N. K. (1977). Getting the bugs out of spelling—Or an alternative to the spelling bee. *Teaching Exceptional Children, 9,* 74-76.

Sullivan, K. (1981). Money: A key to mathematical success. *Arithmetic Teacher, 29,* 34-35.

Suydam, M. N. (1984). Research report: Manipulative materials. *Arithmetic Teacher. 31,* 27.

Suydam, M. N. (1986). Manipulative materials and achievement. *Arithmetic Teacher, 33,* 10, 32.

Swett, S. C. (1978). Math and LD: A new perspective. *Academic Therapy, 14,* 5-13.

Thomas, C. C., Englert, C. S., & Gregg, S. (1987). An analysis of errors and strategies in the expository writing of learning disabled students. *Remedial and Special Education, 8,* 21-30.

Thornton, C. A., Tucker, B. F., Dossey, J. A., & Bazik, E. F. (1983). *Teaching mathematics to children with special needs.* Menlo Park, Calif.: Addison-Wesley.

Thornton, C. A., & Wilmot, B. (1986). Special learners. *Arithmetic Teacher, 33,* 38-41.

Thurber, D. N. (1981). *Teacher's edition. D'Nealian handwriting.* Glenview, Ill.: Scott, Foresman & Co.

Tompkins, G. E., & Friend, M. (1986). On your mark, get set, write! *Teaching Exceptional Children, 18,* 82-89.

Tompkins, G. E., & Friend, M. (1988). After the students write: What's next? *Teaching Exceptional Children, 20,* 4-9.

Traub, N. (1982). Reading, spelling, handwriting: Traub systematic holistic method. *Annals of Dyslexia, 32,* 135-145.

Trueblood, C. R. (1986). Hands on: Help for teachers. *Arithmetic Teacher, 33,* 48-51.

Vaca, J. L., Vaca, R. T., & Gove, M. K. (1987). *Reading and learning to read.* Boston: Little, Brown & Company.

Vallecorsa, A. L., Zigmond, N., & Henderson, L. M. (1985). Spelling instruction in special education classrooms. *Exceptional Children, 52,* 19-24.

Viet, D. T., Scruggs, T. E., & Mastropieri, M. A. (1986). Extended mnemonic instruction with learning disabled students. *Journal of Educational Psychology, 78,* 300-308.

Weiner, H. (1988, April). *Collaborative models revised.* A paper presented at the conference on Writing Models and Programs for the Learning Disabled College Student, New Paltz, New York.

Whitt, J., Paul, P. V., & Reynolds, C. J. (1988). Motivating reluctant learners to write. *Teaching Exceptional Children, 20,* 36–39.

Wiederholt, J. L., Hammill, D. D., & Brown, V. (1978). *The resource teacher: A guide to effective practices.* Boston: Allyn & Bacon.

Williams, D. E. (1986). Activities for algebra. *Arithmetic Teacher, 33,* 42–47.

Witman, C. C., & Riley, J. D. (1978). Colored chalk and messy fingers: A kinesthetic-tactile approach to reading. *The Reading Teacher, 31,* 620–623.

Woodruff, E., Bereiter, C., & Scardamalia, M. (1981). *On the road to computer assisted compositions. Journal of Educational Technology Systems, 10,* 133–148.

Wong, B. Y. L. (1986). A cognitive approach to spelling. *Exceptional Children, 53,* 169–173.

Zigmond, N., Vallecorsa, A., & Leinhardt, G. (1980). Reading instruction for students with learning disabilities. *Topics in Language Disorders, 1,* 89–98.

CHAPTER 8

Adapting Grading and Testing for Mainstreamed Students

(Mimi/Monkmeyer Press Photo Service)

Testing and grading student mastery of specific material is a necessary component of classroom activities. However, for mainstreamed students, traditional testing and grading procedures can be an obstacle to successful functioning in the regular classroom milieu (Salend & Salend, 1985a). Therefore, in addition to modifying the instructional program for mainstreamed students, teachers may need to adapt their evaluation systems. For example, if a teacher modified the instructional program for a mainstreamed student who experiences difficulties in writing, the teacher may need to adapt the ways content mastery will be measured and graded.

Educators must be careful that the testing and grading modifications they institute do not compromise the integrity of the test, course, and curriculum. Therefore, the need for adaptations in testing and grading should be determined by the multidisciplinary placement team and outlined in the student's IEP. It may be valuable for regular classroom teachers to meet with special educators and parents to identify what alternative testing and grading systems have been successful (New York State Education Department, 1986). This chapter presents information educators can use in determining and designing adaptations in testing and grading. Specifically, the chapter offers information on alternative grading systems, factors to consider in designing teacher-made tests, alternative testing techniques, and teaching test-taking and research paper-writing skills to students.

Grading

Although grading presents a problem for many educators, it may be particularly problematic for teachers dealing with mainstreamed students (Harrington & Morrison, 1981; Kinnison, Hayes & Acord, 1981). The major responsibility for assigning grades will lie with the regular classroom teacher, but because mainstreamed students may receive the services of a resource room teacher, the roles of these professionals regarding the assigning of grades should be discussed and delineated (Cohen, 1983). This discussion should include

1. Who is responsible for assigning the report card grade?
2. Should the grade be based on the discrepancy between the student's actual and potential performance, or between the actual performance and grade-level expectancy?
3. What type of grading feedback should be given on a daily basis?
4. What type of descriptive annotation will best complement the system's report card grading procedure?

5. Whom should the parent contact to discuss a grade? (Cohen, 1983, p. 86).

Point Systems

Most teachers use a traditional grading system whereby students are compared and assigned letter or numerical grades based on their performance on tests (Marsh & Price, 1980). However, this system may not be appropriate for many mainstreamed students because it does not allow for grades to be assigned on an individualized scale (Cohen, 1983). Point systems can be made fairer for mainstreamed students by weighing a variety of activities to determine students' grades (Kinnison, Hayes, & Acord, 1981). For example, rather than grades being based solely on test scores, points toward the final grade can be divided so that 40 per cent of the grade is related to projects, 30 per cent to test performance, 10 per cent to class participation, 10 per cent to homework, and 10 per cent to effort.

Alternative Grading Systems

Teachers may have to consider several grading alternatives for use with mainstreamed students (Kinnison, Hayes, & Acord, 1981). Teachers can individualize each grading alternative for mainstreamed students by incorporating descriptive comments on student performance and a listing of skills mastered into the student's report card.

Individualized Educational Program

A grading alternative that allows teachers to individualize the grading procedures for mainstreamed students is the Individualized Educational Program, or IEP (Cohen, 1983; Kinnison, Hayes, & Acord, 1981). Using the IEP as a foundation for grading can help assign meaningful grades that acknowledge student progress in meeting goals established at a certain skill level. Thus, students who are working at their expected ability levels can receive grades that are commensurate with their effort and performance.

The IEP contains objectives and performance criteria that teachers can use to measure students' performance and achievements during the marking period. The students' grades could be a function of the number of objectives mastered and the level of mastery demonstrated for each objective. For example, students who master all their objectives by obtaining a mastery level of 80 per cent might be assigned a grade of B, while students who achieve a mastery level of 95 per cent on all their objectives would be assigned a grade of A. Students who fail to demonstrate mastery of the objectives outlined in their IEPs would be graded accordingly.

To ensure the consistency of this alternative grading system with the school district's policies for grading, the criteria levels specified in the IEP should reflect the performance standards specified in the district's grading procedures (Kinnison, Hayes, & Acord, 1981). For example, if the district's policy states that an A grade is earned when a student achieves at the performance criterion of 90 per cent or better, then the performance standards used in formulating the IEP should be consistent with this criterion.

Student Self-Comparison

A grading policy that is similar to IEP grading is *student self-comparison* (Kinnison, Hayes, & Acord, 1981), a technique that employs elements of mastery learning to individualize the grading process. Students measure their progress by examining their gains relative to the curriculum. Students and teachers meet to determine appropriate instructional goals within the curriculum. They then keep track of the students' progress toward meeting the identified goals, which are reported on the students' report cards.

Contract Grading

In a similar alternative grading procedure that teachers can employ, *contract grading*, teachers and students determine the amount and quality of the work students must complete in order to receive a specific grade. Since the quantity, quality, and method of evaluation are specified in advance, contract grading reduces the subjectivity involved in grading and helps students understand the expectations associated with a specific grade (Vasa, 1981).

In addition to motivating academic performance, contract grading allows students to have input into selecting and evaluating mastery of academic goals. Contract grading can increase student motivation to achieve and promote a sense of responsibility and pride in their work (De Charms, 1971). In framing the contract, both teachers and students should agree on content the students hope to learn; activities, strategies, and resources that will help students acquire the skills; products students will produce to demonstrate mastery; strategies for evaluating students' products; timelines for assignments, including penalties for lateness: and procedures for assigning grades (Jones & Jones, 1986; Vasa, 1981).

One way to implement contract grading in the classroom is to list activities of different degrees of complexity on the blackboard as well as the corresponding grade associated with each assignment. Then explain each assignment to students; each student can select an appropriate skill-level assignment commensurate with the grade they would like to receive (Jones & Jones, 1986). The agreement between students and teachers can then be formalized in a contract.

Pass/Fail Systems

A very popular grading option is *pass/fail grading* (Bellanca & Kirschenbaum, 1976), in which minimum course competencies are specified. Any student who demonstrates mastery receives a "P" grade, while students who fail to meet the minimum standards are given an "F" grade (Vasa, 1981). Pass/fail grading acknowledges that students completed their classes' requirements without being compared to their peers. Some schools have modified traditional pass/fail grading to include such distinctions as honors (HonorP), high pass (HP), pass (P), and low pass (LP).

Mastery Level/Criterion Systems

Mastery and criterion grading alternatives possess elements of the IEP and contract grading systems. Mastery level systems can be highly individualized, with students working on different skills and activities and thus taking different tests. Students and teachers meet to divide the material into a hierarchy of skills and activities based on individual needs and abilities as measured by a pretest. After completing learning activities, the students take a posttest or perform an activity to demonstrate mastery of the content. When students demonstrate mastery, they receive credit for that accomplishment and proceed to the next skill to be mastered. This process is repeated until students master all skill levels. While students can then be graded in traditional ways, mastery of skills can be acknowledged through a pass/fail system. Thus, students who demonstrate mastery of the requisite skills are awarded a pass; those students who do not show proficiency receive a fail.

Another type of criterion grading involves checklists that delineate the competencies associated with teachers' courses (Vasa, 1981). They evaluate each student according to mastery of these competencies. The checklist grading system has several advantages (Vasa, 1981). It provides more specific data on the students' mastery of skills, which facilitates communication with parents. This type of system can also be diagnostic, helping educators identify areas of weakness that need to be targeted for remediation.

Multiple Grading

A *multiple grading system* can reward mainstreamed students for different aspects of their performance and individualize the grading process (Kinnison, Hayes, & Acord, 1981). Rather than receiving a one-dimensional grade, multiple grading provides teachers with the opportunity to grade students in the areas of ability, effort, and achievement. The ability grade is based on students' expected improvements in content area. The effort grade is a measure of the time and energy the students devoted to learning the content. The achievement grade assesses the students' mastery of the material in relation to others. Students' report cards can then include a listing of the three grades for each content area, or grades can be computed by averaging the three areas.

Level Grading

A type of multiple grading, *level grading* allows teachers to individualize the grading system by using a subscript to indicate the level of difficulty at which the students' grades are based (Kinnison, Hayes, & Acord, 1981). For example, a subscript system can be devised so that a B_1, B_2, and B_3 indicate that the student grade is based on content above grade level, at grade level, or below grade level. Similarly, a grade of B_6 might note that a student is working in the B range at the sixth-grade level. In addition to using subscripts to provide additional information, teachers also can supplement quantitative report card grades by writing comments concerning the students' performance and effort (Cohen, 1983).

Shared Grading

Regular and special education teachers who are working together to instruct students in a specific content area may choose a *shared grading* system, in which teachers collaborate to assign students their grades based on both teachers' observations of performance (Kinnison, Hayes, & Acord, 1981). This system requires collaboration between educators, so they should establish guidelines for determining and weighing valid criteria and measuring performance.

Descriptive Grading

Teachers can individualize each grading alternative for mainstreamed students by incorporating descriptive comments on student performance and listing skills mastered on the students' report card. Descriptive grading systems allow teachers to write a detailed description of the students' performance, which provides parents, students, and other educators with information on the students' skills, learning styles, effort, and attitudes. When using descriptive grading, teachers should avoid subjective descriptions and support all statements with examples and behaviors that document their observations.

Designing Teacher-Made Tests

While alternative grading systems are available to teachers, most of these innovative systems rely on data from traditional teacher-made tests. Lee and Alley (1981) found that performance on teacher-made unit tests constituted 60 per cent of students' grades. However, use of teacher-made tests to evaluate performance may be an obstacle for mainstreamed students whose ability to function within the parameters of such tests is limited by their disability (Adelman, 1982). Therefore, consider several factors when constructing tests to accurately assess the performance of mainstreamed students. Questions that can guide teachers in adapting their tests for mainstreamed students are presented in Figure 8.1.

Test Content

The academic component of a teacher-made test should be directly related to the objectives of the instructional program. Prior academic instruction should guide the formation of test items. The test should reflect not only *what* but also *how* content has been taught. Because many mainstreamed students may experience difficulty with generalization (Rose, Lesson, & Gottlieb, 1982; Vaughn, Bos, & Lund, 1986), the application of skills to other conditions should not be tested unless specifically taught. For example, after teaching basic multiplication facts, it would be counterproductive to attempt to test these facts through word problems. Similarly, the types of items should relate to the ways in which students acquired the information (Bloom, 1956; Gagne, 1979). Content taught via analysis, synthesis, or problem-solving techniques is best tested through essay questions, whereas factual and rote material can be tested by multiple

FIGURE 8.1.   Teacher-Made Test Construction Evaluation Questions.

Questions to ask in devising and evaluating teacher-made tests:

Content

- Is the content of the test directly related to the objectives taught?
- Does the test require students to apply skills that they have not been specifically taught?
- Are the types of questions consistent with the strategies used to help students learn the content?
- Are the language and terminology used in both test directions and items consistent with that used in class?
- Is the percentage of items devoted to specific content areas commensurate with the amount of class time spent on those areas?
- Is the scope of the material being tested too broad? too narrow?
- Is the readability of the test appropriate?

Format

- Are directions understandable?
- Are cues provided to indicate a change in directions? alert students to the specifics of each item?
- Is the test too long?
- Is the test neat and free of distracting features?
- Is the test legible?
- Are there a reasonable number of items per page?
- Do items on a page have proper spacing?
- Are items sequenced correctly?
- Do students have to transfer their responses to a separate answer sheet?
- Do students have enough space to record their responses?

Multiple Choice Items

- Are the choices grammatically correct and free of double negatives?
- Is the stem longer than the answer alternatives?
- Does the stem relate to only one point and include only relevant information?
- Are all the choices feasible and the same length?

Matching Items

- Does the matching section include no more than ten items?
- Are there an equal number of choices in both columns?
- Is there only one correct response for each pair?
- Are the directions and the columns presented on the same page?
- Do students respond by writing the letter or number in a blank rather than drawing lines from column to column?
- Are the longer item statements listed in the left-hand column and the shorter statements in the right-hand column?

FIGURE 8.1.   (*continued*)

True-False Items

- Are questions phrased clearly without double negatives?
- Do items relate to relevant information?
- Do students respond by circling their choice of *True* or *False* rather than writing out their response?

Sentence Completion Items

- Do questions relate to meaningful information?
- Are questions understandable to students?

Essay Questions

- Is the readability of the question appropriate?
- Are key words highlighted?
- Are open-ended questions divided into smaller sequential questions?

---

choice, true-false, matching, and short-answer items. Additionally, use language and terminology in both test directions and items that are consistent with that used in class.

Consider another aspect of previous academic instruction when determining the content of a test: the amount of time spent on instructional units. The percentage of test questions related to specific content areas should be commensurate with the amount of class time spent on these topics (Salend & Salend, 1985a). For example, a test following a unit during which 30 per cent of class time was spent on the U.S. Constitution, should contain that percentage of test items assessing mastery of material related to the Constitution. Shorter and more frequent tests that focus on more specific content rather than fewer comprehensive tests of broader scope can assist mainstreamed students who have difficulty remembering large amounts of information. Frequent testing can allay the apprehension produced by unit testing and provide opportunities to develop proper test-taking behaviors.

Format

Even though many mainstreamed students can master the academic content necessary for successful performance on a test, they may experience unusual difficulty with the test format (Beattie, Grise, & Algozzine, 1983). Tests for mainstreamed students should be designed to correspond not only to the testing purpose, but also to the characteristics of the students to be tested. Therefore, to promote optimal student performance, educators should consider several aspects of a test's format (Salend & Salend, 1985a).

The appearance and organization of a test may affect students' scores. Tests that seem overwhelmingly long or that cause confusion and distraction because of poor appearance or spatial design can defeat students before they begin. The test should be neat and free of distracting features. Only information relevant to the test items should appear on the pages. Because many students with disabilities have reading problems, legibility of items is essential. Therefore, items should be clearly and darkly printed on a solid, nondistracting background. A piece of dark paper can be placed under the test as a background (Wood, 1988). Ideally, tests should be typed, but if they must be written, the writing should be in the style (manuscript or cursive) to which the student is accustomed. Finally, making more than one master copy of a test will reduce the number of tests being run from one master, so that printing clarity is preserved. If, however, a ditto of the test does not provide a copy clear enough for mainstreamed students, a xerox copy of the master sheet should be provided.

Many students with specific learning problems lack appropriate organizational skills, which can adversely affect their test performance (Hammill & Bartel, 1978; Wallace & McLoughlin, 1979). The number and types of items on a page, as well as how they are displayed, can have an impact on student performance. Too many items on a page can cause confusion, as can items that are begun on one page and continued on another. Inadequate spacing between items or poor spacing within items can make a test seem overwhelming. Tests that cannot be written on and require students to transfer answers to a separate paper may be especially difficult for mainstreamed students.

Minimize organizational confusion by properly spacing and sequencing items. A minimum of three spaces between items and one and a half spaces within lines of an item can help delineate boundaries between items. Similarly, presenting items in a fixed, predictable, symmetrical sequence that emphasizes the transition from item to item can ensure that mainstreamed students do not skip lines or fail to complete test items. Allowing students to write on the test protocol rather than transferring answers to a separate page can lessen confusion for those students with organizational difficulties. Providing adequate space for the response to items will allow students to complete an answer without continuing on another page, and can structure the length of the students' responses.

Also give consideration to the order in which items are presented, as well as the variety of items presented on a test. Items that measure similar skills should be ordered so that they reflect a progression from easiest to hardest (Beattie, Grise, & Algozzine, 1983). Objective items, such as multiple choice, true-false, or matching, are best suited to the response modes of some students; subjective essays and short answers are best for others. For this reason, a test that requires a variety of responses within a reasonable amount of time will be most fair. Similarly, teachers can structure their tests to allow students to have some choice in responding to items (Sarda, 1988). For example, a test section can comprise twenty items of varying format; students can be directed to respond to any fifteen questions within that section. Those students who are proficient at multiple choice items but have difficulty with true-false questions can choose to answer more of the former and fewer of the latter.

An important aspect of the test format is the manner in which test items are presented to students. Therefore, teachers also should consider their mainstreamed students' needs in phrasing and structuring objective and essay type questions. Guidelines teachers should consider in writing questions are listed below.

MULTIPLE CHOICE ITEMS. Teachers can promote student performance on multiple choice items by considering several factors relating to the stem and the choices. In writing multiple choice tests, teachers should ensure that

- the choices are grammatically correct and free of double negatives;
- the stem is longer than the answer alternatives;
- the stem has only one major point and includes only relevant information;
- the choices are all feasible and the same length;
- the choices are presented to students using a vertical format, with the answer bubble located to the right of each alternative; and
- the correct choice is the best answer (Beattie, Grise, & Algozzine, 1983; Pauk, 1984; New York State Department of Education, 1986).

Multiple choice items also can be tailored to the needs of mainstreamed students by reducing the number of choices to three rather than the more traditional four or five. Eliminating more difficult choices, such as having to select *all of the above, none of the above,* or two of three choices, also can aid the performance of mainstreamed students. Furthermore, allowing students to circle their choice selection can alleviate problems students may encounter in recording their answers (Wood, 1988).

MATCHING ITEMS. The organization of matching item questions can have a significant impact on students' test scores. When constructing matching items, teachers should consider several variables, such as number and organization of items (Wood, 1988). Each matching section of the test should include a maximum of ten items. When the need arises for more than ten items, group the additional items by content area in a separate matching section. There should be an equal number of choices in both columns, with only one correct response for each pair. Because students usually approach matching items by reading an item in the left-hand column, and then reading all the available choices in the right-hand column, teachers can help students save time by listing the longer items in the left-hand column (Shanley, 1988). For example, a matching item designed to assess mastery of vocabulary would have the definitions in the left-hand column and the vocabulary words in the right-hand column.

Organize the matching section of the test to avoid confusing the students (Wood, 1988). Placing the directions and both columns on the same page can prevent the frustration some students encounter when matching tests are presented on more than one page. To avoid the disorganization that can occur when students respond by drawing lines connecting their choices from both columns, locate blanks to the left of the left-hand column, and direct students to record the letter or number of their selection in the blank. Teachers also can facilitate rather than hinder student performance on this type of test question by composing choices that are clear and concise, and organizing both columns in a sensible fashion (such as identifying items in one column in numerical order, and the other in alphabetical order).

TRUE-FALSE ITEMS.   Many students may have difficulty responding to the true-false part of a test. In particular, they may experience problems responding to true-false items that require them to correct all false choices. Teachers can help students perform on true-false items by phrasing questions clearly, briefly, and without double negatives; highlighting critical parts of the true-false statements, such as words like *always* and *never;* eliminating items that assess trivial information or mislead students; avoiding items that ask students to change false statements into true statements; and limiting the number of this type of question to no more than ten items per test (Wood, 1988). Since some students may inadvertently fail to discriminate the *T* and the *F* when working in the pressure situation of a test, the response choices of True or False should be written out completely. Rather than writing out their response, students should be afforded the oppportunity to record their response by circling either True or False.

SENTENCE COMPLETION ITEMS.   Sentence completion items can be especially difficult for mainstreamed students who have memory deficits.

Teachers can lessen the memory requirements of these items by providing several response choices. For example, the sentence completion question, *The outer layer of the atmosphere is called the*—can be modified by listing the choices *stratosphere, exosphere,* and *ionosphere* under the blank. Statements to be completed that come directly from print materials, such as textbooks, can be too vague when taken out of the paragraph or chapter context, so phrase sentence completion clearly so that they are understandable to students (Wood, 1988).

ESSAY QUESTIONS. Essay questions present unique problems for many mainstreamed students because of the numerous skills necessary to answer them. Teachers can adapt essay questions by making sure that the questions are appropriate for students in terms of readability and level of difficulty (Wood, 1988). Highlight and define key words that guide students in analyzing and writing the essay. If it is inconvenient to define a large number of words and concepts on the test itself, allow students to use a word list or dictionary (Sarda, 1988).

Teachers also can help students interpret the question correctly and guide the essay in several ways. Rather than using a single, open-ended essay question, direct the organization and completeness of the response by employing subquestions that divide the open-ended question into smaller sequential questions that can elicit all the components of an accurate, well-structured, detailed answer. Here is an example of an essay question that teachers at Paramus (New Jersey) High School adapted for an English test:

In *By the Waters of Babylon,* John's father says, "If your dreams do not eat you, some day you will be a great man." Using *2* of the following characters—Arthur, Jack, Ralph, and John—discuss:

1. What does each character dream of doing?
2. What must each character do to fulfill his dream?
3. How do the attempts of each character to realize his dream change him as a person?
4. Does each achieve his dream? Explain.
5. Does each character's dream eat up that character? Explain.
6. In what ways does his success or failure make his life better or worse, happier or sadder? (Walla, 1988).

In addition to using subquestions, teachers can structure the students' essays by providing an outline or an answer checklist as a format for writing and sequencing the response (Wood, 1988).

Readability of Items

Another factor to consider when composing tests is the readability of its items, which teachers can assess using a readability formula (see Chapter 2). Teachers can adjust the readability of each item in several ways. Simplify abstract sentences by reducing the complexity of the language and adding examples that illustrate the statements. For example, the essay terms requiring students to compare and contrast two concepts can be simplified by asking students to identify how the concepts are alike and different (Wood, 1988). Similarly, understanding of critical, complicated terms can be facilitated by the use of synonyms and jargon-free explanations. The readability of sentences that are too long can be enhanced by eliminating unnecessary clauses and phrases, or dividing the sentence into two or more sentences. Misunderstandings can be avoided in reading test items by decreasing the number of pronouns used to refer to important points, objects, or events (Simpson, n.d.).

Alternative Testing Techniques

Mainstreamed students' performance on teacher-made and standardized, commercially produced tests may be affected by their specific learning needs. For example, students with reading difficulties may perform below their capabilities on a math test if the test problems and directions are presented solely through reading. PL94–142 mandates the use of alternative testing techniques so that "when a test is administered to a child with impaired sensory, manual, or speaking skills, the test results accurately reflect the child's aptitude or achievement level or whatever other factors the test purports to measure, rather than reflecting the child's impaired sensory, manual, or speaking skills (except where those skills are the factors which the test purports to measure)."

Alternative testing techniques are adaptations in testing administration and procedures that provide students with disabilities with the opportunity to perform at their optimal level (New York State Education Department, 1986). The type of testing modification needed will depend on the individual student's needs, as well as the nature of the test. In the math test example cited above, an appropriate alternative testing technique may be for an adult or peer to read the questions to the students. The multidisciplinary team should determine specific alternative testing techniques that are appropriate for students and list them in the students' IEP. Alternative testing techniques should only be used when necessary, and students should be weaned from their use as they demonstrate success in the mainstreamed setting.

Alternative testing techniques include adaptations in the manner in which test questions and directions are presented to students, or changes in the manner students respond to test items or determine their answers. Any modification in the procedures used to administer and score the test also is considered an alternative testing technique. When using commercially produced, standardized tests, educators should consult the test's manual to determine if the test modification is consistent with the administration procedures outlined by the test developers. Because alternative testing techniques prohibited in the manual may invalidate a student's test results in comparison to the norm group, educators should exercise caution when interpreting these results.

Presentation of Items and Directions

The items and directions for most tests are usually presented to students in print. Because of their problems decoding printed matter, students with visual impairments and reading difficulties will experience problems completing tests that are presented in this fashion. Several modifications are available to educators to help students understand the directions and items of the test: rewriting the test's directions in terminology that the student can read and understand; offering directions for each new section of the test; presenting directions in the sequence in which they should be followed; translating the test directions and items into sign language, Braille, large print, and/or the students' native language; structuring the reading so that each sentence is placed on a single line; avoiding double negatives; omitting items that cannot be modified to address the students' disabilities; and giving additional examples (New York State Education Department, 1986; Wood, 1988).

Incorporate cues into the test that will facilitate the mainstreamed students' understanding and following of test directions. For example, to indicate a change in directions among types of items, provide a sample of each type of problem set off in a box with each change of test directions (Beattie, Grise, & Algozzine, 1983). Similarly, cues such as color coding, underlining, and enlarging key words or highlighting changes in mathematical symbols will alert students to the specifics of each item. If appropriate, highlight and define key terms for students on the test. For example, the directions for a section of a test asking students to find the least common denominator can include a definition of that term. Cues, such as arrows, can be placed at the bottom of the test pages to indicate those pages that are a continuous part of a section of the test; stop signs can indicate ending pages (Beattie, Grise, & Algozzine, 1983).

Some students will require help from school personnel in discerning the test's directions and items. An adult—the teacher, resource room teacher, or teacher's aide—can be an individualized proctor to read the test directions and questions to students. When using this alternative, it may be necessary to read the fixed directions at the beginning of the test repeatedly, and review them when a new set of directions is introduced (New York State Education Department, 1986). In reading test parts to students, adults should be careful not to provide students with cues and additional information that may affect their performance.

In addition to assistance from school personnel, some mainstreamed students may need the help of specialized equipment to gain information about test directions and items. Students with visual impairments may benefit from use of visual magnification aids, while devices that amplify auditory stimuli can help maximize the performance of students with hearing impairments. Audiotapes of tests and markers to focus the students' attention and maintain place during reading can aid students with reading disabilities (New York State Department of Education, 1986).

Responses to Items

Some mainstreamed students, particularly those that have problems writing and speaking, may require alternative testing techniques to respond to test items. Spelling problems can be minimized by placing correct spelling of difficult words necessary for essays or short-answer items on the blackboard. Students who have difficulty with handwriting can be helped in several ways. Use of multiple choice items instead of sentence completion and essay questions can minimize the writing requirements necessary to complete the test. When grammar, punctuation, and spelling are not essential aspects of the response, students can tape-record answers or take an oral test. If the mechanics of written language are important in evaluating the response, students can dictate their response to an adult recorder. Students can then review their response in written form, and direct their recorder on the correct grammar, punctuation, and word choices. Devices such as word processors, pointers, communication boards, and typewriters can help students who have difficulties communicating their answers in written or oral form (New York State Department of Education, 1986).

Because of their unique conditions, some mainstreamed students may need to employ aids to determine their responses to items. Computational aids, such as calculators, software programs, arithmetic tables, word lists, an abacus, and number lines, can be useful for students who have the requisite problem-solving abilities to complete items but lack the necessary memory skills to remember facts or word definitions. For example, a list of arithmetic tables can help students who understand the process of solving word problems but lack the mastery of math facts to compute the correct answer.

Scoring

Teachers also can modify test scoring to address mainstreamed students' unique needs. Teachers can adapt their scoring procedures by scoring only items that are completed, omitting certain questions and prorating credit (Banbury, 1987; New York State Department of Education, 1986). For example, mainstreamed students' scores can be determined by computing the percentage correct out of the number attempted (Gillet, 1986). Tests can be scored so that students who give incorrect answers receive partial credit for showing correct work. For example, when completing math tests, students can earn credit for performing and listing the operations necessary to solve the problem. When grammar, spelling, and punctuation are not the elements being tested, teachers can consider not penalizing students for these errors or giving students separate grades for content and mechanics. For example, if an essay response on a social studies test is correct but contains many misspelled words, the teacher could give the student a separate grade for content and spelling. On essay tests, students initially can be given credit for an outline, web, diagram, or chart in lieu of writing a lengthy response (Fagen, Graves, & Tessier-Switlick, 1984).

Testing Procedures

Although tests are typically administered in large groups during one timed session, educators may need to adjust the procedures they employ to test mainstreamed students. One such testing procedure is the scheduling of tests. Mainstreamed students may not work as fast as their nonhandicapped peers because of difficulties processing information and staying on-task, the time constraints associated with the use of specialized testing techniques (such as dictating answers), and physical needs that cause them to tire easily (New York State Education Department, 1986). Therefore, when planning testing for some mainstreamed students, educators should consider such scheduling alternatives as allocating more time to complete tests, eliminating the time limits on tests, reducing the length of the tests, providing the opportunity for students to take frequent breaks as needed, dividing the testing sessions into separate, short periods within a day, and completing the tests over a period of several days (Banbury, 1987; New York State Department of Education, 1986).

An alternative testing technique that can be appropriate for some mainstreamed students is changing the setting of the test. Students who are easily distracted, have difficulty remaining on-task, and are anxious about taking tests may perform better if they take the test individually in a quiet place free of distractions, such as the resource room (New York

State Education Department, 1986). Similarly, students who have difficulty maintaining on-task behavior should be seated in a nondistracting area of the room (Wood, 1988). Students with physical disabilities may require adaptive furniture or devices; students with sensory impairments may need specific environmental arrangements, such as specialized lighting or acoustics (Banbury, 1987).

Using Microcomputers

Educators have begun to use computers in the area of educational assessment (Hasselbring & Crossland, 1981; Wilson & Fox, 1982). Hasselbring and Crossland (1981) devised a computer-monitored, student-paced spelling assessment called the Computerized Diagnostic Spelling Test. Wilson and Fox (1982) developed a computer-based system to assess students' language skills. Both systems provide raw scores, identify correct and incorrect responses, and perform error analysis. While the main use of microcomputers in educational testing has been with standardized tests, they also can assist teachers in designing, constructing, administering, and scoring teacher-made tests (Salend & Salend, 1985b). However, because students may not efficiently use the keyboard, exercise caution in using microcomputers in the assessment of student skills (Varnhagen & Gerber, 1984).

MODIFYING PRESENTATION MODES.   Presentation mode problems, which some students may encounter with paper-and-pencil, teacher-made tests, can be alleviated by giving students tests via the microcomputer. The computer can aid the teacher by regulating the speed as well as the organization of the presentation, highlighting critical information, and limiting distracting features that may interfere with student performance.

Teachers can use microcomputers to control the speed of the presentation of test questions. Those tests that are not speed-based can be paced by the computer, so that a new question is presented only after a student has responded. In speed tests, the computer can be programmed to introduce the next item at fixed intervals that are appropriate to the students' levels of proficiency. For example, the level of difficulty of a test of addition facts can be individualized by adjusting the speed at which the computer presents new items to students, based on their prior performance. As mainstreamed students master the content at a specific presentation interval, the speed at which they are required to demonstrate mastery can be increased.

Microcomputers can help teachers design tests that facilitate student performance. Items can be presented one at a time to minimize organizational problems. Visual boundaries around items as well as proper spacing can be employed to delineate items when more than one item appears on the screen (Salend & Salend, 1985b).

Microcomputers' graphics and design capabilities can enhance the test's appearance and highlight essential parts of the questions (Salend & Salend, 1985b). High-quality graphics, such as graphs, maps, drawings, and models, can be produced with the microcomputer. The computer monitor offers students a solid, dark screen that can limit distractions and promote legibility. Student awareness of the specifics of items and test directions also can be heightened for students using computer graphics and color.

MODIFYING THE RESPONSE MODES. The unique ways students can enter information into the computer allows teachers the opportunity to offer mainstreamed students several response mode alternatives (Salend & Salend, 1985b). Students can respond to computer-based tests by typing or using such peripheral devices as a mouse, light pen, joystick, and touch screen (see Chapter 6). The light pen, a device that looks like a pen and allows individuals to respond to the computer by touching the monitor, can be particularly helpful for responding to multiple choice items. Computerized speech synthesizers can help nonverbal students respond orally to test questions.

MOTIVATING STUDENTS. Because of prior poor performance on tests, many mainstreamed students may lack the motivation to achieve at their optimal level (Salend, Blackhurst, & Kifer, 1982). The computer can be a vehicle for motivating students to perform on tests. Because feedback can motivate students during testing (Allyon & Kelly, 1972; Salend, et. al., 1982), microcomputer-administered tests can be designed to include feedback and reinforcement to students (Salend & Salend, 1985b). For example, after students answer a fixed number of items, the computer can deliver feedback by flashing a statement of encouragement (*Keep on trying!*) or presenting a novel computer graphic. The frequency and type of feedback statements should be tailored to students' needs. To avoid satiation and maintain student motivation, feedback statements should be varied and delivered after a variable number of responses.

Increase motivation of students to perform at their optimal level on tests by presenting the test as a computer game, with correct responses allowing students to proceed toward winning the game. For example, a tic-tac-toe game can pit students against the computer. Each correct response to a test question can be acknowledged by allowing students to put an X or O on the screen. Video game formats also can foster the motivational appeal of computer-based tests (Chaffin, Maxwell, & Thompson, 1982).

Branching can assist teachers in designing tests that prevent frustration by exploring the students' mastery of specific content (Lord, 1980; Salend & Salend, 1985b). Using the microcomputer's branching capabilities, students' tests can be individualized so that they are channeled to items at their appropriate level before progressing to more difficult items. When the content of a test is sequentially based, ceilings can be programmed into the test so that the test or a section of the test ends when students incorrectly answer a certain number of items.

SCORING.   The computer can also score microcomputer-administered tests. In addition to timeliness, microcomputer scoring can help educators identify diagnostic error patterns. For example, a punctuation test can be designed to list correct and incorrect responses and determine the types of errors made. The pinpointed errors can then form the basis of additional instruction in that area.

Teaching Test-Taking Skills

The ability of students to demonstrate mastery of classroom content covered on tests can be affected by their *test-wiseness* (Scruggs & Mastropieri, 1988). Millman and Pauk (1969) define test-wiseness as "the ability to use the characteristics of tests and test-taking situations to reach the full potential of one's knowledge and aptitude" (p. xiii).

Research indicates that many students with learning problems fail to use appropriate test-taking skills to enhance their test performance (Scruggs, Bennion, & Lifson, 1985; Scruggs & Lifson, 1986; Tolfa & Scruggs, 1986). In an extensive review of the literature on the test-taking skills of students with learning problems, Scruggs and Mastropieri (1988) concluded that

> deficits were found in skills such as use of stem information, elimination of implausible options, deductive reasoning strategies, prior knowledge, self-monitoring, attention to specific format demands, and use of separate answer sheets. All identified deficits, taken together, suggest that test scores of LD students may not be as accurate a reflection of achievement or ability as the scores of nonhandicapped children, who are typically able to use test-taking strategies to maximize their scores. (p. 91)

Mainstreamed students can learn a variety of test-taking skills to increase their test-wiseness and to maximize their performance on tests. Scruggs and Marsing (cited in Scruggs & Mastropieri, 1988) taught adolescents with learning problems to use four test-taking skills effectively.

Scruggs and Tolfa (1985), Scruggs and Mastropieri (1986), and Scruggs, Mastropieri, & Tolfa–Veit (1986) used direct training of test-taking skills to increase the standardized achievement test scores of students with learning problems. Lee and Alley (1981) increased students' performance on teacher-made tests by teaching them to use the SCORER strategy, a first-letter cue strategy that facilitates test performance by reminding students to

S = Schedule your work
C = Clue words
O = Omit difficult questions
R = Read carefully
E = Estimate your answers
R = Review your work
(Carman & Adams, 1972, p. 125).

Several test-taking behaviors that can be taught to students are outlined below.

Study for the Test

Appropriate studying behaviors also can ensure that students perform to the best of their abilities on tests. Therefore, encourage students to

- review content to be studied over a spaced period of time rather than cramming;
- determine the specific objectives to be accomplished in each study session;
- study the most difficult content areas first;
- set up the study area so that it is conducive to studying;
- gather all the materials necessary to facilitate the process, including notebooks, textbooks, paper, writing utensils, reference books, and calculators; and
- learn content-related terminology by creating a word file (Farquhar, Krumboltz, & Wrenn, 1969; Spargo, 1977).

Between ten and twenty minutes after studying content, it is a good technique for students to write out from memory the main points to be remembered and compare them with material from notes and textbooks to note any discrepancies (Chapman, 1969). This review can improve memory and help identify content that needs to be reviewed again.

When preparing to study for a test, students should determine the type(s) of questions that will be included in the test (Spargo, 1977). Because teachers often use tests that have similar formats and repeat questions, they can help students prepare for tests by giving them the opportunity to review prior tests and quizzes (Millman & Pauk, 1969). The review could offer students an explanation of the test's purpose and format. The length of the test, response types, and the completeness of the responses required also should be covered; examples of actual student responses are helpful, too.

In addition to knowing the type of test, students should have an idea of the test's content. One indication of the likelihood of a content area being covered on a test is the amount of class time the teacher has spent teaching it. Typically, important topics that will be covered on tests are those on which the teacher has spent significant amounts of time. An examination of notes and textbooks also can help students determine a test's content (Farquhar, Krumboltz, & Wrenn, 1969). Those topics that appear in both notes and textbooks are likely to be on the test. To ensure that students study relevant content, offer students specific information regarding the chapters and notes that will be covered on the test (Mercer & Mercer, 1985). Humphrey, Hoffman, and Crosby (1984) suggest that teachers give students a written outline or review sheet of material that will be covered on the test at least one week before the test.

Teachers also can provide students with time to work in small groups to prepare for tests. For example, small groups can review notes and chapters, predict possible questions, and quiz members on specific facts, terms, and concepts (Bos & Vaughn, 1988). Similarly, students can work together to develop and study lists of terms that are relevant to the subject matter (Devine, 1981).

Survey the Test

Before beginning a test, students should be taught to survey it (Millman & Pauk, 1969). This survey or preview should help students determine both the number and nature of the items to be answered. If unsure, students also should ask the test administrator how much time they will have to complete the test.

Establish a Plan

Based on the information obtained in surveying the test and reading the directions, students should develop an order and timeline for working on the test. In establishing the plan, students consider the total time allotted to the test, the point values of sections, and the level of difficulty of the items. To ensure that each section of the test is covered, students should allot a certain amount of time for each section based on point values and length. They should work on those sections worth the most points in descending order (Spargo, 1977).

In addition to working on the sections with respect to their point values, another approach students could use is to categorize the items according to their level of difficulty, and work on those items that are the easiest first. Thus, it is recommended that students make three passes through the test (Spargo, 1977). In the first pass, students read all questions and respond to those they know how to answer. They denote those that are somewhat difficult or very difficult with a symbol. During the second pass, students respond to those somewhat difficult questions skipped in the first pass. All unanswered questions are answered during the third and final pass.

Read the Directions

It is essential that students carefully and purposefully read the directions to all parts of the test (Spargo, 1977). In reading the directions, students should identify the nature of the response required, the aids that they will be allowed to use to assist them in answering questions (reference books, calculators, and computers), the sequence to be followed in completing the test, the point values of items and sections of the test, and the time and space constraints (Millman & Pauk, 1969).

To ensure that students understand the test's directions, teachers can use practice items. At the beginning of the test, teachers can assign several practice items relating to the various types of questions on the test. These practice items can be reviewed with students prior to allowing them to proceed with the rest of the test. Once students start the test, teachers can check their understanding of test directions by periodically monitoring the student's answer sheet (Fagen, Graves, and Tessier-Switlick, 1984).

Seek Clarification

During the test, students may forget directions, encounter words that they do not understand, or find questions that they can interpret in several ways. For example, in the question *Show four differences between the ideas of Jefferson and Hamilton,* students may need additional clarification concerning how extensively they should discuss these differences. When these instances arise, students should be allowed to seek clarification from the teacher concerning the specifics of the question or section. Teachers willing to answer questions concerning the test should establish specific procedures for doing so beforehand.

Jot Down Essential Facts

Most tests require the memorization of information, so students initially should write down on the test paper essential facts and formulas that they will use throughout the test (Millman & Pauk, 1969). Therefore, in studying, students might develop and then memorize a list of essential information that is likely to appear on the test.

Use Key Words

The need for teacher assistance during testing can be minimized by teaching students to identify key words in question stems and the definitions of these words. It is recommended that students learn to circle or underline key words as they encounter them, and then determine their definition. A list of key words typically used in phrasing test questions and their meanings with respect to test items is presented in Figure 8.2.

Check Answers

If time remains at the end of the test, students should check that their responses are correct, complete, and neat (Millman & Pauk, 1969). After a page of the test has been reviewed, students should place a notation on it to indicate it has been completed, and checked so that additional time is not spent in reviewing it again. Students should be taught that when they are unsure of an answer, it is best to stay with their first choice (Spargo, 1977). Rather than leaving questions unanswered, students should attempt to answer all questions. However, when they lose points for incorrect responses, students should be taught to answer only those questions that they have a high probability of answering correctly.

Review Returned Tests

Teachers should offer corrective feedback on items in addition to providing students with a score on their tests (Cohen, 1983). When the test is graded and returned to students, it should be reviewed carefully by the class. In addition to checking for scoring errors, students should analyze tests to determine the frequency and types of errors made. If they note patterns of errors, students' preparation for upcoming tests should address the error trends. Error trends also can provide teachers with information for adapting tests to meet students' skills and preparing students for tests. For example, if a student's test shows problems with true-false

FIGURE 8.2.   Key Words in Essay Questions.

Clue Words	Meaning
1. describe define trace discuss examine analyze	Give in words a picture of an idea, a concept, or an object. Give clear, concise definitions. Record careful observation. Give the important ideas and show how they are related.
2. compare and contrast differentiate distinguish	Give likenesses and differences. Show differences between items, groups, or categories.
3. enumerate outline	Use lists, outlines, main and subordinate points, and details.
4. state relate	Write concisely and clearly, connecting ideas or concepts. Use chronology of events or ideas where it applies.
5. prove justify	Use facts, or logic, or cite authorities to justify your thesis.
6. evaluate criticize	Make value judgments but use logic to explain. Criticize, pro or con, the merits of a concept or a theory.
7. review summarize synthesize	Summarize main points concisely, restate judgments or conclusions, integrate arguments from different sources.

Source: M. J. Tonjes and M. V. Zintz. *Teaching Reading/Thinking/Study Skills in Content Classrooms* (Dubuque, Iowa: Wm. C. Brown, 1981), p. 246. Reprinted by permission.

items, the classroom or resource room teacher can assess mastery of this content using other types of items or review with the student the suggested strategies for optimizing performance on true-false items.

Objective Tests

Although several test-taking strategies are relevant for all types of tests (Mastropieri & Scruggs, 1987), taking an objective test is a very different process from taking an essay test. Objective tests include multiple choice, true-false, matching, and sentence completion items. Because objective tests cover a wide range of content areas, students will need to review the specifics to be covered on the test.

When working on any type of item in an objective test, students should identify and analyze critical words, look for word clues, such as *always* and *never*, which indicate extremes and (usually) incorrect answers, and rephrase questions in language they can understand (Spargo, 1977).

MULTIPLE CHOICE ITEMS.   One of the most popular objective test formats is the multiple choice item, which gives a question stem and then requires that the best answer be selected from a series of alternatives. In multiple choice questions, it is often best to read the question and think of the answer before reading and carefully analyzing all the choices. If the anticipated response is not one of the answer alternatives, students should delete obviously incorrect choices and analyze the other available choices.

Students should examine each response alternative to determine if it is true or false and then eliminate choices that are false or incorrect statements, not related to the content covered in class, or silly and deal with nonsense or irrelevant material (Pauk, 1984). However, in choosing correct options, students should examine all the alternatives and select the one that is the most complete and inclusive (Langan, 1982). Students should be aware that the choices of *all of the above,* *none of the above,* and numbers that represent the middle range often are correct (Pauk, 1984). Similarly, alternatives that are unusually long or short are frequently the correct answer (Bragstad & Stumpf, 1987). When response alternatives present contradictory answers, one of them is likely to be the correct response (Langan, 1982). However, when options provide information that is similar, both of them should be eliminated from consideration (Scruggs & Mastropieri, 1988).

Examining other elements of multiple choice items can provide clues to the correct alternative. Sometimes information from one question can assist in determining the correct answer to another question. Occasionally, the stems of questions contain the answer to other questions. According to Millman and Pauk (1969), generally, the correct alternative in a poorly constructed multiple choice test can be identified by considering such variables as length, qualifications, generalization, physical location, logical position, similarity of opposites, phraseology, language, grammar, emotive words, and silly ideas. While these clues are valuable in responding to poorly written multiple choice tests, students should be taught not to rely on them and to exercise caution in generalizing their use on other multiple choice tests.

Occasionally, multiple choice tests are machine graded and require the student to use a special writing utensil to record responses in a grid on a separate answer sheet. Since the transfer of responses from one document (test questions) to another (test answer sheet) can be problematic, students should exercise caution to ensure that they do not lose credit because of this unique format. Therefore, in taking machine-scored tests, students should have the correct writing tool; mark completely the grid that indicates their response; erase changes or mistakes thoroughly; fill in only one answer grid per item; and record answers in the correct space and follow the correct sequence (Carman & Adams, 1972).

TRUE-FALSE ITEMS.   Some true-false tests require students to respond by listing whether a statement is correct or incorrect, while others require students to correct false responses. Because their performance on the test will suffer if they do not read the directions to discern this difference, students should be instructed to determine the type of true-false items on the test before beginning.

When working on true-false items, students should examine the questions for *specific determiners,* which are words that modify or limit a statement (*rarely, usually*) (Millman & Pauk, 1969). Pauk (1984) identified the six most commonly used sets of qualifiers as

All-most-some-none (no)

Always-usually-sometimes-never,

Great-much-little-no

More-equal-less

Good-bad

Is-is not (p. 229)

Learning these sets and analyzing each true-false item by inserting them into the statement can help students determine if a true-false statement is understated, overstated, or correct. In general, false statements often include a qualifier that suggests the statement is extreme, or true 100 per cent of the time (such as *no, never, every, always, all*). Words that moderate a statement (*sometimes, most, many, generally, usually*) often indicate that a statement is true. Similarly, if true-false statements lack a specific determiner, the question should only be marked true if it is always true (Millman & Pauk, 1969).

Some true-false items have several parts. When answering these types of items, students should be careful to read all parts of the statement. If any part of the statement is false, they should make the statement false (Pauk, 1984).

True-false statements that have negative words or prefixes in them can be particularly problematic. In responding to these items, students should highlight the negative terms and identify the meaning of the item while deleting the negatives. Then, they should examine the sentence to determine whether the statement is true or false (Pauk, 1984).

MATCHING.   Matching tests require students to establish a relationship between information presented in left and right columns. Initially, students should determine the parameters of the matching tasks to note if each column has an equal number of items and if they can use an alternative more than once (Langan, 1982). When answering matching questions, it is helpful for students to survey both lists to get an idea of the choices; read the initial item in the left column first; read each choice in the right-hand column before answering; determine and record the correct answer if the answer is readily known; circle or underline the choice in the right-hand column that has been used; skip items that are difficult; and repeat these steps while proceeding down the left-hand column (Pauk, 1984). Students should be taught to avoid guessing until they have worked on all items; an incorrect match can multiply the number or errors by using a possible correct choice from the right-hand column.

SENTENCE COMPLETION ITEMS.   Sentence completion or fill-in-the-blank items require students to write the missing word, phrase, or number that correctly completes a sentence. These types of items often are used to measure the recall of information that is triggered by the stem of the question.

Students can be taught to approach these types of items by converting them into a question (Wood, 1988). For example, the sentence completion question *A large mass of moving air is called a*_____can be transformed into the question *What is a large mass of moving air called?* In responding to these questions, students should use the grammatical structure of the item to assist in formulating the answer (Millman & Pauk, 1969). For example, if the stem ends in *-a* or *-an,* then students can deduce that the correct answer starts with a vowel or a consonant, respectively. Examining the verb form also can cue students to whether the answer is singular or plural (Hook, 1969). Sometimes a hint about the correct answer to this type of item can be found by examining the number and length of the blanks provided by the teacher. Often, two blanks with no words between them indicates that a two-word answer, such as an individual's name, is the answer; two blanks separated by words should be approached as two separate statements. Similarly, a long blank tends to suggest that the correct answer is a phrase or a sentence. Encourage students to choose responses that are logical and consistent with the stem of the question.

Essay Tests

Essay tests necessitate that students write a response to a question. The degree of detail of the response will vary, but students can employ several strategies to improve their performance on this type of test. Initially, students should prepare for an essay test by trying to determine the material that will be covered on the test. Because test content should relate to material presented in classes and textbooks, students can get a good idea of the test's content by reviewing notes for information and topics emphasized in class and textbooks. Once the content has been determined, it is helpful for students to compose and try to answer questions that might be on the test (Spargo, 1977).

Students should approach an essay test in a systematic manner. Millman and Pauk (1969) propose that students answer essay questions using a three-step method. In the first step, students read the questions and record relevant points to be mentioned or addressed next to each question. This technique allows students to make sure that they don't forget essential information from one question as they work on another. In the second step, students start with the easiest questions first, rereading them and adding new or deleting irrelevant information recorded during the first pass. At this time, students also should organize their response into an outline before writing. The outline should use a combined number and letter system to indicate main points (*1, 2, 3*) and secondary supporting arguments (*1a, 1b, 1c*).

During the final step, students use the outline as a guide for composing their answer. In writing responses to essay questions, students should rephrase the question as the initial sentence of the answer, present the answer in a logical order with transitions from paragraph to paragraph, give specifics when necessary, use examples to support statements, and summarize the main points at the end of the essay. To save time, students should cross out mistakes rather than erasing or blacking them out (Carman & Adams, 1972). In terms of appearance of their final product, students should leave room in the left-hand margin for the teacher's comments, provide space between responses, and record their answer on one side of the page (Pauk, 1984). Finally, since the scoring of most essay questions allows for partial credit, students should try to respond to each question in some fashion. Therefore, if they are running out of time, students should be taught to put down their outline rather than leave the question blank.

Open-Ended Tests

Though not as prevalent as objective or essay tests, open-ended tests are preferred by some teachers. In an open-ended test, students are allowed to use reference books, usually their textbooks, to complete the exam. Since open-ended tests measure the ability to organize and interpret information, preparation for taking this type of test is critical for success

(Millman & Pauk, 1969). Therefore, rather than trying to memorize content, students should spend time organizing and reviewing their notes from class and textbooks.

Millman and Pauk (1969) suggested that students develop an outline to index information from their notes and textbooks in order to prepare for open-ended tests. For example, an outline containing main points and secondary points, or key questions and the corresponding pages from textbooks, class notes, and worksheets that address these topics can be developed (see Figure 8.3). When working from reference materials during the test, students should phrase their responses in their own words, rather than copying sentences or quotations verbatim.

Oral Exams

A test modification that some mainstreamed students may need is an oral exam, which is particularly relevant for students who may have difficulty writing responses to test questions. However, oral exams can be intimidating and students may have limited experience with this type of situation, so students should be taught to engage in several behaviors that can aid them in performing on oral exams. These behaviors include determining the content to be covered on the exam, listening carefully to the examiner, seeking clarification from the examiner concerning ambiguous questions and terminology, recording on a pad (if possible) key points to make in answering a question, thinking prior to responding, allowing time for the examiner to respond, distinguishing opinions from

FIGURE 8.3.   Sample Open-Ended Test Study Outline.

Content Area	Textbook Pages	Class Notes	Worksheets	Other Materials
1. Matter				
a. Definition	81–82	10/11	Matter	
b. Characteristics	83–84	10/11	Matter	
2. States of matter				
a. Solid	85–86	10/12	Solids	
b. Liquid	87–89	10/13	Liquids	
c. Gas	90–93	10/14	Gases	
3. Changing states of matter				
a. Freezing points	100–103	10/17	Freezing points	
b. Boiling points	104–106	10/18		Experiment #4
c. Evaporation	107–111	10/20		Experiment #5

facts, staying on task, and displaying appropriate manners (Millman & Pauk, 1969). Allowing students to supplement their oral responses with visual aids and manipulatives also may facilitate their performance on oral tests (Fagen, Graves, & Tessier–Switlick, 1984).

Writing Research Papers

Another form of evaluation in the regular classroom is the research paper. Teachers assign research papers to assess mastery of content, as well as organizational and writing skills. In planning and writing their papers, students should follow several guidelines (Pauk, 1984; Yaggy, 1969). These guidelines are described below.

Selecting a Topic

The initial step in writing a paper is to choose a topic (Yaggy, 1969). In selecting a topic, students should choose one that is of interest to them and relates to the assignment. Before selecting a topic, students also should consider whether they have the capabilities to comprehend it. If undecided, students should try to select a topic that relates to an interest or a hobby. Teacher consultation can help students generate ideas for topics. After choosing one, students should try to establish the paper's focus by narrowing the topic. For example, a paper on the general topic of the brain could be narrowed to focus on the left-brain, right-brain theory.

Gaining and Organizing Information

Information on the topic will be available in several resources. The school librarian can be helpful in identifying and obtaining a wide range of resources for the paper. As students read the material, they should record relevant points and facts on note cards (Yaggy, 1969). Note cards facilitate easy retrieval of information and sources for later use. In preparing note cards, it is recommended that students use a three-by-five-inch card; write on only one side of the card; use a separate card for each topic; list the reference at the top of the card and the page number in parentheses; record concise notes in their own language; write neatly; limit the number of direct quotations; and employ a system to indicate direct quotes, paraphrased statements, and original notes (Pauk, 1984).

Outlining the Paper

Note cards also can help students organize their papers into a skeletal outline (Yaggy, 1969). Therefore, students should review their notes to determine the focus of the paper as well as the main points and corresponding supporting points. Both main and supporting points should then be organized in an outline that provides a framework for the content and sequence of the paper (Pauk, 1984).

Writing the Paper

Starting with the introductory statement, students should prepare a draft by following the sequence of the outline. In writing the paper, students should present each point of the outline in a clear, direct manner; elaborate on and support each point with quotes, statistics, facts, and examples; use transitions to connect main points that have relationships; and avoid extraneous information (Pauk, 1984). Once the draft is complete, it is a good idea for students to wait at least a day before revising and editing their work (Pauk, 1984). In addition to modifying the paper's content, students should examine it closely for grammar, word usage, spelling, references, and organization. When the revision is completed, students should prepare the final paper according to the specifications outlined by the teacher.

Summary

Traditional methods of testing and grading can create frustration for teachers and students, and serve as a stumbling block to successful mainstreaming. Teachers can ease this frustration by using a variety of alternative grading procedures that more accurately reflect student performance. Since grades are often based primarily on test performance, teachers can help mainstreamed students maximize their test performance by carefully designing their tests to address the unique needs of mainstreamed students, employing alternative testing techniques, using the microcomputer to develop and administer tests, and teaching test-taking skills.

References

Adelman, M. J. (1982, April). *Making mainstreaming work: A collaborative consulting model for secondary schools.* Paper presented at the meeting of the Council for Exceptional Children, Houston.

Allyon, T., & Kelly, K. (1972). Effects of reinforcement on standardized test performance. *Journal of Applied Behavior Analysis, 5,* 477–484.

Banbury, M. (1987). Testing and grading mainstreamed students in regular education subjects. In A. Rotatori, M. M. Banbury, R. A. Fox (Eds.), *Issues in special education* (pp. 177–186). Mountain View, Calif.: Mayfield.

Beattie, S., Grise, P., & Algozzine, B. (1983). Effects of test modification on minimum competency performance of learning disabled students. *Learning Disability Quarterly, 6,* 75–77.

Bellanca, J. A., & Kirschenbaum, H. (1976). An overview of grading alternatives. In S. B. Simon and J. A. Bellanca (Eds.), *Grading the grading myths: Primer of alternatives to grades and marks.* Washington, D.C.: Association for Supervision and Curriculum Development.

Bloom, B. (1956). *Taxonomy of educational objectives: Handbook 1: Cognitive domain.* New York: David McKay.

Bos, C. S., & Vaughn, S. (1988). *Strategies for teaching students with learning and behavior problems.* Boston: Allyn and Bacon.

Bragstad, B. J., & Stumpf, S. M. (1987). *A guidebook for teaching study skills and motivation.* Boston: Allyn & Bacon.

Carman, R. A., & Adams, W. R. (1972). *Study skills. A student's guide for survival.* New York: John Wiley & Sons.

Chaffin, J. D., Maxwell, B., & Thompson, B. (1982). ARC-ED curriculum: The application of video game formats to educational software. *Exceptional Children, 49,* 173–178.

Chapman, E. N. (1969). The time message. In F.L. Christ (Ed.), *SR/SE resource book* (pp. 3–8). Chicago: Science Research Associates.

Cohen, S. B. (1983). Assigning report card grades to the mainstreamed child. *Teaching Exceptional Children, 15,* 86–89.

DeCharms, R. (1971). From pawns to origins: Toward self-motivation. In G.S. Lesser (Ed.), *Psychology and educational practice.* (pp. 380–407). Glenview, Ill.: Scott, Foresman.

Devine, T. G. (1981). *Teaching study skills.* Boston: Allyn and Bacon.

Fagen, S. A., Graves, D. L., & Tessier-Switlick, D. (1984). *Promoting successful mainstreaming: Reasonable classroom accommodations for learning disabled students.* Rockville, Md.: Montgomery County Public Schools.

Farquhar, W. W., Krumboltz, J. D., & Wrenn, C. G. (1969). Prepare for examinations. In F. L. Christ (Ed.), *SR/SE resource book* (pp. 63–69). Chicago: Science Research Associates.

Gagne, R. (1979). *The conditions of learning.* New York: Holt, Rinehart and Winston.

Gillet, P. (1986). Mainstreaming techniques for LD students. *Academic Therapy, 21,* 389–399.

Hammill, D., & Bartel, N. R. (1978). *Teaching children with learning and behavior problems.* Boston: Allyn & Bacon.

Harrington, A. M., & Morrison, R. A. (1981). Modifying classroom exams for secondary LD students. *Academic Therapy, 16,* 571–577.

Hasselbring, T., & Crossland, C. (1981). Using microcomputers for diagnosing spelling problems in learning-handicapped children. *Educational Technology, 21,* 37–39.

Hook, J. N. (1969). Read carefully. In F.L. Christ (Ed.), *SR/SE resource book* (pp. 55–62). Chicago: Science Research Associates.

Humphrey, M. J., Hoffman, E., & Crosby, B. M. (1984). Mainstreaming LD students. *Academic Therapy, 19,* 321–327.

Jones, V. I., & Jones, L. S. (1986). *Comprehensive classroom management: Creating positive learning environments* (2nd Ed.). Boston: Allyn & Bacon.

Kinnison, L. R., Hayes, C., & Acord, J. (1981). Evaluating student progress in mainstream classes. *Teaching Exceptional Children, 13,* 97–99.

Langan, J. (1982). *Reading and study skills. 2nd ed.* New York: McGraw-Hill.

Lee, P., & Alley, G. R. (1981). *Training junior high LD students to use a test-taking strategy (Research Report No. 38).* Lawrence: University of Kansas, Institute for Research in Learning Disabilities.

Lord, F. (1980). Some how and what for practical tailored testing. In L. Th. Van Der Kamp, W. Langerak, & D. DeGruyter (Eds.), *Psychometrics for educational debates* (pp. 189–205). New York: Wiley.

Marsh, G. E., & Price, B. J. (1980). *Methods for teaching the mildly handicapped adolescent.* St. Louis: C. V. Mosby.

Mastropieri, M. A., & Scruggs, T. E. (1987). *Effective instruction for special education.* Boston: College-Hill.

Mercer, C. D., & Mercer, A. R. (1985). *Teaching students with learning problems. 2nd ed.* Columbus: Charles E. Merrill.

Millman, J., & Pauk, W. (1969). *How to take tests.* New York: McGraw-Hill.

New York State Department of Education. (1986). *Alternative testing techniques for students with handicapping conditions.* Albany: Author.

Pauk, W. (1984). *How to study in college.* Boston: Houghton Mifflin.

Rose, T. L., Lesson, E. I., & Gottlieb, J. (1982). A discussion of transfer of training in mainstreaming programs. *Journal of Learning Disabilities, 15,* 162–165.

Salend, S. J., Blackhurst, A. E., & Kifer, E. (1982). Effects of systematic reinforcement conditions on the test scores of children labeled learning and behaviorally disordered. *Measurement and Evaluation in Guidance, 15,* 133–140.

Salend, S. J., & Salend, S. M. (1985b). Implications of using microcomputers in classroom testing. *Journal of Learning Disabilities, 18,* 51–53.

Salend, S. M., & Salend, S. J. (1985a). Adapting teacher-made tests for mainstreamed students. *Journal of Learning Disabilities, 18,* 373–375.

Sarda, L. Personal communication, May 18, 1988.

Scruggs, T. E., Bennion, K., & Lifson, S. (1985). Learning disabled students' spontaneous use of test-taking skills on reading achievement tests. *Learning Disability Quarterly, 8,* 205–210.

Scruggs, T. E., & Lifson, S. (1986). Are learning disabled students "test-wise"?: An inquiry into reading comprehension test items. *Educational and Psychological Measurement, 46,* 1075–1082.

Scruggs, T. E., & Mastropieri, M. A. (1986). Improving the test-taking skills of behaviorally disordered and learning disabled students. *Exceptional Children, 53,* 63–68.

Scruggs, T. E., & Mastropieri, M. A. (1988). Are learning disabled students "test-wise"?: A review of recent research. *Learning Disabilities Focus, 3*(2), 87–97.

Scruggs, T. E., Mastropieri, M. A., & Tolfa-Veit, D. (1986). The effects of coaching on the standardized test performance of learning disabled and behaviorally disordered students. *Remedial and Special Education, 7,* 37–41.

Scruggs, T. E., & Tolfa, D. (1985). Improving the test-taking skills of learning disabled students. *Perceptual and Motor Skills, 60,* 847–850.

Shanley, D. (1988, November). *Techniques and strategies for secondary level resource rooms.* A paper presented at the convention of the New York State Council for Exceptional Children, Buffalo.

Simpson, M. n.d. *Writing effective teacher-made tests for slow learning and mainstreamed students.* Unpublished manuscript.

Spargo, E. (1977). *The now student: Reading and study skills.* Jamestown, R.I.: Jamestown.

Tolfa, D., & Scruggs, T. E. (1986). Can LD students effectively use separate answer sheets? *Perceptual and Motor Skills, 63,* 155–160.

Varnhagen, S., & Gerber, M. M. (1984). Use of microcomputers for spelling assessment: Reasons to be cautious. *Learning Disability Quarterly, 7,* 266–270.

Vasa, S. F. (1981). Alternative procedures for grading handicapped students in the secondary schools. *Education Unlimited, 3,* 16–23.

Vaughn, S., Bos, C. S., & Lund, K. A. (1986). . . . But they can do it in my room: Strategies for promoting generalization. *Teaching Exceptional Children, 18,* 176–180.

Walla, D. (1988, April). *A secondary modified program in English/Language Arts.* A paper presented at the conference on Writing Models and Programs for the Learning Disabled College Student, New Paltz, New York.

Wallace, G., & McLoughlin, J. A. (1979). *Learning disabilities concepts and characteristics.* Columbus: Charles E. Merrill.

Wilson, M. S., & Fox, B. J. (1982). Computerized bilingual language assessment and intervention. *Exceptional Children, 49,* 145–148.

Wood, J. W. (1988, March). *Adapting instruction for the mildly handicapped student: A national perspective.* Paper presented at the meeting of the Council for Exceptional Children, Washington, D.C.

Yaggy, E. (1969). Writing a research paper. In F.L. Christ, ed. *SR/SE resource book* (pp. 79–84). Chicago: Science Research Associates.

CHAPTER 9

Evaluating the Progress of Mainstreamed Students

(Photo: Alan Carey/The Image Works)

Once students are placed in the mainstream, teachers should monitor their progress to determine if the mainstreamed placement is achieving its intended academic and social outcomes (Bender, 1987; Hundert, 1982; Ledeber & Azzara, 1980). If problems are found, follow-up information can be gathered to develop new strategies to intervene in and minimize the identified problem areas. For example, a mainstreaming followup may indicate that a student is not completing homework assignments. This problem can then be addressed by setting up a communication system between parents and teachers to assist and monitor the student's completion of homework (Schloss, Schloss, & Segraves, 1983). A follow-up examination of students' progress should be directed at providing educators with data to evaluate the school district's mainstreaming procedures (Bender, 1987). Such data can help educators validate successful mainstreaming policies that should be continued, as well as pinpoint procedures that need to be revised.

This chapter offers information to assist educators in evaluating the progress of mainstreamed students. Specifically, the chapter presents guidelines for designing follow-up evaluations, using standardized tests, assessing the progress of students from multicultural backgrounds, using curriculum-based assessment and minimum competency testing, obtaining information from regular educators, parents, and mainstreamed students, and examining the effectiveness of instructional modifications, adaptive devices, and medical interventions.

Designing Evaluation of Mainstreaming Placements

Wang, Anderson, and Bram (1985) identified three aspects of student performance that should be assessed in evaluating mainstream programs: performance, attitude, and process. *Performance measures* relate to achievement in the content areas. *Attitudinal measures* include the mainstreamed student's self-concept as well as attitudes toward school and peers. The attitudes of nonhandicapped peers, teachers, and parents toward mainstreaming and the mainstreamed student also are important attitudinal variables. *Process measures* encompass the types of interactions mainstreamed students have with their teachers and peers.

Bender (1988) proposes that teachers, administrators, and multidisciplinary teams—or a combination of these three groups—periodically conduct a determination of student progress in the mainstream. The frequency of follow-up evaluations will depend on the needs and skill levels of the students, parents, and educators. Salend (1983) suggests that the initial evaluation of student progress occur three to four weeks after students have been placed in the mainstreamed milieu. This amount of time will allow educators to distinguish substantive mainstreaming problems from the short-term problems that can be associated with any type of new class placement. However, the three- to four-week span allows educators to resolve problems in a timely fashion and thus minimize any long-term deleterious effects.

The follow-up evaluation of student progress should be carefully planned and implemented by the multidisciplinary IEP planning team. The team should determine the areas to be evaluated and by specific criteria, as well as the procedures for measuring student progress. They can obtain information on student progress via standardized tests, curriculum-based assessment, observation, and interviews with educators, parents, and students. These assessments can be performed by special educators, regular educators, and placement team members with specific areas of expertise.

Using Standardized Tests

Educators make many critical decisions about student educational programs based on data collected frɔm norm-referenced and criterion-referenced standardized tests. Both types of tests can assess student progress in the mainstreamed setting. For example, a criterion-referenced test like the *Brigance Inventory of Essential Skills* (Brigance, 1980) can be employed to document students' mastery of specific objectives outlined in their IEPs; a norm-referenced test such as the *Woodcock-Johnson Psychoeducational Assessment* (Woodcock & Johnson, 1977) can assess academic growth in the regular education setting. A listing of standardized tests by area is presented in Figure 9.1. Information and reviews of these tests can be obtained by consulting McLoughlin and Lewis (1986), Salvia and Ysseldyke (1985), and Sattler (1988).

Norm-Referenced Testing

Norm-referenced tests provide measures of performance that allow educators to compare an individual's score to the scores of others (McLoughlin & Lewis, 1986). Norms are determined by analyzing the scores of students from different ages, grades, geographical regions, cultural and economic backgrounds, and settings (such as urban, suburban, and rural). These norms are then used to compare students, schools, school districts, and geographical regions in terms of such variables as age and grade level (Wallace & Larsen, 1978). For example, norm-referenced test-

FIGURE 9.1.   List of Standardized Tests.

Name	Content Areas	Type	Ages/Grade Levels
Achievement Tests			
Woodcock–Johnson Psycho-Educational Test of Achievement, Part 2 (Woodcock & Johnson, 1977)	Reading, written language, math, science, social studies, and humanities	Norm-Referenced	3 to 80+ years; Grade K to 12
Kaufman Test of Educational Achievement (K-TEA) (Kaufman & Kaufman, 1985)	Math, reading, spelling	Norm-Referenced	6 to 17–11 years
Peabody Individual Achievement Test (Dunn & Markwardt, 1970)	Math, reading, spelling, general information	Norm-Referenced	5–3 to 18–3 years; Grade K to 12
Brigance Diagnostic Inventory of Basic Skills (Brigance, 1977)	Reading, math, spelling, writing, readiness, reference skills	Criterion-Referenced	Grade K to 6
Brigance Comprehensive Inventory of Basic Skills (Brigance, 1983)	Reading, math, spelling, writing, spoken language, readiness, reference skills, graphs and maps	Criterion-Referenced	Grade K to 9
Brigance Inventory of Essential Skills (Brigance, 1980)	Reading, math, spelling, writing, reference skills, vocational, graphs, schedules	Criterion-Referenced	Grade 4 to 12
Mathematics Tests			
Keymath Diagnostic Inventory of Essential Mathematics (Connolly, 1988)	Basic concepts, computations, applications	Norm-and Criterion-Referenced	Grade K to 10
Stanford Diagnostic Mathematics Test (Beatty, Madden, Gardner, & Karlsen, 1984)	Number system, numeration, computation, applications	Norm-Referenced	Grade 1.5 to 12.9
Test of Mathematics Ability (Brown & McEntire, 1984)	Attitude toward math, math vocabulary, computation, word problems, general information	Norm-Referenced	Grade 3 to 12; 8–6 to 18–11 years
Enright Diagnostic Inventory of Basic Mathematics Skills (Enright, 1983)	Number facts, computation with whole numbers, fractions, and decimals	Criterion-Referenced	Grade 1 to 6

FIGURE 9.1. (*continued*)

Name	Content Areas	Type	Ages/Grade Levels
Written Language Tests			
Test of Written Language (Hammill & Larsen, 1983)	Word usage, punctuation, capitalization, spelling, handwriting, vocabulary, thematic vocabulary	Norm-Referenced	7 to 18–11 years
Picture Story Language Test (Myklebust, 1973)	Productivity, syntax, content	Norm-Referenced	7 to 17 years
Zaner–Bloser Evaluation Scales (1984)	Letter formation, spacing, alignment, proportion, line quality	Rating Scale	Grade 1 to 8
Test of Written Spelling (Larsen & Hammill, 1986)	Spelling of rule and non-rule based words	Norm-Referenced	Grade 1 to 8; 5 to 13–5 years
Spoken Language			
Test of Language Development—Primary (Newcomer & Hammill, 1982)	Syntax, semantics, articulation, word discrimination	Norm-Referenced	4 to 8–11 years
Clinical Evaluation of Language Functions (CELF) (Semel & Wiig, 1980)	Phonology, syntax, semantics, memory, word finding and retrieval	Norm-Referenced	Grade K to 12
Boehm Test of Basic Concepts (Boehm, 1971)	Basic concepts of space, quantity, time, etc.	Norm-Referenced	Grade K to 2
Peabody Picture Vocabulary (Dunn & Dunn, 1981)	English vocabulary	Norm-Referenced	2–5 to 40 years
Adaptive Behavior			
Adaptive Behavior Scale—School Edition (Lambert, Windmiller, Tharinger, & Cole, 1981)	Adaptive and inappropriate behavior	Norm-Referenced	3–3 to 17–2 years
Vineland Adaptive Behavior Scale—Classroom Edition (Sparrow, Balla, & Cicchetti, 1984)	Communication, daily living, socialization, motor skills	Norm-Referenced	3 to 12–11 years

ing may yield that a student is reading at a third-grade level and performing at a fifth-grade level in mathematics.

Norm-referenced tests are the basis for many educational decisions. They can be employed in the initial screening of students to determine if their performance warrants a more extensive evaluation. They also can be employed to determine if a student's performance makes him or her eligible for special education services. Norm-referenced tests can help educators determine the general curricular areas in which students excel or need remedial instruction, as well as evaluate whether or not the instructional program has resulted in a change in the students' performance. The advantages and disadvantages of norm-referenced testing are summarized in Figure 9.2.

Criterion-Referenced Testing

As opposed to norm-referenced testing, *criterion-referenced testing* compares an individual's performance to a specific level of mastery in relation to a curriculum. Rather than giving a grade level at which students are functioning, criterion-referenced testing yields information to determine the specific skills mastered and not mastered by students. For example, the results of a criterion-referenced test may show that a student can add and subtract decimals and fractions, but cannot multiply or divide them.

FIGURE 9.2.　Advantages and Disadvantages of Norm-Referenced Testing.

Advantages	Disadvantages
1. Provides basis for comparisons with other students.	1. Fails to provide data for teaching and planning an instructional program.
2. Offers general measures of progress.	2. Findings can be overgeneralized and used to make incorrect decisions.
3. Reliability and validity are usually reported in the manual.	3. Often lacks adequate reliability and validity.
4. Provides educators with a capsule description of a student's performance.	4. Provides global information rather than looking at each item.
5. Can pinpoint areas where student needs remediation or more intensive assessment.	5. Format of test can be difficult for exceptional students.
6. Usually easy to administer, score, and interpret.	6. Test items and standardization do not reflect a multicultural perspective.
	7. Can be biased with respect to curriculum content.

FIGURE 9.3.   Advantages and Disadvantages of Criterion-Referenced Testing.

Advantages	Disadvantages
1. Students are judged on their own strengths and weaknesses. 2. Facilitates teaching and the planning of instructional programs. 3. Allows for ongoing assessment of students' progress. 4. Teacher-made criterion-referenced tests can be adapted to a variety of curricular areas and have a direct link to the curriculum.	1. Content of commercially produced tests may not match the teachers' curriculum. 2. Teacher-made, criterion-referenced tests can be time consuming to construct and are only as good as the teacher's competence. 3. The behavioral levels for mastery and the skill sequence may be inappropriate.

The advantages and disadvantages of using criterion-referenced testing are presented in Figure 9.3.

Many criterion-referenced tests measuring a range of content areas are available (See Figure 9.1), but educators may need to develop their own criterion-referenced tests tailored to their unique curriculum. The steps involved in devising teacher-made criterion-referenced tests are

1. Determine the curriculum area to be assessed (for example, addition and subtraction of decimals).
2. Develop a skill sequence for the curriculum area. Make sure the skill sequence is complete and ordered from easiest to hardest.
3. Task analyze each skill into subskills, if necessary.
4. State each skill as a behavioral objective.
5. Determine a level of mastery for each objective.
6. Construct items to reflect the objectives. Consider:
   - Do items match the objectives?
   - Are there a sufficient number of items per objective?
   - What materials are needed?
   - What is the teacher's role?
   - Are the presentation and response modes consistent with the objectives?
   - How are items scored?
7. Construct a scoring and descriptive data sheet.
8. Conduct the assessment.
9. Revise the assessment device.

McCormack (1978) provides additional guidelines for constructing teacher-made, criterion-referenced tests.

Evaluating Standardized Tests

The usefulness and value of data on students' progress will depend on the assessment instruments selected and administered (Otto, McMenemy, & Smith, 1973). Since even widely used tests may not be appropriate, educators need to be good test consumers in terms of selecting tests with good attributes. While most of the information needed to evaluate a test can be found in the test's manual, teachers can obtain additional data by interviewing others who have used the test and by examining professional resources (such as the *Mental Measurements Yearbook* or assessment textbooks). Several factors to consider in selecting and evaluating standardized tests include test design and construction, examinee and examiner characteristics, and economics (Mehrens & Lehman, 1969; Salend, 1984a).

TEST DESIGN VARIABLES.   Test design variables help to determine the objectives and nature of the instrument as well as the content areas addressed by the test. Knowledge of these variables allows educators to match a test to the specific purpose of the assesssment. In evaluating these variables, educators should address the following:

- Who developed the test? When was it developed?
- Who is the publisher?
- What are the stated objectives of the test?
- What are the unstated or derived objectives of the test?
- What type of test is it (norm-referenced, criterion-referenced, speed, power, or the like)?

TEST CONSTRUCTION VARIABLES.   The value of a test in monitoring student progress and providing relevant information will depend on the manner and care in which the test was constructed. For example, a test that is neither reliable nor valid will be of little use to educators in monitoring student progress.

RELIABILITY.   *Reliability* refers to consistency and stability of an individual's score from one administration of the test to another (McLoughlin & Lewis, 1986). Typically, the reliability coefficient is presented in the test's manual in terms of a correlational coefficient; the higher the coefficient, the more reliable the test. For example, a test that has a correlational coefficient of .88 would be more reliable than a test that has a reliability coefficient of .61. A test that has a reliability coefficient below .90 should not be used for making important educational decisions about students (Salvia & Ysseldyke, 1985).

VALIDITY.   *Validity* examines what the test measures and how well it does that job. There are several types of validity: content, criterion-related, and construct. *Content validity* relates to the extent a test covers the content area it purports to assess. Content validity is measured by examining the test to determine What is the content outline of the test?; Is the content complete and sequenced appropriately?; Do the test items reflect the stated objectives?; and Are there a sufficient number of items per objective? For example, a math test to assess the progress of a mainstreamed second grader that does not include items related to subtraction lacks content validity.

Criterion-related validity provides educators with information to estimate how performance on a test will relate to performance in other areas, such as other tests, report card grades, and peer relationships. One type of criterion-related validity is *predictive validity,* which refers to a test's ability to predict the future performance of a student. The other type of criterion-related validity, *concurrent validity,* relates to the comparison between performance on one test with performance on another test that has demonstrated validity.

An examination of the psychological assumptions and ideas on which a test is based is called *construct validity.* For example, a test that presumes that intelligence is related to school learning will be very different from a test that defines intelligence in terms of an appreciation of art, music, and dance. To evaluate construct validity, educators can identify the constructs on which the test is based, derive a hypothesis regarding test performance that is associated with the construct, and verify or dispute the construct via logic and research.

STANDARDIZATION.   The norms for a test are standardized by administering the test to a group of students. However, many of the groups used to standardize tests do not include individuals with disabilities or individuals from multicultural backgrounds. Consequently, the use of tests whose standardization group does not reflect the characteristics of the students being tested may not be appropriate. Therefore, in selecting tests to measure the progress of mainstreamed students and students from multicultural backgrounds, educators should carefully evaluate the standardization of the test to determine if it is appropriate for use.

STANDARD ERROR OF MEASUREMENT.   No matter how reliable or valid a test, every test will have some margin of error. Thus, an individual's score is thought to be composed of the true score and some error in measurement (McLoughlin & Lewis, 1986). The *standard error of measurement,* a statistic that estimates the amount of measurement error in a score, is important in interpreting test results. A test with a large standard error of measurement might not provide an accurate assessment of student performance.

A review of a test in terms of test construction variables should address

- Does the test have adequate reliability?
- Is the test valid?
  1. content validity?
  2. predictive validity?
  3. concurrent validity?
  4. construct validity?
- What is the standard error of measurement?
- What are the results of the standardization?
- How was the standardization group selected?
- What are the characteristics (age, sex, race, socio-economic status, languages spoken, geographic region, disabilities of the standardization group?

EXAMINEE-RELATED VARIABLES.   Educators should consider several student characteristics in choosing and evaluating a standardized test (Salend, 1984a):

- What prerequisite skills are needed by the examinee to complete the test?
- In what languages or modes of communication can the test be administered?
- Is the vocabulary of the test's directions appropriate?
- What are the presentation modes of test items?
- What are the response modes of the items?
- What stated and unstated adaptations can be made in the presentation and response modes of the test?
- Is the test free of sex and ethnic biases?
- Is the test motivating?
- Are opportunities to give feedback to students provided?
- Is the test suitable for individual or group use?
- Are there multiple entry points to begin testing?

EXAMINER-RELATED VARIABLES.   The amount of preparation necessary to administer the test is another important factor in selecting and evaluating an assessment instrument (Salend, 1984a). Evaluation questions that relate to examiner variables include

- What preparation and skills does the examiner need to administer, score, and interpret the test?
- Does the manual provide specific instructions for use?
- Is the manual complete and understandable?
- Are the timing and pacing of the test appropriate?
- Are procedures for recording student performance suitable?
- Are guidelines for interpreting student performance appropriate?

ECONOMIC VARIABLES.   Economic variables, such as cost, time, and available personnel, can affect the choice of tests (Compton, 1980). Tests that require several examiners may not be feasible in many settings due to personnel shortages. Additionally, assessment instruments that are not durable and have costly replacement materials can be impractical. In evaluating the economics of a test, educators can consider these questions:

- What is the cost of the test?
- What is the approximate time required for use?
- What staff is required?
- What media and supplementary materials are required?
- Are materials free of distracting features?
- What consumable and permanent materials are required?
- Is the test durable? attractive? portable?
- Are materials packaged for easy use?

Assessing the Progress of Students from Multicultural Backgrounds

Educators should exercise caution when using standardized tests to assess the progress of mainstreamed students from multicultural backgrounds (Laosa, 1977; Oakland, 1980). This section describes some of the issues to which teachers must be alerted.

Nondiscriminatory Testing

While PL94-142 mandates that assessment materials and procedures be selected and administered so that they are not racially and culturally discriminary, research indicates that standardized tests *are* culturally and socially biased, resulting in a disproportionate number of minority students being misclassified as handicapped (Heller, Holtzman, & Messick, 1982). Additionally, several court cases have established the need for nondiscriminatory testing (Galagan, 1985). In the landmark case relating to nondiscriminatory assessment, *Diana v. California State Board of Education,* nine Spanish-speaking Mexican–American students were classified as mentally retarded as a result of their performance on English-language standardized tests. The students' attorneys argued that the evaluation procedures were discriminatory in terms of standardization and their dependence on English-language skills. To support this contention, they produced evidence that showed that when seven of the nine students were retested in Spanish, they scored in the average range. In an out-of-court settlement, it was agreed that students must be assessed in their native language, in addition to English; assessments should include a measure of student performance on nonverbal subtests; Mexican–American students in classes for the educable mentally retarded must be retested, and plans for placing students no longer eligible for these services in regular education classrooms must be developed; educators will develop an IQ test that is consistent with the Mexican–American culture and normed using Mexican–American students; and school districts must examine the racial and ethnic balance in their classes for educable mentally retarded students and establish plans for any inequities that are found. The findings of the Diana case were extended to black students in the *Larry P. v. Riles* case, and to Chinese–American students in *Lau v. Nichols.* Although these cases took place in California, similar cases have been initiated in other states (Fradd, Vega, & Hallman, 1985; Galagan, 1985).

Several alternatives to traditional assessments for students from multicultural backgrounds have been proposed: culture-free/fair tests, culture-specific tests, translations, and pluralistic assessment (Guerin & Maier, 1983; McLoughlin & Lewis, 1986).

CULTURE-FREE/FAIR TESTS.   *Culture-free* or *culture-fair tests* seek to measure aspects of growth that are presumed to be unrelated to culture, such as perceptual and motor growth. For example, the Cattell Culture-Free Test of Intelligence (Cattell & Cattell, 1963) attempts to minimize the influences of language and school learning in assessing intelligence by asking students to select the appropriate visual stimuli that completes a visual pattern. However, research on these types of tests indicates they are *not* free of bias (Galagan, 1985; Gonzales, 1982) because perceptual and test-taking skills *are* related to culture (Guerin & Maier, 1983).

CULTURE-SPECIFIC TESTS. *Culture-specific tests* measure knowledge of and competence within the minority culture (McLoughlin & Lewis, 1986). These tests give a measure of the student's understanding of the culture, but their use is limited because their relationship to school learning is minimal and their content is only related to a small region (Guerin & Maier, 1983).

TEST TRANSLATION. PL94–142 requires school districts to establish procedures so that students from multicultural backgrounds are administered tests in their native language or preferred mode of communication. As a result, some educators have sought to minimize the bias in English-language assessment instruments by translating them into the student's dominant language. However, translations do not remove the bias in tests that are related to item and task selection. Thus, despite the translation, the constructs on which the test items are based still reflect the dominant culture and may not be appropriate for students from minority backgrounds. Also, translation does not account for experiences and words that have different or multiple meanings in different cultures.

PLURALISTIC ASSESSMENT. *Pluralistic assessment* seeks to reduce the bias in testing by assessing several domains and using norms developed for multicultural populations. One type of pluralistic assessment, the System of Multicultural Pluralistic Assessment (SOMPA) (Mercer & Lewis, 1977), provides data on students' medical status, social performance, and learning potential using standardized tests with norms established on minority group populations. The SOMPA also includes a parent interview.

ADAPTIVE BEHAVIOR. A key component of the SOMPA is the measurement of *adaptive behavior,* the "effectiveness with which individuals can cope with the social and cultural demands of their environments" (Knapp & Salend, 1983, p. 63). Because adaptive behavior instruments examine domains outside the traditional educational setting, they can be instrumental in giving a more accurate and diverse profile of student performance (Coulter & Morrow, 1978). This is especially important for many minority students whose lifestyles provide them with a range of experiences and create a demand for them to perform a variety of roles, which may differ significantly from their middle-class peers. However, educators should interpret the results of adaptive behavior measurements with care, as behavior is culture-bound (Trueba, 1983) and these instruments are based on a cultural perspective of adaptive behavior. Therefore, they are not completely free of cultural bias. Additional potential problems in the administration and interpretation of adaptive behavior measurements have been identified, and solutions offered (Knapp & Salend, 1983).

Assessing Limited English-Proficient (LEP) Students

A growing number of students from minority backgrounds also are from limited English-proficient (LEP) backgrounds (Salend & Fradd, 1986; Waggoner, 1984). To meet the needs of LEP students with disabilities, PL94–142 and the Civil Rights Act of 1964 mandate that school districts develop a pedagogically sound program that meets the student's English learning needs, offer instruction in content areas so that learning is not hindered by language differences, and assess student progress regularly and provide programmatic adjustments if assessment results reflect lack of educational success (Roos, 1984).

Therefore, in addition to academic and social progress, educators also should assess the language skill progress of students from multicultural backgrounds. Such an evaluation should examine the students' language dominance, preference, and proficiency. *Language dominance* refers to the language in which the individual is most fluent; *language preference* identifies the language in which the individual chooses to communicate. *Language proficiency* relates to the degree of skill an individual possesses in a specific language. A variety of tests are available in these areas (McLoughlin & Lewis, 1986), as shown in Figure 9.4.

Coballes–Vega and Salend (in press) propose a two-phase model for assessing language skills. In step one, information on the student's use of language outside the school is obtained by observation or interviews. The observations and interviews should address these questions:

- What language or dialect is spoken by the parents?
- What language is spoken by the student and the siblings?
- What language or dialect is used in the family's community?
- Is a distinction made among the uses of the primary language or dialect and English? If so, how is that division made? (For example, the non-English language is used at home, but children speak English when playing with friends.)
- What is the student's language preference in the home and community?

In the second phase, educators identify the student's language skills in school by identifying

FIGURE 9.4.   Bilingual Language Proficiency Tests.

Name (Authors)	Ages or Grades	Language(s)	Oral Language Skills Assessed
Basic Inventory of Natural Language (Herbert, 1979)	Grades K-12	Spanish and 31 other languages	A language sample is scored for fluency, complexity, and average sentence length
Ber-Sil Spanish Test (rev. ed.) (Beringer, 1976)	Ages 4 to 12	Spanish (versions also available in Chinese, Philippine, Korean, and Persian)	Receptive vocabulary
Bilingual Syntax Measure (Burt, Dulay, & Chávez, 1978)	Grades K-12	Spanish, English	Expressive syntax
Del Rio Language Screening Test (Toronto, Leverman, Hanna, Rosenzweig, & Maldonado, 1975)	Ages 3 to 7	Spanish, English	Expressive syntax, receptive and expressive semantics
Dos Amigos Verbal Language Scales (Critchlow, 1973)	Ages 5 to 12	Spanish, English	Expressive vocabulary
Language Assessment Scales (DeAvila & Duncan, 1981)	Grades K-12+	Spanish, English	Auditory discrimination, articulation of speech sounds, receptive syntax, expressive vocabulary, oral production
Prueba de Desarrollo Inicial de Leguaje (Hresko, Reid, & Hammall, 1982)	Ages 3 to 7	Spanish	Receptive and expressive syntax and semantics
Woodcock Language Proficiency Battery, English Form and Spanish Form, (Woodcock, 1980, 1981)	Ages 3 to 80+	Spanish, English	Receptive and expressive semantics

Source: J. A. McLoughlin and R. B. Lewis, *Assessing Special Students,* second edition, (Columbus, Ohio: Merrill, 1986), p. 379. Reprinted by permission of the publisher.

- Was the student born in the United States? If not, how long has he or she been living in the United States?
- Has the student's language dominance been established? If so, what is it? If not, a language proficiency test should be administered.
- Has the student's language of instruction always been English? If not, did the student receive previous instruction in the primary language and in English as a second language? For how long?
- Does the student interact with peers in the primary language and/or English?
- Is the student able to engage in simplified interactions in English with school personnel?
- Can the student answer basic questions relating to self, family, health, and school?

These data, coupled with performance on language skill tests, can then be used to plan instructional procedures, determine appropriate languages for instruction, and evaluate student progress. For example, if the student functions in the primary language in a number of domains (home, school, and community) and the skills in English appear limited, then the student might benefit from academic instruction in the primary language and supplemental instruction in English as a second language (Wilkinson & Ortiz, 1986).

Using Curriculum-Based Assessment

Although student progress traditionally has been assessed via standardized tests, it can also be examined in relation to the curriculum of the class, grade, school, or district through use of *curriculum-based assessment* (CBA) (Germann & Tindal, 1985; Tucker, 1985). Glicking and Thompson (1985) define CBA as "a procedure for determining the instructional needs of students based on the student's ongoing performance in existing course content" (p. 206).

CBA provides individualized, direct, and repeated measures of students' levels of proficiency and progress in the curriculum. CBA's content is derived directly from students' instructional programs (Tucker, 1985). For example, a CBA to assess progress in reading requires students to read selections from the reader they use every day. Rather than assessing students once in a while, teachers using CBA sample student performance of typical classroom tasks on a regular basis. Because CBA is an ongoing, dynamic process, it provides teachers with a continuous measurement of student progress.

CBA has several advantages over other methods of assessment including linking testing, teaching, and evaluation; improving communication between professionals; being sensitive to changes in student performance over brief periods of time; facilitating decisions regarding instructional placement; and being cost-effective in terms of ease of administration and economics (Deno, 1985; Deno & Fuchs, 1988). CBA provides teachers with information on the demands of instructional tasks, allowing them to determine the content and pace of an instructional program. Thus, in addition to providing data on student progress, CBA can help teachers match specific instructional practices and materials to mainstreamed students' learning needs, which results in improved performance on school-related tasks (Gickling & Thompson, 1985). CBA also can help develop norms for school districts to provide a database for decisions to classify students and develop IEPs (Germann & Tindal, 1985; Peterson, Heistad, Peterson, & Reynolds, 1985).

Blankenship (1985) and Deno and Fuchs (1988) offer educators guidelines for conducting a CBA:

1. *Identify the content area(s) to be assessed.* CBA has been used to assess a variety of content areas, including speech, vocational education, secondary content areas, independent living skills, reading, math, and social skills (Germann & Tindal, 1985).

2. *Define the school-related tasks that will constitute the assessment and the sample duration.* For example, measure reading by having students read aloud from their readers for a sample duration of one minute, spelling by the number of words from the spelling list spelled correctly, and writing by the number of words in a story during a sample duration of five minutes (Deno & Fuchs, 1988). The content level will vary depending on the ability of the individual student.

3. *Determine if performance or progress measurement will be used.* Performance measurement involves changes on a specific task over a period of time, while progress measurement evaluates student progress on sequentially ordered levels or objectives within the curriculum (Deno & Fuchs, 1988; Germann & Tindal, 1985). If performance measurement is selected, then the task that constitutes the assessment will remain constant throughout the CBA. If progress measurement is chosen, then the objectives in the curriculum should be placed in sequential order, mastery levels determined, and corresponding tasks identified.

4. *Prepare and organize the necessary materials.*

5. *Administer the CBA.* Students should be informed that the goal of the assessment is to help teachers decide what needs to be taught,

they may not know the answers to every question, and they should do their best (Blankenship, 1985).

6. *Decide how frequently the CBA will be re-administered.* Depending on teacher time, student skill, and the nature of the task, educators should decide how frequently the CBA will be re-administered to students.

7. *Graph student performance.* A sample graph is presented in Figure 9.5. The vertical axis represents the student's performance on the school-related task (the number of words read or the number of words spelled). The horizontal axis indicates the day on which the measurement is taken. Data points on the graph measure the correct and incorrect responses. The diagonal broken line starting at the left side of the graph and ending on the right is called the *aimline.* Germann and Tindal (1985) define aimlines as "visual illustrations of estimated or predicted progress/performance and indicate the general trend and direction that the data must take" (p. 246). The vertical broken lines indicate changes in the instructional program.

8. *Analyze the results to determine student progress in terms of skills mastered and not mastered.* Identify the students who evidence mastery of the skills and are ready for new instructional objectives, are progressing but need additional instruction to demonstrate mastery

FIGURE 9.5.   Curriculum-Based Assessment of Spelling.

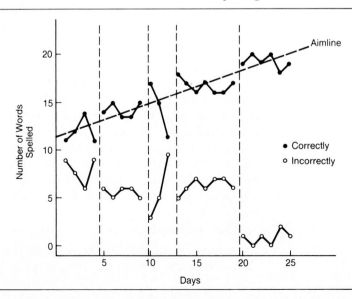

of skills, and have not progressed and need modifications in their instructional program (Blankenship, 1985).

9. *Compare the efficacy of different instructional strategies.* Several rules for using CBA to determine the need for changes in instructional strategies have been suggested (Germann & Tindal, 1985; White & Haring, 1981). White and Haring (1981) recommend that educators use a different instructional program when students' levels of performance are below the predicted performance level (aimline) for three consecutive days. Similarly, Mirkin et. al. (1981) propose that teachers examine performance for a period of seven to ten days before modifying the instructional program. Germann & Tindal (1985) believe that teachers should change their instructional strategies every three weeks to determine the effectiveness and efficiency of a variety of instructional procedures.

Error Analysis

Educators using norm- and criterion-referenced testing and CBA to evaluate student progress in the mainstreamed setting can increase the amount of information obtained from these procedures by employing *error analysis* (Gickling & Thompson, 1985; Grimes, 1981). Data provided via error analysis can help teachers make decisions that significantly improve student performance (Grimes, 1981). Error analysis allows teachers to examine students' responses to identify areas of difficulty and patterns in the ways students approach a task.

The technique usually focuses on identifying errors related to inappropriate applications of rules and concepts, rather than careless random errors or errors caused by lack of training (Cox, 1975). For example, an error analysis of the subtraction problem

$$
\begin{array}{r}
4265 \\
- \ 3197 \\
\hline
1132
\end{array}
$$

may indicate that the student has mastered the subtraction facts, but subtracts the smaller number from the larger number rather than the subtrahend from the minuend. Thus, rather than teaching the student subtraction facts, the teacher would focus instruction on subtracting the subtrahend from the minuend.

Educators can conduct an error analysis by

1. Giving the student a series of problems or questions.

2. Recording the student's responses so that they can be analyzed. When a written response is not produced by the student, such as when reading, teachers should convert the student's response to a permanent product.

3. Analyzing errors by looking for patterns in the student's responses.
4. Probing further to confirm error patterns by having the student respond to additional items.
5. Reviewing with the student how she or he approached the task and arrived at answers.
6. Instructing the student to remediate the error pattern.

Think-Aloud Techniques

Information on the ways students approach a task also can be obtained through *think-aloud techniques,* which ask students to state the process they are employing while working on a task (Meyers & Lytle, 1986). For example, Meyers and Lytle (1986) propose think-aloud techniques to assess reading comprehension. Students are instructed to read each sentence individually, then state their thoughts, which are then categorized as indicating understanding, expressing doubt or lack of understanding, analyzing text features, expanding on text, or judging the text and reasoning. These data are then used to assist students in improving their reading comprehension skills.

Using Minimum Competency Testing

While *minimum competency testing (MCT)* has been employed by many school districts to ensure that students exit high school with a minimum set of skills to function successfully in society, it also has been used to measure the progress of students and determine their promotion to the next grade (McCarthy, 1980). Gallagher and Hall (1979) suggest that competency testing also can evaluate the success of mainstreaming programs. They note that competency testing can assess the extent to which students with disabilities have mastered the basic skills of the regular education curriculum. Additionally, they propose that competency testing can provide educators with a measure of the mainstreamed students' performance in comparison to that of their regular education peers.

However, the advent of MCT creates several problems for mainstreamed students. First, if promotion to the next grade is contingent on passing the MCT rather than identifying instructional needs, then many mainstreamed students face the prospect of not being promoted or being segregated into special education classes (McCarthy, 1980). Second, use of tests that reflect middle-class norms and lack reliability and validity can prevent mainstreamed students and students from multicultural backgrounds from receiving a high school diploma, and thus limit their employability (Safer, 1980).

In light of the problems MCT can create for students with disabilities, educators will need to consider several procedures to lessen its potential deleterious effects. Although mainstreamed students should be granted exemptions from MCT when it can have a negative impact on the students' families and self-concept and when they lack the skills to pass the test (Amos, 1980), all mainstreamed students should have an opportunity to take the test using any alternative testing techniques they require (McCarthy, 1980). Mainstreamed students who fail the test should receive remedial instruction and be allowed to retake the test as many times as necessary (McCarthy, 1980).

Multidisciplinary teams also can address issues related to students' performance on MCT through the IEP process (Amos, 1980; Safer, 1980). The IEP could contain information on which MCT requirements are valid for a specific mainstreamed student, and the best procedures to assess mastery of these requirements (Safer, 1980). Amos (1980) suggests several modifications that multidisciplinary teams can consider when adapting the MCT process for mainstreamed students. These modifications include allowing the student's IEP committee to

1. review the MCT and select the test items that will best evaluate the objectives of his or her plan;

2. choose a test that will best evaluate the child's mastery of basic skills; and

3. develop a comparable test that will clearly demonstrate the outcome of his or her objectives or goals (Amos, 1980, p. 197).

Graduation Requirements

As mainstreamed students achieve success in and progress through the regular education system, the likelihood that they will graduate with a diploma or some type of recognition increases. While variations exist in the ways mainstreamed students demonstrate mastery of graduation requirements, several approaches to granting some type of diploma to acknowledge completion of graduation requirements have been identified (Ross & Weintraub, 1980). Ross and Weintraub (1980) have delineated five alternative approaches related to graduation requirements for students with disabilities:

1. *Pass/Fail approach.* Upon completing their individualized course of study, all students receive a standard diploma. Individualized achieve-

ments, courses completed, and scores on minimum competency tests are specified on the students' transcripts.

2. *Certificate of attendance approach.* Students who do not meet graduation requirements receive a certificate to document that they participated in and attended a specific educational program for a specified period of time. In using this alternative, educators should be careful that it does not demean students, lessen the availability of services to disabled and minority students, and limit the post-secondary opportunities for disabled students.

3. *IEP approach.* Students' IEPs act as the framework for establishing and individualizing eligibility for graduation and receipt of a diploma. The IEP's goals and objectives parallel the standard diploma requirements and serve as a document listing the minimum competencies a mainstreamed student must complete in order to graduate. If the students complete the goals and objectives specified in their IEPs, they earn diplomas. Diplomas can be supplemented by transcripts indicating courses taken, IEP objectives mastered, and instructional adaptations employed.

4. *Special education diploma approach.* Students who do not complete the standardized graduation requirements receive a specialized diploma based on mastery of goals and objectives outlined in their IEP. A transcript listing mastery of objectives and goals could accompany the diploma to provide additional information to prospective employers.

5. *Curricular approach.* Students and parents, with the assistance of educators, select a course of study related to their needs and career goals (college preparation, vocational education, basic skills, or life management). Each course of study has a prescribed set of requirements and strategies for assessing mastery of identified competencies. When requirements are met, students receive a diploma documenting their mastery of the competencies of the plan of study they have selected.

Obtaining Follow-up Information

Follow-up information on a student's progress in the mainstreamed setting can be obtained from regular educators, parents, and mainstreamed students.

Information from Regular Educators

Students' regular classroom teachers are a primary source of information concerning their progress in mainstreamed settings (Salend, 1983).

Through observation, teachers can obtain valuable data that can pinpoint existing or potential problems in the academic, behavioral, social, and emotional adjustment of mainstreamed students that can be shared with special educators, parents, and other members of the mainstreaming communication network (see Chapter 5). For example, a teacher may notice that a mainstreamed student is performing well academically but has few social interactions with peers during free time, recess, and lunch. Interventions to increase the mainstreamed student's social interactions with peers can then be initiated.

Regular educators also can share information concerning student progress by meeting with the multidisciplinary placement team (Salend, 1983). However, scheduling problems may make direct communication between educators problematic. If direct communication is not possible, audiotapes (Salend, 1980) or written responses can be used to share information. Regardless of the communication format employed, teachers should respond to the following:

1. How is the student performing academically in your class?
2. Does the student complete classwork, homework, or other assigned projects?
3. Was the student academically ready for entry into your class?
4. In what behavioral areas does the student demonstrate proficiency?
5. With what behavioral areas does the student experience difficulty?
6. How are the student's study skills and work habits?
7. How does the student react to your classroom management system?
8. Was the student behaviorally prepared for entry into your class?
9. How does the student get along with his or her peers?
10. In what school clubs or extracurricular activities does the student participate?
11. How do you think the new placement is affecting the student's self-concept?
12. Was the student socially and emotionally prepared for entry into your class?
13. How are the student's hygiene and health-related habits?
14. What, if any, architectural barriers exist in your classroom?
15. Is the student receiving the necessary services from ancillary support personnel?
16. How is the communication system between school personnel functioning?
17. How is the communication system with the student's parents functioning?

18. Are you satisfied with the student's progress in your class?

19. What solutions would you suggest to remediate identified problem areas?

20. What school-wide mainstreaming policies would you like to see retained? revised?

TEACHER ATTITUDES.   Teacher attitude has been identified as a critical variable in the success of mainstreaming (Gickling, Murphy, & Mallory, 1979; Larrivee & Cook, 1979). Therefore, an evaluation of mainstreaming should include an assessment of teacher attitude (Bender, 1987). While attitudes of teachers toward mainstreamed students can be assessed via questionnaires, Salend and Johns (1983) suggest that change in attitudes be measured through teacher behaviors, since it is teacher behavior rather than questionnaire responses that affect the progress of mainstreamed students.

Teacher attitude can be defined in terms of discrete behaviors that attest to an individual's commitment toward a specific issue or program. These specific behaviors could include describing verbally mainstreamed students, writing anecdotal records or other school-based reports concerning the behavior and progress of mainstreamed students, making comments to other professionals in support of mainstreaming, asserting confidence in their ability to teach mainstreamed students, becoming an advocate for mainstreamed students, seeking additional training, providing support to others involved in mainstreaming, and presenting a mainstreaming-related project at a faculty or in-service meeting.

Information from Parents

Parents are often a good source of information concerning their children's reactions to the mainstreamed setting and relationships with classroom peers (Salend, 1983). They can be especially informative in providing information concerning the social and emotional adjustment of the student. For example, parents may notice that a recently mainstreamed student is now reluctant to go to school, and has little contact with classmates outside of school. Similarly, parents can inform educators that their child is spending excessive amounts of time on homework and is having difficulty with the academic requirements of the mainstreamed setting. Therefore, follow-up evaluation should also assess parent satisfaction with respect to the child's social-emotional adjustment and academic progress, as well as the communication between home and school. Salend (1983) suggests that parents can provide useful information concerning the progress of a mainstreamed student by responding to the following:

1. What is your reaction to your child's new class placement?
2. How do you think your child feels about his or her new class placement?
3. How is your child coping with the academic demands of the new class placement?
4. How would you rate your child's progress in interacting with his or her peers?
5. Do you notice any changes in your child since he or she has been placed in the mainstreamed setting?
6. Are you satisfied with your role in the mainstreaming process?
7. How is the communication system between you and school personnel working?
8. Could you suggest any strategies that would be helpful in facilitating the child's adjustment to his or her new setting?
9. What school-wide mainstreaming policies would you like to see retained? revised? (Salend, 1983).

Information from Mainstreamed Students

Feedback from mainstreamed students can provide a novel perspective on student progress and validate the perceptions of others (Salend, 1983). Students can be interviewed regarding their perceptions of their academic, behavioral, and social-emotional adjustment to the regular classroom. Interview questions could include

1. How do you feel about your new class?
2. Were you academically prepared for entry into your new class?
3. In what academic areas are you doing well?
4. With what academic areas are you having difficulty?
5. Are the academic modifications and adaptations that are being implemented helping you?
6. Are you receiving the necessary services and assistance from ancillary support personnel? (Specify support personnel for the student.)
7. How would you rate your behavior in the new class? (Be specific.)
8. Briefly describe your study skills and work habits.
9. Are you completing all classwork, homework, and assigned projects? If not, why not?
10. How do you get along with other students in your class?
11. In what school clubs or activities do you participate? If none, why?

12. Could you suggest any strategies that would help your adjustment to your new class?

Student responses to more formal measures can be particularly helpful in evaluating students' social-emotional progress in the new setting. A Q-Sort comparing students' self perceptions prior to and after the mainstreaming placement can identify target behaviors in need of intervention (Kroth, 1973). Similarly, a self-report (Wallace & Larsen, 1978) or a self-concept measure such as the Piers-Harris Self-Concept Scale (Piers & Harris, 1969) can be administered to obtain a measure of social-emotional progress in the mainstream. Additional strategies for assessing self-concept have been identified by McLoughlin and Lewis (1986) and Smith (1969). In follow-up evaluation, problems with self-concept should be identified and strategies to remediate these areas should be formulated and implemented (Salend, 1983).

Student attitudes and reactions to the social and academic environment of the mainstreamed placement can be assessed by asking students to complete a *classroom climate inventory*, which examines the student's satisfaction with specific aspects of the classroom (Wallace & Larsen, 1978). Fox, Schmuck, van Egmond, Ritvo, and Jung (1975) and Fox, Luszki, and Schmuck (1966) have developed inventories for assessing satisfaction with a new classroom environment. Hawisher (1975) has devised a format for soliciting the perceptions of secondary-level students toward their new placements. Fox, et. al. (1975) have provided guidelines for conducting a classroom climate inventory. Generally, classroom climate assessments are easy to administer, score, and interpret, and can help educators identify the components of classroom environments that are causing difficulties for mainstreamed students (Wallace & Larsen, 1978). Negative discrepancies between student reactions to school before and after the initiation of the mainstreamed placement should be resolved.

The ability of mainstreamed students to meet the behavioral demands of a new classroom setting can be asssessed in several other ways (Bender, 1987). The mainstreaming social skill competencies identified on the IEP can be converted into a checklist, and students can be rated on their level of mastery of these skills. Social skills not mastered can be targeted for remediation. Fagen and Long (1979) have presented guidelines for measuring students' perceived competence in self-control. The Fagen and Long model can be easily adapted to the needs of a variety of students, and can assist professionals in identifying behavioral deficiencies that interfere with student performance. Students' perception of their behavior also can be obtained by having students complete the Student Rating Scale of the Behavior Rating Profile (Brown & Hammill, 1978). Similarly, Brown (1978) has offered a student self-assessment strategy for determining proficiency in independent study behaviors.

Examining the Effectiveness of Instructional Modifications, Adaptive Devices, and Medical Interventions

Because mainstreamed students may require instructional modifications, adaptive devices, and medical interventions to be successful in the mainstream, information to examine the effectiveness of these adaptations should be an integral part of the follow-up evaluation.

Implementation of Instructional Modifications

Although many students will require specific instructional procedures and modifications in order to function successfully in mainstreamed settings, research indicates that many elementary and secondary teachers are not instituting these accommodations for their mainstreamed students (Ammer, 1984; Zigmond, Levin, & Laurie, 1985). Therefore, data should be collected on the types of instructional strategies and adaptations teachers are employing (Bender, 1987). Educators can help teachers who are not employing planned modifications by offering assistance to help regular classroom teachers implement the strategy and providing praise and recognition to teachers for strategy use (Margolis & McGettigan, 1988).

Use of effective teaching practices can be evaluated in several ways (Bender, 1987). A special educator, principal, or member of the multidisciplinary team can observe in the mainstream setting. Bender (1987) suggests that the observation focus on the teacher's management procedures, instructional materials used, and instructional strategies and modifications employed. Measurement of the teacher's adherence to specific instructional procedures, also referred to as *procedural reliability* (Billingsley, White, & Munson, 1980; Peterson, Homer, & Wonderlich, 1982), can be obtained by having the observer record the number of times the instructional procedure was implemented and the number of times the procedure should have been implemented (Salend, 1984b).

However, since these types of observation may result in problems related to professional reviews (Bender, 1987), another method of evaluating use of teaching strategies is self-rating (Darling–Hammond, Wise, & Pease, 1983; Gibson & Dembo, 1984). Teachers are given a rating scale listing effective instructional strategies; they rate themselves on the use of each strategy. Results of observations and self-ratings are then shared with teachers, and plans to promote the use of targeted strategies are identified and implemented.

The effectiveness and efficiency of suggested instructional practices and adaptations also should be evaluated. Since there is a positive relationship between academic learning time and student achievement (Leinhardt, Zigmond, & Cooley, 1981; Rosenberg, Sindelar, & Stedt, 1985), a factor to consider in evaluating the efficacy of appropriate interventions for mainstreamed students is *academic learning time,* which Wilson (1987) defines as the "amount of time students spend successfully performing relevant academic tasks" (p. 13). Academic learning time is usually measured by determining the actual instructional time, student's on-task behavior, and student success rate. Actual instruction time is determined by recording the length of time students spend learning. On-task behavior relates to the time a student is engaged looking at the teacher or the instructional materials that make up the lesson. Student success rate is examined by calculating the percentage of correct responses to oral or written questions and problems.

Curriculum-based assessment data can give educators a measure of the academic and social outcomes of instructional strategies, so data on the effectiveness of these strategies from the perspective of the teachers implementing them should be collected (Greenwood & Hops, 1981; Kazdin, 1977). These data can be collected by having teachers respond to the following:

1. How does the strategy affect you?
2. What are the strengths of the strategy?
3. What factors contribute to the success of the strategy?
4. What are the weaknesses of the strategy?
5. How does the strategy affect the mainstreamed student? other students? other adults in the room?
6. How does the strategy affect other behaviors?
7. Do the effects of the strategy generalize to other situations?

SCHEDULES. In order to implement the IEPs of mainstreamed students, special and regular educators will have to plan carefully and implement schedules that allow these students to receive the necessary related services to help them master content presented in their regular classes. Therefore, educators should examine schedules to ensure that students are receiving the related services specified in the IEP, and that sufficient time is allocated for these services. Educators can evaluate mainstreamed students' schedules in these terms:

1. Does the schedule allow time for meeting the students' IEP goals?
2. Is the length of time for each component appropriate for the students?
3. Does the sequence of events provide for a variety of learning experiences?
4. Does the sequence flow in a logical progression?
5. Do the components vary from one-to-one to group activities?
6. Are transitions between activities planned to minimize confusion?
7. Does the schedule provide a stable routine? (Lund & Bos, 1981, p. 121).

Because many mainstreamed students may receive supplementary instruction and services from ancillary support personnel, regular classroom teachers should coordinate their schedules with other professionals. Additionally, since these students will miss work and assignments while outside the room, procedures for making up these assignments should be established (Everston, Emmer, Clements, Sanford, & Worsham, 1989).

Adaptive Device Monitoring

The progress of some mainstreamed students, particularly those with sensory and physical disabilities, also will depend on their use of adaptive and prosthetic devices. Since failure of these devices to work properly can limit the likelihood of success for mainstreamed students, educators will need to monitor the working condition of these devices. For example, a malfunctioning hearing aid can hinder the academic progress of a student with a hearing impairment; the wear and tear on a wheelchair and other prostheses can limit a student's mobility and ability to interact with peers. Obtain information concerning prostheses and adaptive devices by consulting the student, parents, special educators, ancillary support personnel, or medical personnel.

Educators can periodically examine a student's hearing aid by using an inexpensive plastic stethoscope, which may be obtained from the speech and hearing specialist. The stethoscope allows the educator to hear what the student using the hearing aid hears, and can help detect malfunctions and their causes. Madell (cited in Cartwright, Cartwright, & Ward, 1985) provides guidelines for determining and solving problems with hearing aids. A whistling sound may indicate that the earmold doesn't fit, the battery or the receiver is malfunctioning, or that the volume control is too loud. No sound often suggests that the cord or the battery is not working. If a faint sound is heard from the aid, it may be the result of a worn or incorrect battery, a broken cord, or an incorrect setting for the volume or tone control. When the sound varies from on to off, the battery and cord connections may be loose or corroded. If the battery and cord are connected properly, the varying signals may be caused by a broken receiver. Finally, a sound that is distorted or too loud can be caused by a weak battery, improper battery or cord connections, incorrect tone control setting, damaged earphone, or a wax clogged earmold or earphone.

Teachers can help maintain the hearing aid in working condition for students by keeping it out of excessively hot or cold locations and making sure it does not get wet (Gearheart, Weishahn, & Gearheart, 1988). When teachers suspect that an aid is malfunctioning and they cannot correct the problem, the student's parents and speech or hearing therapist should be contacted immediately for assistance.

Venn, Morganstern, and Dykes (1979) suggest that teachers examine ambulatory devices used by students. If they note problems, they should contact parents or appropriate medical personnel. Checklists to assist teachers in determining the condition of lower extremity braces, prostheses, and wheelchairs are presented in Figure 9.6.

Medication Monitoring

Some mainstreamed students may take prescription drugs to enhance their school performance. For example, physicians may prescribe medication for students to control seizures and students with attention deficits to increase their ability to pay attention (Courtnage, Stainback, & Stainback, 1982). Educators serving these students should be aware of the school district's policies regarding drug management. Specifically, educators should consider

1. Who is allowed to administer drugs to students?
2. Does the school district have a form that empowers school personnel to dispense medications?
3. Does the school district have a form for obtaining the approval of physicians to dispense medications to students?
4. Does the school district have a procedure for obtaining information from physicians and parents concerning the name of medication, dosage, frequency, duration, and possible side effects?
5. Does the school have a format for maintaining records on medications administered to students?
6. Does the school have established procedures for receiving, labeling, storing, dispensing, and disposing of medications?
7. Does the school have procedures concerning the self-administration of drugs? (Courtnage, Stainback, & Stainback, 1982).

FIGURE 9.6.   Lower Extremity Braces, Prostheses, and Wheelchairs Condition Checklist.

Minicheck—Lower Extremity Orthoses (For Use in the Classroom)

	No	Yes	Comments
I. AFO (ankle-foot orthosis) Short Leg Brace			
A. With the brace off the student			
1. Do joints work easily?			
2. Can shoes be easily removed?			
3. Is the workmanship good?			
a. No rough edges			
b. Straps secure			
c. Leather work stitched properly			
B. Student standing with brace on			
1. Are the sole and heel flat on the floor?			
2. Are the ankle joints aligned so that they coincide with the anatomical joints?			
3. Is there ample clearance between the leg and the brace (one finger width)?			
4. Does the T-strap exert enough force for correction without causing deformity?			
5. Do the uprights conform to the contour of the leg?			
6. Do the uprights coincide with the midline of the leg when viewed from the side?			
7. Is the brace long enough?			
a. It should be below the bend of the knee so the student can bend the knee comfortably to 120°.			
b. It should not be lower than the bulky part of the calf muscle.			
C. Student walking with brace on			
1. Is there clearance between the up-rights and the leg?			
2. Are there any gait deviations?			
3. Is the brace quiet?			

FIGURE 9.6.   *(continued)*

	No	Yes	Comments
II. KAFO (knee-ankle-foot orthosis) Long Leg Brace A. With the brace off the student			
1. Do joints work easily?			
2. Can the shoes be easily removed?			
3. Is the workmanship good?			
a. No rough edges			
b. Straps secure			
c. Leather work stitched properly			
B. Student standing with brace on			
1. Are the knee joints aligned at the approximate anatomical joints?			
a. There should be no pressure from thigh band when knee is bent (if so the joints are too high).			
b. There should be no pressure from calf band when knee is bent (if so the joints are too low).			
c. There should be no pressure on calf (if so the joints are too far forward).			
d. There should be no pressure on shin or knee cap (if so the joints are too far backward).			
2. Are locks secure and easy to work?			
3. Is the brace long enough?			
a. Medial upright should be up into groin region but should not cause pain.			
b. Lateral upright should be 1 inch longer.			
4. Are the thigh bands and calf bands about equal distance from the knee?			
III. HKAFO (hip-knee-ankle-foot orthosis) Long Leg Brace with Pelvic Band A. With the brace off the student			
1. Do joints work easily?			
2. Can shoes be easily removed?			
3. Is the workmanship good?			
a. No rough edges			
b. Straps secure			
c. Leather work stitched properly			

FIGURE 9.6. (*continued*)

	No	Yes	Comments
B. Student with brace on 1. Is the pelvic band located below the waist?			
2. Is the student comfortable sitting and standing?			
3. Are the hip joints in the right place and do the locks work easily?			
IV. Other joints to check A. Do the shoes fit and are they in good repair?			
B. Do reddened areas go away after the brace has been off 20 minutes?			
C. Is the student comfortable?			
D. Is the brace helping the student?			
V. Plastic Braces A. Does the brace conform and contact the extremity?			
B. Is the student wearing a sock between his foot and the brace?			
C. Does the brace pull away from the leg excessively when the student walks?			
D. Do reddened areas go away after the brace has been off 20 minutes?			

Minicheck—Lower Extremity Prostheses (For Use in the Classroom)

	No	Yes	Comments
I. Lower Extremity Prosthetics A. Is the student wearing prosthesis (frequency)?			
B. Does the student use assistive devices with prosthesis (crutches, canes, one cane, other)? If so, what does he or she use and how often.			
C. Is the prosthesis on correctly? 1. Is the toe turned out about the same as the other foot?			
2. When the student sits is the knee in alignment?			

FIGURE 9.6.   *(continued)*

	No	Yes	Comments
D. Does the leg appear the same length as the normal leg?			
1. Does the student stand straight when bearing weight on the prosthesis?			
2. Are the shoulders even when weight bearing (one shoulder should not drop)?			
3. Does the knee stay straight when walking without turning out or in?			
II. Gait Deviations			
A. Does the student stand straight when bearing weight on the prosthesis?			
B. Does the artificial leg swing forward without turning in or out?			
C. Does the student swing the artificial leg through without rising up on the foot of the normal leg?			
D. Does the leg swing straight forward when walking? (It should not swing out in an arc.)			
E. When standing are the feet a normal distance apart? (The stance should not be too wide.)			
F. Does the knee bend and straighten like a normal leg?			
III. Condition of the Prosthesis			
A. Do the suspension joints appear to be in good condition (leather, joint, band)?			
B. Does the leg stay in place when the student is standing and sitting?			
C. Does the knee bend appropriately?			
D. Are the joints quiet when the joint is moved?			
E. Do the foot and ankle appear to be in one piece?			
F. Is the shoe in good condition (heel, sole)?			

FIGURE 9.6.   (*continued*)

Minicheck—Wheelchairs (For Use in the Classroom—Wheelchair Prescriptions, 1968, 1976)			
	No	Yes	Comments

I. With the student out of the wheelchair
  A. Arms
    1. Are the armrests and side panels secure and free of sharp edges and cracks?			

2. Do the armlocks function properly?			
B. Backs 1. Is the upholstery free of rips and tears?			
2. Is the back taut from top to bottom?			
3. Is the safety belt attached tightly and not frayed?			
C. Seat and frame 1. Is the upholstery free of rips and tears?			
2. Does the chair fold easily without sticking?			
3. When the chair is folded fully are the front post slides straight and round?			
D. Wheel locks 1. Do the wheel locks securely engage the tire surfaces and prevent the wheel from turning?			
E. Large wheels 1. Are the wheels free from wobble or sideplay when spun?			
2. Are the spokes equally tight and without any missing spokes?			
3. Are the tires free from excessive wear and gaps at the joined section?			
F. Casters 1. Is the stem firmly attached to the fork?			
2. Are the forks straight on sides and stem so that the caster swivels easily?			

FIGURE 9.6.   (*continued*)

	No	Yes	Comments
3. Is the caster assembly free from excessive play both up and down as well as backward and forward?			
4. Are the wheels free of excessive play and wobble?			
5. Are the tires in good condition?			
G. Footrest/Legrest			
1. Does the lock mechanism fit securely?			
2. Are the heel loops secure and correctly installed?			
3. Do the footplates fold easily and hold in any position?			
4. Are the legrest panels free of cracks and sharp edges?			
II. With the student sitting in the chair			
A. Seat width			
1. When your palms are placed between the patient's hip and the side of the chair (skirtguard), do the hands contact the hip and the skirtguard at the same time without pressure?			
2. Or, is the clearance between the patient's widest point of either hips or thigh and the skirtguard approximately 1 inch on either side?			
B. Seat depth			
1. Can you place your hand, with fingers extended, between the front edge of the seat upholstery and to the rear of the knee with a clearance of three or four fingers?			
2. Or, is the seat upholstery approximately 2 to 3 inches less than the student's thigh measurement?			
C. Seat height and footrest			
1. Is the lowest part of the stepplates no closer than 2 inches from the floor?			
2. Or, is the student's thigh elevated slightly above the front edge of the seat upholstery?			

FIGURE 9.6.   (*continued*)

	No	Yes	Comments
D. Arm height 1. Does the arm height not force the shoulders up or allow them to drop significantly when in a normal sitting position?			
2. Is the elbow positioned slightly forward of the trunk midline when the student is in a normal sitting position?			
E. Back height 1. Can you insert four or five fingers between the patient's armpit area and the top of the back upholstery touching both at the same time?			
2. Is the top of the back upholstery approximately 4 inches below the armpit for the student who needs only minimum trunk support?			
III. With the student pushing or riding in the wheelchair A. Is the wheelchair free from squeaks or rattles?			
B. Does the chair roll easily without pulling to either side?			
C. Are the large wheels and casters free of play and wobble?			

Source: J. Venn, L. Morganstern, and M. K. Dykes, *Teaching Exceptional Children*, Vol. 11 (Reston, Virginia: Council for Exceptional Children), pp. 54–56. Reprinted by permission of the publisher.

Educators serving mainstreamed students who require medication should carefully monitor student progress and behavior throughout the drug treatment, and maintain communication with parents and medical professionals. To effectively monitor students, teachers should receive information from the student's doctor, school physician, or school nurse concerning the name or type of medication, dosage, frequency, and duration of the administration, and anticipated symptoms and side effects (Courtnage, Stainback, & Stainback, 1982). When changes occur in students' medication schedule and dosage level, teachers should be informed.

Because side effects are possible with many medications, Courtnage, Stainback, and Stainback (1982) suggest that teachers maintain an anecdotal record of student behavior in school, including statements concerning the students' academic performance, social skills, notable changes in behavior, and possible symptoms associated with the use of medications (Sprague & Gadow, 1976). This record should be shared with parents and medical personnel with the consent of parents to assist them in evaluating the efficacy and need for continued use of the medication (Courtnage, Stainback, & Stainback, 1982). A sample anecdotal record is presented in Figure 9.7.

Educators should avoid dispensing medications, but occasionally the drug treatment schedule may necessitate the school nurse administering medication to students during school hours. If the school nurse cannot dispense the medication, teachers may be asked to do so. However, before dispensing medication, obtain the permission of parents and the appropriate medical personnel. All medications should be stored together in a secured location that is open only to school personnel involved in the administration of medications. To avoid confusion, each student's medication should be clearly labeled, including the name of the student, physician, pharmacy, type of medication, the telephone number

FIGURE 9.7.   Sample Drug Anecdotal Record.

| Name of Student | Henry Jones | | Grade | 6 |
| School | Pine Lake Elementary | | Recorded by | Ms. Healy |

Date	Observations
10-8-81	Henry seems to have lost his appetite. He didn't eat much of his lunch Tuesday and Wednesday. Today he did manage to eat everything, but it did demand encouragement on my part. If this continues much longer I will contact the parents.
10-12-81	Henry was not very accepting of the idea of taking medication but since my contact with the parents on October 5th, he seems to be less resistant.
10-15-81	Henry did eat his lunch today. He also did attend better in his morning reading and social studies classes, but had two fights with his classmates at lunch break and was irritable during the afternoon.

Source: L. Courtnage, W. Stainback, and S. Stainback, *Teaching Exceptional Children*, Vol. 15 (Reston, Virginia: Council for Exceptional Children), p. 9. Reprinted by permission of the publisher.

FIGURE 9.8.   Record of Drug Administration.

Name of Student _____ Henry Jones _____   **Birthdate** __July 25, 1970__

Address _____ Holcomb Avenue _____   **Phone** __(515) 832-6111__

_____ Des Moines, Iowa _____

School _____ Pine Lake Elementary _____   **Grade** _____ 6 _____

Date	Time	Name of Medication	Dosage	Signature of Person Administering Medication	Comments
10-5-81	11:20	Ritalin Initiated	20 mg.	H. Healy	Henry questioned the need for medication. Parents notified.
10-6-81	11:20	Ritalin	20 mg.	H. Healy	—
10-7-81	11:20	Ritalin	20 mg.	H. Healy	—
10-8-81	11:20	Ritalin	20 mg.	H. Healy	—
10-9-81	Absent				—
10-12-81	11:20	Ritalin	20 mg.	H. Healy	—
10-13-81	11:20	Ritalin	20 mg.	H. Healy	—
10-14-81	11:20	Ritalin	20 mg.	H. Healy	Henry spit out pill. Said didn't need it—took it second time.
10-15-81	11:20	Ritalin Discontinued	—	H. Healy	—
10-15-81	9:15	Cylert Initiated	37.5 mg.	H. Healy	Hesitant about taking new medication.

Source: L. Courtnage, W. Stainback, and S. Stainback, *Teaching Exceptional Children,*
Vol. 15 (Reston, Virginia: Council for Exceptional Children), p. 8. Reprinted by
permission of the publisher.

of the physician and the pharmacy, date, dosage, and frequency of
administration (Kinnison & Nimmer, 1979). A record of the medications
dispensed also should be maintained (see Figure 9.8).

Summary

Student progress in the regular classroom setting should be evaluated
periodically to determine if the mainstreamed placement is achieving
its intended academic and social outcomes. Educators can assess student

progress by administering standardized and minimum competency tests, employing curriculum-based assessment, analyzing error patterns, and examining the effectiveness of instructional modifications, adaptive devices, and medical interventions. Information on student progress in the mainstream also can be obtained from regular educators, parents, and the mainstreamed students themselves.

References

Ammer, J. J. (1984). The mechanics of mainstreaming: Considering the regular educators' perspective. *Remedial and Special Education, 5,* 15–20.

Amos, K. M. (1980). Competency testing: Will the LD student be included? *Exceptional Children, 47,* 194–197.

Beatty, L. S., Madden, R., Gardner, E. F., & Karlsen, B. (1984). *Stanford diagnostic mathematics tests. 3rd ed.* Cleveland: Psychological Corporation.

Bender, W. N. (1987). Effective educational practices in the mainstream setting: Recommended model for evaluation of mainstream teacher classes. *Journal of Special Education, 20,* 475–488.

Bender, W. N. (1988). The other side of placement decisions: Assessment of the mainstream learning environment. *Remedial and Special Education, 9* (5), 28–33.

Billingsley, F., White, D. R., & Munson, R. (1980). Procedural reliability: A rationale and an example. *Behavioral Assessment, 2,* 229–241.

Blankenship, C. S. (1985). Using curriculum-based assessment data to make instructional decisions. *Exceptional Children, 52,* 233–238.

Boehm, A. E. (1971). *Boehm Test of Basic Concepts.* Cleveland: Psychological Corporation.

Brigance, A. H. (1977). *Brigance Diagnostic Inventory of Basic Skills.* North Billerica, Mass.: Curriculum Associates.

Brigance, A. H. (1980). *Brigance Diagnostic Inventory of Essential Skills.* North Billerica, Mass.: Curriculum Associates.

Brigance, A. H. (1983). *Brigance Diagnostic Comprehensive Inventory of Basic Skills.* North Billerica, Mass.: Curriculum Associates.

Brown, L. L., & Hammill, D. D. (1978). *Behavior Rating Profile.* Austin, Tex.: Pro-Ed.

Brown, V. (1978). Independent study behaviors: A framework for curriculum development. *Learning Disability Quarterly, 1,* 78–84.

Brown, V., & McEntire, E. (1984). *Test of Mathematical Abilities.* Austin, Tex.: Pro-Ed.

Cartwright, G. P., Cartwright, C. A., & Ward, M. E. (1985). *Educating special learners.* Belmont, Calif.: Wadsworth.

Cattell, R. B., & Cattell, A. K. S. (1963). *Culture fair intelligence test: Scale 3.* Champaign, Ill.: Institute for Personality and Ability Testing.

Coballes-Vega, C., & Salend, S. J. (in press). Guidelines for assessing migrant handicapped students. *Diagnostique.*

Compton, C. (1980). *A guide to 65 tests for special education.* Belmont, Calif.: Pitman Learning.

Connolly, A. J. (1988). *Keymath: A Diagnostic Inventory of Essential Mathematics.* Circle Pines, Minn.: American Guidance Service.

Coulter, W. A., & Morrow, H. W. (1978). *Adaptive behavior.* New York: Grune & Stratton.

Courtnage, L., Stainback, W., & Stainback, S. (1982). Managing prescription drugs in schools. *Teaching Exceptional Children, 15,* 5–9.

Cox, L. S. (1975). Diagnosing and remediating systematic errors in addition and subtraction computations. *The Arithmetic Teacher, 22,* 151–157.

Darling-Hammond, L., Wise, A. E., & Pease, S. R. (1983). Teacher evaluation in the organizational context: A review of the literature. *Review of Educational Research, 53,* 285–328.

Deno, S. L. (1985). Curriculum-based measurement: The emerging alternative. *Exceptional Children, 52,* 219–232.

Deno, S. L., & Fuchs, L. S. (1988). Developing curriculum-based measurement systems for data-based special education problem solving. In E.L. Meyen, G.A. Vergason, & R. J. Whelan (Eds.), *Effective instructional strategies for exceptional children* (pp. 481–504). Denver: Love Publishing.

Dunn, L. M., & Dunn, L. M. (1981). *Peabody Picture Vocabulary Test.* Circle Pines, Minn.: American Guidance Service.

Dunn, L. M., & Markwardt, F. C. (1970). *Peabody Individual Achievement Test.* Circle Pines, Minn.: American Guidance Service.

Enright, B. E. (1983). *Enright Diagnostic Inventory of Basic Arithmetic Skills.* North Billerica, Mass.: Curriculum Associates.

Everston, C. M., Emmer, E. T., Clements, B. S., Sanford, J. P., & Worsham, M. E. (1989). *Classroom management for elementary teachers (2nd ed.).* Englewood Cliffs, N.J.: Prentice Hall.

Fagen, S. A., & Long, N. J. (1979). A psychoeducational curriculum approach to teaching self-control. *Behavioral Disorders 4,* 68–82.

Fox, R. S., Luszki, M. B., & Schmuck, R. (1966). *Diagnosing classroom learning environments.* Chicago: Science Research Associates.

Fox, R. S., Schmuck, R., van Egmond, E., Ritvo, M., & Jung, C. (1975). *Diagnosing professional climates of schools.* Fairfax, Va.: NTL Learning Resources Corporation.

Fradd, S. H., Vega, J. E., & Hallman, C. L. (1985). *Meeting the educational needs of limited English proficient students: Policy issues and perspectives.* Gainesville, Fla.: College of Education.

Galagan, J. E. (1985). Psychological testing: Turn out the lights, the party's over: *Exceptional Children, 52,* 288–299.

Gallagher, J. J., & Hall, J. (1979). The benefits of competency testing for the exceptional student. *Education Unlimited, 1,* 71–72.

Gearheart, B. R., Weishahn, M. W., & Gearheart, C. J. (1988). *The exceptional student in the classroom (4th. ed.).* Columbus: Charles E. Merrill.

Germann, G., & Tindal, G. (1985). An application of curriculum-based assessment: The use of direct and repeated measurement. *Exceptional Children, 52,* 244–265.

Gibson, S., & Dembo, M. H. (1984). Teacher efficacy: A construct validation. *Journal of Educational Psychology, 4,* 569–582.

Gickling, E. E., Murphy, L. C., & Mallory, D. W. (1979). Teachers' preferences for resource services. *Exceptional Children, 45,* 442–449.

Gickling, E. E., & Thompson, V. P. (1985). A personal view of curriculum-based assessment. *Exceptional Children, 52,* 205–218.

Gonzales, E. (1982). Issues in the assessment of minorities. In H.L. Swanson & B.L. Watson (Eds.), *Educational and psychological assessment of exceptional children* (pp. 375–389). St. Louis: C. V. Mosby.

Greenwood, C. R., & Hops, H. (1981). Group-oriented contingencies and peer behavior change. In P. Strain (Ed.), *The utilization of classroom peers as behavior change agents* (pp. 189–259). New York: Plenum.

Grimes, L. (1981). Error analysis and error correction procedures. *Teaching Exceptional Children, 14,* 17–21.

Guerin, G. R., & Maier, A. S. (1983). *Informal assessment in education.* Palo Alto, Calif.: Mayfield.

Hammill, D. D., & Larsen, S. C. (1983). *Test of Written Language.* Austin, Tex.: Pro-Ed.

Hawisher, M. F. (1975). *The resource room: An access to excellence.* Lancaster: South Carolina Region V Educational Services Center.

Heller, K., Holtzman, W. H., & Messick, N. (1982). *National Research Council Special Task Force Report.* Washington, D.C.: National Academy Press.

Hundert, J. (1982). Some considerations of planning the integration of handicapped children into the mainstream. *Journal of Learning Disabilities, 15,* 73–80.

Kaufman, A. S., & Kaufman, N. L. (1985). *Kaufman Test of Educational Achievement.* Circle Pines, Minn.: American Guidance Service.

Kazdin, A. E. (1977). Assessing the clinical or applied importance of behavior change through social validation. *Behavior Modification, 4,* 427–452.

Kinnison, L., & Nimmer, D. (1979). An analysis of policies regulating medication in schools. *The Journal of School Health, 49,* 280–287.

Knapp, S., & Salend, S. J. (1983). Adapting the adaptive behavior scale. *Mental Retardation, 21,* 63–67.

Kroth, R. (1973). The behavioral Q-Sort as a diagnostic tool. *Academic Therapy, 8,* 317–324.

Lambert, N. M., Windmiller, M., Tharinger, D., & Cole, L. J. (1981). *AAMD Adaptive Behavior Scale—School Edition.* Monterey, Calif.: CTB/McGraw-Hill.

Laosa, L. M. (1977). Nonbiased assessment of children's abilities: Historical antecedents and current issues. In T. Oakland (Ed.), *Psychological and education assessment of minority children* (pp. 1–20). New York: Brunner/Mazel.

Larsen, S. C., & Hamill, D. D. (1986). *Test of Written Spelling-2.* Austin, Tex.: Pro-ED.

Larrivee, B., & Cook, C. (1979). Mainstreaming: A study of teacher attitudes toward handicapped children. *The Journal of Special Education, 13,* 313–324.

Ledeber, J., & Azzara, C. (1980, April). *Mainstreaming for emotionally disturbed students.* Paper presented at the annual meeting of Council for Exceptional Children, Philadelphia.

Leinhardt, G., Zigmond, N., & Cooley, W. (1981). Reading instruction and its effects. *American Educational Research Journal, 18,* 343–361.

Lund, K. A., & Bos, C. S. (1981). Orchestrating the preschool classroom: The daily schedule. *Teaching Exceptional Children, 14,* 120–125.

Margolis, H., & McGettigan, J. (1988). Managing resistance to instructional modifications in mainstreamed environments. *Remedial and Special Education, 9*(4), 15–21.

McCarthy, M. (1980). Minimum competency testing and handicapped students. *Exceptional Children, 47,* 166–173.

McCormack, J. E. (1978). The assessment tool that meets your needs: The one you construct. *Teaching Exceptional Children, 8,* 106–109.

McLoughlin, J. A., & Lewis, R. B. (1986). *Assessing special students.* Columbus: Charles E. Merrill.

Mehrens, W. A., & Lehman, I. J. (1969). *Standardized tests in education.* New York: Holt, Rinehart and Winston.

Mercer, J. R., & Lewis, J. F. (1977). *System of multicultural pluralistic assessment.* Cleveland: Psychological Corporation.

Meyers, J., & Lytle, S. (1986). Assessment of the learning process. *Exceptional Children, 53,* 138–144.

Mirkin, P., Deno, S. L., Fuchs, L., Wesson, C., Tindal, G., Marston, D., & Kuehnle, K. (1981). *Procedures to monitor student progress on IEP goals.* Minneapolis: University of Minnesota, Institute for Research on Learning Disabilities.

Myklebust, H. R. (1973). *Development and disorders of written language, Volume two: Studies of normal and exceptional children.* New York: Grune & Stratton.

Newcomer, P. L., & Hammill, D. D. (1982). *Test of Language Development-Primary.* Austin, Tex.: Pro-Ed.

Oakland, T. (1980). Nonbiased assessment of minority group children. *Exceptional Education Quarterly, 1*(3), 31–46.

Otto, W., Mcmenemy, R. A., & Smith, R. J. (1973). *Corrective and remedial teaching.* Boston: Houghton Mifflin.

Peterson, J., Heistad, D., Peterson, D., & Reynolds, M. (1985). Montevideo individualized prescriptive instructional management system. *Exceptional Children, 52,* 239–243.

Peterson, L., Homer, A. L., & Wonderlich, S. A. (1982). The integrity of the independent variables in behavior analysis. *Journal of Applied Behavior Analysis, 15,* 477–492.

Piers, E. V., & Harris, D. B. (1969). *The Piers-Harris Self-Concept Scale.* Nashville: Counselor Recordings and Tests.

Roos, P. D. (1984). *The handicapped limited English proficient student: A school district's obligation.* Tallahassee, Fla.: State Education Department.

Rosenberg, M., Sindelar, P., & Stedt, J. (1985). The effects of supplemental on-task contingencies upon the acquisition of simple and difficult academic tasks. *Journal of Special Education, 19,* 189–203.

Ross, J. W., & Weintraub, F. J. (1980). Policy approaches regarding the impact of graduation requirements on handicapped students. *Exceptional Children, 47,* 200–203.

Safer, N. (1980). Implications of minimum competency standards and testing for handicapped students. *Exceptional Children, 46,* 288–290.

Salend, S. J. (1980). How to mainstream teachers. *Education Unlimited, 2,* 31–33.

Salend, S. J. (1983). Mainstreaming: Sharpening up follow-up. *Academic Therapy, 18,* 299–304.

Salend, S. J. (1984a). Selecting and evaluating educational assessment instruments. *The Pointer, 28,* 20–22.

Salend, S. J. (1984b). Therapy outcome research: Threats to treatment integrity. *Behavior Modification, 8,* 211–222.

Salend, S. J., & Fradd, S. (1986). Nationwide availability of services for limited English-proficient handicapped students. *Journal of Special Education, 20,* 127–135.

Salend, S. J., & Johns, J. (1983). A tale of two teachers: Changing teacher commitment to mainstreaming. *Teaching Exceptional Children, 15,* 82–85.

Salvia, J., & Ysseldyke, J. E. (1985). *Assessment in special and remedial education* (3rd ed.). Boston: Houghton Mifflin.

Sattler, J. M. (1988). *Assessment of children (3rd ed.).* San Diego: Sattler.

Schloss, P. J., Schloss, C. N., & Segraves, G. (1983). Home-school cooperation in motivating homework completion. *Journal for Special Educators, 20,* 23–27.

Semel, E., & Wiig, E. (1980). *Clinical Evaluation of Language Functions.* Columbus: Charles E. Merrill.

Smith, R. M. (1969). *Teacher diagnosis of educational difficulties.* Columbus: Charles E. Merrill.

Sparrow, S., Balla, D., & Cicchetti, D. (1984). *Vineland Adaptive Behavior Scales.* Circle Pines, Minn.: American Guidance Service.

Sprague, R., & Gadow, K. (1976). The role of the teacher in drug treatment. *School Review, 85,* 109–140.

Trueba, H. T. (1983). Adjustment problems in Mexican and Mexican-American students: An anthropological study. *Learning Disability Quarterly, 6,* 395–415.

Tucker, J. A. (1985). Curriculum-based assessment: An introduction. *Exceptional Children, 52,* 199–204.

Venn, J., Morganstern, L., & Dykes, M. K. (1979). Checklists for evaluating the fit and function of orthoses, prostheses, and wheelchairs in the classroom. *Teaching Exceptional Children, 11,* 51–56.

Waggoner, D. (1984). The need for bilingual education: Estimates for the 1980 census. *Journal of the National Association for Bilingual Education, 8,* 1–14.

Wallace, G., & Larsen, S. C. (1978). *Educational assessment of learning problems: Testing for teaching.* Boston: Allyn & Bacon.

Wang, M. C., Anderson, K. A., & Bram, P. (1985). *Toward an empirical data base on mainstreaming: A research synthesis of program implementation and effects.* Pittsburgh: Learning Research and Development Center, University of Pittsburgh.

White, O. R., & Haring, N. G. (1981). *Exceptional teaching.* Columbus: Charles E. Merrill.

Wilkinson, C. Y., & Ortiz, A. A. (1986). Reevaluation of learning disabled Hispanic students: Changes over three years. *Bilingual Special Education Newsletter.* Austin, Tex.: Bilingual Special Education Training Program at the University of Texas at Austin.

Wilson, R. (1987). Direct observation of academic learning time. *Teaching Exceptional Children, 19,* 13–17.

Woodcock, R. W., & Johnson, M. B. (1977). *Woodcock-Johnson Psychoeducational Battery.* Allen, Tex.: DLM Teaching Resources.

Zaner-Bloser Evaluation Scale. (1984). Columbus: Zaner-Bloser.

Zigmond, N., Levin, E., & Laurie, T. E. (1985). Managing the mainstream: An analysis of teacher attitudes and student performance in mainstream high school programs. *Journal of Learning Disabilities, 18,* 535–541.

Appendix:
Parental, Professional, and Advocacy Organizations

Compiled by Lynn Sarda, Lynne Crockett, Veronica Lazzaro, Cathy Mastrocola, Susan Richmann, Joan Neugebauer, and Merrily Warren-Blum.

Advocates * Resources * Counseling
ARC of King County
2230 Eighth Avenue
Seattle, WA 98121   206-622-9324

Maintains a Parent-to-Parent Support Program, trains parents to work with parents whose children have similar disabilities. Disseminates a newsletter for parents and for grandparents of children with special needs.

Alexander Graham Bell Association for the Deaf
3417 Volta Place, NW
Washington, DC 20007   202-337-5220

Answers inquiries from parents, offers information on educational options and consultation services, disseminates a journal and newsletter.

American Association on Mental Retardation
1719 Kalorama Road, NW
Washington, DC 20009   800-424-3688

Distributes information about programs and research, sponsors conferences, and serves as a clearinghouse on various aspects of mental retardation. A publications list and newsletter are available.

American Cancer Society
90 Park Avenue
New York, NY 10016   212-599-8200

Provides information, direct services, and referrals. Some materials are available in Spanish.

American Cleft Palate Association
331 Salk Hall, University of Pittsburgh
Pittsburgh, PA 15213   412-681-9620

Provides publications, referrals for services, and free pamphlets for parents. Puts parents in touch with others who have children with cleft palates.

American Council for the Blind
1010 Vermont Avenue, NW, Suite 1100   800-424-8666, 3–5 P.M.
Washington, DC 20005   202-393-3666

Serves people who are visually impaired or deaf/blind. Offers a parent organization, legal assistance, a newsletter, and free magazine. Some information is available in Braille, Spanish.

American Council on Rural Special Education
National Rural Development Institute
Western Washington University
Bellingham, WA 98225   206-676-3576

Focuses on improving services for students with disabilities living in rural areas.

American Foundation for the Blind, Inc.   232-5463
15 West 16th Street   800-AFBLIND
New York, NY 10011   212-620-2000

Serves people who are visually impaired or deaf/blind. Provides information on education and employment and daily living activities. Pamphlets, films, and publications are available including some in Braille and Spanish.

American Heart Association
7320 Greenville Avenue
Dallas, TX 75231   214-750-5300

Provides information and referral services for individuals with cardiovascular disorders, stroke, and aphasia. There is a small charge for some materials. Some materials are available in Spanish.

American Lung Association
1740 Broadway
New York, NY 10019   212-315-8700

Provides information on respiratory conditions, tuberculosis, and asthma. Most resources and materials are free. Several pamphlets in Spanish are available.

American Physical Therapy Association
1111 North Fairfax Street
Alexandria, VA 22314   703-684-2782

Provides pamphlets, newsletter, and free bibliographies. Refers to facilities offering physical therapy services.

American Printing House for the Blind
P.O. Box 6085, 1839 Frankfort Avenue
Louisville, KY 40206-0085   502-895-2405

Offers lists of books, brochures, catalogues in Braille and large print publications. Serves as the largest publishing house for people who are blind or visually impaired.

American Society for Deaf Children   800-942-273
814 Thayer Avenue
Silver Springs, MD 20910   301-585-5400

Provides parents and families of children who are hard of hearing or deaf with support and information. Offers networking referral and advocacy services. Publishes a newsletter, legislative information, and position papers.

American Speech, Language & Hearing Association
10801 Rockville Pike
Rockville, MD 20852   301-897-5700

A professional organization that disseminates research and information on communication disorders. Publishes journals and serves as an advocacy group.

Association of Birth Defects Children, Inc. (ABDC)
3526 Emerywood Lane
Orlando, FL 32806   407-859-2821

Provides information about birth defects associated with environmental factors and disseminates information related to effects of environmental agents. Publishes a quarterly newsletter.

Association for Children and Adults with Learning Disabilities
4156 Library Road
Pittsburgh, PA 15234   412-341-1515/8077

Provides general information and referrals. Offers free pamphlets, lists of special schools, colleges, and camps for students with learning disabilities.

Association for Persons with Severe Handicaps
7010 Roosevelt Way, N.E.
Seattle, WA 98115   206-523-8446

Offers parent-to-parent support and communication network. Assists with referrals and publishes a journal, newsletter, and bibliographies.

Association for Retarded Citizens of the United States
National Headquarters
2501 Avenue J   800-433-5255
Arlington, TX 76006   817-640-0204

Provides services and referrals. Publishes pamphlets, books, and a newsletter. There is a nominal charge for publications. Some publications in Spanish are available.

Bilingual Special Education
Department of Special Education
EDB 306
University of Texas
Austin, TX 78710

Provides newsletter and bulletin board for information on the identification, assessment, placement, and educational planning for special needs language minority students.

Blind Children's Fund
International Institute for Visually Impaired, 0-7, Inc.
230 Central Street
Auburndale, MA 02166-2399

Develops and disseminates information, materials, and services for individuals with visual impairments. Provides support services to parents and professionals, programs, a newsletter, publications. Some publications in Spanish are available.

The Candlelighters
Childhood Cancer Foundation
Suite 1001
1901 Pennsylvania Avenue, NW
Washington, DC 20006   202-659-5136

For parents and their children with cancer. Produces a quarterly newsletter and a youth newsletter. Provides support, information services, and lobbying groups.

Children's Defense Fund
122 C Street NW
Washington, DC 20001

Attends to the needs of minority children and children with special needs through public education, awareness, and preventive programs. Provides information on legislation and specific projects. Charges for some publications and newsletter.

Children with Attention Deficit Disorders (CHADD)
1859 North Pine Island Road
Suite 185   305-384-6869
Plantation, FL 33322   305-792-8100

Serves parents of children with attention deficit disorders by offering informational meetings, a support group, and newsletters.

Citizens Alliance to Uphold Special Education (CAUSE)
313 South Washington Square, Suite 040
Lansing, MI 48917   Voice/TDD   800-221-9105

Provides information and training for parents interested in helping other parents through workshops and support groups. Maintains a resource library, transition and minority outreach programs, and a program of parents training parents.

Clearinghouse on the Handicapped
Office of Special Education and Rehabilitative Services
U.S. Department of Education
Switzer Building, Room 3132
Washington, DC 20202-2319   202-732-1214

Answers inquiries regarding programs, housing, transportation, legislation, funding, etc. A newsletter, referrals to parents, publication list are some of the free services available.

Collaboration Among Parents and Health Professionals Project (CAPP)
P.O. Box 992
Westfield, MA 01086   413-562-5521

Promotes communication among parents and health care providers. Encourages parent involvement in the health care of their children with special needs. Provides listings of regional and national parent centers.

Coordinating Council for Handicapped Children
20 East Jackson Boulevard, Room 900
Chicago, IL 60604   312-939-3513

Publishes pamphlets, training manuals, fact sheets, and newsletters for parents of children with special needs. Provides an information and referral service and an outreach program for minority parents. Materials are available in Spanish.

Council for Exceptional Children
1920 Association Drive
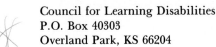Reston, VA 22091   703-620-3660

Provides an information service on special education, laws, and policy. Advocates for legislation and services to benefit individuals with special needs and their families. Materials and bibliographies are available.

Council for Learning Disabilities
P.O. Box 40303
Overland Park, KS 66204   913-492-8755

Functions as a professional organization that publishes journals and disseminates information and research concerning individuals with learning disabilities.

Easter Seal Society
National Headquarters
2023 West Ogden Avenue   800-211-6827
Chicago, IL 60612   312-243-8400

Provides services, journals, newsletters, and bibliographies for parents. There is a small charge for some information. Some materials in Spanish are available.

Epilepsy Foundation of America
4351 Garden City Drive, Suite 406   800-EFA-1000
Landover, MD 20785   301-459-3700

Serves individuals with epilepsy or seizure disorders. Provides services, programs, as well as information on education, health, and employment. Pamphlets, newsletters and bibliographies are available in Braille, Spanish, and other languages.

Father's Program
Merrywood School
16120 NE 8th Street
Bellevue, WA 98008   206-747-4004

Provides training for forming support groups to meet the needs of fathers of children with special needs. Suggests developmentally appropriate activities that fathers and their children can enjoy together. Lists current related books and materials and publishes a newsletter.

Federation for Children with Special Needs
312 Stuart Street 2nd Fl.
Boston, MA 02116   617-482-2915

Provides child advocacy and information centers for parents and parent organizations. Conducts workshops and provides technical assistance for parents.

The Genesis Fund
30 Warren Street
Brighton, MA 02135   800-225-5995

Provides genetic counseling; funding for diagnosis, care and treatment of children born with genetic diseases, birth defects, and mental retardation.

HEATH Resource Center
Higher Education and Adult Training for People with Handicaps
One Dupont Circle, Suite 670   800-544-3284
Washington, DC 20036-1193   202-939-9320

Serves as an information center for higher education and people with special needs. Publications, fact sheets, and newsletters are available at no cost.

Helen Keller National Center for Deaf-Blind Youths and Adults
111 Middle Neck Road
Sands Point, NY 11050   516-944-8900

Serves students aged 18 and up. Provides information on communication, mobility, and life skills. Pamphlets, articles, and bibliographies are available for a nominal fee.

International Rett Syndrome Association
8511 Rose Marie Drive
Fort Washington, MD 20744   301-284-7031

Provides information and referral services and offers direct and parent-to-parent support systems. Encourages research, promotes awareness, disseminates information through brochures and a quarterly newsletter.

Juvenile Diabetes Foundation
60 Madison Avenue
New York, NY 10010   212-689-2860

Disseminates research and information on juvenile diabetes.

The Kids on the Block, Inc.
9385-C Gerwig Lane
Columbia, MD 21045

Provides educational puppeteering programs that include topics on disability awareness, medical issues, and social concerns.

KIDS Project, Inc.
1720 Oregon Street
Berkeley, CA 94703   415-548-4121

Develops and presents inclusive, non-discriminatory materials dealing with individuals with disabilities in society. Provides free informational brochures, pamphlets, articles, and a price list of other games, books, and materials.

Leukemia Society of America
733 Third Avenue
New York, NY 10017   212-573-8484

Disseminates research and information and offers a variety of services to individuals with leukemia and their families.

March of Dimes Birth Defects Foundation
1275 Mamaroneck Avenue
White Plains, NY 10605   914-428-7100

Provides information for the public as well as prospective parents on how to protect mother's and baby's health. Printed materials are available.

Ronald McDonald House
500 North Michigan Avenue
Chicago, IL 60611

Offers temporary housing near hospitals for families of children who are seriously ill and must be hospitalized or receive outpatient care for an extended period of time at a site far from home.

Migrant Education Resource List Information Network (MERLIN)
Pennsylvania Department of Education
8th Floor, 333 Market Street   800-233-0306
Harrisburg, PA 17018   717-783-7121

Provides information on migrant education. Identifies and links national resources that support the educational needs of migrant children.

Muscular Dystrophy Association
810 Seventh Avenue
New York, NY 10019   212-586-0808

Provides services, materials, magazine, and free brochures.

National Amputation Foundation
12-45 150th Street
Whitestone, NY 11367   718-767-8400

Provides assistance and legal, financial, and employment information.

National Association for Bilingual Education
Room 407, 1201 16th Street, NW
Washington, DC 20036   202-822-7870

Addresses educational needs of minority populations. Programs, materials, and newsletters are available.

National Association of the Deaf
814 Thayer Avenue
Silver Spring, MD 20910   301-587-1788

Serves individuals who are deaf or hearing impaired. Provides information on programs and services, legislation and legal rights. Newsletter, books, publications lists are available.

National Association for the Education of Young Children
1834 Connecticut Avenue, NW
Washington, DC 20009   202-323-8777

Focuses on improving the quality and availability of child care and early education for young children (0–8 years). Provides referrals, books, kits, brochures, bibliographies, and directories.

National Association for Hearing and Speech Action   AM Sp. LANG
10801 Rockville Pike
Rockville, MD 20855   800-638-TALK

Disseminates brochures on hearing, listening devices, communication disorders, and on role of speech pathologists and audiologists. Publishes a newsletter on services, products, programs, and activities for individuals and families. Provides information on legislation and insurance coverage for speech/language pathology and audiology services. Some materials in Spanish are available.

National Association for Parents of the Visually Impaired, Inc.
P.O. Box 562
Camden, NY 13316   800-562-6265

Promotes the development of state and local organizations of, by, and for parents of children who are visually impaired. Provides support and increases public awareness. Publishes quarterly newsletter.

National Association of Protection and Advocacy Systems (NAPAS)
300 I Street, NE
Suite 212
Washington, DC 20002   202-546-8202

Provides a listing of advocacy agencies by state.

National Association for Sickle Cell Disease, Inc.
4221 Wilshire Boulevard, Suite 360
Los Angeles, CA 90010

800-421-8453
213-936-7205

Provides services, fact sheets, brochures, and a newsletter. Most materials are available at no charge.

National Association for the Visually Handicapped
22 West 21st Street
New York, NY 10010

212-889-3141

Serves those with partial vision. Provides information, referrals, services, materials, and newsletters. Some materials in Spanish are available.

National Ataxia Foundation
600 Twelve Oaks Center
15500 Wayzata Boulevard
Wayzata, MN 55391

612-473-7666

Offers counseling, support, and referrals. Free booklets, brochures, and fact sheets are disseminated.

National Birth Defects Center
c/o Kennedy Memorial Hospital
30 Warren Street
Brighton, MA 02135

800-322-5014

Offers diagnostic and evaluation clinics. Maintains parent support groups. Houses the Pregnancy Environmental Hotline for information about drugs, medications, chemicals, and other environmental agents that are potentially harmful to a pregnant woman and her child.

National Captioning Institute
5203 Leesburg Pike
Falls Church, VA 22041

Voice/TTY   703-998-2400

Provides cable and network listings two times a year for closed-captioned programming and a closed-captioned videocassette listing six times a year.

National Center for Education in Maternal and Child Health
38th and R Streets, NW
Washington, DC 20007

202-625-8400

Provides research, information services, and educational materials on pregnancy, high risk infants, nutrition, genetics, and disabling conditions. Some publications are available in Spanish.

National Center for Research in Vocational Education
The Ohio State University
1960 Kenny Road
Columbus, OH 43210-1090

800-848-4815
614-486-3655

Provides publications list, data bases, catalogs of products, and services for professionals in employment-related education and training.

National Clearinghouse for Bilingual Education
11501 Georgia Avenue, Suite 102   800-647-0123
Wheaton, MD 20902   301-933-9448

Has information on bilingual education programs and legislation.

National Committee for Citizens in Education
10840 Little Patuxent Parkway, Suite 301   800-NET-WORK
Columbia, MD 21044-3199   301-997-9300

Focuses on improving quality of public schools through increased public involvement. Publications, newsletter, special education checklist, parents' rights, and legal information are available.

National Cystic Fibrosis Foundation
6000 Executive Boulevard   800-FIGHTCF
Rockville, MD 20855   301-881-9130

Has information on local chapters, materials, publications list, and publishes a newsletter. Most information is available free.

National Down Syndrome Congress
1800 Dempster Street   800-232-NDSC
Park Ridge, IL 60068-1146   312-823-7550

Provides opportunities for parents and professionals to work towards improving education, stimulating research, and promoting the rights and welfare of individuals with Down syndrome. Sponsors national and international conferences, publishes a monthly newsletter, fact sheets, brochures, and bibliographies.

National Down Syndrome Society
141 Fifth Avenue   800-221-4602
New York, NY 10010   212-460-9330

Provides information, services and referrals, booklets, materials, bibliography, fact sheets, and a newsletter. Some materials in Spanish are available. Maintains 24-hour hotline.

National Head Injury Foundation, Inc.
333 Turnpike Road   800-444-NHIF
Southborough, MA 01772   617-485-9950

Increases public, family, and professional awareness. Publishes a newsletter and brochures. Provides a resource center and disseminates legislative information.

National Hearing Aid Society
20361 Middlebelt
Livonia, MI 48152   800-521-5247

Provides listing of professional hearing instrument specialists, informational booklet on signs and types of hearing loss, recommendations for choosing and evaluating a specialist, and consumer information on hearing aids. Maintains a hotline for further information.

National Hemophilia Foundation
The Soho Building
110 Greene Street, Room 406
New York, NY 10012   212-219-8180

Provides referrals, materials, publications and a newsletter.

National Information Center for Children and Youth With Handicaps (NICHCY)
PO Box 1492   800-999-5599
Washington, DC 20013   Voice/TDD   703-893-6061

Answers questions, connects individuals with similar needs, provides advice, and directories of agencies and organizations. Some materials in Spanish are available.

National Institute of Neurological and Communicative Disorders and Stroke
National Institute of Health
U.S. Department of Health and Human Services   list ✓
Building 31, Room 8A-16
Bethesda, MD 20814   301-496-5751

Serves people with neurological and communicative disorders, cerebrovascular disease, metabolic disorders, head and spinal cord injury. Answers question, provides publications, pamphlets, and fact sheets. Maintains publications list and single pamphlets free.

National Legal Resource Center for Child Advocacy
1800 M Street, NW
Washington, DC 20036   202-331-2250

Provides information and educational services on issues relating to children with special needs and their parents.

National Library Service for the Blind and Physically Handicapped   returning my call
Library of Congress
1291 Taylor Street, NW   800-424-8567
Washington, DC 20011   212-287-5100

Has a collection of Braille, talking books, magazines, and playback equipment that is loaned. Articles, fact sheets, brochures, bibliographies, and directories are free.

National Mental Health Association
1021 Prince Street   WRITE
Alexandria, VA 22314

Serves people with mental and emotional disorders. Provides information on services, research, rehabilitation, legislation, and employment. Publications and materials list are available.

National Rehabilitation Information Center
4407 Eight Street, NE   800-43-NARIC
Washington, DC 20017   202-635-5826

Provides brochures, publications, newsletter, information, and catalogs on products and equipment. Most resources are available at no cost.

National Rural Development Institute
Western Washington University
Bellingham, WA 98225   206-676-3576

Provides copies of published and unpublished articles on specific topics, notices of upcoming conferences of possible interest, and personnel recruitment services. Supports parental and professional involvement in research, program, and staff development.

National Society for Children and Adults with Autism
1234 Massachusetts Avenue, NW, Suite 1017
Washington, DC 20005-4599   202-783-0125

Provides information, services, referrals, parent support groups, public education, and advocacy. Offers a catalog of books, pamphlets on autism, and a newsletter. Some materials in Spanish are available.

National Spinal Cord Injury Association
149 California Street
Newton, MA 02158   617-965-0521

Disseminates fact sheets on spinal cord injury, publications list, newsletter, and a list of state chapters.

National Tay-Sachs and Allied Diseases Association, Inc.
385 Elliot Street
Newton, MA 02164   617-964-5508

Provides information and education about Tay-Sachs and allied diseases. Promotion of carrier screening, a parent support group, and research are other activities sponsored by this organization.

National Wheelchair Athletic Association—Junior Division
3617 Betty Drive, Suite S
Colorado Springs, CO 80907

Provides organized athletic opportunities for physically disabled youth and listings of videotapes including integrated recreation. A newsletter is available.

New Eyes for the Needy
549 Millburn Avenue
Short Hills, NJ 07078   201-376-4903

Provides funds to individuals not eligible for other sources of financial aid for glasses, artificial eyes, and contact lenses for cataract patients.

Orton Dyslexia Society
724 York Road
Baltimore, MD 21204   301-296-0232

Provides information and guidance to resources. Pamphlets and articles are available at a small charge.

PACER Center, Inc.
Parent Advocacy Coalition for Educational Rights
4826 Chicago Avenue South   800-53-PACER
Minneapolis, MN 55417   612-827-2966

Provides information on infants, toddlers, and preschoolers with special needs. Offers a free newsletter, workshops, lists, and brochures. Disseminates information about laws, parents' rights and responsibilities. Some materials in Spanish are available.

Parent Information Center
P.O. Box 1422
Concord, NH 03301   603-224-7005

Provides support, information, and training to families of children with disabilities. Provides technical assistance to parents/parent groups interested in establishing parent training and information programs.

Parents Helping Parents, Inc.
535 Race Street, # 220
San Jose, CA 95126   408-288-5010

Offers services to special needs families. Includes information packets, peer counseling, home visits, public meetings, social gatherings, family support sessions, training, advocacy, and sibling support groups. Publishes a quarterly newsletter.

PEAK Parent Center, Inc.
6055 Lehman Drive, Suite 101   800-426-2466 ex. 423
Colorado Springs, CO 80918   713-531-9400

Provides parents with answers to questions about children, location of services/resources, parent networks, state and federal laws, educational issues, and integration.

Perkins School for the Blind
175 N. Beacon Street
Watertown, MA 02172   617-924-3434

Serves people who are blind, deaf/blind, or multihandicapped/blind. Lists of curriculum materials and publications, brochures, books, newsletters are available in Braille, large type, and Spanish.

Pilot Parents
Central Palm Plaza
2005 N. Central Avenue, Suite 100
Phoenix, AZ 85004   602-271-4012

Offers family-to-family support, information, and education for families of children with disabilities. Publishes a newsletter and maintains a lending library.

Prader-Willi Syndrome Association
6439 Excelsior Boulevard, E-102
St. Paul, MN 55426   612-926-1947

Provides a bimonthly newsletter, a materials list, and information for persons interested in Prader-Willi syndrome. Local chapters of the organization have been formed throughout the United States and Canada. A national annual conference is held.

Shriners Hospitals for Crippled Children
2900 Rocky Point Drive
Tampa, FL 33607   813-885-2575

Offers free orthopedic and severe burn care to children.

Sibling Information Network
Connecticut's University Affiliated Facility
University of Connecticut
249 Glenbrook Road U-64
Storrs, CT 06268   203-486-4034

Serves as a clearinghouse for information, research and activities relating to siblings of children with special needs.

Speech Foundation of America
5139 Lingle Street NW
Washington, DC 20016

Publishes current information on prevention and treatment of stuttering; some for parents, some for professionals. Some materials are available in Spanish, French, and Vietnamese.

Spina Bifida Association of America
1700 Rockville Pike, Suite 540   800-621-3141
Rockville, MD 20852   301-770-SBAA

Provides public education, research, referrals. Disseminates publications, newsletter, and manuals. Some materials are available in Spanish.

Tourette Syndrome Association
42-40 Bell Boulevard
Bayside, NY 11361   718-224-2999

Serves persons interested in Tourette syndrome. Programs, brochures, research
materials, videotapes and films, and legal aid publications are available.

Travel Information Center
Moss Rehabilitation Hospital
12th Street and Tabor Road
Philadelphia, PA 19141

Provides a listing of airlines and trains having accommodations for individuals
with special needs. Offers a listing of hotel chains that offer accommodations for
people with special needs.

United Cerebral Palsy Association
666 E. 34th Street
New York, NY 10016   212-947-5770

Disseminates information and delivers services to individuals with cerebral palsy
and their families.

Very Special Arts
1825 Connecticut Avenue, NW, Suite 417
Washington, DC 20009   202-662-8899

Provides information on curriculum and instruction in arts for individuals
with special needs. Lists of organizations with art programs, brochures, and
a newsletter are available.

Index